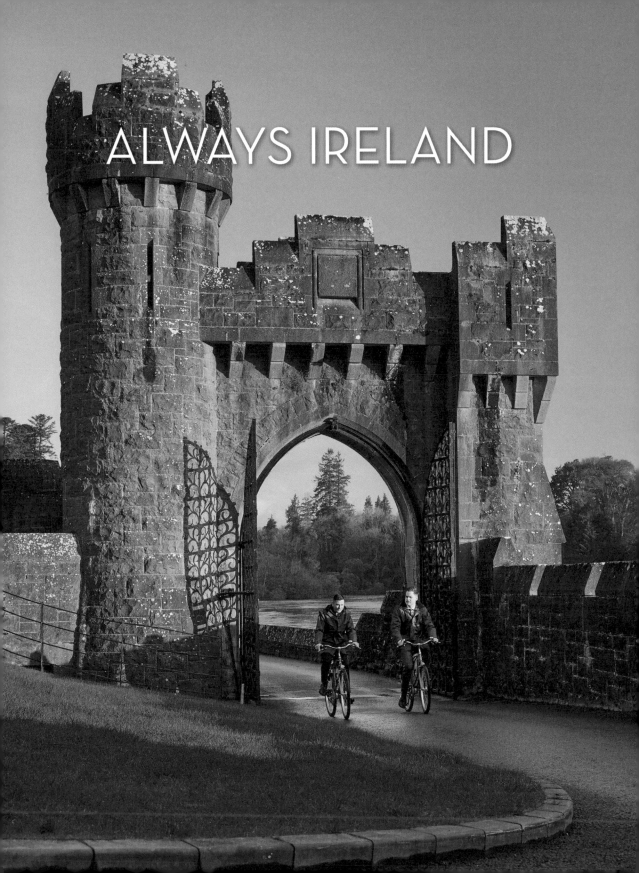

ALWAYS IRELAND

ALWAYS IRELAND

An Insider's Tour of the Emerald Isle

JACK KAVANAGH

NATIONAL GEOGRAPHIC

WASHINGTON, D.C.

CONTENTS

Titanic Belfast PAGE 1: Ashford Castle Estate, Counties Galway and Mayo PAGES 2-3: St. Finbarr's Oratory, Gougane Barra, County Cork

Introduction

The Spirit of Ireland

This book, *Always Ireland,* was born of my experiences as a native as well as the many trips I've made around my homeland over the last 25 years. In 1995 I emigrated from Dublin to work first in London, then in the United States. But though I left Ireland, Ireland never left me. I often returned to join old friends for weddings, vacations, or wakes (always a lively Irish event). Other times, I'd welcome American friends to the old country, or report on various sites for feature stories or guidebooks. Recently, I've had the pleasure of seeing Ireland through the eyes of many first-time visitors, as I accompany them on National Geographic Expeditions' "Tales and Traditions of the Emerald Isle" tour.

If you travel there seeking the soul of Ireland today, you'll find many clues in the island's stunning landscapes. The essence of what many consider the world's only Celtic nation resounds in the dolmens and burial chambers of ancient kings and chieftains, lingering along the rugged coastlines dotted with offshore islands where Irish-speaking communities keep its language alive. Irish is one of three Gaelic languages; Scots Gaelic and Manx are the others. Ireland's spirit of independence still swirls like mist high in many of the mountain regions—Kerry's Macgillycuddys Reeks, Down's Mountains of Mourne, and the Wicklow Mountains—that once gave refuge to the country's revolutionaries.

The long struggle for independence gave the Irish a special talent for subversion and challenging orthodoxies, and Irish minds like to reinvent their world imaginatively when things get stale. Historically, Ireland is divided into 32 counties, and native Irish identify by their county, its accent, and its idioms: Because I'm from Wicklow, I might greet my brother-in-law "Good, Daithi," which means "Hello, David"; because he is a Meath man, he will respond "Are ye fit?" which translates to "How are you?" These 32 Irish counties (26 in the Republic and six in Northern Ireland; see map, page 9) are grouped into four provinces: Leinster, Munster, Connacht, and Ulster. But recently, the Irish have reimagined their island into newly delineated geographical and cultural/historical regions (see map inset, page 9).

This book follows these newly reimagined regions: Part One covers the ancient east, with its rich traditions of monastic settlement and learning. Next come the agricultural heartlands of Munster and the south, where the spirit of independence is as strong as the lilting Cork and Kerry accents. In Part Three, the Munster counties of Cork, Kerry, Limerick, and Clare are linked to the coastal route of the Wild Atlantic Way, which stretches along the western seaboard through Connacht and up to Donegal in the province of Ulster. The bulk of Ulster

Stone walls crisscross Inisheer, the easternmost Aran island.

follows in Part Four: the six counties that are now in Northern Ireland. Here, the Causeway Coast stretches along the island's northernmost edge, providing yet another unforgettable Irish drive. And finally, we visit the seascapes encompassing several island groups, along with Ireland's other offshore areas, in Part Five.

These days, of course, you can also use the internet to orient yourself, to wonder at Ireland's natural beauty, or to study its rich history. The Irish have long since colonized cyberspace as storytellers supreme, just as they once did with the English language and English literature. Modern Ireland adapted easily to the internet era, and its well-educated workforce now helps tell global stories in the digital age: Google has its European headquarters in Dublin's Silicon Docks, while LinkedIn's Europe, Middle East, and Africa HQ is located nearby.

While modern Ireland connects with the world on digital highways, much of its history is written in bricks and mortar. Everywhere you go, Ireland's landscapes and landmarks are shaded by its storied past. The influence of outsiders still haunts the ruins of ancient Norman castles scattered across this fertile land and lives on in Dublin's finest architecture, from the Customs House to the city's tall Georgian mansions.

Walk the streets of Dublin and you'll soon realize that the way many Irish people greet each other is not "How are you?" but "What's the story?" Psychogeographers—who study how places and landscapes impact our thoughts, feelings, and behaviors—quickly become mired in Ireland's mythical, historical, and storytelling traditions. I tried it myself recently, walking through Galway with a local historian. We were soon lost in a fog of legends about the visit of John F. Kennedy, in poetic flights of fancy courtesy of William Butler Yeats, and in fantastic tales about the Otherworld, realm of the fairies. One such story matter-of-factly described the absence of a musician for three days: This fiddle player fell into a fairy ring—an enchanted portal to the spirit state of Irish sprites—and was taken to play at a wedding of these otherworldly beings. Just listening to this prolific historian spinning his wondrous web made me realize that he was also a *seanchaí* (a Gaelic storyteller), and that I was bound up in *his* spell, lost in his labyrinth of tales—some historic, some mythic, all entrancing.

Of course, few people are as connected to the spiritual realm as the Irish. The country could adopt William Faulkner's famous quote as its national axiom: "The past is never dead. It's not even past." Like Yeats, Faulkner's family tree had many Irish branches, the Butlers among them. Even in exile, the Gael is spirited toward the future by past accomplices—note how another Irishman, the actor Gabriel Byrne, called his recent memoir *Walking With Ghosts*.

This Celtic closeness to the spiritual world is not just nostalgic. It also lends the Irish imagination a liberating advantage. Irish myths are filled with fantastical worlds such as Tír na nÓg ("land of eternal youth"), where life is better than here on our rain-plagued island. The ancient saints honored the Christian tradition of the "green martyrdom," an ascetic retreat into nature to get closer to God. The Irish monks retreated into places such as Clonmacnoise and Glendalough, complete with round tower refuges, to re-create the Gospels in manuscript form, for preservation as Rome fell and Europe was pillaged first by barbarians, then by Vikings.

Later, Irish poets, including Yeats, were also drawn to towers, where they invoked new spirit worlds into a rich heritage of literature, most of it in their conquerors' language. In the late 1970s a gang of young Dubliners, bored within the bland anonymity of suburban life, dreamt up an alternative reality they called Lypton Village, adopting colorful names such as Bono Vox, the Edge, Gavin Friday, and Guggi. Out of this rock 'n' roll dreamscape sprung U2. Bono later bought a Martello tower in my hometown of Bray, and beat his own artistic retreat. One of the songs composed there, "Promenade," celebrates reaching the spiritual "higher ground" via a "spiral staircase" of the imagination.

When the Irish don't like the world they live in, they simply make up another one to inhabit imaginatively. It helps them in exile, of course. The Gael's ease of movement between the real and the imagined is doubtless

THE ISLAND OF IRELAND
From an ancient land of Celtic kingdoms, Ireland became a country divided into four provinces: Leinster, Munster, Connacht, and Ulster. Together they have a combined 32 counties, with six making up Northern Ireland (light green on map opposite), part of the United Kingdom.

the foundation for the country's overachievement in the arts. A small country of just five million, Ireland boasts four winners of the Nobel Prize in Literature: William Butler Yeats (1923), George Bernard Shaw (1925), Samuel Beckett (1969), and Seamus Heaney (1995).

A curious traveler will find many clues to the Irish soul in the country's rich literature, its music, and its song; these days, you'll also enjoy Ireland's storytelling traditions in contemporary forms such as film, comedy monologues, travel blogs, and television dramas. To get to the very essence of Ireland, I often encourage guests to spend an hour or two just listening to the Irish talk. And you never have to go too far to hear the Irish talk.

The Irish are, at heart, indefatigable storytellers, and the best place to eavesdrop among them is the local pub. The public house in Ireland is a uniquely Gaelic institution that is part drinking emporium, part social center, part music hall, part private parlor, and—if it boasts a snug (a secluded booth) and a trusty barman—part secular confessional box. My own "local" is Bray's Harbour Bar, which is all these things, with the added attraction of an in-house "chipper." Fresh fish and chips (thick potato fries) washed down with a satisfying stout followed by a Jameson on the rocks is my taste of home. The Harbour is just a short walk from Bono's tower; the higher ground is never far away in Ireland.

Opening this book, I hope, will be like visiting *your* favorite Irish pub: Cracking its covers should evoke a wall of noise as the revelers within make a happy racket on a Friday night, when the local band—*céilí*, country, or rock 'n' roll—is in full flow. You might spot Bono and Enya, or Christy Moore and Shane MacGowan over near the stage discussing favorite Irish songs; in the snug, Willie Henry, the Galway historian and *seanchaí*, might be spinning folktales. And there's Fionnán O'Connor, the garrulous academic over in the far corner, intriguing all with his insights into Irish whiskey; the vinegary smell of chips and cod deep-fried in batter wafts in from the outer courtyard, where an Irish wolfhound is charming scraps from admiring diners; and the engaging barman is asking you where you're from. He'll soon be telling you of his time spent "over beyond" in London or "across in America," while you wait for the creamy head to settle on your Guinness.

You're always welcome here. This is *Always Ireland*. *Sláinte!* ∎

Irish pubs, such as Dick Mack's in Dingle, County Kerry, often resound with song, and sometimes even dancers' shoes. OPPOSITE: Ancient volcanic activity shaped Hamilton's Seat, a rugged and romantic highpoint of the Causeway Coast in County Antrim.

Part One
Ireland's Ancient East

Glendalough, in County Wicklow, is a centuries-old monastic settlement with farms, a cathedral, and a 100-foot-tall (30 m) round tower that still stands today.

The ancient Gaelic sport of hurling
OPPOSITE: Trinity Library, Dublin

Wander through every era of Irish history

Céad míle fáilte, a hundred thousand welcomes, to Ireland's ancient east. Here you can wander through every era of Irish history, from Neolithic monuments at Newgrange to the Norman castle in bewitching Kilkenny. Stroll through the Georgian splendor of colonial-era Dublin, then step up to the 21st-century futurism of the capital's financial district or into the space-age Aviva Stadium to cheer on the national soccer (aka football hereabouts) or rugby teams.

In Ireland, fiction is celebrated as much as fact. Visit Dublin around Bloomsday, June 16, and enter into the world of James Joyce's *Ulysses;* you can follow in the footsteps of Leopold Bloom, the only literary character celebrated worldwide with his own feast day. This city is filled with literary history, and most pubs boast of a poet or a novelist who sought inspiration in its libations. Dublin's lively music scene covers all genres and has nurtured generations of celebrated musicians from the Dubliners to Phil Lynott to U2. A visit to the Guinness Brewery is the perfect prelude to a performance at the Olympia Theatre or Vicar Street.

The Neolithic burial sites of Brú na Bóinne are a leisurely day's drive from Dublin, including a lunch stop at Slane Castle. Take in the Battle of the Boyne Visitor Centre to learn the history of this 1690 clash and why it still resonates, north and south. The Hill of Tara, crowning site of Ireland's High Kings, imbues a more positive energy, while nearby Kells and Clonmacnoise offer insights into monastic Ireland. Glendalough in County Wicklow, where St. Kevin founded his monastery in the sixth century, may be Ireland's most sacred site. The call to a life of asceticism is palpable here, but don't deny yourself the seafood delicacies found farther southeast.

Outdoor types will find mountain, shore, and cliff walks and sea-based adventures throughout the east, and lakes and forest parks as far west as Longford and Westmeath. Horse lovers in particular should head for Kildare, where a day at the races is a great way to encounter the full spectrum of Irish humanity, usually at its most vocal and vibrant. ∎

DUBLIN

Like many invaders of Ireland, the Vikings who helped establish Dublin circa 841 eventually settled there. Following defeat by the Irish High King Brian Boru at the Battle of Clontarf in 1014, many Vikings stayed on as traders, disarmed by the charm of the native Gaels. Modern-day invading hordes consist mainly of stag (bachelor) and hen (bachelorette) parties from England and Europe, carousing late into the night around the city's Temple Bar district. Those venturing into Dublin by day will find a contemporary city of coffee bars, artisan foods, and craft beer.

While not the prettiest city, Dublin may well be the most social. Ask any Dubliner and they'll not only name their favorite pub, they'll probably insist on taking you there, too. Many a local's perfect day would be an afternoon spent in Fleet Street's Palace Bar with a newspaper followed by a night in Mulligans of Poolbeg Street, where you'll be served the best "pint of plain" on Earth. To seek out its source, follow your nose to the Guinness Brewery, about a mile up the River Liffey; you'll be reliably led by the scent of roasting barley, the ingredient that gives stout its rich blackness.

Another of Dublin's "disarming charms" was once the malodorous whiff of the Liffey. Happily, the river, personified as Anna Livia Plurabelle by James Joyce, has been cleaned up for the 21st century. Now you can breathe deeply as you stroll across the modern Millennium Bridge or the old Ha'penny Bridge, or whenever you cross the harp-shaped Samuel Beckett Bridge.

North of the river lies Croke Park, home of the Gaelic Athletic Association (GAA) and sacred ground for all Gaels. If you're in Dublin in September, walk alongside the crowds making their way to an All-Ireland final (hurling or football) to hear Irish banter at its best. The ironic jeers of Dubliners have been well-honed through the ages, going all the way back to the founding father of Irish satire, Jonathan Swift (1667–1745), dean of St. Patrick's Cathedral. The mockery is always fond and friendly, and the Dublin welcome is always warm. ∎

The Ha'penny Bridge, named for the toll Dubliners paid to cross the River Liffey

Insider's Guide

Literary Dublin

Dublin is perhaps the only capital in the world where the best known tourist attraction is not a beautiful building or boulevard, but a book: the *Book of Kells.* Or, in its proper "Dubbalin" pronunciation, "De Buke a Kells." The Irish capital was, in Georgian times, a major British city, and it's often said that Ireland's revenge was to colonize the English language. Dublin has an incredible literary heritage, and Dubliners have their own particular mastery of the rhythms and cadences of the English language. Conversations in bars and barbershops reveal a richness in imagery and imagination to the outsider who eavesdrops (or "earwigs" in Dublinese).

After viewing the *Book of Kells* (see page 56) at **Trinity College,** the **Museum of Literature Ireland** on St. Stephen's Green is just the place to soak up the storytelling traditions that have mesmerized readers for centuries. En route between these two attractions, you'll find Dublin's finest bookstore, the four-story **Hodges & Figgis** on Nassau Street.

If you're looking for a view of Irish literature from a Dubliner's perspective, the **Dublin Writers' Museum** at 18 Parnell Square is "your only man" (meaning "your best option" in a favored Dublin idiom of novelist and playwright Flann O'Brien). Here you can discover how Jonathan Swift popularized satire in Ireland with works such as *Gulliver's Travels,* how Bram Stoker conjured up *Dracula* in Victorian Dublin, and, of course, how James Joyce's *Ulysses* became the city's love letter from exile. This museum is sited in a beautifully decorated 18th-century mansion and hosts exhibitions, lunchtime theater, tours, and readings; downstairs are a bookshop and the Michelin-starred Chapter One restaurant. It also has a fine replica of the *Book of Kells* that facilitates a more leisurely look at the monks' handiwork.

The nearby **Abbey Theatre** on Abbey Street Lower has hosted historic opening nights of plays by Nobel Prize winners W. B. Yeats and Samuel Beckett.

Scholars and revelers from around the world celebrate Joyce's renowned novel, *Ulysses,* each Bloomsday (June 16).

The ghost of James Joyce (1882–1941) happily haunts literary Dublin. His 1922 masterpiece *Ulysses* still attracts scholars from around the world each Bloomsday, June 16. Dressed as characters from the novel, readers pay homage on the **James Joyce Trail,** which follows the perambulations of the novel's hero, Leopold Bloom, around Dublin's streets and pubs. The midpoint is a reenactment of Bloom's lunch of a Gorgonzola and mustard sandwich and a glass of burgundy in **Davy Byrne's** pub on Duke Street.

On any day of the year, drop into **Sweny's Pharmacy** on Lincoln Place for a Joyce reading with host P. J. Murphy. If you have time, jump on a DART (local train) and head for the **James Joyce Tower and Museum** in nearby Sandycove.

In **Merrion Square,** you'll find a statue of Oscar Wilde (1854–1900) lounging louchely on a rock. Near Baggot Street Bridge, a sculpture of Monaghan-born poet Patrick Kavanagh (1904–1967) contemplates his beloved **Grand Canal.**

As you chase the greats of Irish literature, check out some of their modern-day heirs in the works of writers such as Dermot Bolger, Roddy Doyle, and Anne Enright, whose stories evoke rich flavors of Irish speech and storytelling. ∎

TASTE OF IRELAND: COCKLES & MUSSELS WITH BACON

Dublin's anthem is "Molly Malone," the ballad of a poor fishmonger who wheeled her wheelbarrow through streets broad and narrow, crying "cockles and mussels, alive, a-live, oh." You'll hear this song roared aloud by thousands at Irish sporting occasions, and its heroine is fondly honored with a statue outside St. Andrew's Church on Suffolk Street. Here's a taste of her Dublin Bay seafood delicacy.

"Cockles and mussels, alive, a-live, oh . . ."

INGREDIENTS

- 50 fresh, live mussels, washed and scrubbed
- 30 cockles, washed and scrubbed
- 8 rashers (streaky bacon), rinds removed
- 1 stick (113 g) Kerrygold Irish butter
- 1 onion, finely chopped
- 2 tablespoons chopped parsley
- 1 tablespoon chopped chives
- Salt and pepper
- 4 sprigs of watercress

DIRECTIONS

- Boil the mussels in a large saucepan of water for 5 minutes, shaking the pan occasionally. Add the cockles and cook an additional 3 to 5 minutes. The shellfish are cooked when the shells open; discard any that remain closed. Remove the cockles and mussels from the shells.
- Slice the bacon rashers in half, widthwise. Roll each piece and secure with a cocktail stick. Cook in a pan for 2 to 3 minutes to remove the salt and set the rolls before draining and drying. Discard the cocktail sticks.
- In a large frying pan, melt the butter and fry the bacon rolls until colored. Remove from the pan and keep warm. Fry the onion until soft and then add the cockles, mussels, and herbs and season with salt and pepper. Toss in the butter to heat thoroughly, about 2 to 3 minutes.
- Combine seafood mixture with the bacon rolls on a warmed plate; garnish with watercress and serve immediately with Irish soda bread to absorb the flavorful juices. Serves 3 to 4 hungry Dubliners as an appetizer.

TIP: For a main course, add some boiled potatoes and double the quantities.

The Guinness Brewery at St. James's Gate, Dublin; the firm was led by family scions from its inception by Arthur Guinness in 1759 until 1992.

'Tis Only Noble: The Goodness of Guinness

One family name is uttered thousands of times daily in Dublin: Guinness.

The iconic Irish brewing business was led by family scions from its inception in 1759 by Arthur Guinness right up to 1992. Still in operation today, the Dublin brewery at St. James's Gate is a curious cluster of industrial and Georgian structures, with massive vats among a network of pipes. The whole operation is driven by an on-site power station. While railway tracks still line the cobbled streets, trucks now transport the black nectar around the

country. The heady aroma of hops wafts along the River Liffey quays, a comforting reassurance of reward come the end of the Dublin workday.

The Guinnesses were Protestant, and, as Anglo-Irish landowners, their interests lay in maintaining the union with Britain. Yet they skillfully negotiated the land wars and the political turmoil of 19th-century Ireland and simultaneously endeared themselves to the Irish people. Guinness was known as an excellent employer, offering workers above-average wages, yearly bonuses, health care, and generous pensions for widows. A

Dublin adage held that "a Guinness man meant money, dead or alive." The Guinnesses were also generous philanthropists. St. Patrick's Cathedral, built in 1190 on a Dublin marsh, had fallen into disrepair before it was saved at huge cost by Arthur's grandson, Benjamin Lee Guinness, in 1860.

Although the family struggled against English society's disdain of new money made from "trade," they were eventually accepted into the British establishment as members of Parliament (MPs) and peers. Benjamin Lee Guinness became Lord Mayor of Dublin in 1851 and was elected Conservative MP for the city in 1868. His daughter Anne married the aristocrat Reverend William Conyngham, and subsequent Guinnesses would be educated at top English schools, such as Eton. The next generation reached the highest echelons of Edwardian aristocracy. Sir Arthur bought his elder brother Edward out of his share of the brewery. As Lord Ardilaun, Arthur hosted shooting parties at his hunting lodge, Ashford Castle, in County Mayo. The visit of Prince of Wales George V to Ashford in 1906 marked a social high-water mark for the Guinnesses. Both siblings, high-profile socialites

in Dublin and London, are immortalized as the "cunning brothers" in Joyce's *Ulysses*.

By 1886, Guinness was floated on the London Stock Exchange and vast wealth flowed to the family. While many Guinness heirs lived the high life, a "curse of the Guinnesses" legend began in the early 1900s when brothers Rupert and Ernest both survived shipwrecks. A third brother, Walter Edward Guinness, also known as the first Baron Moyne, cruised the world seeking unknown tribes and collecting unusual wildlife and plants. He was assassinated in Cairo while serving as a British cabinet minister

in 1944. Ernest's daughters, Aileen, Maureen, and Oonagh—known as the Golden Guinness Girls—all divorced in their twenties. Oonagh took up residence in the fairytale Wicklow estate of Luggala. Her son, Tara Browne, a darling of Swinging London who died tragically in 1966, would be immortalized in the Beatles' song "A Day in the Life."

The family's motto, *"Spes Mea in Deo"* ("'Tis Only Noble to Be Good"), lives on today through Sir Arthur's gift of St. Stephen's Green to the people of Dublin in 1880 and the trusts Edward established to house the poor in London and Dublin. ∎

IN THE KNOW: GREAT PUBS OF DUBLIN

The Guinness harp became the company's trademark in 1862, modeled on the instrument of Brian Boru, the Irish warrior who routed the Vikings from Dublin in 1014. The harp now adorns the signage outside Dublin pubs, where you're guaranteed a decent "pint of plain," as writer Brian O'Nolan (Flann O'Brien) eulogized the famous stout. The **Guinness Storehouse** at St. James's Gate brewery is the obvious place of pilgrimage for visiting aficionados. After taking the tour and visiting the museum, you can relax in one of several bars on the premises. Or strike out and visit one of Dublin's great hostelries, including:

- **The Abbey Tavern,** 28 Abbey Street, Howth: An ancient pub, perfect for a Sunday roast and pint after a seaside walk.
- **The Bar With No Name,** Fade Street: Go underneath the snail and venture up the stairs for tempting and tantalizing cocktails at Dublin's best kept secret.
- **The Brazen Head,** Bridge Street Lower: Ireland's oldest pub. Good Guinness, great food.
- **The Dawson Lounge,** Dawson Street: A tiny downstairs bar, where the chat is intimate, even among strangers.
- **Devitts,** Lower Camden Street: *The* Dublin venue for a trad music session, with multi-instrumentalist locals aplenty.
- **Doheny & Nesbitt,** 5 Baggot Street Lower: Here's another wonderful snug, with intimate leather seating for six.

- **The Gravediggers,** Prospect Square: A traditional treasure beside the Botanical Gardens.
- **Johnnie Fox's Pub,** Glencullen: Enjoy fine city views from this 220-year-old pub in the Dublin mountains, with a turf fire, music, and a great pint.
- **Kehoe's,** Anne Street South: A city center gem, just off Grafton Street, with cozy snugs.
- **Kennedy's Bar,** Westland Row: Dublin's lesser known Joycean pub, opposite Sweny's Pharmacy, where Bloom bought his wife's lemon soap.
- **Mulligan's,** Poolbeg Street: The best pint in Dublin, no arguments. And none better anywhere else.
- **Neary's,** Chatham Street: Toast the ghost of poet Patrick Kavanagh and other scribes who frequented this artists' haven.
- **O'Reilly's,** Tara Street (DART) Station: Down a tiny alley, perfect for a quiet pint.
- **The Palace Bar,** 21 Fleet Street: No better Dublin pub for reading the *Irish Times* (published nearby) or a good book.
- **Pavilion Bar,** Trinity College Green: Join students on the steps above the cricket field amidst age-old Trinity architecture.
- **The Stag's Head,** Dame Court: A beautiful Victorian labyrinth of a pub. Happy hunting.

Ireland On Screen

Dublin in the Movies

The history of "dear, auld, durty Dublin," as James Joyce once memorably called it, has been richly portrayed in a multitude of fine films spanning various eras in Ireland's capital city. Incidentally, the first cinema in Dublin was managed by none other than Joyce himself. The Volta was opened in December 1909 by the struggling writer with the backing of a group of businessmen from Trieste, where he then lived. Despite the capital's embrace of the form in subsequent decades, Joyce's venture was not a success.

Dublin's best loved film is a screen adaptation of a story from Joyce's *Dubliners*. John Huston's cinematic version of *The Dead* (1987) would prove to be the director's swan song, an evocative movie starring his daughter Angelica (who was raised in Ireland) and Donal McCann.

Joyce's short story, set on a snowy night at a Feast of the Epiphany dinner party in the town house of two elderly spinster sisters, contains one of the most moving closing paragraphs ever written. Huston captures Joyce's heartbreaking finale wonderfully through his redolent re-creation of Edwardian Dublin and McCann's wistful monologue.

The turmoil of Dublin during the War of Independence was re-created on screen by Neil Jordan in *Michael Collins* (1996). The film tells the story of the eponymous Irish soldier and politician who waged a daring guerrilla warfare campaign that led to a negotiated peace treaty and the eventual withdrawal of British troops from Ireland in the 1920s. It dramatizes the assassination of British spies and the retaliatory slaughter at a GAA match in Croke Park that became known as

Bloody Sunday. Liam Neeson plays the Irish hero and Julia Roberts his love interest, Kitty Kiernan. Director Neil Jordan has established himself among Ireland's leading writers and garlanded filmmakers, with a long career, including many films examining the role of political violence in Ireland's troubled history.

A lesser known gem directed by Jordan is *The Miracle* (1991). This coming-of-age story swirls around the return of a glamorous American woman (Beverly D'Angelo) to a Wicklow seaside resort one summer. The scenes of escaped circus animals wandering the town exemplify the Irish magical realism that Jordan brings so powerfully to the screen in many of his works.

Another celebrated Irish filmmaker, Jim Sheridan, co-wrote the screenplay for *My Left Foot* (1989), an adaptation of the 1970 biography of a celebrated Dublin writer. Christy Brown was born with cerebral palsy and learned to paint and write with his only controllable limb—his left foot. Method-acting his way through an astonishing performance, Daniel Day-Lewis plays the lead role, alongside Brenda Fricker as Brown's mother. They respectively won best actor and best supporting actress awards at the 1990 Oscars. The screenplay by Sheridan and Shane Connaughton evokes the hardscrabble life and street humor of Dublin in the middle of the 20th century.

A scene from the film *Once*, a tale of two lovelorn musicians in Dublin

Quirke tells the stories of 1950s Irish society through the eyes of the eponymous antihero, a lugubrious state pathologist played by Gabriel Byrne.

A more contemporary capital is captured by John Carney in *Once* (2007), the story of two lovelorn musicians in 21st-century Dublin. You can stroll through its still recognizable street scenes today, starting in St. Stephen's Green, where a thief tries to steal Glen Hansard's guitar; then amble along Grafton Street, where Hansard's character and Markéta Irglová's young immigrant musician first meet. Lastly, be sure to visit Waltons music shop on Georges Street, where the pair play the Oscar-winning song "Falling Slowly."

A faster-paced vision of life in Ireland's capital city is unleashed in John Crowley's *Intermission* (2003). This collage of interwoven stories sets Colin Farrell, Cillian Murphy, and Colm Meaney on a conclusive collision course that takes in surrealism (kissing buses!) and typical Dublin gallows-humor crime along the way.

Storytelling, of course, is part of life in Ireland, and one of Dublin's best known storytellers is Roddy Doyle. His marvelously humorous novels capture Dublin's satirical wit and working-class patois "to a bleedin' tee," with three of them adapted onto the big screen. *The Barrytown Trilogy* is worth seeking out to get the full flavor of Doyle's beloved Dublinese: *The Commitments* (1991) tells the tall tale of Jimmy Rabbitte (played by Robert Arkins), a would-be rock impresario who decides to form Ireland's ultimate soul band. *The Snapper* (1993) and *The Van* (1996) tell the respective stories of an unplanned pregnancy and an ill-planned mobile food truck purchase amid the inhabitants of Doyle's Barrytown, a fictional northside suburb of Dublin.

For crime-show fans, the Dublin noir novels of Booker Prize winner John Banville, writing as Benjamin Black, have been adapted into the dark and brooding TV series *Quirke*, set amid the austerity of 1950s Dublin. Black's eponymous antihero, a lugubrious state pathologist, is played by one of Ireland's finest actors, Gabriel Byrne. In his role administering postmortems on Dublin's dead bodies, Quirke witnesses all the malevolence caused by the then ubiquitous power of the Catholic Church, the knee-bending ethos of Ireland's government, and a cowed citizenry. ∎

The band U2 emerged from a depressed Dublin in the late 1970s, offering songs of hope on an island divided by sectarian violence.

Songlines

Dubliners With Big Dreams

They started out in hard times, young contrarians hollering about hope on a divided island. Five decades later, their dreams of rock 'n' roll redemption live on in the spiritual message of U2's music, their inspired stage shows, and Bono's social activism.

The early U2, inspired by punk, raged against the despair of '70s Dublin. As they navigated the urban inevitabilities of gangs, dole queues, and drugs, the band subverted their world, reinventing it as a mythical mindscape called Lypton Village. In this dreamt-up alt-reality, they adopted names like Bono Vox (Latin for "good voice") and the Edge. They were a gang of outsiders: Paul Hewson (Bono) is the son of a Catholic father and a Protestant mother. The parents of David Evans (the Edge) are Welsh. Adam Clayton is the son of an English RAF pilot. (Larry Mullen Jr. is from Dublin.)

From the start, Bono shared deep Christian beliefs with the Edge and Mullen, and many U2 songs reflect the fervor of their faith: "Gone" echoes the hymn "Nearer My God to Thee." "Please" appealed to Northern Ireland's politicians at the time of the 1998 Good Friday Agreement. As they conquered the world, the band's horizons expanded to take in other world events, from Hiroshima's holocaust ("The Unforgettable Fire") to Martin Luther King ("Pride") to third-world hunger ("Crumbs From Your Table"). "Mothers of the Disappeared" was a lament for the victims of violence in South America.

In the 1990s, Bono shape-shifted from Christian shaman to hedonistic devil-in-disguise, and U2 pioneered groundbreaking stage sets: The ZOO TV tour broadcast a sensory overload of fast-edit images and ironically sloganeered words (EVERY-THING YOU KNOW IS WRONG—WATCH MORE TV—BELIEVE EVERYTHING) on a plethora of large screens. The message was that the medium becomes the message if you let it; Bono would adopt a demonic persona called MacPhisto to prank-call the White House or the Vatican. The PopMart extravaganza used the world's largest screen, crowned by a yellow arch, to parody the age of mass consumerism. Beneath the glamorous disguises, U2 used their global platform to preach their own Christian, turn-of-the-millennium message: IT'S YOUR WORLD—YOU CAN CHANGE IT.

Another of their slogans—MOCK THE DEVIL AND HE WILL FLEE—was a phrase favored by St. Patrick 1,500 years ago to convert the pagan Irish; the band used it to mock their own fame and ambition.

Their shows illuminated serious causes, from the Declaration of Human Rights to the names of victims of IRA atrocities, to a list of the names of the victims of 9/11. Bono's activism took him to Ethiopia and Latin America in the 1980s; more recently, he has amazed Washington and London politicians with his articulate and informed demands on behalf of the world's poor, aided by

another outspoken Dublin singer-songwriter, Bob Geldof.

Yet broach the topic of Bono's activism in any Dublin pub, and you'll doubtless hear a searing critique of alleged tax evasion by the multimillionaire behind the DATA and ONE campaigns. Despite such hometown begrudgery, the band members remain residents of Ireland, creating employment and investing in local businesses and properties. The reality is that the members of U2 *have* changed their world—both locally and globally. The success of these four hometown heroes will soon be celebrated in a U2 museum. ∎

IRISH HISTORY: SUNDAY BLOODY SUNDAY

In 1983, one of Ireland's most historically charged terms gave U2 a title for a global hit. "Sunday Bloody Sunday," the opening song on the album *War,* was inspired by Ireland's Troubles and by singer Bono's early experience of watching his parents go to different churches throughout his childhood.

Incidents several decades apart mark two distinct Bloody Sundays. On the morning of November 21, 1920, during the Irish War of Independence, IRA units killed 14 British undercover agents in Dublin. In the afternoon, 14 civilians attending a Gaelic football match at Croke Park were killed by the Royal Irish Constabulary, aided by British Auxiliary and Black and Tan soldiers. That evening, three IRA prisoners in Dublin Castle were murdered by their interrogators.

Derry's notorious Bloody Sunday took place on January 30, 1972, when Parachute Regiment soldiers, in an action subsequently labeled by British Prime Minister David Cameron as "unjustified and unjustifiable," shot 26 civilians—14 of whom later died from their injuries—at a civil rights march in the city.

U2's statement on the spiral of murderous revenge in Northern Ireland opens with an echo of their pacifist hero John Lennon's line about reading the news today, in despair. Over the rousing tattoo of a military drumbeat, Bono decries a bewildering political landscape that offered no hope of

escape. This is a protest song against violence, an anthem for peace, but the band was careful it was not misinterpreted as a call for a united Ireland. Bono would introduce it to American audiences by saying, "This is *not* a rebel song."

The chorus of "Sunday Bloody Sunday" begged the question of how long Irish people must sing the tired song of violence. An answer came in the closing song of the album, "40," which drew its inspiration from the biblical passage of Psalm 40. This tells of God putting "a new song in my mouth," offering hope for an Ireland that was, at the time, hopelessly divided. ∎

The film *Bloody Sunday* retells the events of January 30, 1972.

IRISH VOICES: THE HISTORIAN OF MODERN IRELAND

For most Irish citizens, the history of modern Ireland begins in 1916, when rebels took over the center of Dublin and declared nationhood. The British, although engaged in a fierce war on the European continent, quelled the Easter Rising within a week, Some 200,000 men from Ireland had served in World War I, yet Ireland's War of Independence followed fast and lasted from 1919 to 1921. The end of British rule in 1921 and the divisive decision to sign a treaty with England turned the dream of nationhood into bitter civil war.

Compromise with the "auld enemy" would always be contentious, as professor of modern Irish history Diarmaid Ferriter notes in A Nation and Not a Rabble: "Veteran Irish republican Denis McCullough recalled in old age 'We lived in dreams always; I dreamt of an Ireland that never existed and never could exist.' The Irish, like all revolutionaries, had their dreams but some turned into nightmares when the challenge of compromise intruded."

The Irish Free State was created as a self-governing dominion in 1922, and so began a long, hard transition toward full statehood. When Ireland became an independent republic in 1949, the six counties of Northern Ireland, created in 1921, remained part of Britain. These counties were Antrim, Armagh, Down, Derry (or Londonderry), Fermanagh, and Tyrone.

In his study of the revolution and its aftermath, Ferriter explores the stories of ordinary Irish people. As a broadcaster as well as a university professor, Ferriter has delved deep into the national archives to exhume many personal narratives of the nascent nation. "History is often written by elite victors without the perspective of the men and women who suffer the consequences of their leaders' decisions," he explains. "That imbalance is now being corrected as we find in newly released archives the military service pension applications of the men and women active on the ground from 1913–23 and we hear their voices, often the despairing voices of the losers."

Despair, of course, is often laced with denial: "Unionists have written their own history; often a history which does not include an honesty about their own internal divisions," Ferriter says. "The Irish nationalist versions were simplistic

> "The rebels would be aghast that Ireland remains partitioned, but seeing a prosperous Republic of Ireland in the EU would give some of them satisfaction."
>
> — *Diarmaid Ferriter*

too, emphasizing the idea of one Irish 'nation' without a nuanced enough definition of what might constitute an Irish 'nation' and how it might be realistically shared; and with insufficient appreciation of the Unionist mindset." A truly "united Ireland" has remained a mirage.

The revolutionary period has been romanticized, not least of all by movies, such as Neil Jordan's *Michael Collins* (see page 22). Ferriter makes the case that if Collins (assassinated at 31) is the James Dean of Irish history, Eamon "Dev" de Valera was Ireland's Gregory Peck. (Dev, the young American-born mathematics teacher who would become Ireland's greatest statesman, was a major player in the sweeping drama of the Irish Revolution.) "The rebels were poets, teachers, trade unionists," says Ferriter. "The 1916 Rising was consciously staged as a drama and had the desired, dramatic effect." In its aftermath, it became clear that the stage had been set for what now seems, in retrospect, the inexorable march toward full independence for Ireland.

Initially, however, public sympathy for the rebels was sparse, but the British backlash swung the pendulum of history toward their cause. "Certainly, British minds saturated with imperial thinking contributed to radicalizing the Irish," says Ferriter. "By executing the 1916 leaders and arresting indiscriminately, they overreached and underestimated; and by not recognizing the results of the 1918 general election, in which Sinn Féin triumphed, they made a war of independence inevitable."

A century on from Ireland's revolution, how would the rebels view the nation's progress? "They would be conscious that many of their promises remained unfulfilled and that while the ideals they articulated were poetic, the post-revolutionary governing was done in prose," says Ferriter. "The awesome power exercised by the Catholic Church would have troubled some of them, and abuses of power— both religious *and* political—had grave consequences for women and children in particular. Ireland has had a remarkably stable democracy for a century and in international terms, that is no mean achievement." ∎

Diarmaid Ferriter is a historian, broadcaster, author, and professor of modern history at University College Dublin.

Battle-scarred Sackville Street, Dublin, during the 1916 Easter Rising

British forces behind barricades as the War of Independence loomed

Entertaining a brighter future: The colorful facade of the Bord Gáis Energy Theatre illuminates Dublin's Grand Canal Square.

Irish Heritage

Dublin Through the Ages

Dublin is a modern, future-looking European capital with a rich past. From the southside of this river-split city, a walk across the harp-shaped **Samuel Beckett Bridge** leads you into Dublin's Docklands, the city's financial district where glass towers stand alongside the **Custom House** as well as other stately 18th-century structures.

The industrial **Boland's Mill,** where Eamon de Valera fought in the Easter Rising of 1916, has been redeveloped as the centerpiece of **Boland's Quay,** a residential and commercial hub; the occupancy of high-tech giants Google and Facebook has resulted in this district being dubbed Ireland's Silicon Docks.

Yet even as Dublin reinvents itself, the past is ever present. Stroll down O'Connell Street, the city's main thoroughfare, and stop to read the Proclamation of Independence outside the **General Post Office.** It was here that Padraig Pearse, leader of the 1916 Rising, read aloud that document's clarion call. Remarkably for its time, the proclamation acknowledged the equality of women, the protection of the nation's children, and even the nascent nation's solidarity with "her exiled children in America." The 1916 rebels were imprisoned a few miles away in **Kilmainham Gaol,** where many were executed. Previous insurrectionists in 1798, 1803, 1848, and 1867 met a similar fate, and a tour of Kilmainham's bleak gray buildings offers chilling insight into Irish history.

To understand "Dubs" a little deeper, visit the **Little Museum of Dublin.** Spread across two rooms of a Georgian building on St. Stephen's Green is the story of the capital in the 20th century. Visitors who want to delve deeper into Ireland's past should round the corner to Kildare Street, where the **National Museum of Ireland (Archaeology)** displays the treasures of this storied island. The 12th-century Ardagh Chalice and the eighth-century Tara Brooch are among the beautifully crafted artifacts on display. The museum also offers visitors the unusual opportunity to gaze upon the bodies of Irish men and women from Celtic times: The "Kingship and Sacrifice" exhibit displays corpses retrieved from midland bogs, preserved for millennia and thought to be victims of ritualistic sacrifice.

The crypt in **Christchurch Cathedral** is another place where Ireland's past is preserved for perpetuity; this medieval church has loomed over the capital since its foundation in 1030 and its rebuilding by Richard de Clare (Strongbow), the Anglo-Norman nobleman who invaded Ireland in 1170. Cross a bridge from Christchurch and you're in **Dublinia,** a

re-creation of the city in medieval times that includes Viking World.

Any typical social media photo posted from here epitomizes Dublin today, a city that often seems to transcend time. Or, as the quintessential Dubliner, James Joyce, once wrote: "I am tomorrow, or some future day, what I establish today. I am today what I established yesterday or some previous day." ∎

IRISH HISTORY: THE PRESIDENT & THE CANDLE IN THE WINDOW

The president is Ireland's head of state, elected to perform largely ceremonial duties for a term of seven years (the Taoiseach, or prime minister, leads the government). Since 1990, however, presidents have used the office symbolically to effect significant social changes.

If you visit Dublin's Phoenix Park, close to the American ambassador's mansion, you'll pass the official residence, Áras an Uachtaráin. In the kitchen window is a perpetually lit candle, a symbol of solidarity with Ireland's emigrants abroad initiated by President Mary Robinson in 1990. The status of the world's outsiders has always been important to Robinson, Ireland's first female president, a former United Nations High Commissioner for Human Rights, and, more recently, a UN Special Envoy for Climate Change.

The candle in the window is an ancient Celtic tradition, a sign of welcome to wandering wayfarers. It is now tended by poet and President Michael D. Higgins (see page 187), a Galwayman whose presidency has also been marked by his support for social equality and justice. The president has encouraged the expression of the island's artistic community, while strongly supporting the humane treatment of refugees and minorities in a changing Ireland. His predecessor, Mary McAleese, made the building of bridges between Ireland's polarized religious communities her mission.

But it was Ireland's third president who was perhaps its most influential political figure. Eamon de Valera—or "Dev," as he was affectionately known—held the presidency from 1959 to 1973, having served three terms as Taoiseach. De Valera was one of the leaders of the 1916 Easter Rising con-

demned to death in the aftermath by British authorities. His life was spared, it was believed, due to representations made by the U.S. Consulate, who argued against the execution of the New York–born de Valera. He would later introduce the Irish Constitution, in 1937, and steer his small ship of state on a course of neutrality during World War II (known as "The Emergency" in Ireland). Once considered a radical—he refused to ratify the Anglo-Irish Treaty of 1921, sparking the civil war—de Valera came to be respected globally as an elder statesman among postcolonial countries. One British politician who negotiated with Dev described him as the "Spanish onion in the Irish stew."

The candle in the window is a reminder of that diversity in Ireland's diaspora, and the warm welcome home that is now afforded to all. ∎

A burning lantern set in the kitchen window of the president's residence serves as a symbol of solidarity with Ireland's émigrés abroad.

WICKLOW

Most visitors to Ireland land in Dublin, so the county of Wicklow, 12 miles (19 km) south of the capital, acts as a portal to the southeast. After landing, head for the coastal town of Bray, then take the back roads through some of Ireland's most scenic countryside. These high roads bring you through Wicklow Mountains National Park. In the heart of summer, when these granite elevations are ablaze with heather and gorse, nature paints spectacular vistas of purple and yellow. But any time of year, Ireland's sunshine and shadow cast their moody hues over the mountainsides, and crystalline rock faces glisten then suddenly darken under rain cloud. The peaks of Lugnaquilla and Scarr Mountain stand out for their top layers of shiny schist.

Historically, County Wicklow fell within the Pale, a jurisdiction of English rule, and the gardens of its great houses were well tended. This horticultural tradition, nurtured alongside the natural beauty of the wilderness, earned Wicklow the title Garden of Ireland. Many mansions still maintain public grounds; the Powerscourt Estate, outside the village of Enniskerry, boasts the crown jewel of Irish gardens, designed in a multiplicity of European and Asian styles.

Wicklow provides hikers with many challenging climbs, chief among them the six-day Wicklow Way. Another trek, St. Kevin's Way, traces the sixth-century saint's footsteps through the hills to the monastic ruins in Glendalough; or take one of the trails within Avondale Forest Park. The county's towns include Wicklow, with its historic jail; Bray, with its Victorian esplanade; and the lesser visited destination of Arklow, which Van Morrison celebrated in song. The town of Avoca, located near the Meeting of the Waters, the confluence of the Avonmore and Avonbeg Rivers, hosts a treasure trove of Irish artisanship at Avoca Mill.

Alongside traditional craft, Irish innovation is blossoming across the county these days. Craft beers flow plentifully, such as those brewed by Wicklow Wolf in Bray, while Glendalough Distillery produces a creative variety of whiskeys and gins. ∎

Glenealo Valley Trail in Wicklow Mountains National Park offers spectacular vistas.

IRISH GARDENS: WICKLOW, GARDEN OF IRELAND

Ireland's temperate climate, mild and mainly damp, makes for a gardeners' Eden. The warm waters of the Gulf Stream inoculate a 10-mile (16 km) band of coastline against frost. All kinds of subtropical plants flourish here, and Irish gardens, long the preserve of the landed Anglo-Irish aristocracy, are liberally laced with exotic species garnered on global travels. Known as the Garden of Ireland because of its dramatic countryside, County Wicklow is home to several of the most beautiful Irish gardens.

Bray's **Killruddery House,** the home of the Brabazon family since 1618, boasts a 300-year-old garden that nestles in the foothills of the Little Sugar Loaf and Bray Head Mountains. Killruddery offers the local community a farm shop, the Grain Store Restaurant, a tearoom, house tours, and a farm market selling produce from the 800-acre (324 ha) estate. Its baroque gardens, a symmetrical web of walks, woods, and water, were designed as an extension of Killruddery's elegant Tudor Revival mansion. Statues of Venus, a dying war-

rior, and the four seasons set the mood for strolls through gardens started in 1682 by Capt. Edward Brabazon.

Brabazon employed a Versailles-trained gardener known today only as Monsieur Bonet, and the French influence is everywhere. The *miroirs d'eaux* (water mirrors), two long ponds 550 feet (168 m) in length, reflect the house and the shifting Wicklow skies. A mountain spring sends water through a half-mile (0.8 km) aqueduct to the Cascades, a series of decorative waterfalls; the flow then continues into the Ace of Clubs and lily-filled Beech Hedge ponds, where a French fountain is surrounded by nymphs at play.

The Sylvan Theatre is a grassy amphitheater surrounded by bay hedges, beyond which stretches the Wilderness, a woodland of shady walks in green, gold, or russet red, depending on the season. Look out for the Florence Court yews (*Taxus baccata,* the oldest Irish yew species) that line the path to the Orangery. Head gardener Daragh Farren has been carefully restoring these, pinching them back each year,

removing deadwood, and paring them into a more fastigiate shape. The Statue Gallery in the house's conservatory, with its impressive glass dome, is a perfect finale to your visit.

In contrast to the horticultural order of Powerscourt (see page 34) and Killruddery, **Mount Usher** in Ashford is Ireland's wildest garden. A riot of plant life, this garden is set astride a series of colorful walkways on a verdant stretch of the River Vartry. Here abundant birdsong prevails, and two suspension bridges provide fine vistas of nature's lushness. A variety of trees and plants from around the globe decorate the meadows, including a Montezuma pine, liquidambar, eucalyptus, and an enormous dawn redwood, a species once thought to be extinct. The Azalea Walk is a spectacular stroll in springtime.

A melancholic mood pervades the **National Botanic Gardens** in Kilbride. Here the ruin of Kilmacurragh, an 18th-century Queen Anne–style mansion, casts a haunted air over a meadow filled with 117 species of wildflowers and grasses, including twayblade, yarrow, and devil's bit scabious. Take the Monk's Walk through a leafy avenue of *Podocarpus salignus,* a Chilean evergreen. Elsewhere, look out for the Prince Albert yew. Victorian-era reseedings from the Americas, Asia, and the Antipodes abound, making a visit to the National Botanic Gardens a horticultural stroll through the British Empire.

If far-flung exotica appeal to your wandering spirit, head for **Victor's Way** in Roundwood, where an Indian spiritual garden provides delightful Asian spice amongst Wicklow's classical European gardens. ■

The expansive estate of Killruddery House welcomes visitors with walks, farm markets, and a range of events year-round. OPPOSITE: Walkways span the River Vartry at Mount Usher in Ashford.

Powerscourt Waterfall is the highest in Ireland, cascading dramatically from an elevation of 398 feet (121 m).

Special Places

Powerscourt House & Gardens

The 62-acre (25 ha) Powerscourt Estate near Enniskerry is a must stop on any gardener's gambol through the Emerald Isle. Visitors arrive via a fine beech avenue leading to the estate's modern mansion, the five-star Powerscourt Hotel. Farther on, the 13th-century castle, **Powerscourt House,** was extensively remodeled in the 18th century into a vast Palladian mansion. The family seat of the viscounts of Powerscourt, the estate has been owned by the Slazenger family, founders of the sporting goods business, since 1961. In 1974,

a fire gutted the house, which was completely renovated in 1996. Today the estate includes an elegant hotel with shops and the Avoca Terrace Café. Also on-site is **Tara's Palace Museum of Childhood,** featuring one of the world's greatest dollhouses. But it is the estate's grandiose gardens that take center stage, inviting visitors to step out onto a sweeping scene from a bygone age.

Created in the Victorian tradition by the sixth and seventh viscounts of Powerscourt, the tiered **Italian Garden** cascades from the house's southeast facade down to a lake-like

pond, with the Japanese Garden to one side and the Victorian Walled Garden to the other. Classical statues commissioned from European sculptors decorate the sweeping amphitheater, which lies luxuriant against the stunning natural backdrop of Great Sugar Loaf Mountain.

This is a garden of slopes, terraces, and wonderful walkways. You descend from the house's terrace, where stones collected from nearby Bray beach have been laid in an elegant mosaic that shows the date of the garden's completion: 1875. Beneath the terrace, on the retaining wall of the perron, sits the sundial of astronomer Francis Cranmer Penrose. Look out, too, for the statues of Victory and Fame, crafted in Berlin in 1866 by sculptor Daniel Rauch.

Flights of steps take you down to the 2.5-acre (1 ha) oval pond, which is ringed with tall North American conifers. A statuesque pair of winged horses guard the watery expanse, which melds into a Monet masterpiece when the water lilies bloom. Next, explore the Gothic boathouse with its margin of local tufa rocks hanging down from the archway like a monster's fangs, and listen to the watery splash of the Triton fountain spouting water from his conch.

While the main amphitheater and the Walled Garden date from the 1730s, the garden's Italianate flourish dates from around 1840, inspired by the sixth viscount of Powerscourt's visit to Villa Butera (now Villa Trabia) in Sicily. His architect, Daniel Robertson, suffered from gout and was wheeled around in a wheelbarrow, a fortifying bottle of sherry in hand as he directed teams of workmen. The roads around Powerscourt gave much needed employment throughout the famine years of the 1840s. The garden was completed by the seventh viscount and his architect, Alexander Robertson (no relation to his barrowbound predecessor).

The **Japanese Garden** was created in 1908. Its centerpiece, the **Pepperpot Tower,** is surrounded by fine Italian cypresses and guarded by a circle of cannons, one of which dates from the Battle of the Boyne in 1690. The tower was built by the eighth viscount, Mervyn Richard

Wingfield, to celebrate the visit of King George V in 1911; the surrounding garden is a clutter of cherry trees, bridges, and a pagoda. Near the tower grows a Torrey pine, an endangered California species. Powerscourt Estate is also home to Ireland's tallest tree, a Douglas fir towering nearly 200 feet (62 m) in height. You'll also come across spiky monkey puzzle trees from South America, fine Sitka spruce, and a giant redwood.

The Japanese Garden leads to the **first viscount's grotto,** a somewhat spooky place with moss-covered walls and arches, darkened by the dense green shades of *Soleirolia soleirolii.* Farther along, the splendid rhododendron walk is flanked by a pet cemetery, where for centuries the estate's owners, the Wingfields and the Slazengers, buried their dogs, ponies, cows, and other best

friends. Perusing the headstones here makes for a poignant pause.

Past the Dolphin Pond, named for its Parisian fountain, lies the wonderful **Walled Garden,** a staple of many Victorian gardens. Look for the metal-worked roses, thistles, and shamrocks on the wrought-iron gate, symbols of England, Scotland, and Ireland, respectively. Inside, the long herbaceous border hosts more than a thousand varieties.

Away from the garden, but a focal point of the estate, is **Powerscourt Waterfall.** Located some three miles (5 km) from the house in the Deer Park, these are the tallest falls in Britain and Ireland, tumbling over rocks some 398 feet (121 m) high. This force of nature provides a cascading crash into the Wicklow wilderness after all the refined elegance and manicured magnificence of Powerscourt's gardens. ∎

The 62-acre (25 ha) Powerscourt Estate is the jewel in the crown of Irish horticulture.

Special Places

Glendalough

Glendalough is among the most sacred places in Ireland. This tranquil monastic site lies nestled in a valley alongside two glacial lakes (Glendalough is Gaelic for "valley of the two lakes"). Protected by steep wooded mountainsides that rise toward heaven, these monastic ruins host a dozen or more 10th-, 11th-, and 12th-century buildings, including one of Ireland's most iconic round towers.

The monastery was founded by St. Kevin in the sixth century. This shy young monk had sought his "green martyrdom" (a total dedication to a spiritual life, lived in nature) by inhabiting a hollow tree to escape his burgeoning renown as a miracle worker. In 570, Kevin became abbot of Glendalough's growing monastic community. His successors suffered repeated attacks from overseas when medieval Europe descended into chaos: The Danes ransacked Glendalough in 922, as did Norman adventurers in 1176. But the resilient holy men rebuilt, largely under the direction of Abbot Lorcan O'Tuathail (St. Laurence O'Toole, 1128–1180).

When you visit this place of pilgrimage today, follow the well-marked footpath through the granite double arch—the only surviving monastic gateway in Ireland.

This path winds around the riverside site, where you'll pass St. Kevin's Kitchen, a cramped oratory with an 11th-century belfry. Wander in awe among the ruins and ponder the lives of the faithfully departed, the dates of whose earthly existences are now erased from the many weathered gravestones.

The remains of the complex include the shell of a 10th-century cathedral, a 12th-century priest's house whose east wall invites you beneath a dogtooth arch, and the 10th-century round tower where monks took refuge from the Norse and the Normans.

The tower tapers 110 feet (33 m) up to its conical top, affording a panoramic lookout; its stairless door hovered some 12 feet (3.5 m) above ground level, accessed probably by rope ladders that could be drawn up before any marauding hordes reached the base. ∎

St. Kevin's monastery in Glendalough ("valley of the two lakes") sits alongside the upper and lower glacial loughs.

GREAT IRISH DRIVES: THE WICKLOW MOUNTAINS

Starting in the seaside town of Bray, this spectacular driving route takes you, in the words of Irish poet William Allingham, "Up the airy mountain, Down the rushy glen . . ." Keep an eye out for hidden mountain lakes as you traverse the Old Military Road and the scenic Sally Gap before descending into the sacred valley of Glendalough. Watch out too for roaming sheep in the road. The beautiful vale of Avoca awaits farther along; then return via Roundwood, Ireland's highest village.

From Bray, first take the N11 south, then turn off onto the R117 for Enniskerry. In the center of this quaint village—a recent set for Disney's *Disenchanted* (2022) film—turn right at the fountain onto the L1011; this climbs steeply up to the smaller village of Glencree. Stop at the **Glencree Centre for Peace and Reconciliation** and the **German Military Cemetery,** where 134 World War II soldiers are buried. During the First World War, this hilltop village also hosted German POWs, mainly unlucky aviators who soon discovered there were worse places to spend the war. Local legend has it that the prisoners—known officially in neutral Ireland as "guests of the nation"—were even allowed to visit the village pub on certain occasions, on a collective promise that they return by midnight. Some even married locals and stayed on after the war.

At the top of the hill, turn left onto the R115. This blacktop, the **Old Military Road,** stretches over gorgeous bogland, passing the mountain lakes of upper and lower Lough Bray and sweeping through **Wicklow Mountains National Park.** This is among Ireland's most scenic stretches of road. At Sally Gap, admire the views of **Lough Tay,** otherwise known as the Guinness Lake, where Ireland's famous brewing family once held legendary parties on the fairy-tale estate of Luggala. If you have binoculars, try to spot peregrine falcons high on the steep cliffs. Farther south, the pull-off on the left at **Glenmacnass Waterfall** affords spectacular views of the cascades and the valley below.

Continue on to Laragh, then turn right onto the R756 for **Glendalough** (see opposite page). Here you can stretch your legs among the medieval ruins and enjoy tea or fine dining at the **Wicklow Heather Restaurant & House** in Laragh. Bibliophiles should peep inside the restaurant's Irish Writers Room to see first editions of several masterworks, including a *Ulysses* printed in Paris in 1922.

From Laragh, follow the R755 south, passing Clara Lara Funpark on your left. This road takes you through bucolic **Vale of Clara Nature Reserve.** At Rathdrum, turn right onto the R752; or, if you have time, continue straight for a mile (0.6 km) to visit **Avondale House and Forest Park,** former home of Charles Stewart Parnell, the man once called the "uncrowned king of Ireland." The R752 leads past the Meeting of the Waters and into the village of Avoca, which may look familiar to viewers of the TV series *Ballykissangel*. Don't miss a visit to **Avoca Mill** for fine clothes and a variety of handcrafted gifts.

Backtrack to Laragh, take the R756 to Annamoe, then the R755 north to Roundwood, where you can view the eclectic mix at Victor's Way Indian Sculpture Park. Continue on the R755, turning left onto the R760 to visit **Powerscourt House and Gardens** (see page 34). Then return via the N11 back to Bray, where **SEA LIFE Bray** is well worth a visit. ∎

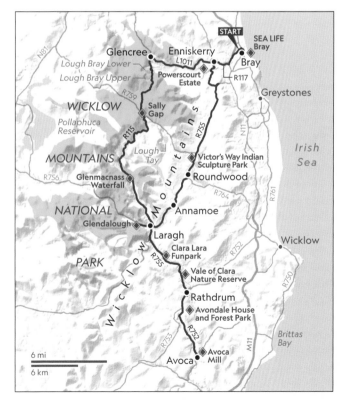

The Wicklow Mountains Drive loops around the Garden of Ireland.

Bray's eclectic Harbour Bar, a labyrinth of rooms dedicated to *caint, craic,* and *ceoíl* (chat, fun, and music)

Insider's Guide

The Best Bar in the World?

No visit to Wicklow is complete without a visit to Bray's **Harbour Bar,** regularly named one of the best bars in the world. This lively venue lies at the end of the seaside town's Victorian promenade, just around the corner from Bray's DART station, making for an easy night out for visitors staying in Dublin's city center. The building was originally a terrace of fishermen's houses, and its many endearingly eclectic rooms make a visit here more like a pub crawl than a pub call. You can sip a creamy Guinness while you watch the harbor swans and ducks in the front courtyard, and order from one of several eateries run by the Duggan family along the seafront (deep-dish pizza, gourmet burgers, etc.). There's also a fish-and-chips stall in Harbour Bar's yard. Another excellent option is to walk the quarter mile (0.4 km) to Daata, one of Ireland's finest Pakistani restaurants.

While there's no shortage of memorable eateries to try, the Harbour Bar is truly an unpredictable adventure in the wild swirl of Wicklow social life. Inside, the middle bar is usually occupied by colorful local characters who'll share Bray tales of local celebs (Bono and Sinéad O'Connor lived nearby for years). The main bar has a dartboard, frequent trad music sessions, and a cozy snug (booth), ideal for secret-sharing. A stage area hosts comedy and live music acts, as well as poetry and book readings. The lounge is warm and welcoming in winter with its coal fire—the perfect place to sip a hot whiskey or port after a cliff walk around Bray Head. Upstairs, you might stray into a party or reunion. Arrive thirsty, order one of the barman's fine cocktail concoctions—the Dark & Stormy is recommended—and wander through a labyrinth where lounging with the locals is an entertaining art form. ■

IRISH VOICES: THE HARPMAKER

The harps in Kevin Harrington's workshop are solid, beautifully crafted instruments: three pieces of carved wood framing strings that resonate with the ancient music of Ireland and as the symbol of a nation. The harp is also the icon of Guinness and the emblem on Ryanair planes. An Irish envelope with a harp shouldn't be ignored—the letter within is from the government. For Harrington, a musician and craftsman from a family of carpenters, the instrument is how he makes his living, creating both modern and Celtic harps for a younger generation.

Harrington was himself a performing musician. He studied and played orchestral music at the Cork School of Music before learning to make instruments at London Metropolitan University and the Newark School of Violin Making. He recalls wielding his double bass through London's Underground for gigs with his band the Small Horses (a nod to Irish writer Flann O'Brien). "I wouldn't be too popular in a packed tube train when the doors opened and I'd squeeze in at Camden Town with the big black case," he laughs.

> "Honestly, hearing one of my harps played well is the ultimate job satisfaction for me."
>
> *— Kevin Harrington*

True to form, a double bass loiters bulkily against a bench in his workshop, but the room is filled mainly with the elegant shapes of harps in various stages of completion. Harrington explains the three wooden parts of a harp: The hollow soundbox, covered by the flat soundboard, lies at a 45-degree angle to the column, or pillar, which rises parallel to the longest string. The swanlike neck, or harmonic curve, that forms the top of the instrument connects the soundbox and pillar and acts also as a board for the tuning and bridge pins, which regulate the strings.

For the soundbox and soundboard, Harrington uses the finest spruce, imported from Switzerland. The wood is harvested from north-facing slopes, where trees age slowly, making it dense, seasoned, and richly resonant for this hollow part that gives the instrument its sound.

"The ancient Celtic harps would have soundboards made of one piece of wood, hollowed out like a canoe," he explains. In the modern harp it's a box with a flat piece glued on top. Even this wood needs time to settle, and new harps frequently go out of tune. "The flat top of the soundboard can belly up [swell]," he says, "so only hard, seasoned spruce is used."

The pillar and the neck are made of local walnut or cherry wood, often sourced locally from Killruddery in Bray. Modern strings are made of carbon fiber, which gives a bright sound and produces more tension than historically used materials, such as nylon or goats' intestines. "Traditional Irish musicians love the tension of carbon fiber strings, as it helps the fingers skip easily across the strings on high-tempo tunes," says Harrington.

The ancient instrument has evolved much since the medieval era of the Trinity College harp (Brian Boru's Harp). This early Irish harp, or wire-strung *cláirseach,* came from an age when powerful chieftains gave patronage to musicians and their castles housed finely decorated instruments. The Anglo-Norman conquest saw the harp decline in popularity, with Irish culture forced underground by the Penal Laws. Traveling musicians carried rudimentary harps, such as the 17th-century harp of the blind Turlough O'Carolan, now on display at the National Museum in Dublin. Happily for Harrington, and music lovers everywhere, the harp has enjoyed a recent resurgence in popularity in Ireland. ∎

Harrington crafted this harp for 10-year-old Muireann Ní Mhuirthile, who was inspired by Disney character Clarabelle Cow's playing of her "Golden Harp Song" on *Mickey Mouse Clubhouse.*

KILDARE

Located just west of Dublin, Kildare is a county of many charms. The market town of Kildare is home to St. Brigid's Cathedral, where you can climb the 108-foot-tall (33 m) round tower to view the surrounding green plains. This was the lookout point for the monks and nuns of a mixed monastery founded by the saint in A.D. 490.

Kildare is known for the Curragh, vast grasslands that constitute the home of Irish horse racing and host some of the world's most successful bloodstock breeding centers. High levels of calcium carbonate in the waters of the River Tully and Curragh grass are credited with increasing the bone strength of horses raised here. Local winners can be backed at the Curragh Racecourse (*cuirrech* means "racecourse" in Irish), while the Irish National Stud & Gardens in the village of Tully provides an equine education with a museum and an array of creatures great and small. The National Stud's Japanese Gardens, dating from 1906, are an exotic delight, designed by renowned horticulturist Tassa Eida. Garden lovers should also visit the Celtic water and rock garden, centered around a monastic cell and dedicated to the patron saint of Irish gardens, St. Fiachra.

The Bog of Allen Nature Centre in Lullymore offers a more expansive landscape. This bogland stretches more than 235,000 acres (115,000 ha) and across nine counties of the Irish midlands. Industrial harvesting of peat fueled power stations, agribusinesses, and urban homes throughout the 20th century, but left much of the fragile ecosystems devastated. The nature center was established to restore the bog as a wetland wilderness and to educate visitors about the ecological values of the boglands.

Just outside the town of Celbridge stands the impressive Palladian mansion of Castletown House, built between 1722 and 1732 for William Conolly, speaker of the Irish House of Commons. The house, rescued from ruin by Desmond Guinness and the Irish Georgian Society, now belongs to the state. Celbridge is known as the home of Georgian Ireland. ∎

A treat for the senses, the serene landscape of the Irish National Stud & Gardens invites relaxation and reflection for the visiting equine enthusiast.

Irish Heritage

The Horse in Ireland

Irish people love horses. It's not unusual to pass children leading a horse through an Irish town to a lush field where their outsize pet can graze. Or even to see youngsters speed through the streets of Dublin with a horse and buggy.

The Irish home of all things equine is the Irish National Stud & Gardens in County Kildare, which also hosts an equine museum. After the museum, take the tour of the grounds and you'll encounter many horses, none more impressive than a stallion called Invincible Spirit. This "Sire of Sires," a champion racehorse who commands a cool $140,000 (€120,000) in stud fees, is owned by Saudi Prince A. A. Faisal. Horse racing in Ireland is a global affair, and horse racing abroad is a strangely Irish affair—attend a meet anywhere in the world and you'll encounter an Irish contingent. Invincible Spirit now leads the Hollywood lifestyle of a retired champion in the heart of Kildare, a county with several private stud farms. At the National Stud, the euphemism of "covering" is used to describe the deed that is now the bay horse's raison d'être. At the height of the breeding season, this temperamental Thoroughbred is led to the "covering shed" up to four times a day. Wander the grounds and you may also meet a tiny Falabella horse called Homer (named after Mr. Simpson). This Argentine breed stands between 25 and 34 inches (63–86 cm) high—about five to seven hands in equine measurements.

Another famously compact animal is the Connemara pony, a hardy native of Ireland's rugged west. Like every good Irish story, the breed's origins are murky and much disputed. Some believe they derived from Scandinavian ponies imported by Vikings. The legend that stuck, however, is that galleons from the Spanish Armada ran aground off Connemara in 1588, and the Andalusian horses on board were set loose. These bred with native horses, resulting in the sturdy, versatile ponies now used for show jumping, dressage, and eventing. The Connemara Pony Breeders' Society holds an annual fair for the sale of the breed. Much less official horse fairs are held each summer in places such as Killorglin in County Kerry (see page 134) and Ballinasloe in County Galway.

The Curragh Racecourse in County Kildare is the home of Irish racing, and any meeting here or at nearby Punchestown Racecourse offers visitors a fascinating glimpse of the Irish (of all social strata) at play. Ireland's wildest equine festival is the weeklong Galway Races. Laytown, in County Meath, is unique in the racing calendar as the only beach race run under the Rules of Racing, the guidelines stipulated by the Irish Horseracing Regulatory Board.

Another summer fixture is the Dublin Horse Show, a show jumping gala that culminates in a contest for the Aga Khan Trophy by teams from around the world, including the U.S. and Mexico. ∎

Horses and ponies are often an Irish child's best friend. OPPOSITE: John O'Sullivan, from Skibbereen, West Cork, stays dry as he keeps a tight rein on his steadfast pair of plow horses.

Joe Strummer of the Clash (back row, second from left) joins the Pogues lineup for a short period: The band married punk with traditional Irish music.

Songlines

The Great Irish Songs

The Irish are a musical, lyrical, and storytelling people, and songwriting is a much prized craft in Irish culture. The web of Ireland's "songlines" winds around the globe, spun by the country's storied diaspora, with many tangled strands of sad ballads, celebratory odes, and country tunes hearkening back to a mist-shrouded homeland.

The land of poets inspires musicians to set verse to music, as evidenced by Mike Scott's interpretations of W. B. Yeats' works on the Waterboys' album *An Appointment With Mr. Yeats*. A recent national poll revealed that Ireland's favorite song was the musical rendition of Patrick Kavanagh's poem "On Raglan Road." The Monaghan poet set his lyrics to an old Irish tune, "The Dawning of the Day," and his ode to a lost love was immortalized by folksinger Luke Kelly (of the Dubliners); Van Morrison (accompanied by the Chieftains) and Sinéad O'Connor have also recorded the song. The sheer lyricism of Kavanagh's words demands a slow, soulful delivery, which, when sung in the *sean-nós* (unaccompanied) style, can hush the rowdiest pub.

Another Irish favorite is "The Green Fields of France" by the Furey Brothers, a wistful ballad about the senseless slaughter of World War I, in which 40,000 Irishmen died, including the song's hero, young Willie McBride.

If you visit Strokestown House (see page 227) or other sites related to the Great Famine, listen to the Pogues' song "Thousands Are Sailing" to get a sense of Ireland's harrowing history of exile. Phil Chevron's lyrics about Irish émigrés' sense of displacement in New York are both exhilarating and heartbreaking—a perfect evocation of the emigrant's dichotomy.

The musical sirens of the homeland for such exiles are, of course, "the pipes, the pipes" that call the wanderer home in one of the most famous of all Irish songs, "Danny Boy." Yet the writer of its well-worn words was an English lawyer named Frederick Edward Weatherly. "The Derry Air" (or "Londonderry Air"), which Weatherly used as the melody for his lyrics, originated in that contentiously named city in the 17th century. "Danny Boy" was written just before World War I, a lament for a young man answering the call of duty, and it articulated his parents'—or maybe his lover's—wish for a safe return. Weatherly's lyrics were ambiguous, but he made clear his "humble hope" that great singers might sing his song. Count Basie, Elvis Presley, Johnny Cash, and Sinéad O'Connor, among many others, have all honored that wish. And many a not-so-gifted guest has performed "this perfect song," as actor Gabriel Byrne described it, as their party piece at an Irish wedding or funeral. ∎

IRISH VOICES: IRELAND'S SINGER-SONGWRITER LAUREATE

If you want to know what's happening in Ireland, you can read the *Irish Times* or the *Irish Independent*. You can watch the RTE News. Or you can listen to Christy Moore sing about it.

Christy Moore, from the Curragh of Kildare, has been telling the story of Irish society in song since the 1960s. His voice is a force of nature, often accompanied only by his guitar. His lyrics are a source of celebration, conflagration, and oftentimes righteous indignation at the world's injustices. Christy tells it like it is, and isn't afraid to tell off others—mainly politicians—for telling it like it isn't. He has celebrated everyone from St. Brendan to Steve Biko; he has castigated everyone from Margaret Thatcher to Irish bishops to the owners of Guinness.

His songs (and cover versions) are a running commentary on every aspect of Irish life, covering a swath of topics: music festivals ("Lisdoonvarna") and Irish school days ("All I Remember"), gangland crime ("Veronica") and the miraculous or the malicious mischief of the Catholic Church ("Casey," "Knock," and "Magdalene Laundries"). His ability to see all sides of an argument was expressed in "North and South of the River," a song he co-wrote with Bono.

A Christy concert is a major musical event in Ireland, an evening of storytelling and *craic* (high spirits), and an enthralling emotional roller-coaster ride. One minute you're laughing at stories of self-induced delusions ("Delirium Tremens"), next minute you're nearly in tears at exiles' laments ("City of Chicago"); then you're swept back to the Irish fighting in the Spanish Civil War ("Vive la Quinte Brigada") or moved by tales of the sufferings of others, such as Ireland's Travelers ("Go Move Shift").

At the center of this swirl of stories and songs sits a man and his guitar. "An Ordinary Man," according to his signature song, but an extraordinary songwriter and storyteller. Christy Moore is no ordinary musician; like the *filés* (poets) of ancient Ireland, he is a traveling entertainer, a provocateur unafraid to speak truth to power. And he is one powerful performer.

Christy Moore is a national treasure. ∎

Christy Moore, who hails from Newbridge, County Kildare, is a singer, songwriter, and *seanchaí* (storyteller) supreme.

"If I had to live again I would do exactly the same thing. Of course I have regrets, but if you are 60 years old and you have no regrets then you haven't lived."

— *Christy Moore*

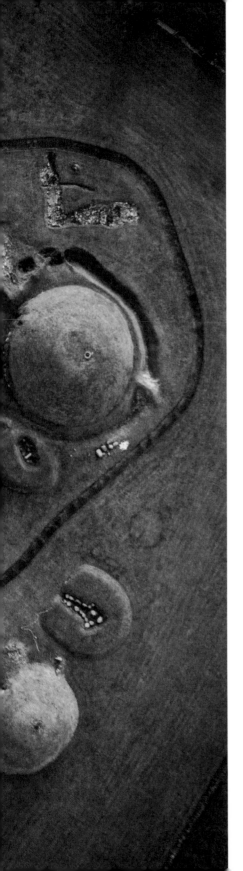

LOUTH & MEATH

Louth, known as the Wee County, is the smallest in Ireland. Yet it looms large in history, legend, and myth. Louth is the setting of *Táin Bó Cúailnge* (aka *The Táin*), Ireland's national epic, and Carlingford Lough was a landing place for the Vikings at a time when the region was a maze of kingdoms. Neighboring Meath has been dubbed the Royal County, its history long shaped by sovereign rulers, both Irish and foreign.

Brú na Bóinne ("palace of the Boyne") is one of the key prehistoric landscapes on Earth. This complex puzzle of passage tombs and monuments centers around the burial chambers at Newgrange, Knowth, and Dowth. Extensive artwork carved in stones honors the sovereign leaders of a Neolithic people who dwelt here 5,300 years ago. The nearby Hill of Tara was the ritual center of Irish monarchy, a sacred "higher ground" where temples, palaces, and tombs marked the lives and deaths of the High Kings of Ireland. Today, grass grows over Ráith na Ríg ("fort of the kings"), but an old yew (a fairy tree) ablaze with prayer ribbons demonstrates the power that this landscape still exerts on the Irish psyche.

Foreign royalty exerted physical power from strongholds such as the Norman-built Trim Castle and Anglo-Irish Slane Castle, seat of the Conynghams, a Scottish Protestant family. In 1690, the armies of the warring kings, Catholic James II and Protestant William III, clashed at the Battle of the Boyne, delineating that river forevermore as a defining political, religious, and historical fault line of Ireland.

Today, the crowds massing atop the Hill of Tara are New Age travelers seeking earthly power from this "energy vortex." Rock fans who flock to Slane Castle for Ireland's biggest gig find there an ancient fortification attuned to the demands of the 21st century, with a restaurant, tours, and a whiskey distillery. Slane Castle, like the Wee County and the Royal County, is now ruled by the future as much as the region's storied past. ∎

The Great Mound at Knowth measures 130 feet (40 m), making it the longest known megalithic passage in western Europe.

Special Places

Brú na Bóinne

In Ireland, the thin veil between the present and the past is all around you. There are few places on Earth, however, where you can step further back in time than at the archaeological wonderworld of Brú na Bóinne.

Brú na Bóinne means "palace of the Boyne" and refers to the sacred prehistoric landscape that encompasses a vast complex of tombs and monuments. The site can only be accessed through its visitors center, which offers a fine introduction to the archaeology and history of the landscape. The Boyne Valley is also a treasure trove of megalithic art, and the center's exhibits supply a quick education on the meaning of the swirls and symbols that the layperson will soon encounter.

Newgrange's main Neolithic passage tomb, believed to have been constructed for ancient Ireland's kings, dates from circa 3300 B.C., making it older than Stonehenge or the Pyramids at Giza. Step inside and you pass through a portal taking you back to the time of Ireland's earliest inhabitants.

This passage tomb is one of the first known instances of humankind's mastery of astronomy. Professor M. J. O'Kelly, who directed the excavations, deduced that the "roofbox" above the tomb's entrance was designed to align with the midwinter sun. At the winter solstice (December 21), the rising sun's rays pierce the roofbox and sunlight edges along the passageway before filling the chamber with light. The ancient

Neolithic people could thus pinpoint nature's turning from the darkness of winter to the lengthening daylight hours of spring.

The mound—312 feet (95 m) in diameter and standing 36 feet (11 m) high—is built of a cairn of stones covered in earth. The outer curbstones have been re-created, and many are decorated with Neolithic art replicated from stones found at the site. The passageway runs for 62 feet (19 m), leading into a cruciform chamber with a corbelled stone roof. Several cremated remains were found here, suggestive of a royal burial chamber. Other Neolithic tombs here are connected to the main mound by a cursus monument (long linear parallel earthen banks) that was probably used for ritual processions.

Knowth holds two passage tombs, found at the western edge of the Boyne Valley. These back-to-back chambers face east and west, with passageways of more than 100 feet (30 m). Several satellite tombs surround the main mound. This sacred site later became the royal residence of the Síl nÁedo Sláine, rulers of the kingdom of North Brega.

About one mile (1.6 km) north of Newgrange lies Dowth, the final piece of the archaeological puzzle of Brú na Bóinne. Dowth is the only mound yet to be excavated and, for now, remains cloaked in mystery. It is thought to be around 5,000 years old. ∎

A 21st-century light show at Knowth, part of the Neolithic tomb complex built for Ireland's kings, circa 3200 B.C. OPPOSITE: The passageway to Newgrange's main tomb utilizes the sun's lowest position in the sky to light the chamber on the winter solstice.

GREAT IRISH DRIVES: THE BOYNE VALLEY

The Boyne Valley is probably the most historically resonant drive you can take anywhere in Ireland. This bucolic route spirits you through dark Cromwellian times via the churches and museums of Drogheda; traveling along the banks of the River Boyne, scene of Ireland's most significant battle; through medieval monastic settlements and Anglo-Norman castles; and back to the ancient burial sites of Neolithic royalty. The drive also takes in stately Slane Castle, where modern-day rock 'n' roll sovereignty are feted each year. The castle, or nearby Slane village, is a perfect place to break for lunch. The sheer beauty of the rolling hills and the river hereabouts are a reminder of why this part of Ireland became the ancient seat of kings and why vast armies vied to rule these rich agricultural lands.

Built of gray stone on the River Boyne, the town of Drogheda has the fine **Millmount Museum** and, on West Street, **St. Peter's Church,** notable for displaying the leathery brown severed head of St. Oliver Plunkett (1629–1681). The saint was hanged, drawn, and quartered here for treason and canonized three centuries later.

From here take the R132 north and follow the signs to **Monasterboice,** the sixth-century site of St. Buite's monastery. Monasterboice is an evocative monastic site, famed for Muiredach's Cross, a 10th-century masterpiece of the stone-carver's art. The site's 110-foot-tall (33 m) round tower is also beautifully crafted from curved stones. From Monasterboice, follow the Boyne Valley Drive signs onto R168 south to **Old Mellifont Abbey,** St. Malachy's Cistercian monastery. This was the center of the Cistercian order (a stricter branch of the Benedictines) in Ireland, having been its pioneer house when established in 1142 by St. Malachy.

Backtrack to the R168 and go south before turning right onto the N51 toward the village of Slane. At the sign, turn left over the bridge to the Battle of the Boyne site at Oldbridge House, where King William of Orange routed the armies of Catholic King James II on July 12, 1690. Cannons guard the **Battle of the Boyne Visitor Centre,** which tells the story of the event and gives demonstrations of the weapons and military equipment used.

The Boyne Valley's past includes the Neolithic sites of Newgrange, Knowth, and Dowth, several monastic sites, and the ruins of Dunmoe Castle (pictured).

Backtrack to the N51 and head west for **Slane Castle,** where the Gandon Room Restaurant offers a set lunch menu in resplendent surrounds. The grounds form a natural amphitheater sweeping down to the river, and rock royalty, including the Rolling Stones, David Bowie, Bob Dylan, Bruce Springsteen, and U2, have played huge concerts here.

Between Oldbridge and Slane, stop off at the **Francis Ledwidge Museum** at Janeville and contemplate the story of a poet caught between the forces of Irish history. Francis Ledwidge grew up here, a dedicated nationalist compelled to fight in World War I for the British Army: He was killed at the Battle of Passchendaele. Ledwidge's "Lament for Thomas MacDonagh" is among many poems celebrating the beauty of the Boyne landscape even as they are tinged with the sadness of the sacrifices made by so many in Ireland's name.

Continue on the N51 through Navan, then take the R147 for Kells, home to a fine set of Celtic high crosses. **Kells Monastery** was founded here by monks from St. Colmcille's (Columba's) monastery on Scotland's Isle of Iona, where they created the famous *Book of Kells* (see page 56). Next, take the R163 past Ballinlough and then the R154 to Oldcastle. You'll soon see signs for **Loughcrew Cairns,** Neolithic passage tombs dating from 3000 B.C. At Cairn T, you'll find some of the finest Neolithic art in Ireland. From here, follow the R154 south through Athboy to the town of **Trim.** If you happen to spot Mel Gibson grazing his sheep on the commons, that's because the actor was made a Freeman of the town, after shooting much of the Oscar-winning *Braveheart* at formidable **Trim Castle.** Another setting used for the film, **Bective Abbey,** lies to the east along R161. The abbey sits by the River Boyne, which supplied the Cistercian monks with water and fish. Bective was the second Cistercian settlement in Ireland, established in 1147.

From here, follow the L4010 to the mythic **Hill of Tara** (see page 52), one of Ireland's sacred places. Tara is considered "higher ground," and from the Meath plains it commands a view of 100 miles (160 km). For a thousand years, throughout the first millennium, Tara was the seat of the High Kings of Ireland. Many Irish people believe the hill is a natural vortex, a focal point of earthly and psychic energy. It is certainly a powerfully evocative place, steeped in history and heroic myth.

The N3 to Navan and the L1600 land you at the Neolithic monuments of **Brú na Bóinne,** the palace of the Boyne (see page 48), where the visitors center will lead you into an ancient Celtic netherworld. Here, at a long bend of the River Boyne, Ireland's pre-Christian dwellers of 5,000 years ago constructed more than 50 monuments that today give us insight into their beliefs and religious practices. This vast complex of tombs, henges, forts, and standing stones is Europe's primary archaeological site. A visit to the massive passage grave of **Newgrange** is particularly enchanting, like stepping into prehistory. The main chamber fills with sunlight on the day of the winter solstice, making its builders among the first humans known to have figured out the sun's seasonal shifts. A small number of visitors are allowed to witness this ancient marvel of astrological and architectural precision each year; you can enter the lottery to be among them at the visitors center.

The L1601 will bring you back to the 21st century, and back to Drogheda, at the end of your day trip through seven millennia of Irish history. ∎

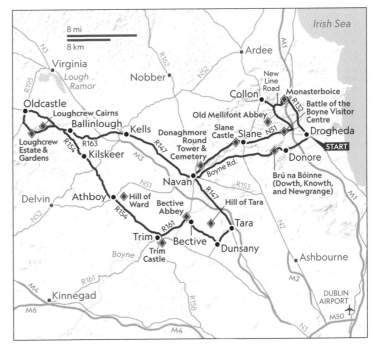

The Boyne Valley Drive leads visitors on a spin through Irish history.

The Lia Fáil ("stone of destiny") rises from the Forradh, a mound where Ireland's High Kings are thought to have been crowned.

Special Places

The Hill of Tara

Ask any Irish person where the spiritual center of Ireland is, and, regardless of religion, they will probably point you toward the Hill of Tara. Rising from the plains of Meath, this was the symbol and seat of Irish government for the first millennium A.D., during which Ireland converted from a pagan to a Christian land.

The harbinger of this change was St. Patrick, who recognized the importance of Tara and approached Laoghaire, the Irish High King, in A.D. 435 to smooth the path for Christi-
anity. On the Hill of Slane, Patrick lit a paschal fire to challenge the pagan fires on Tara. This alarmed the Druids of the king, who summoned the newcomer to the royal court. Patrick so impressed the king that the new faith was soon given the sovereign's approval. Today, St. Patrick's Church, built in 1822-23, acts as the visitors center for the site. Just outside the churchyard, a statue honors the nation's patron saint.

In pagan Ireland, Tara's geography and topology made it a natural choice for the crowning of kings.
From its apex, one can see parts of all four provinces on a clear day, a vital advantage in ancient times when the early warning of approaching enemies was necessary. The hill is also believed to sit at the intersection of several of nature's life force lines, making it an energy vortex, a swirling center of Earth's healing powers.

Various inhabitants occupied the Hill of Tara for at least 3,000 years prior to its abandonment in 1022. Today, you enter through the visitors center, where maps are available that trace the subterranean layout of this largely grass-covered site of burial mounds and covered monuments and trenches. Before you exit, look out for Irish artist Evie Hone's fine stained-glass window.

The northern side of the hill contains the massive trenches of a sunken entrance to Tara, 750 feet (230 m) long, known as the Tech Midchúarta ("banquet hall"). Nearby is Gráinne's Fort, a ditched mound, and the circular Sloping Trenches where Dúnlaing, the king of Ulster, massacred 30 princesses of Tara in A.D. 222.

As you reach the top of the slope, Tara's oldest monument, the **Mound of the Hostages,** comes into view. Before reaching this, however, you must pass the remains of **Ráith na Ríg** (Fort of the Kings). This vast enclosure measures approximately 1,045 feet (320 m) north-south by 866 feet (264 m) east-west and incorporates most of the key monuments of Tara. It is believed to have been used for ritualistic or ceremonial purposes.

Continue south along the hill, past the three-ringed Iron Age hill fort known as **Ráith na Senad** ("rath of the synods"), where two beautiful gold collars, or torques, were discovered in 1810. This is thought to have been another great feasting hall, where kings and their warriors were feted. Excavations unearthed fragments of imported fine glass goblets.

Alas, the site was badly damaged in the early 1900s, when a group of British Israelites roughly ransacked an adjacent graveyard in their search for the Ark of the Covenant.

Next to this is the **Royal Enclosure,** the largest embanked area, which encloses three sites. **Dumha**

na nGaill, the Mound of the Hostages, a grass-covered hummock with a low entranceway, is a Neolithic passage tomb where High King Cormac mac Airt (A.D. 227–266) imprisoned captives from Connacht. Side by side to the south are **Cormac's House** and the **Royal Seat,** two ring forts. King Cormac ruled during the Iron Age, and he is remembered in the Annals of Clonmacnoise (a 17th-century English translation of a lost Irish chronicle) as "absolutely the best king that ever ruled in Ireland . . . wise, learned, valiant and mild, not given causelessly to be bloody as many of his ancestors were, he reigned majestically and magnificently."

Farther south you'll come across the **Forradh,** a mysterious mound that is the subject of intense speculation. It is thought to have been the ceremonial place of inauguration where High Kings were crowned. Rising from this mound, the Lia Fáil, or "stone of destiny"—a somewhat phallic pillar stone—points skyward. Irish legend relates that this stone would cry out when the rightful king of Ireland put his foot on it. Even farther south, outside of the Royal Enclosure, stands another ring fort, **Rath Laoghaire,** where the Druid-cursed King Laoghaire is believed to be buried upright in full battle regalia.

The legendary political and psychic power of Tara has cast its spell down the centuries of Irish history. Hugh O'Neill rallied his troops here before the Battle of Kinsale in 1601. A group of rebels are buried where they were slaughtered on the hill during the 1798 Rebellion. And the Catholic Emancipator, Daniel O'Connell, held his largest "Monster Meeting" here in 1843 as he sought to repeal the Act of Union.

The Hill of Tara looms large in the Irish psyche. ∎

ABOVE: A detail from the Book of Kells, the famous biblical tome crafted by Irish monks

Insider's Guide

The Boyne's Lingering Legacies

To drive along the green farmlands of the Boyne Valley is to journey through the vast sweep of Irish history. To the west lie the ruins of several medieval monasteries. **Monasterboice** was founded by St. Buite in the sixth century; its round tower and Celtic high crosses evoke an age when Christianity stood firm against Norse raiders as Rome was ransacked and Western civilization overrun. At monasteries such as Monasterboice and **Kells,** monks recorded the Gospels for posterity; the round tower of Monasterboice, burned in 1097, is believed to have housed a library and other treasures. On nearby **Muiredach's Cross,** however, biblical stories survive in carved stonework: Sts. Paul and Anthony in the desert, the damned entering hell, and Adam and Eve in the Garden of Eden are among the panels still visible on this fine Celtic cross.

A short drive away is **Mellifont Abbey,** the motherhouse of the Cistercians in Ireland. The abbey was established by St. Malachy, who gathered Irish and French monks to the hard-working and disciplined order founded by St. Bernard of Clairvaux in France. From here, the Cistercians added "daughter houses" such as nearby **Bective Abbey.** The success of Mellifont would lead to its confiscation in 1539, when Henry VIII ordered the dissolution of the monasteries.

Henry's break with Rome led to the schism that would divide Ireland for centuries along sectarian lines. This schism was reinforced in 1690 at the Battle of the Boyne, which would also shape the future of Europe. Decades earlier, Oliver Cromwell's conquest of Ireland began with the massacre of Drogheda, where Irish Catholic and English royalist forces, along with many townspeople, were savagely butchered. The **Millmount Museum,** located in the old fort, recounts this dreadful day in Irish history: September 11, 1649.

Centuries later it is a different day that is still celebrated by Ulster Unionists—and dreaded by Irish Republicans. On July 12, 1690, the Protestant forces of William of Orange routed those of James II, the Catholic king who controlled all of Ireland except Ulster. The Jacobites were fighting for Irish sovereignty, Catholic rights, and land ownership. The death toll was relatively small— only an estimated 2,000 of the 23,500 Jacobites and 36,000 Williamites who took part were killed. But William's triumph resulted in vast tracts of land being granted to his supporters and the ascent of the Anglo-Irish aristocracy to power. As King of England, Scotland, Wales, and Ireland, William implemented the Penal Laws, which would suppress Catholics for centuries. The day's narrative and outsize ramifications are recounted at the **Battle of the Boyne Visitor Centre** at Oldbridge House.

As you walk through these now bucolic battlefields, you cannot but consider all the lives still affected in Ireland, north and south, by the divisions sown so long ago. ∎

Muiredach's Cross, a medieval Celtic high cross at the monastic site of Monasterboice

Irish icon Bono attains elevation at stately Slane Castle, home of Henry Mountcharles and host to rock's biggest acts.

IN THE KNOW: SLANE CASTLE

One of Ireland's most beautiful—and accessible—castles, the imposing hilltop fortification at Slane has been the home of the Conynghams, a Scottish Protestant family, since 1703.

Visitors can take a guided tour of the castle to learn of its storied history, which includes tales of major rock concerts hosted by the current lord of the estate, Henry Mountcharles, the eighth Marquess Conyngham. The concerts began in 1981, when Irish band Thin Lizzy were supported by a relatively unknown young Dublin act called U2. The Rolling Stones, supported by the Chieftains, headlined in 1982 (and later in 2007). Future Nobel laureate Bob Dylan played chess with a youthful Bono before taking the stage in 1984, to be joined for an encore by the young Dublin singer along with Belfast veteran Van Morrison. Bruce Springsteen, David Bowie, R.E.M., and Madonna have also entertained the happy masses on the castle grounds. Many performers have noted that the setting's natural amphitheater sweeping down to the Boyne River makes Slane one of the world's most appealing music venues. In 2001, U2 returned for a memorably emotional homecoming on the week that Bono's father was laid to rest. The castle was a second home for the band, who had used its elegant library to record their 1984 album, *The Unforgettable Fire.*

Tours can also be taken of the Slane Whiskey distillery. The heritage room, barley room, cooperage, and maturation warehouse are preludes to a tasting of Slane's signature triple-blend casked whiskey. If you time your tour well, you can enjoy lunch or supper at the castle's superb Gandon Room restaurant before a farewell cocktail (or more Slane Irish Whiskey) at Browne's Bar, which also offers light meals. Accommodations are also available at the organic Rock Farm on the estate. ■

Every dazzling page showcases the painstaking detail that the monks of Kells and the Scottish isle of Iona imbued in their mesmerizing masterpiece.

Irish Heritage

The *Book of Kells*

The town of Kells in County Meath is known worldwide for the book that was probably written, and most likely conceived, somewhere else. Like Joyce's *Ulysses,* the *Book of Kells* was likely created far from Ireland, yet both these works continue to lure people to Dublin from all over the world.

While scholars debate its origins, many concur that this glorious 680-page rendering of the four Christian Gospels was probably begun at St.

Columba's monastic island settlement at Iona Abbey (established off the west coast of Scotland circa 563) and continued at Kells.

Monastic life during the sixth to ninth centuries was marked by rigid training in the arts of calligraphy and illustration, and religious orders dedicated long hours to the preservation of the Gospels and the Latin language. Monks toiled by candlelight in scriptoriums, copying ancient texts onto durable vellum pages and rein-

venting ways to illustrate the Bible.

The *Book of Kells* was kept at Kells Monastery from around A.D. 800, at the height of Ireland's golden age of monastic talent and influence, until Oliver Cromwell arrived in the town in 1654. It was sent to Dublin for safekeeping and presented to Trinity College in 1661, where it has been kept ever since, under glass in a special display area in the Old Library. In 1953, it was rebound in four volumes, two of which are always on display—one open to a sumptuously illuminated page, the other to a page of text. While the egg-white fixative employed by the monks 1,200 years ago has proved remarkably effective in keeping details sharp, the pages on display are changed every few months to prevent the illuminated script from fading due to overexposure. Whichever pages are on view, visitors are always awestruck by the wit, intricate beauty, and inspiring power of the imagination that shines through the patina of the centuries.

The artistic brilliance of the monks of Iona and Kells shows in the freedom of line and intricacy of detail that draw the viewer into every page. At first sight, the illuminated capital letters may seem an inextricable riot of circles, rectangles, and curlicued bits of foliage, tangled up in red, gold, and blue. But study them further and you'll discern more devils in the details: beasts with open mouths, misshapen demons, domestic cameos, and figures passionately embracing. You'll also see huge-eyed angels, heavenly flowers, and fruit, all cunningly hidden in uprights or packed into round spaces. A single page thus becomes either an admonishing or encouraging sermon on the pitfalls and pleasures of life in this earthly realm. Every dazzling page shows the infinite pains the ancient monks must have taken in making their mesmerizing masterpiece—and many demonstrate their mischievous delight, too.

To achieve the luminous colors, the monks used whatever natural resources they had access to or could obtain by barter, purchase, or gift, such as gold leaf, chalk for white, and copper verdigris for green. Reds came from lead, shades of black from charcoal, and blues were wrought from either ground-up lapis lazuli or woad, a European plant. No doubt a fair number of monks went blind in the making of their masterpiece, just like Joyce would while working on his, 1,100 years later. ■

IN THE KNOW: *THE SECRET OF KELLS*

In 2009, the creation of the *Book of Kells* was daringly reimagined in *The Secret of Kells*, a movie produced by Kilkenny-based animation studio Cartoon Saloon, directed by Tomm Moore. Using decorative animation to mirror its subject matter, this enchanting film tells the story of Brendan, a 12-year-old boy given the task of completing the legendary book. Brendan's challenge to complete Brother Aidan's lifelong labor takes him beyond the abbey walls at Kells into the enchanted woods, where mythical monsters dwell. The young boy must fight Vikings and a serpent god in his search for a crystal that holds the key to his quest. He must also overcome his own fears and turn darkness into light. The narrative details the painstaking labors of the monks and their ingenuity in sourcing nature's rich color palette for the pages of their manuscripts. The animation also delightfully relates how this rich array of color and luminescence was applied to the pages that still inspire awe in the eye of the beholder. The resulting rich fantasy is a delight for children and adults alike, and heralded Cartoon Saloon as one of the great success stories in Irish cinema history. ■

A scene from *The Secret of Kells,* a daring and imaginative animation of the monks' tale

Historic Drogheda

The medieval town of Drogheda was founded in the 12th century by the Lord of Meath, Hugh de Lacy, near the mouth of the River Boyne. This Norman stronghold was protected by walls built between 1234 and 1424 and withheld an Irish rebel army in 1641. By the time Oliver Cromwell arrived to quell the rebellion in 1649, Drogheda was defended by the Irish Catholic Confederation and English royalist forces who had fled to Ireland after the English Civil War.

Cromwell's New Model Army attacked Drogheda, butchering an estimated 3,000 royalists, priests, women, and children in a period of hours. The royalists took final refuge in Millmount Fort on an ancient mound south of the river. Sir Arthur Aston, who had refused to surrender, was reportedly beaten to death with his own wooden leg. The massacre of Drogheda marked September 11, 1649, as one of Ireland's darkest days. In 1808, Millmount Fort was replaced by a Martello tower built to protect against Napoleonic invasion. Today the tower holds the **Millmount Museum,** which tells the story of the massacre and Drogheda's role in the Irish Civil War (1922–23).

On the town's east side, the 13th-century barbican St. Laurence's Gate once welcomed visitors through an arched entrance flanked by five-storied towers. The cemetery of **St. Peter's (Protestant) Church,** originally built by Hugh de Lacy and rebuilt in 1747, is also worth a visit to see the ghoulish "cadaver tombs" of Sir Edmond Goldyng and his wife, Elizabeth Fleming, which depict in stone the decomposing bodies of these 16th-century nobles.

An even more gruesome reminder of mankind's mortality is on display in a golden shrine at the 19th-century **St. Peter's Roman Catholic Church:** the leathery brown severed head of St. Oliver Plunkett. Plunkett, who established a Jesuit college in Drogheda, was executed for treason on the orders of King Charles II. ■

The Millmount Museum towers above Drogheda; the medieval town was founded in the 12th century by the Lord of Meath.

IN THE KNOW: DROGHEDA'S FESTIVALS

The Fleadh Cheoil (Festival of Music) comes to Drogheda.

The Drogheda Arts Festival hosts live music, poetry, and performance.

Like towns all over Ireland, Drogheda regularly welcomes visitors to its many festivals. Throughout the summer, the **Drogheda Arts Festival** hosts theater, live music, film, poetry, and workshops such as silk painting. The **Drogheda Traditional Music Weekend** (usually held in November) attracts some of the most accomplished and talented traditional musicians, singers, and dancers to the old town. The **Boyne Music Festival** (a monthlong event during July and August) brings chamber music concerts, jazz, and poetry readings to the Boyne Valley, and it's a joy to find yourself in the parlor of fine old Townley Hall, listening to a quartet, followed by an Irish poet. A rather more raucous outdoor musical experience is the annual **Slane summer concert** (see page 55), where global superstars rock the castle grounds by the serene waters of the Boyne.

Drogheda also hosts **An Chúirt Chruitireachta** (International Festival for Irish Harp), a multiday event during which practitioners and makers of the ancient Gaelic musical instrument come to celebrate the soothing sound of the strings. You'll hear solo performances of the harp, as well as concerts where the instrument's fluid music mixes with uilleann (elbow) pipes, concertinas, flutes, vocal groups, and even electronic instruments that propel the harp into new musical spheres.

Drogheda has twice been chosen to stage Ireland's largest traditional music festival, **The All-Ireland Fleadh Cheoil** (Festival of Music). The Fleadh is run by Comhaltas Ceoltóirí Éireann (Society of the Musicians of Ireland), an organization founded in 1951 to promote Irish music and culture in Ireland and among the diaspora. The weeklong festival—usually held near the beginning of August—seeks out the finest exponents of music, singing traditions, and Irish dancing. Drogheda's successful first hosting of the competition in 2018 attracted a record crowd of half a million to the small town over the eight days of the festival, and the warm local hospitality was rewarded with the honor of hosting a second Fleadh Cheoil the following year. Drogheda's Fleadhs included participants from as far afield as the United States, Canada, Australia, and Japan.

Traditional Irish music and dance have become a truly global phenomenon in the 21st century. In Britain and North America, as in Ireland, regional competitions are held as qualifiers for the All-Ireland Fleadh. So in the year leading to the main event, the parish halls and schoolrooms of small towns and villages resound with the practice sessions of young singers, fiddlers, uilleann pipers, and dancers, all vying for the honor of representing their county or province in this high summer festival.

Although the Fleadh has a competitive side, the real joy comes from taking part in the celebration. Wander the streets of whichever town is hosting the All-Ireland Fleadh and you'll come across buskers filling the summer air with lively reels, jigs, and hornpipes. In the town square you'll likely find a line of steel-tipped dancing shoes clacking out an irresistible rhythm on a wooden stage. Or you can settle into a corner of a pub pulsing with the sounds of a traditional session, and listen in wonder as a fiddle player, an accordionist, or a *sean-nós* (unaccompanied) singer enchants the crowd into a hushed silence worthy of church. ∎

Trailheads around Carlingford lead to several hikes tracing the footsteps of pillaging Vikings and folkloric Irish legends.

Walking Around Carlingford

If walking is your pleasure, head for the medieval village of Carlingford in County Louth. There you'll find the trailheads of hikes that follow in the footsteps of pillaging Vikings and folkloric Irish legends. The Norse invaders used the shelter of Carlingford Lough to land in eastern Ireland before plundering towns and monasteries. From Carlingford they headed south to the nascent citadel of Dubh Linn (Black Pool), where many eventually set up as traders among the native Irish. They would not be the last invaders to be absorbed by the Celts' civilization.

The **Táin Trail** on the Cooley Peninsula is an easy climb that rewards with spectacular views. It starts at Carlingford Village, where you'll see the Mountains of Mourne in County Down rising across the lough (and across Britain's problematic border with the European Union).

The town's harbor is dominated by the 12th-century **King John's Castle,** built by Hugh de Lacy, Lord of Meath, shortly after the Norman invasion. Also on the waterfront stands the forbidding **Taafe's Castle,** a 16th-century tower house.

The Táin Trail is signposted from the Village Hotel on the town square. The trail zigzags gradually and you'll soon reach the saddle of the pass at the top of the path, where Carlingford Mountain rises to your right and the lower shoulder of Barnavave to your left. The trail celebrates *The*

Táin, an early Irish epic about the Cattle Raid of Cooley. In it, the mythic hero Cúchulainn enjoys his finest hour when the treacherous Queen Medb of Connacht launches a cattle raid upon Ulster. The queen covets a fabulous bull, the White-horned One, that belongs to her husband, King Ailill. She hatches a plan to steal a beast that would match it: Ulster's renowned Brown Bull of Cooley.

Medb casts a spell to weaken Ulster's warriors, leaving the 17-year-old Cúchulainn to defend the province single-handedly. Wielding his sword, slingshot, and the dreaded spear Gae, he heroically defeats Medb's armies. The wicked queen returns to Connacht with her stolen Brown Bull of Cooley, only to see her prize kill the White-horned One and rampage through Ireland before dropping dead. The queen would later avenge Cúchulainn (Irish women usually have the last word in such disputes).

If you are as fit as the young Cúchulainn (who took his name from a hound), you can attempt trails that take you farther into this mountainous terrain. One leads to the peak of Slieve Foye; at 1,932 feet (589 m), this is the highest point of Carlingford Mountain. From here you'll gaze across two countries and the border between the Republic and Northern Ireland that to this day proves as divisive as the Brown Bull of Cooley. ∎

TASTE OF IRELAND: COOLE SWAN WHITE RABBIT

The Boyne Valley has long been a source of fine food products and is especially renowned for its honey. The medieval monks in settlements such as Mellifont Abbey and Monasterboice were well versed in the ancient art of apiculture (beekeeping). St. Colmcille's brotherhood, having fled Viking raids on the Scottish island of Iona, were granted rich farmlands around the village of Kells, where pastures for cattle were plentiful.

In modern times, the Boyne Valley continues to delight the epicurean traveler. One recent success story is Coole Swan, a quality liqueur that blends rich cream with Irish whiskey. There are many great ways to savor this delicious taste of Ireland: on the rocks in summer, or in a warming Irish coffee on a cold winter's night. Here's an easy way to make a colorful cocktail that blends several tastes of Ireland's ancient east.

INGREDIENTS

- 1⅓ ounces (40 mL) Coole Swan Irish cream liqueur
- ¾ ounce (25 mL) gin (Glendalough recommended)
- ¾ ounce (25 mL) amaretto (Disaronno Originale recommended)
- 1 teaspoon lemon curd (Big Red Kitchen recommended)
- Edible flowers for garnish (such as Sweet William, cornflower, elderflower, dame's rocket, or nasturtium), optional

DIRECTIONS

- Pour the Coole Swan, gin, and amaretto into a shaker.
- Add the lemon curd and ice, and shake well.
- Strain into a chilled cocktail glass, then garnish with edible flowers if using.

Coole Swan makes a refreshing summer cocktail and gives added warmth to an Irish coffee, perfect on a cold winter's night.

Eamon Doherty's sculpture "To the Skelligs" rises high above the landscape in County Kerry, honoring globe-trotting local St. Brendan the Navigator.

The Diaspora in Europe

The Irish have always seen themselves as Europeans. The island was settled first by Celts from northern Europe, and other ethnic groups later assimilated, including Scandinavian Vikings and French Normans. These historical links, and strong bonds with Catholic Rome, meant Ireland's participation in the European Economic Community (later the European Union, or EU) proved less contentious than that of Britain.

Christianity came to Ireland in the fifth century through the returning British slave Patricius (St. Patrick), who had previously escaped his Irish captivity to study for a bishopric in France. Patrick was the first missionary to convert pagans beyond Roman borders. In the fifth and sixth centuries, as barbarians descended on the great cities of the Roman Empire, looting and burning libraries, Irish monks took on the task of transcribing the literature of Europe. As the Pax Romana shattered and the early Middle Ages descended, these men of peace copied classical works by candlelight. Ireland became Europe's

publisher, and many beautifully decorated Irish manuscripts now grace the libraries of France, Switzerland, Italy, and Russia.

St. Colmcille founded his monastery in Iona, Scotland, in 564, where the *Book of Kells* (see page 56) was probably begun. Other Irish monks fanned out across Europe: Columbanus went to Gaul (France) in 590 and founded forest monasteries in Annegay, Fontaines, and Luxeuil.

He also established the first Irish-Italian brotherhood at Bobbio in 612. Irish missionaries reached as far as Modra (Moravia) and Kiev (Ukraine). Monasteries such as Clonmacnoise, Monasterboice, and Mellifont Abbey maintained links with their European brotherhoods, and the Irish founded continental schools to spread the faith via literacy and a love of learning. The first medieval geographer was an Irishman, Dicuil, who studied at St. Denis, France; his *Measurement of the Globe* showed the imaginative sweep of the Irish mind.

Ireland survived later invasions by the Vikings, who plundered the monasteries, and Anglo-Normans, who were largely assimilated. By 1607, however, the English crown sent the Irish aristocracy into permanent exile. Hugh O'Neill, Rory O'Donnell, and Hugh Maguire were among the Ulster lords who boarded a Spanish ship on Lough Swilly in Donegal in that year. Spirited to Rome, they would never see their homeland again, and their lands became the Ulster plantations granted to English and Scottish settlers. Rome and London would thereafter dominate the mindsets of a divided Ulster.

The Flight of the Earls left the Irish lords forever after known as the Wild Geese. They scattered across Europe, many eventually settling in Catholic Spain or France, where they founded vineyards that enjoyed worldwide success with brands such as B&G (Barton & Guestier) and Hennessy (brandy).

In the early 20th century, two Irish writers in European exile revolutionized modern English literature. Dubliner James Joyce left his native city in 1904 and wandered the continent, living in Trieste, Rome, Paris, and Zurich. Yet Dublin was all he wrote about. The multilingual Joyce reinvented language as he went, tapping into Europe's newest science of psychoanalysis to give voice to his characters' streams of consciousness with riverine linguistic fluidity. Joyce was a great European who described multilingualism and exile as forcing one into "two thinks at a time." Joyce believed that history was a nightmare from which we were trying to wake (he would witness the advent of two world wars).

His young acolyte, Samuel Beckett, another Dubliner, worked for Joyce in Paris as he set about his own literary revolution. Writing in both English and French, he pared all but the bare essentials of language from his works. In a desolated post–World War II Europe, Beckett imagined a world of absurdities without God, without meaning, but not without hope.

Like the monks transcribing their medieval manuscripts, the Irish remain adept at absorbing other cultures and creatively mixing them: As war raged in the Balkans in the 1990s, Bono joined with Luciano Pavarotti to record a song for those under siege, "Miss Sarajevo." The Dublin singer and the Italian tenor melded rock 'n' roll with opera in their plea for peace.

Many Irish are now schooled and seasoned in European settings: Killarney Park Hotel's head chef, Sean Doyle, for example, learned his culinary skills in London, Stockholm, and Paris before bringing his expertise back home.

The Irish are committed Europeans; a recent survey showed 82 percent consider themselves "a citizen of the EU." In 2021, President Michael D. Higgins released a book titled *Reclaiming the European Street*. Today, the islanders from Europe's western edge move fluidly throughout the continent, and Europe's most successful airline, Ryanair, displays Ireland's national symbol, the harp, as it flies workers and holidaymakers to Brussels, Trieste, Rome, and beyond. ∎

The Europhile James Joyce with Sylvia Beach, proprietor of the Shakespeare and Company bookstore in Paris and first publisher of *Ulysses,* in 1922

LAOIS & OFFALY

The counties of Laois and Offaly are often overlooked by travelers who cleave to the more dramatic scenery around Ireland's rugged coastlines. Yet time spent here in the heart of Ireland will transport you back through centuries of history and heritage. The monastic settlement of Clonmacnoise in Offaly, with its superbly carved Celtic high crosses, is Ireland's best preserved site of the medieval era. This was a time when Irish monks sacrificed their sleep and their sight to transcribe biblical scripts by candlelight. They labored in fear of Viking attacks, keeping lookouts posted in round towers, which also offered sanctuary from marauding Norsemen. One that remains, the Timahoe Round Tower near Abbeyleix, boasts one of Ireland's finest Romanesque doorways.

Stand atop the Rock of Dunamase in neighboring County Laois and you'll hear the whisperings of two and a half thousand years of Irish history in the wind blowing up from the plains. Iron Age settlers are believed to have first constructed a wall around the summit of the rock sometime around 500 B.C. In A.D. 845 the Vikings plundered the rock's medieval settlement. In the 12th century, Dermot MacMurrough, King of Leinster, built his castle here, a structure later fortified by the Norman warlord Richard de Clare (aka Strongbow) only to be destroyed by Oliver Cromwell's forces in 1650. One Anglo-Norman stronghold does survive in Offaly: stately Birr Castle. Today visitors enjoy the estate's beautiful gardens and viewing the huge, historic telescope designed and built by the third Earl of Rosse. Concerts are also regularly held on the grounds, and a visit to the castle's Science Centre is a rewarding educational experience for all ages.

For the midlands' more recent natural history, head for Lough Boora Discovery Park, on land reclaimed from long-harvested boglands. The park now hosts a string of human-made lakes, looped by cycle and hiking trails, and provides vital habitats for many species of birds, insects, and wild animals. ∎

The reflecting telescope known as the Leviathan of Parsonstown, once the largest in the world, stands on the grounds of Birr Castle.

Built on ancient battlements, the ruins seen today on the Rock of Dunamase are remnants of one of the key Norman castles in the conquest of Ireland.

Saints & Scholars

Travel across Ireland's ancient east and you trace the archaeological footprints from centuries of history. The counties of Laois and Offaly encompass many key epochal sites sure to fill modern-day visitors with a sense of wonder, as they ponder the lives of those who have conquered, defended, and settled these storied lands.

The monastic site at **Clonmacnoise** in County Offaly is one of the most evocative ruins from the age of Irish saints and scholars. The monastery was founded by St. Ciarán in the sixth century. In early medieval Ireland, Clonmacnoise sat at the crossroads of transport and power: The River Shannon ran half the length of Ireland, while the Slí Mór pilgrim's road ("Great Way") connected the kingdoms of Mide (Meath) and Connacht, transecting the midland bogs. With Clonmacnoise's shrewd location, Ciarán kept a foot in both camps.

His brotherhood's loyalty was rewarded in 909, when King Flann of Mide commissioned a cathedral and a stunning Celtic high cross, the Cross of the Scriptures. Other patron kings followed suit, as Clonmacnoise gained in stature as a center of prayer and learning. Burial alongside St. Ciarán was coveted by the powerful as the belief spread that the saint had the ear of St. Peter, keeper of records at the Gates of Paradise. Alas, Clonmacnoise suffered the fate of other monasteries as the Vikings attacked in search of plunder in 842 and 845, and today only roofless ruins hint at the site's former grandeur.

In neighboring Laois, we find **Timahoe Round Tower,** one of the finest monastic towers built during Viking times. It dates from the 12th century and is distinguished by a detailed Romanesque doorway depicting interwoven chevrons and human heads. The structure rises almost 98 feet (30 m), with the doorway located 16 feet (5 m) off the ground.

The surrounding monastery was founded in the seventh century by St. Mochua, a warrior turned holy man who lived the life of a hermit, keeping just three earthly companions. His rooster roused him for morning prayer, his mouse kept him awake by licking his ear, and his pet fly marked his place as he read his missal. The **Timahoe Heritage Centre,** located in the 19th-century church next to the round tower, has all the stories.

High atop the **Rock of Dunamase,** located three miles (5 km) east of Portlaois, sits a fortification that has witnessed 2,500 years of human drama from its strategically advantageous elevation on Ireland's central plain.

The Rock is a palimpsest of Irish history, with its three wards, or defensive enclosures divided by walls, inviting you into the heart of the island's Viking, Norman, and Cromwellian past. The Inner Ward boasts three angles of Strongbow's castle still standing firm against the elements. Strongbow was the nickname of Richard de Clare, the formidable Anglo-Norman warlord who ruled his eastern terrain from this ringed fortress. Peer out the round-arched windows onto sweeping farmlands below and imagine a nervous Norman knight wondering who was friend and who was foe in this strange land of clannish Celts.

The Strongbow nickname stemmed from de Clare's preference for Welsh archers during his Irish wars. He found a ready-made site for such defensive warfare on Ireland's central plain: The Rock of Dunamase offered sight lines for spotting attackers all the way to the Wicklow Mountains in the east and the Slieve Bloom Mountains to the west.

The hillock was originally the site of an Iron Age ring fort. The Rock was attacked by Vikings, and the 13th-century Norman castle that Strongbow built was virtually destroyed by Cromwell's forces in 1650. Today, the raw cawing of the crows that now claim these ruins gives this elevated seat of Norman power an eerie afterlife. ∎

IRISH GARDENS: BIRR CASTLE

Birr Castle in County Offaly is an outstanding destination for an entertaining and educational day out. This well-preserved Gothic pile has been the seat of the Parsons family, the earls of Rosse, since 1620. The castle today is still a private house, but it is the beautiful grounds, and the Parsons' active encouragement of their public use, that sets Birr apart as a thoroughly modern Irish estate. The gardens offer several beautiful walks lined with rare plants and trees gleaned from the global travels of Parsons past. Bucolic vistas open up as you stroll around a series of formal gardens, waterfalls, lakes, and rivers. You'll also pass between the world's tallest box hedges, standing some 36 feet (11 m) high.

The focal point of the parklands is the Leviathan of Parsonstown, the great telescope constructed by William, third Earl of Rosse, a dedicated astronomer. Housed between two miniature castle towers, the telescope has the largest cast-metal mirror ever made. When William Parsons peered into what was then the world's largest telescope for the first time in 1845, he discovered a "whirlpool nebula," the light of another galaxy 40 million light years from Earth. The excellent Science Centre on the castle grounds tells the story of the Parsons family's many contributions to scientific learning. ∎

Birr Castle's extensive gardens, some peppered with statuary, may be experienced via walks themed around distinctive trees and the solar system.

Camogie teams from Galway (maroon) and Kilkenny (yellow and black) contest a recent All-Ireland Senior Camogie Championship final.

Irish Heritage

Hurling: Heroic Game of Ancient Myth

Like other GAA sports, hurling is played only by amateurs, yet the game is endlessly discussed and analyzed all over Ireland and has been for generations. Stories about the game graced the country's ancient epics long before they became the stuff of Monday's sports pages and internet posts. Ulster hero Cúchulainn (Hound of Culann), was born Sétanta, and gained his name by killing the fierce guard dog of the royal blacksmith Culann with a *camán* (hurley stick) and *sliotar* (ball).

As with Gaelic football, a game invented in the 19th century, hurling is now played by teams of 15, on a field 476 feet (145 m) long and 295 feet (90 m) wide. The H-shaped goalposts have nets below the crossbar; players strive to score goals into the net (worth three points) and gain single points above the crossbar. They can use their *camán* or their feet to propel the ball, and can run with the ball balanced on their *camán*—an amazingly skillful and brave feat—as opponents try to whack it away. All players wear protective helmets as they compete in a sport dubbed the "clash of the ash" (for the wood used to make *camáns*).

A version of the game for women is called camogie, and many Irish towns run club teams for both genders, which compete for county and provincial honors.

The ultimate goal is to represent one's county in the All-Ireland Championship, which pits all 32 counties (plus teams from London and New York) in an annual competition culminating in the final each September in Dublin's Croke Park. The men's champions are awarded the Liam MacCarthy Cup; the women's winning team collects the Brendan Martin Cup. ∎

IRISH VOICES: THE HURLEYMAKER

Hurling may be played by amateurs, yet as commentator Mícheál Ó Muircheartaigh observed, "When the Gods come out to play, they play hurling." Every visitor to Ireland should try to witness the sheer speed, tribalism, and excitement of an intercounty match and see the current crop of gods who come out to play—bank tellers, teachers, barmen, farmers—all local heroes who grace the beloved national sport.

Joseph Fitzpatrick, who proudly represented the county of Laois at senior hurling, now makes hurling sticks ("hurleys," or camáns) for the next generation. To witness Fitzpatrick craft the instrument of Ireland's ancient sport, you can visit his home workshop, Fitz Hurleys in Brocka, Rathdowney, in County Laois. Here Fitzpatrick produces 3,000 to 4,000 hurleys a year, each crafted from a block of ash, the "wood that gives the greatest spring" to launch a sliotar (small leather ball) 70 yards (64 m) downfield. He explains that the "blocking" of the wood (cutting into a block) by a supplier is key to the process, as the cut must follow the grain down through the "turn" in the wood to the root. He finds 30- to 40-year-old ash is best, with the wood dried to 18 to 20 percent moisture. Much of Ireland's ash has been cut by now, so French wood is a popular alternative.

"A well balanced camán is everything for the hurler," Fitzpatrick says as he takes a plank of springy ash and carves using a scroll saw. He edges the heel, explaining that more needs to come out of older ash, as it's heavier. As he shaves the wood, the ancient artifact takes form. He gently smooths the stick with sandpaper, then binds the handle with a rubber grip, adds two bands to the head to bind the wood, and there it is: a durable Gaelic artwork in ash, crafted by Joseph Fitzpatrick, hurler and artisan, in 15 minutes flat.

"That's a camán that I'd take into battle playing for the county," he says, testing its strength and its spring against the ground. The hurler in him still recalls stepping onto the field at Croke Park in the blue and white of Laois: "Oh God, my heart was racing. It meant everything to me and my family." The calm craftsman recalls how the ancient craft of hurleymaking was passed along to him: Joe Fitz, as he's warmly known in these parts, speaks fondly of a local craftsman named Peter Bergin, who repaired his favored sticks. "It's like a musician with a favorite guitar, I suppose. You tend to just keep on patching up the camán you love," he says, "or the one that brings you luck." In the process, Bergin imparted the "knowledge" to the young, receptive student of the sport.

Lastly, what about that daunting-looking scar running up Joe Fitzpatrick's hand and wrist? "No, that's no old battle wound," he laughs. "That was from the sandpaper strip coming off the machine, a while back—36 stitches, all told." That's Joe Fitz for you; still putting his body on the line for the game he loves so much. ∎

Joe Fitzpatrick, avid hurler and hurleymaker, in his workshop in Brocka, County Laois

"The stopwatch has stopped. It's up to God and the referee now. The referee is Pat Horan. God is God."

— *Mícheál Ó Muircheartaigh, GAA commentator*

KILKENNY

Kilkenny is a medieval town with a thoroughly modern outlook. Here, you can wander across the limestone and marble Green's Bridge, and listen to the whispers of history that swirl in the eddies of the River Nore below. Yet step through Kilkenny's maze of streets and narrow lanes and, if it's August, you'll lose yourself in the sway of one of Ireland's liveliest arts festivals.

Kilkenny was historically the seat of the Butlers, the earls of Ormond, one of the great Norman families to settle in Ireland. Their stately stronghold, Kilkenny Castle, towers over the town and has hosted many a royal revelry, not to mention the odd rock 'n' roll rowdy: Mick Jagger raised hell here in the Swinging Sixties. But sympathy for the devil is a centuries-old practice in Kilkenny. The city came under a spell of suspicion in the 1300s, when Alice Kyteler, the "Witch of Kilkenny," was accused of wicked deeds, including multiple murders. The shadowy cellar of 14th-century Kyteler's Inn, where she lived, is a spirited site for supper, an atmospheric place to ponder Alice's story and that of her maidservant Petronella, who was burned at the stake on High Street.

Kilkenny's higher spiritual ground is attained up on the hill of Irishtown, where St. Canice's Cathedral was built in the 1250s on the site of its namesake's monastery. You can enjoy a panoramic view from the cathedral's 101-foot-high (31 m) round tower. Below you'll see the walled boundaries of the old medieval town, which is laid out in model form inside the cathedral. For the history of the Butlers and Kilkenny's merchants, the Medieval Mile Museum and Rothe House Museum are imperative. Foodies can also plan their visit around one of Kilkenny Castle's great feasts or food markets. And discerning shoppers head across the Parade from the castle to the 18th-century stables, which now house the headquarters of the Kilkenny Design Centre, one of Ireland's finest stores for modern jewelry, fine ceramics, and fashions. ∎

The Kilkenny Arts Festival, one of Ireland's liveliest summer events

Insider's Guide

A Wander Through Kilkenny

Meander along the old streets and narrow lanes of Kilkenny, known as the Marble City for its streets paved with local marble, and step back in time. You will pass such fine Victorian buildings as **Left Bank** on High Street, perhaps pausing for a pint of Smithwick's in Kyteler's, a medieval inn. Sure to stop you in your tracks, however, is the majesty of **Kilkenny Castle;** the imposing Norman fortress towers over the town and dominates its history.

This ancestral home of the Butlers was established on the west bank of the River Nore in 1172. Richard de Clare, the Norman baron known as Strongbow, constructed a wooden fort on this site, later replaced by the stone castle built by his son-in-law William Marshal. The castle was a seat of regional parliaments when the Butlers, the earls of Ormond, bought the castle and the lordship of Kilkenny in 1392.

Among laws passed here were the 1366 Statutes of Kilkenny, which sought to keep Anglo-Norman culture free of all Irish influence. The statutes prohibited the invaders from marrying the natives, speaking Irish, or playing Gaelic games or music. These laws were ignored; the Irish have the best parties, after all. In the words of one observer, the Normans became *"Hiberniores*

Hibernis ipsis—more Irish than the Irish themselves."

Today's Kilkenny Castle is a three-sided fortification: Oliver Cromwell's troops knocked down the fourth (westward-facing) wing in the 1650s, when they passed through Ireland looting cathedrals and monasteries. A tour of the castle is a wonderful procession through historic settings: the Victorian library and drawing room; a massive tapestry parlor; the

dainty bedrooms; and a room with a Kilkenny marble table used by the Butlers to lay out their dead.

Many of the former residents can be admired in portrait form in the Long Gallery, the tour's grand finale. The Butler portraits hang below a finely carved 19th-century hammer-beam roof that resembles an upturned Viking longboat. The castle grounds are equally impressive.

Downtown Kilkenny is a maze of historical cottages, merchants' houses, and medieval churches. The

14th-century **Kyteler's Inn** was the birthplace and home of the town's most notorious citizen, Alice Kyteler, the "Witch of Kilkenny." The wealthy, well-bred Alice married four times, gaining great wealth from a series of sudden, rather convenient widowhoods. She was overheard offering peacocks' eyes and nine red cocks to a sprite named Robin Artisson, whom she would meet at the crossroads. Bishop Ledrede tried her for witchcraft, along with her maid Petronella and her son William Outlawe. Dame Alice escaped to England but poor Petronella was burned at the stake. Outlawe was sentenced to a year's penance—attending mass thrice daily, feeding the poor, and covering the roof of St. Canice's Cathedral with lead. Four years later, the roof mysteriously collapsed.

For more Kilkenny history, head to the **Rothe House Museum** on Parliament Street. Built in the 1590s for a wealthy merchant, the house hosts antique treasures, furniture, and artwork of the Marble City. To get a taste of modern-day Kilkenny, visit in August when the Arts Festival animates the town, or in September, when the Kilkenny "Cats" are usually contesting yet another All-Ireland Hurling Final. ∎

ABOVE: A 13th-century tome from Kilkenny's Medieval Mile Museum OPPOSITE: St. Canice's Cathedral

St. Canice's Cathedral sits high above Kilkenny, preserving the spirit of the medieval era and the storied history of the city thereafter.

Irish Heritage

Medieval Kilkenny

The name Kilkenny is the anglicization of Cill Cainnigh, the Church of Cainneach. St. Canice was a sixth-century monk who established the monastic site high on the hill now known as Irishtown. In Norman times, the native Irish were confined to this ghetto just outside the city walls. Here stands **St. Canice's Cathedral,** a beautiful place of worship that dates from the 13th century but has been renovated throughout its storied history. The Anglo-Norman lord, William Marshal, funded the construction circa 1202; he was also patron of Kilkenny Castle and the Black Abbey, founded nearby circa 1235 by Dominican monks. Both the abbey and the cathedral retain many medieval architectural features alongside more recent stained-glass windows of note.

St. Canice's Cathedral invokes a hushed reverence for the medieval era, with an evocative array of tombs and effigies within its walls. Those laid to rest here were the wealthy and powerful of Anglo-Norman life, among them a number from the Butler family. Many are depicted in full armor with dogs lying at their feet, symbolizing their loyalty.

Take note especially of the beatific effigies of Piers Butler, Earl of Ormond and Ossory (d. 1539) in his domed helmet and elaborate breastplate, alongside his wife, Margaret Fitzgerald, with her horned headdress and puffy sleeves. These memorials are carved in the shiny local limestone called Kilkenny marble, one of many aspects of the cathedral entertainingly explained by the engaging deacon who leads the tours. (His sermon on campanology, the art of bell-ringing, is a real comedic blessing.) Musically inclined visitors should also attend one of the numerous choral recitals held in the cathedral; the acoustics are magnificent and the setting is sublime. St. Canice's has rejoiced in an almost uninterrupted choral tradition dating back to the 13th century.

The cathedral is overlooked by a well-preserved **round tower,** which stands about 100 feet (30 m) tall. The tower is one of only two in Ireland that can still be climbed (the other being St. Brigid's Cathedral in Kildare). For the reasonably agile, the view from on high is worth the somewhat tricky climb involving internal ladders and comprising seven floors and 121 steps in total. From here, you'll be able to view **St. Mary's,** Kilkenny's other cathedral, built in 1857.

St. Mary's Church and **St. John's Priory** are two more sites that reveal the importance of religion in medieval Kilkenny. St. Mary's is now home to one of Ireland's finest visitor experiences, the **Medieval Mile Museum,** where an interactive exhibit reconstructs the history of the medieval city and introduces its key families, including the Rothes, the wealthy Tudor merchants who built the Rothe Chapel. The museum is superbly designed to accommodate the church setting. On weekends, it offers walking tours along Kilkenny's **Medieval Mile Trail,** guided by museum experts. ∎

IRISH GARDENS: WOODSTOCK

The great house of Woodstock in Inistioge may have been burned by Irish Republicans during the civil war in 1922, but recent conservation work by the Kilkenny County Council has restored the grounds into one of Ireland's finest gardens.

Many trees from Asia and the Americas were planted here in the 19th century, including huge Monterey pines sourced in California by horticulturalist David Douglas. Redwoods from the Golden State also tower over the gardens, planted mainly during the residency of William Frederick Fownes Tighe and his wife, Lady Louisa, whom he married in 1825. After Lady Louisa died at Woodstock in 1900, aged 96, the house was left unoccupied and was ultimately razed.

Lady Louisa's long, box-outlined flower beds still grace the terraces outside Woodstock's Victorian walled garden, shaped in chain patterns of circles, diamonds, and T's. Today, the old glass greenhouse has been replaced by the circular, high-domed Turner Conservatory, and the two-acre (0.8 ha) walled garden is abloom once more, its double herbaceous border filled with Victorian perennials and vegetables springing from the loamy, well-drained soil of Kilkenny.

Woodstock's modern garden follows the design of the head gardeners of Lady Louisa's heyday (1840–1890), Pierce Butler and later Charles McDonald, with every effort made to use plants and materials typical of that era. The Winter Garden was laid out by McDonald, a man once described as having "the enthusiasm of a poet, the eye of a painter, and the genius of the artist."

The long-term vision of McDonald, and that of his employer, William Tighe, resulted in the two tree-lined walks that now distinguish Woodstock Gardens. The 1,805-foot-long (550 m) Monkey Puzzle Avenue cuts a path through columns of *Araucaria araucana*—an evergreen commonly known as monkey puzzle—that seem to rise from some forest primeval, but in fact lead visitors into a modest stand of beech and oak.

The Noble Fir Walk amazes with its bolt-upright, skyscraping red firs (*Abies procera*) lining a shaded pathway. This would prove to be the colonel's swan song—he died in 1878, shortly after planting these 44 pairs of trees. ∎

Woodstock's modern garden follows the design of the head gardeners of Lady Louisa's heyday (1840–1890).

IN THE KNOW: BEST PUBS & EATS IN KILKENNY

The old town of Kilkenny pulses with cozy pubs and fine restaurants. If you happen to be here on a weekend when the county hurlers are in action, every pub will be buzzing, and any local will happily tell you why Kilkenny's "Cats" are Ireland's most successful hurlers. Time spent among the array of GAA memorabilia in **Lanigans Bar & Restaurant,** on Rose Inn Street, is an excellent introduction to the Marble City's number one sporting obsession.

If the Cats are victorious, be sure to raise a glass to their success at **Tynan's Bridge House Bar.** Dating from 1703 and located next to St. John's Bridge, this is one of Kilkenny's most atmospheric pubs, with regular music sessions introduced (and sometimes hilariously critiqued) by charismatic bar manager Liam Phelan.

Kyteler's Inn on St. Kieran's Street is famous for its bewitched history, and you'll find your ease somewhere amid two floors of stone floors and wood-beamed bars. This medieval venue—in parts dating to the 14th century—has good food and a wide selection of wines and beers. A meal in its atmospheric cellar will certainly cast you back to the age when inns were places of refuge and sustenance from the long, hungry journeys along dark country roads. The menu at **Matt the Millers** also satisfies most modern-day appetites, and the pub's Lower John Street location offers the option of outdoor dining alongside the River Nore.

Also on Lower John Street is the **Dylan Whiskey Bar,** an enticing Victorian-style bar with more than 280 whiskeys and 60 premium gins. Slide into a leather seat and enjoy the comforting aroma of the open turf fire while perusing the memorabilia of arguably America's greatest songwriter—and Nobel laureate—on the walls. Live music is performed after 9 p.m. most weeknights, and the staff are up for the challenge of mixing any craft cocktail.

For a quiet afternoon tipple in one of the most intriguing bars in all of Ireland, sneak through the tiny alleyway to the **Hole in the Wall,** perhaps the country's most secretive pub. This tiny bar has a secluded patio, where you'll see the outline of the infamous gap, used long ago as a bolt-hole by imbibers who wished to remain incognito. Ask the barkeep for the full, funny history of this time-warp portal of a bar. Kilkenny also has a long tradition of brewing: Smithwick's ale has been a local mainstay for centuries. And **Brewery Corner** now serves craft-beer enthusiasts a selection of modern Irish brews on tap. The venue also hosts local acts and DJs, and offers tasty made-to-order pizzas.

For dining or drinks, the **Left Bank** is an impressive venue consisting of nine bars spread throughout an elegant Victorian building, all offering a full bar menu. Situated at the east end of High Street and the corner of the Parade, this is an ideal place to start—or finish—any night out in Kilkenny. The building was a bank built in 1870. **Louie's Backyard** is an outdoor area of the Left Bank, a fully heated and covered lounge with its own outdoor fireplace and an outdoor bar. Around the corner on the Parade, the Left Bank's sister restaurant, **Rive Gauche,** combines fine French cuisine with Irish artisan produce.

For a memorable Marble City supper, **Rinuccini** on the Parade is hard to beat. The Cavaliere family has been serving classic Italian food with an Irish twist here for three decades. The spaghettini with Kilmore Quay prawns is delicious. For a taste of Kilkenny's Norman heritage, head for **Campagne** in the Arches, with offerings such as roast pheasant and sausage or loin of wild venison with chestnuts. Or try **Anocht** ("tonight") in the Kilkenny Design Centre, a beautiful setting for a meal among oak beam ceilings and cartwheel windows. The menu here relies on seasonal local produce with an extensive wine and beer list, and fine ciders from the local Highbank Orchards. ∎

Rive Gauche offers fine French cuisine with an Irish twist. OPPOSITE: Jim Croke prepares Lanigans Bar for an All-Ireland appearance by Kilkenny hurlers.

CARLOW

Carlow is a quiet, unassuming county without major towns but possessing several fascinating yet little-known gems well worth a visit. Wherever you wander in this largely rolling, agricultural countryside, you'll come across farmers with tales that grow taller as you listen; friendly vets on the hoof to their latest lambing, calving, or equine appointment; and archaeological enthusiasts seeking out the county's ancient dolmens.

Carlow also has an alluringly dark and intriguing side. The county ends to the south at the bleak beauty of the Blackstairs Mountains, stepping south into Wexford. And no visitor to the ruins of ominous Duckett's Grove will fail to be chilled by this stunning Gothic Revival pile. Built by the wealthy Duckett family in the 18th century, the castle was abandoned in 1916 and destroyed by fire in 1933. If "The Fall of the House of Usher" had been set in Ireland, Edgar Allan Poe would have found his inspiration at Duckett's Grove.

Just off the main street of Clonegal village stands Huntington Castle, home of the Esmondes since 1625. A stroll through the gardens leads you through a haunting tunnel of yew trees, whose branches threaten to close in as you pass beneath. Members of the Durdin Robertson branch of the family guide you through the castle, explaining its eclectic mix of styles and influences. Descend to the basement and you enter the realm of the truly esoteric: The Temple of the Goddess here is the spiritual home to a modern global worldwide religion, an unexpected sacred site to find in the cellar of an Irish castle. Elsewhere in Carlow, the medieval monastic ruins at St. Mullins date from the seventh century and sit on sacred grounds where several kings of Leinster are buried.

Ancient royalty likely lay for millennia in the portal tombs of Brownshill and Haroldstown Dolmens, and their tilted capstones and vertical supports are well-loved landmarks. For horticultural enthusiasts, Altamont House and Gardens provides a relaxing repose within the county whose people—historically known as great onion growers—were once called the "scallion eaters." ∎

Kayaking at Clashganny Lock near Borris, County Carlow

The Brownshill portal tomb, or dolmen, a prehistoric landmark located east of Carlow town, attracts archaeologists, dreamers, and picnickers.

Insider's Guide

A Ramble Around County Carlow

The Neolithic Irish provide the earliest human footprint in County Carlow, where the **Brownshill Dolmen,** Ireland's largest portal tomb, dates back 5,000 years. How early Irish builders moved such a deadweight is a mystery: Its massive capstone weighs more than 100 tons (90 metric tonnes). Another Neolithic wonder is found farther east at **Haroldstown,** where two huge, slightly tilted capstones sit atop 10 vertical stones. An impoverished family used the dolmen as a dwelling during the 19th century.

Another Victorian-era County Carlow resident lived somewhat larger at the more salubrious setting of **Borris House.** However, Arthur MacMurrough Kavanagh (1831–1889) had many obstacles to overcome in life. Born with only stumps for arms and legs, he nonetheless became an excellent hunter and horseman; Kavanagh also enjoyed a long career in politics. His Borris demesne now hosts weddings and corporate events.

Farther south along the Barrow River is St. Mullins, a village named for St. Moling (614–697), who founded his monastery here in the seventh century. After wandering through its ruins, walk to the valley below to see **St. Moling's Well,** a place of pilgrimage in later medieval times when the plague swept across Ireland. Pilgrims still circle the well in a clockwise direction (circumambulation) while reciting prayers.

Huntington Castle, in Clonegal, was built in 1625 for the aristocratic Esmondes and today is home to the Durdin Robertsons, who personally give guided tours of their eclectic castle. Visitors approach along a lime tree–lined avenue; elsewhere in the gardens a row of English yews creates an enchanting natural tunnel for walkers. But it is deep in the basement where visitors will find another sacred site that has attracted pilgrims from afar: the **Temple of the Goddess.** Established in 1976, this is home to a world religion celebrating the female aspects of divinities, founded by Huntington's owner, Olivia Robertson, with her brother, Lawrence (Derry), and Derry's wife, Bobby. The castle is sited near the **Well of St. Brigid** and features a main altar framed by dozens of side altars honoring a multitude of goddesses and zodiac signs.

No visit to Carlow should bypass the ominous allure of **Duckett's Grove.** This Gothic Revival castle dates back to the early 18th century, when it was part of an estate of more than 12,000 acres (4,850 ha). The Ducketts' wealth and generosity made them popular employers up to the 20th century, but by 1916, the year of the Easter Rising in Dublin, Mrs. Maria Duckett had abandoned the house in fear of the changing political climate. The fertile Carlow lands of the estate were subsequently distributed among local farmers, and the great house was

burned to a shell in 1933, leaving behind atmospheric ruins. Today visitors can take guided tours of the estate gardens, including two recently restored walled gardens. Come summer, the **Upper Walled Garden** is abloom with historic varieties of shrub roses, a collection of Chinese and Japanese peonies, and various perennials and flowering shrubs. The **Lower Walled Garden** is planted with an assortment of fruits, including figs and historical varieties of Irish apples. The blossoms offer the promise of rebirth amidst the Gothic gloom of the Duckett's Grove ruins. ∎

IRISH GARDENS: ALTAMONT

The beautiful gardens of Altamont, near Ballon, revolve around a human-made lake created as part of an employment scheme during the post-famine era of the 1850s. Dawson Borrow, then Altamont's owner, made many such improvements to his estate, adding the yew-lined broad walk and the fascinating Ice Age Glen path around the far lakeshore. This walk winds through a landscape of massive, mossy boulders, shaded by rare and ancient sessile (Irish) oaks (*Quercus petraea*). The track then leads the intrepid hiker along the banks of the River Slaney and rises sharply through the granite stairway eponymously dubbed the One Hundred Steps.

Altamont House dates from around 1720, and the presence of an avenue of beech trees resembling a cloister, called Nun's Walk, suggests it may have previously been the site of a convent. A walled garden, added in the late 18th century, adds to the estate's peaceful atmosphere of spiritual repose.

A 20th-century resident of Altamont, Corona North, spent years importing rhododendron hybrids to plant haphazardly around the lake, as well as rare tree species such as the dawn redwood (*Metasequoia glyptostroboides*) that she managed to source through Kew Gardens in London. She surrounded the lily-carpeted lake with stands of cedars, chestnuts, limes, and Lawson cypresses, making Altamont a lush, shadowy escape. Visitors may well call to mind the words of the

17th-century English poet, Andrew Marvel: "Annihilating all that's made / To a green thought in a green shade."

Corona North's horticultural legacy is today marked in a commemorative border by the gate leading to Altamont's walled garden. This 230-by-23-foot (70 m x 7 m) herbaceous border was created in 2000, one year after Corona North died and left the house and its famous gardens to the Irish state. By midsummer, the Corona North Commemorative Border becomes a riot of color with the flowering of multiple plants donated by admirers of the great lady. ∎

Altamont Gardens, an enchanting blend of formal and informal gardens with riverside walks, covers more than 40 acres (16 ha).

WEXFORD

Ireland's sunny southeast is a gateway for visitors arriving on ferries from Britain and the continent. The Vikings and the Normans plied these coasts, too, whether they came to plunder and quickly depart, to conquer, or to settle.

The town of Wexford was founded by Vikings in the ninth century, and its old quays still bustle with the industry of seafarers. Narrow covered alleys such as Keyser's Lane are trooped by weary fishermen heading into town, where pubs resound with the lively, playfully ironic banter you'd expect to find in places called the Mocking Monck, Maggie May's, the Undertaker, and the Foggy Dew Inn. Just outside Wexford, the Irish National Heritage Park offers a walk through history with reproductions ranging from a Stone Age circle to a Viking shipyard and a moored longboat.

At Ferns, the ruins of St. Aidan's seventh-century Augustine monastery testify to the damage the Norsemen wrought. In Enniscorthy, the castle of Robert de Quincey is a well-preserved example of the wealth and power of later Anglo-Norman invaders. Some streets and bridges survive from the 13th-century Norman town, while others are recognizable as locations in the 2015 film *Brooklyn,* based on Colm Tóibín's novel about a young girl who leaves Enniscorthy to live in New York.

Ireland's most famous returning son of emigrants is commemorated just outside the town of New Ross. It was from here that the forefather of President John F. Kennedy set sail for America. The Kennedy Homestead is located five miles (8 km) south of the town, as is the JFK Arboretum. New Ross is also home to the Dunbrody Famine Ship, moored on the quay, and the Emigrant Flame that burns in memory of emigrants who fled the Great Famine of the 1840s. Opposite the replica ship hangs the Ros Tapestry, a series of embroidered tapestries depicting the Norman arrival in Ireland. History is everywhere in coastal Wexford, a county forever marked by fateful arrivals and departures. ■

The boldly striped Hook Lighthouse is considered the oldest continuously operating lighthouse in the world. The current structure has stood for 800 years.

Opera buffs flock to Wexford's famous festival of opera, held each year in the coastal town between October and November.

Insider's Guide

The Drama of County Wexford

Wexford is a port city clustered around long quays on the Slaney Estuary. Travelers are warmly welcomed here, despite the city's historically bloody dealings with outsiders. In 1649, Oliver Cromwell's men decimated the 12th-century **Selskar Abbey,** leaving only red stone ruins on Abbey Street as his New Model Army massacred 1,500 citizens. The 1798 Rebellion brought more bloodshed, and a statue of a peasant pikeman now stands in the **Bullring,** the city center district, to honor the sac-

rifice of the United Irishmen rebels. Stop at the **West Gate,** a Norman tower, where a visitors center will guide you to other historic Wexford sites. Opera lovers flock here in autumn, when the two-week **Wexford Festival Opera** brings greasepaint, glamor, and dramatic arias to this workaday Irish town.

Fifteen miles (24 km) north of Wexford, **Enniscorthy Castle,** built in the 1190s by the Norman knight Philip De Prendergast, sits at the heart of the medieval town of Enniscorthy. The town was founded by St.

Senan in A.D. 510. In the 1960s, the father of renowned local author Colm Tóibín joined forces with a willful parish priest to preserve the castle, and today the square-shaped fortress houses the **Wexford County Museum.** Exhibits recount the region's 1,500-year history, including the story of the castle's last residents, the Roche family, as well as that of Tóibín's successful novel turned movie *Brooklyn.*

Elsewhere in the town, the **National 1798 Rebellion Centre** relates the history and aftermath of that bloody uprising, explaining the events in the broader European context of the Age of Revolution. The United Irishmen's rebellion was finally crushed on **Vinegar Hill** on the east bank of the River Slaney. Some 500 people were killed there, many of them the fleeing wives and children of the rebels; a round tower and memorial plaque now mark the site.

North of Enniscorthy sits the ancient religious center of Ferns, where St. Aidan founded his monastery in the seventh century. The ruins of the **Augustinian Abbey,**
founded in 1150, still stand today. The town was home to the powerful MacMurchadas, kings of medieval Leinster. Visitors can also tour the ruins of **Ferns Castle,** starting from the interpretive center, where exhibits explain how Diarmait MacMurchada, buried here, made the fateful alliance with Richard de Clare—aka Strongbow—that led to the Norman conquest of Ireland.

For a peaceful respite from the county's war-torn past, head for the **Wexford Wildfowl Reserve.** Find a perch along the seawall to watch
thousands of Greenland white-fronted geese as they take to the southeastern skies at dusk; the whoosh of their winged ascent is a wondrous, unforgettable sound. About 10,000 of these impressive geese winter here.

Other migrants passing through this marshy coastal reserve include black swans, greenshanks, and redshanks, as well as reed warblers and reed buntings. Bring your binoculars, a flask of tea (or something stronger), and a warm coat—the sunny southeast gets cold in the winter. ◾

TASTE OF IRELAND: SMOKED MACKEREL, HORSERADISH PÂTÉ & BROWN BREAD

Ireland's southeastern coastline is ideal for summer picnics on the long sandy beaches that stretch south from Kilmuckridge to Rosslare. Here's a simple but delicious way to make a seafood sandwich using smoked mackerel in a horseradish pâté with Dijon mustard—a culinary tribute to both the Norse seafarers who founded Wexford and the Norman settlers who later settled the southeast and beyond.

juice, and black pepper, and blend to a rough paste. Add the butter and blend until smooth. Season to taste with salt. Serve on brown bread sprinkled with spring onions.

• Serves 2 to 4 Wexford day-trippers.

TIP: Fresh Wexford strawberries are sold along southeastern roads in summer—just add Murphy's Irish ice cream for the perfect picnic dessert.

INGREDIENTS

• 2 whole smoked mackerel (or 4 fillets)
• 1 teaspoon freshly grated horseradish (or 2 tsp "hot" horseradish sauce)
• 2 teaspoons Dijon mustard
• 2 tablespoons crème fraîche
• Juice of ½ lemon
• Freshly ground black pepper
• 1 stick (113 g) unsalted Kerrygold butter, chopped
• Irish brown bread, cut into slices
• Spring onions, chopped

DIRECTIONS

• Remove the skin from the fish (the odd piece is acceptable as the mixture will be blended). Add the fish to a blender.
• Add the horseradish, mustard, crème fraîche, lemon

A taste of summer in the sunny southeast: Smoked mackerel goes perfectly with horseradish pâté and Dijon mustard.

Insider's Guide

Ancient Abbeys & a Haunted House

The county of Wexford has a range of storied architectural curiosities sure to satisfy any traveler equipped with an interest in archaic buildings, a car, and a camera. Near the Campile River stand the ruins of **Dunbrody Abbey,** founded in 1170 by Hervey de Montmorency under the instruction of Strongbow. This Gothic Cistercian monastery expanded the brotherhood of St. Mary's Abbey in Dublin. (The crossing tower was a later addition.) The cloisters are still visible, and one can picture pensive monks going about their daily duties.

Nearby **Tintern Abbey** was founded in 1200, when the Norman knight William Marshal took command of Leinster. Legend has it that Marshal prayed for deliverance from a storm on his crossing from England, vowing to God that he would found a monastery wherever his ship reached safety. That place was Bannow Bay, where he promptly granted lands to the Cistercian Order. As Earl of Pembroke, Marshal was also patron of Tintern Abbey in Monmouthshire in Wales. That Welsh brotherhood helped populate his new monastery, which became known as Tintern of the Vow. Built on fertile farmlands, Tintern became wealthy and powerful, keeping close ties with St. Mary's and Mellifont Abbey in neighboring Waterford (see page 54). The layout closely followed that of Mellifont, with cloisters located to the south and a cruciform church to the north.

The desire for land caused conflict between Dunbrody and Tintern Abbey, particularly when the abbot of Dunbrody imprisoned one of Tintern's visiting monks and confiscated his money and livestock. Dunbrody went the way of many monasteries in the 1540s and was dissolved under Henry VIII. It then became the residence of Sir Osborne Etchingham.

Like Dunbrody, Tintern Abbey was disbanded and turned into a fortified home under Henry VIII. The castellated bridge over the stream dates from the 18th century, and the walled garden from the 19th century. Tintern was granted to the Irish state in 1959, and the gardens have since been extensively restored.

Loftus Hall, on the Hook Head Peninsula, is another storied Wexford demesne. Having previously belonged to the Redmonds, a family of Anglo-Irish aristocrats, it was granted to Sir Nicholas Loftus in 1666. Legend tells of a wild storm at sea in 1775, one that brought a ship ashore at Hook Head, whereupon a dashing young man sought shelter at Loftus Hall. Charles Tottenham, his second wife, Jane Cliffe (née Loftus), and his daughter Anne played cards with this charming stranger, until Anne accidentally dropped a card. On retrieving it, she saw that the guest had hooves instead of feet.

She shrieked, and the man disappeared in a cloud of sulfurous smoke, leaving a hole in the roof that proved impossible to repair. Anne suffered a nervous breakdown and an exorcism before dying at 31. Her ghost is said to still haunt Loftus, although the old house was demolished in 1870 and replaced by the current hall. ∎

Dunbrody Abbey, founded in 1170 by Anglo-Norman invaders, is now largely in ruins; restoration work continues. OPPOSITE: Tintern Abbey today includes beautifully restored exhibition spaces.

In 1963, the U.S. president was rapturously received in Galway following tea with his Irish cousins at the Kennedy Homestead in Dunganstown.

Irish Heritage

The Homecoming of JFK

Ireland has many memorials to victims of the Great Famine of the 1840s (see page 227), many of whom left for America on infamous "coffin ships," so called because of the many who died during the passage. On the quayside of New Ross sits the **Dunbrody Famine Ship,** a replica of such doomed vessels. But its location in this Wexford town has an alternate message of hope and historic destiny fulfilled. For it was from this quayside in 1848 that Patrick Kennedy sailed to Boston to become a cooper. As his great-grandson,

President John F. Kennedy, would observe when he visited here more than a century later, "He carried nothing with him except two things: a strong religious faith and a strong desire for liberty."

A year after landing in Boston, Patrick Kennedy married Bridget Murphy, a native of Ballycullane, County Wexford. But he died a poor man in 1858, leaving his young bride with four children to rear without income. He was just 35 years old, and the date of his death was November 22, a day that would be seared into history some 105 years later.

In June 1963, the president made a longed-for return to his ancestors' homeland and was rapturously received across the country. The welcome was especially heartfelt in New Ross. The visit was viewed in Ireland as a homecoming for the Irish diaspora. Ireland was a young state in the 1960s, and the president's speech at New Ross bolstered its burgeoning sense of identity: "In the years since independence, you have undergone a new and peaceful revolution . . . transforming the face of this land, while still holding on to the old spiritual and cultural values." JFK's full speech is inscribed on the cast-bronze podium that stands on the quayside. The podium is a reminder that Kennedy spoke for generations of Irish Americans who followed in the wake of those fleeing the Great Famine from a country stricken by starvation, disease, and death.

The president also visited the **Kennedy Homestead** in Dunganstown, New Ross, and was warmly welcomed by relatives. The public can now visit the homestead, and a small museum examines the story of the Kennedy dynasty on both sides of the Atlantic. Nearby, the **John F. Kennedy Arboretum** is a fine woodland park with walking trails and 4,500 species of trees and plants spread across 623 acres (252 ha) of forests and gardens. A memorial wall and statue of JFK in New Ross also stand as a lasting legacy of the homecoming.

Thomas Kiernan, the Irish ambassador to the United States at the time of the visit, observed: "I think his coming back was a closing of a chapter that began in the famine. . . . Here was a fellow who came from famine stock on both paternal and maternal sides and who reached the very top in the United States." One could well imagine an elderly JFK savoring a return to Wexford in later life, with all the time in the world to stop in on relatives without handlers rushing him on to his next public engagement. But, as American scholar and politician Daniel Patrick Moynihan said after his great friend's assassination, to be Irish is to know that, in the end, the world will break your heart.

Just south of the quayside podium is the **New Ross Emigrant Flame,** lit from the eternal flame at the president's graveside in Arlington, Virginia. It's a touching memorial to the man who symbolized the American Dream for generations of Irish emigrants. ∎

IN THE KNOW: WHERE TO STAY & EAT IN WEXFORD

To witness the Irish on vacation, head for the family-run **Kelly's Resort Hotel** in Rosslare. Located on Rosslare's sandy strand, this is a hotel where the home fires always burn, the barkeep is always friendly, and the food is always hearty. Small wonder it's been called "Ireland's favorite place to stay" by the *Irish Times*. **La Côte** on Custom House Quay in Wexford is an intimate seafood restaurant on the waterfront, where Chef Paul Hynes and his wife, Edwina, combine local surf and turf produce to delicious effect. The torched Kilmore cod with Ard Mhacha shiitake mushrooms is one such tasty creation. The **Aldridge Lodge** in the fishing village of Duncannon is a great weekend stay, with cozy double rooms upstairs and fine dining downstairs. Try the Hook Head lobster with *pommes duchesse,* lobster bisque, or the roast loin of wild venison with hazelnuts and mushrooms, all exquisite tastes of Wexford. **Dunbrody Country House** in Arthurstown, New Ross, is an elegant hotel where morning walks on a spacious estate are the perfect prelude to a sumptuous buffet breakfast. For supper, Kevin Dundon's eight-course tasting menu is temptation on a plate, while his seafood bar options present the best of Wexford's catch. The caramelized Dunmore East scallops are simply unmissable. ∎

Dunbrody Country House in the Arthurstown neighborhood of New Ross, an elegant country house located on a spacious estate

WATERFORD

Waterford is a workaday port city famous for its crystal, and the surrounding county provides hidden treasures for travelers. Waterford was founded by the Vikings in the ninth century. The city's many facets glitter within the three museums of the Waterford Treasures complex that spirit visitors through 11 centuries of history: Reginald's Tower exhibits artifacts from the Viking era, the Medieval Museum takes you through the Middle Ages, and Bishop's Palace reflects the Georgian and Victorian periods.

Modern-day Waterford is distinguished by its glassblowers and designers, whose celebrated skills can be seen on a guided House of Waterford Crystal factory tour. Those who appreciate the best things in life should also head to the Cliff House Hotel in Ardmore, about 45 miles (73 km) southwest of Waterford. Here, you'll relish one of Ireland's top restaurants, both for its food and its stunning coastal vistas. The luxurious spa hotel is located close to a bracing cliff walk and Ardmore's monastic site, where a 12th-century round tower—97 feet (29 m) tall—guards the haunting ruins of St. Declan's Cathedral.

Lovers of geology can explore the Copper Coast UNESCO Global Geopark, which stretches from Ballyvoile Beach near Stradbally eastward to Kilfarrasy Beach, near Fenor. Visitors follow the self-guided Copper Coast Trail armed with walking cards from the Geopark Centre in Bunmahon.

Elsewhere in County Waterford rise the towers of Ballysaggartmore, magnificent follies, and Lismore Castle, once owned by Sir Walter Raleigh, high on a bluff above the River Blackwater. From Lismore, motorists can complete the scenic Vee Drive, taking in Feddaun, Clogheen, Ardfinnan, Newcastle, and Cappoquin. For a quiet off-road experience, head for Gaulstown Dolmen, dating to about 3500 B.C. This imposing portal tomb is bewitchingly situated in a wooded glade at the base of Cnoc na Cailligh ("hill of the hag"). This is Ireland's ancient east at its most transcendental, taking you back through time and into the mystic. ∎

Lismore Castle, Irish home of the dukes of Devonshire since 1753

Insider's Guide

Waterford City

Waterford, like every port city, has been shaped by its exposure to the winds of global change and the vicissitudes of time. The **Waterford Treasures** museum complex is a trip through the centuries that have molded this city since it was founded by Vikings in the 800s. The city and county are often referred to as the Déise (pronounced DESH), from the medieval kingdom of the Déisi. Safe within the **Medieval Museum** lies an artifact that heralded submission to a distant kingdom: the Great Charter Roll of 1372, the 13-foot-long (4 m) illustrated roll that validated the power of the English crown.

English architecture gives the city much of its distinctive appearance, with the Georgian style (from the 18th and early 19th centuries) particularly noticeable along the Mall and O'Connell Street. The Protestant **Christ Church Cathedral,** completed in 1779, has been described by architectural historian Mark Girouard as the finest 18th-century ecclesiastical building in Ireland. Here you'll come across another reminder of man's susceptibility to the scythe of Father Time: The morbid effigy of James Rice, seven times Lord Mayor of 15th-century Waterford, is depicted as a shrunken corpse gouged by toads and worms.

The **Cathedral of the Most Holy Trinity,** completed in 1793, is the oldest Catholic cathedral in Ireland. Look for its 10 crystal chandeliers, presented as a gift from Waterford Crystal in the 1970s. The company reached peaks of employment, production, and profitability in the following decades.

By 2010, Waterford Crystal was a globalized firm, with much of the manufacturing being done abroad, and the Irish operation relocated back to the roots of glassmaking in the city center. The current Mall location has both a manufacturing facility that melts more than 825 tons (750 metric tonnes) of crystal annually and a visitors center that offers popular tours.

The city's lead crystal still sparkles around the world. Waterford chandeliers were installed in Westminster Abbey in 1966, paid for by the ever beneficent Guinness family. The halls of Windsor Castle in London and the Kennedy Center in Washington, D.C., also glisten with chandeliers made here. Waterford glassmakers crafted the 2,688 crystals for the New Year's Eve Ball that drops in New York's Times Square.

Also in Waterford is the **Irish Museum of the Science and Story of Time,** hosting the largest collection of Irish-made clocks in the world. Here, exhibitions also tell the 5,000-year story of how the passage of time was marked and recorded in Ireland. One such display, called "When Times Runs Out," explores how the Irish landscape and the Irish mind have been shaped throughout the ages by the rituals and superstitions of the Irish wake. ■

Tours allow visitors to watch artisans creating world-famous glass products at the House of Waterford Crystal. OPPOSITE: Winterval heralds Christmas in Waterford.

Recognized as a UNESCO Geopark, the scalloped Copper Coast offers many invigorating walks along the shorelines of County Waterford.

The Copper Coast & Lismore Castle

Following one of the many trails along the **Copper Coast UNESCO Global Geopark** (essentially an outdoor geology museum) is an invigorating way to experience the county of Waterford and the south coast of Ireland. The winds from the Celtic Sea blow away the cobwebs of life's cares, the terrain is easy on the limbs, and the wondrous geology and birdlife all around are fillips for the spirit.

Hikers should stop first at the **Geopark Centre** in Bunmahon, where walking cards for trails are available.

The center also has an informative exhibition on the history and geology of the copper mining industry that thrived here in the 19th century.

While in Bunmahon, check out the **Geological Garden,** which explains much about the minerals and rocks of the region. In this part of the Irish countryside, 460-million-year-old mudstones, sandstones, and lavas were buckled by a continental clash; into the strata rushed hot, metal-rich fluids that formed quartz veins rich in copper minerals as they cooled.

Then, follow the R675 along the coastline from Tramore to Dungarvan and choose your own path(s) to wander. On a clear day, the green hills, azure Celtic Sea, and rust red or ochre yellow cliffs provide a colorful canvas for the geology or geography enthusiast.

Just to the east of Bunmahon, the Cornish-style winding **engine house** at Tankardstown evinces this coastline's historical parallels with the coast of Cornwall across the Irish Sea. The engine house pumped water from the bottom of the 84-foot (256 m) mine shaft and powered the cages that lowered miners and supplies into the mines. Before it closed around 1850, Knockmahon was regarded as one of the key mining districts in the British Empire. Many of the miners, unemployed after its closure, emigrated to work in the copper mines of Butte, Montana.

Venturing inland, the N72 will take you to the Irish Heritage Town of **Lismore** (from the Irish Lios Mór, or "great fort"). The medieval settlement sprang up around the monastery founded by St. Mochuda in 636, but the modern town is named for imposing **Lismore Castle,** which towers above the River Blackwater.

Built in 1185 by the Anglo-Norman Prince John, the fortification was attacked several times throughout history, notably during the Desmond Rebellion of the late 1500s. Lismore Castle is also the birthplace of Robert Boyle (1627–1691), the father of modern chemistry. Open to the public, the beautiful castle gardens will surprise visitors with two concrete relics from the 20th century: slabs of the Berlin Wall.

During 19th-century renovations, the quill-written *Lismore Crozier* and the *Book of Lismore* were discovered in blocked-off passageways. Now on display at the National Museum in Dublin, the crozier dates from about

1100. The *Book of Lismore* was probably crafted in the 15th century; in its pages, scholars detailed the lives of several Irish saints, including Patrick, Columba, and Brigid.

Lismore's rich history can be explored in the **Lismore Heritage Centre,** located in the town's 19th-century courthouse. A few miles outside town, you'll find the fabulous follies of **Ballysaggartmore Towers,** the gate lodge and tower bridge constructed for a house that was dreamed of yet never built. The spendthrift ways of the estate's owner, Arthur Kiely-Usher, came to typify the cruelty of the landlord classes in famine-era Ireland. ∎

IRISH GARDENS: MOUNT CONGREVE

A stroll through the lush gardens of Mount Congreve at Kilmeaden is a southeastern treat: an easy amble amid rolling landscape with views of the River Suir. Located five miles (8 km) from Waterford City, the gardens offer 10 miles (16 km) of sporadically shaded pathways through stands of beech, oak, and conifers. The gardener whose vision sculpted these walks was London-born Ambrose Congreve, a bon vivant with an impeccable eye for horticultural beauty. (His birthplace, 3 Savile Row, would later become part of pop music history as headquarters of the Beatles' Apple corporation and the location of their last live concert, on its rooftop.) The river walkways are a riot of seasonal purple when plantings of Campbell's magnolia and Sargent's magnolia blossom. The large-leaved great Chinese rhododendron in the woods are another wondrous sight in full bloom.

Ambrose was not an idle gardener, nor was he afraid of excess: Mount Congreve's color-filled estate encompasses more than 3,000 different trees and shrubs, more than 2,000 rhododendrons, 600 camellias, 300 Acer cultivars, 600 conifers, 250 climbers, and 1,500 herbaceous plants. The lawns sloping down to the river are planted with hundreds of snake's head fritillaries. Masses of white Japanese wisteria

within the Walled Garden bloom like floral waterfalls in spring. Fluvial cascades and arches and pagodas and temples are dotted around the garden, punctuation marks in Congreve's engrossing compositions.

The effusive planter died in 2011, but his gardens still give joy, with concerts and other activities, including yoga, held regularly. His estate is bordered by the Waterford Greenway, a walking and cycling path with an adjacent access point, for those who wish to extend their walk. ∎

The lush southern gardens of Mount Congreve

The Irish Abroad

The Irish in Africa

The Irish share a strong connection with many Africans, a bond long fostered by the missionary programs of many Catholic orders. From the 19th century, Irish lay teachers were dispatched alongside priests and nuns to teach in cities. Others helped build and run schools in remote bush regions in Kenya, Liberia, and Tanzania.

Back at Blackrock College, Dublin, the Holy Ghost Fathers educated an unlikely hero of the Ethiopian people in rebel rock star Bob Geldof, who would go on to organize a global response to the famine in Ethiopia in 1985. Live Aid raised millions for crisis relief, nowhere more so than in Ireland, where folk memories of the Great Famine still linger.

Geldof's commitment to Ethiopia was no fleeting fancy: He has recently invested in an Ethiopian winery. His fellow Dubliner, Bono, has long spearheaded the One and Red campaigns to alleviate poverty across Africa. His interest has intensified since he and his wife, Ali, first volunteered in an Ethiopian refugee camp in 1984, where a man begged them to take his starving child back to Ireland. Bono's counsel also guided President George W. Bush's African AIDS policy.

In Dublin, former Irish president Mary Robinson resigned to become UN High Commissioner for Human Rights in 1997. Her work in Africa and her stance against human rights abuses by major powers caused controversy. Undeterred, Robinson, alongside Kofi Annan, Nelson Mandela, and Desmond Tutu, founded a group called the Elders to contribute wisdom and leadership to global debates. This respect for societal elders echoes ancient Irish Brehon Law, and African tribal traditions. ∎

Great minds, thinking aloud: Former Irish president Mary Robinson greets Nelson Mandela at a meeting of the Elders in 2010.

IRISH VOICES: THE PROTECTOR OF FANTASTIC BEASTS

A longtime National Geographic contributor, David O'Connor is a conservationist whose work protecting large mammals and their habitats has spanned five continents. Born in the U.S. to parents who eventually returned to their native Ireland, O'Connor has worked in Europe, North America, Australia, Southeast Asia, and Africa. His Irish upbringing, he claims, gave him an open-minded perspective for a life lived without borders as a global citizen of the 21st century.

"I remember staring at this strange, prehistoric-looking creature in Fota Wildlife Park in Cork, and him staring back," says O'Connor in a mischievous Irish accent. "That's one thing I learned early: You'll never win a staring match with a giraffe."

O'Connor studies large mammal conservation and movement ecology, and loves Africa's endless wild spaces—and their endless possibilities. "Growing up in Ireland means you are always looking outward, always open to the world and its wonders. Irish people have a natural curiosity and I find the Africans I work with very much akin in that spirit of openness and sheer fun." His family settled in rural Woodstown, near Waterford, when he was three. The idyllic rustic setting led to O'Connor's lifelong love of animals. "I was always out in the wild. One spring, I discovered a fox's den in a hedgerow, and I spent that summer watching the vixen raise her cubs. I remember the smell of wet earth as I lay watching those rust red mammals with their foxy, musky scent."

Ireland is, of course, a small island, and the young O'Connor learned that in a very short time the country had lost most of its big wildlife species—including wolves, giant elk, and golden eagles—when their habitats were cleared for agriculture. "You get places like the Burren that were cleared by invaders, but we still treasure our wildlife and our wild lands in Ireland."

A degree in zoology and earth science from University College Cork paved a path to a career in conservation. O'Connor worked for San Diego Zoo Global (SDZG), a zoological institution with a mission to save endangered species. "I began the giraffe conservation initiative in northern Kenya with pastoralists, and I've also helped SDZG begin support-

O'Connor's conservation work focuses on endangered types of giraffes.

ing the Reteti Elephant Sanctuary, Sera Rhino Sanctuary, Ishaqbini Hirola Sanctuary, and other programs. The giraffes are hunted as bush meat, so we work to give locals alternative economic incentives to keep populations healthy and to preserve habitats through training and education." O'Connor recently became president of Save Giraffes Now, an organization dedicated to working with local communities to conserve these threatened animals across the continent.

O'Connor is still staring up at the dinosaur-like creatures he saw in Fota as a child. But these days, he says, we must also look to the *Homo sapiens* who share the giraffes' habitat to ensure their future. "It is the people who live alongside the wildlife who will ultimately determine whether they survive, so we must work with them to find the right ways to preserve the wilderness." ∎

"Most people think that conservation is all about wildlife.
In fact, conservation is about people."

— *David O'Connor*

St. Declan's Way is an ancient pilgrim path linking Cashel in County Tipperary with the monastic settlement at Ardmore.

Insider's Guide

Ardmore's Monastic Ruins & Cliff Walk

The little village of Ardmore offers a perfect Irish escape from the stresses of modern life. Perched high on the bluffs leading out toward Ardmore Head, the town is a picturesque parade of thatched cottages and small pubs thrumming with traditional music at night. During the day, pay a visit to **Ardmore Pottery and Gallery,** a fine store with authentic Irish arts and crafts.

A weekend here can be spent exploring the ancient monastic ruin of **St. Declan's Monastery** and ambling along the three-mile (5 km) **Ardmore Cliff Walk,** a breathtaking foray into nature and history. The trail starts from the Cliff House Hotel and takes you first to the ruin of **St. Declan's Church,** where you'll also find **St. Declan's Well.** The saint's feast day, July 24, is celebrated at the well, with pilgrims walking in a patterned series around the holy site and holding concerts, lectures, sports events, guided tours, and storytelling jags.

The main monastic building here is **Ardmore Cathedral,** which dates from the 12th century. With its long nave, chancel, and intricate stone carvings of biblical scenes, this is one of the most remarkable examples of Romanesque architecture in Ireland. The ogham (medieval Irish alphabet) inscription on one of the cathedral's two ancient stones reads "the stone of Lugaid, grandson of Nia-Segmon."

The monks who established their monastery here in the fifth century were no doubt seeking the "green martyrdom" that St. Kevin advocated when he lived the life of a hermit in Glendalough, County Wicklow. The aim was to get closer to God, and the round tower here certainly served that purpose, rising heavenward to a height of 98 feet (30 m). It tapers upward, marked by three outer stone rings as it narrows. Capped in stone, the tower is believed to date from the 12th century.

A cloudless day on the cliffs should allow you to spot the shipwreck of the *Samson,* driven onto the rocks during a storm in 1987. The walk continues up **Ram's Head** for a fine view of Capel Island off the coast of Cork, with Ballycotton Island visible farther along. A tower that served as a lookout post during the Napoleonic wars can also be seen, and all around you will hear the calling of seabirds, including nesting fulmars, choughs, kittiwakes, sand martins, migrant warblers, goldcrests, and even Manx shearwaters. A capped natural spring marks the far point on the walk as you loop around and head back toward the landmark round tower at the monastery.

Time spent walking these cliffs suggests that the old Irish saints were on to something in their quest for the divine in nature. It is little surprise to discover that the well-known Molly Keane Writers' Retreat is located on the inspiring higher ground around Ardmore. ∎

IN THE KNOW: WHERE TO STAY & EAT IN WATERFORD

The **Cliff House Hotel** at Ardmore is one of Ireland's great boutique hotels, a clifftop aerie overlooking the Celtic Sea with every luxury you could wish for: a spa offering seaweed baths (an Irish specialty), peat baths for feet, and the Cliff's signature couple's massage, complete with soothing ocean views.

You won't even have to leave the hotel for Michelin-star dining. Just take a seat at the **Cliff House Restaurant,** where Chef Ian Doyle serves up stunning culinary creations using local Irish ingredients and a boundless imagination. The menu is a carousel of seasonal selections that might include delights such as raw langoustine with pear, sorrel, and cucumber and gin sauce, or mussel puree, tagetes, sea beet, and mussel cream.

Those in the know consult the hotel to book a foraging tour with Andrew Malcolm, a local who will guide you through Waterford's wonderful range of edible flowers, mushrooms, seaweeds, and other freshly picked delicacies that will later adorn your plate. Elsewhere at the Cliff, the **Bar Restaurant** offers a more informal, but no less mouthwatering dining experience. The menu offers a selection of sandwiches and seafood dishes, including monkfish, Helvick cod, local crab, and chowder. The rib-eye steak is a carnivore's delight, and a classic Irish dessert rounds out what is a truly memorable supper.

For an old-fashioned Irish pub meal and a few drinks, head for the **Spinnaker** in Dunmore East, where the welcome is always warm and the servings are always satisfying. Choose from classic fish-and-chips, gourmet burgers, a three-fish catch, garlic mussels with fries, or handmade pizzas. The Spinnaker also has an excellent array of beers on tap and an exten-sive selection of wines and cocktails. You can enjoy live music while you inhale the sea breezes outside in the beer garden.

The **Tannery** is another popular dining destination for Waterford gourmands. Chef-owner Paul Flynn serves up generous portions of rustic Irish fare in an attractive setting. The menu might include wild Atlantic cod and Dollar Bay clams with white beans, sea greens, and butter sauce, or Irish mountain lamb, glazed carrot, sorrel, and velvet cloud yogurt. If you overindulge (and frankly, why wouldn't you?), there are accommodations available just around the corner at the **Townhouse,** and a wine bar for a nightcap. Flynn also runs a cooking school, so stick around and you might also learn a thing or two about fine Celtic cooking. ∎

The Cliff House Restaurant provides a mouthwatering dining experience.

Part Two

Munster & the South

Blarney Castle, home to the
famous Blarney Stone, is steeped
in history and local legend.

BEST TIME TO VISIT: Spectacular Kerry, and particularly Killarney, gets crowded in summer, but Cork offers quieter roads and less crowded hotels and bars. Summer is fun anywhere in this sports-mad province, when Tipperary and Limerick also buzz with festivals. Cork is a lively night out in fall and winter, especially around Christmas.

SPECIAL EVENTS: Kinsale Restaurant Week (February); Clonmel Junction Festival (July); Puck Fair, Killorglin, Kerry (August); Clonmel Busking Festival (August); Cork Folk Festival (September–October); Cork Jazz Festival (October); Kinsale Gourmet Festival, Cork (October)

GETTING THERE: Shannon Airport, in County Clare, is the main portal to Munster. Cork has a smaller airport also serving transatlantic travelers. Car rental is imperative for sightseeing on the southern seaboard, with its strings of villages spaced along magnificent mountain drives.

A jaunting car ride in Killarney National Park OPPOSITE: The English Market has served the people of Cork through famine, flood, war, and several recessions.

Hearing the heartbeat of Ireland

The southern province of Munster is where the Irish heartbeat can best be felt. Although the Easter Rising of 1916 erupted in Dublin, many of the future Free State's leaders, including Michael Collins, were cunning Munster men. Stepping onto Cork soil is to enter not just Ireland's largest county, but a different mindset entirely. For Cork is the "rebel county," the Texas of Ireland. Some even call it the People's Republic of Cork; while in Cork City, locals will welcome you sardonically to the "*real* capital of Ireland."

That's a sentiment that will raise eyes to heaven in mountainous County Kerry next door, a region also known as the Kingdom. Here it's said that while a Corkman thinks he's better than everyone else, a Kerryman *knows* he is. Both counties' natives generally have plenty to say for themselves. Suffice to say that wherever you travel in Cork and Kerry, you need to bring your listening ears. And maybe a translator. In theory, English is spoken here, but it's actually a highly poetic interpretation of ancient Irish turns of phrase and rhythms of speech delivered with lengthy lyricism and a delightfully lilting, singsong accent.

In the county of Tipperary, the Rock of Cashel was in medieval times the spiritual center of Ireland. It was here that St. Patrick converted the king of Munster. These days, the hurlers of Tipp usually inspire half the county to make the pilgrimage up to Croke Park in Dublin for the All-Ireland final Sunday come September.

County Limerick, another hurling stronghold, historically was the seat of kings and a land of legends. The Shannonside town of the same name is known as the Treaty City because of the agreement signed here in 1691 on behalf of King William III and his wife, Mary II. This gave the Catholic Jacobite forces safe passage to France, the diaspora known as the Flight of the Earls.

Celtic Ireland was ended . . . but it seems nobody told the good people of Munster. ∎

CORK

The county of Cork, especially West Cork, holds some of Ireland's most beautiful landscapes. Strolling down St. Patrick's Street in Cork City, however, is more an aural and linguistic experience than a visual delight. As you're doing *pana* (Cork for "walking"), be *doggy wide* (pay attention) to the wildly lyrical idioms bantered between locals, all delivered in the singsong undulations of the Cork accent. And fear not if a street trader offers you *the blood-and-bandages*—they're just trying to hawk a deep-red Cork GAA jersey. Just tell them you've nothing in your *conjun box* (savings) right now. The Corkonian might then commiserate with your current state of *loberty* (penury) and then proceed to drop the price.

Haggling and verbal jousting are raised to an art form once you enter the English Market. This covered arcade is a trove of tasty local produce and the kind of improvised banter that charmed the Queen of England herself. The market is the perfect spot to put together a mighty Munster picnic before leaving the city to explore the Rebel County's many delights. In fine weather, head for Fota Wildlife Park. If it's a rainy day, visit one of Cork's many Anglo-Irish estates, none finer than Bantry House, with its magnificent Italian gardens. If the rapid-fire patter and strange cadences of Cork leave you somewhat speechless, head for Blarney Castle and kiss the famous stone for the "gift of the gab" (eloquence). Blarney's Tudor-style village square is a reminder of the significant English influence on Cork's history.

The English presence is also evident in the twin fortresses, Charles Fort and James Fort, at the entrance to Kinsale Harbour. Today, this historic town welcomes weekend invasions of foodies seeking the best tables in Ireland's culinary capital.

If you seek your leisure away from the crowds, follow in the sandaled footsteps of St. Finbarr and head for the site of his monastic settlement in the valley of Gougane Barra. The forest park has many trails by which to seek your own green escape. ∎

The copper mining town of Allihies sits serenely near the southwestern tip of the Beara Peninsula; the mines here closed in 1884.

With the help of an ugly monkfish, Pat O'Connell turns on the Cork charm to welcome Queen Elizabeth II to the English Market.

Insider's Guide

The English Market

The beautiful old covered food bazaar known as the English Market sits in the heart (or maybe the belly) of Cork City. Built in 1788 by the Protestant, or "English," corporation that controlled the city at that time, the large market was surrounded by the homes and businesses of Cork's wealthy merchants, most belonging to the English ruling classes. The name "English market" was initially just a popular appellation; it became official sometime around the 1850s.

The market stalls sold local meats, fish, fruit, and vegetables. Sales of fish increased in the 19th century, as the Catholic population abstained from meat on holy days, Fridays, and the 40 days of Lent. This penitent branding led to a doldrums for fish sales in the mid-20th century. But the city's newly globalized range of cuisines has revolutionized the seafood market in recent decades.

The market's ornamental front on Princes Street and most of its roof date from 1862. Following Ireland's War of Independence and civil war, the market's profitability became a barometer of Cork's economic health. A fire in 1980 badly damaged the Princes Street end, but the market building was eventually restored, complete with brick entrance, fountain, and first floor gallery of shops, stalls, and cafés.

With a wealth of Munster meats, seafood, dairy foods, and a variety of bric-a-brac in its tempting stalls—not to mention the priceless Cork wit ringing through its halls—the English Market is *the* place for the savvy visitor to go to experience the very essence of Cork City. ∎

IRISH VOICES: THE MAN WHO CHARMED THE QUEEN

Most people remember the day they met the Queen of England. And most people in Cork remember May 20, 2011, as the day the queen met Pat O'Connell.

O'Connell is used to being around powerful women: His mother, Kay, started K. O'Connell Fish Merchants in Cork's English Market in 1962. "She had a fruit and veg stall on George's Quay beforehand," he recalls, "but when the chance of renting a 12-by-12-foot [3.6 m x 3.6 m] fish stall in the English Market came up, she didn't hesitate. And that was a brave move for a woman at that time.

"As a teenager, I, of course was trying to avoid fish at all costs," O'Connell goes on to say, with an eruption of his infectious laughter. "It wasn't the best aftershave to be wearing as a young fella."

A business degree led to a stint on the Cork City Council, but fish was in his blood, and at 24, Pat joined his brother Paul in the famous old market on Grand Parade. O'Connell brought to the business the bigger picture of a changing Cork. "When we started out," he explains, "we'd get most of our fish from one boat, the *Mona Lisa,* in Castletownbere [on the Beara Peninsula in West Cork]. We would basically sell what they caught. But my mother saw the limitations of that."

Since then, O'Connell Fish Merchants has constantly adapted to Cork's changing demographics. "We get all kinds of fish from different sources now," Pat explains, "such as freshwater salmon from the communal fisheries on the River Lee and the River Blackwater." The stall also sources organic salmon from farms in Donegal, and sea bass from French waters. More recently they've bought more red snapper to satisfy the demands of a growing Asian population in the city. The arrival of more Africans has led to a burgeoning demand for tilapia and halibut.

"Like every good business," says Pat, "we've adapted to a changing clientele, but we're traditional fishmongers in that our business is based on trust. Our customers trust us to source the best fish in a sustainable way."

The rebound of cod populations in Irish waters is one happy outcome of such tradition and trust. "We'll respond to customers' preferences, but we'll also encourage them to try new fish, in new recipes, and to be open to new culinary ideas."

Persuasion comes easy to O'Connell, a former city councilor with a warm laugh and contagious charm. His business card, after all, shows the now globally known photo of Queen Elizabeth II and O'Connell in stitches. When invited to a rehearsal at City Hall for the Queen of England's 2011 visit, O'Connell had felt that rigid niceties were not really what the English Market was all about. So he took a chance on the big day. "Because of the person I was speaking to and because the world was looking on and because I was in some ways representing the English Market, the city, and the fish industry, I had to be diplomatic, didn't I?" he asks, a twinkle in his eye the size of a beam from the Fastnet Rock Lighthouse. "You must be joking, boy!" he chuckles with a burst of true Corkonian contrariness. (Comic timing is a treasured trait here in the Rebel County.)

So O'Connell greeted the queen by telling her that he hadn't been so nervous since the day of his wedding, 30 years ago that week. The queen warmed to such candor, and they were soon discussing the ugly-looking monkfish on prominent display. "That, Your Majesty, is what we in Cork call a mother-in-law fish," said O'Connell. "That was a bit of a gamble," he reflects now. "Fortunately, she has a *great* sense of humor and the banter flowed from there."

O'Connell so charmed the queen that he and his wife, Margaret, were invited to a celebration of the U.K.'s Irish community at Buckingham Palace in 2014. "The chef in the palace invited us upstairs before the event began," says O'Connell with pride. Apparently "Herself" had been "rocked by her visit to the English Market," and she even asked O'Connell to sign a copy of the famous market photo for her private collection.

The queen's, and Cork's, favorite fishmonger now looks to the future. "The next generation is what's important. My daughter Emma might follow us into the fish business, if she wants. So we've opened a fish smokery in Bandon to serve that growing new market for smoked seafood in Ireland." ∎

> "Shopping for fish should be fun, and what's the point of visiting the market without experiencing the *craic* among the characters who work here?"
>
> — *Pat O'Connell*

The verdant grounds of Blarney Castle include horticultural curiosities such as the Poison Garden, the Fern Garden, and the Himalayan Walk.

Special Places

Blarney Village & Castle

The peaceful village of Blarney, located six miles (10 km) northwest of Cork, is steeped in legends. Built around a walled, English-style village green, and overlooked by its famous medieval castle, Blarney seems to exist outside of time.

Blarney Castle was built upon a rock outcrop overlooking the River Martin in 1446 by Dermot Laidhir ("The Strong") McCarthy. The original tower dates from the time of Cormac McCarthy, King of Munster. He is believed to have supplied four thousand Munster men to fight for Scotland's Robert the Bruce at the Battle of Bannockburn in 1314. Bruce supposedly gave half of the Stone of Scone (also known as the Coronation Stone, what we now call the **Blarney Stone**) to McCarthy in gratitude. Another legend suggests the stone was brought to Ireland by the prophet Jeremiah, and yet another tale proffers that Cormac was given the stone by an old witch he had saved from drowning. A more likely account is that the stone was brought to Ireland from the Holy Land by an unnamed crusader. Like every good Irish story, the legend has only grown with the retelling. Truth, if such a thing exists in Blarney, depends very much on who you're talking to.

While most visitors head first for the Blarney Stone, the grounds of the castle are worth exploring, with several specialty gardens, including the Poison Garden, the Bog Garden, and the Jungle. Wander here to stand atop the druidic foundations of the Rock Close, make your own offering at the sacrificial altar of the Fairy Glade, or receive your dearest desires by negotiating the Wishing Steps backward with your eyes closed.

Of course, if your heart's desire is the gift of the gab, simply climb the stairs of the old castle keep, passing the Great Hall with its huge fireplace, where the McCarthy clan no doubt gathered to discuss their plans of love and war. An early morning visit will help you avoid long lines of tongue-tied visitors before you find yourself lying on your back over the 83-foot (29 m) drop to the ground and kissing the Blarney Stone. This is safer than it sounds: A metal grille protects you, as does the grip of a beefy security man. Your first words of newfound eloquence should be in praise of modern-day health and safety standards: In the olden days, the guards simply grabbed you by the ankles and held you upside down over the side of the castle.

Most travelers' next stop is **Blarney Woollen Mills,** the largest Irish store in the world, located a short stroll along the trout-filled River Martin. The stone mill buildings date from 1823, when production of world-famous Blarney tweed began. Later the *báinín* (Aran) yarn produced by the mill was turned into Aran sweaters by teams of local knitters. Although the decline in demand for Irish wool led to the closure of the mill in the early 1970s, the long-term vision of owner Christy Kelleher soon secured the firm's future as international purveyors of the best of Irish clothing and traditional crafted wares. Today, Blarney Woollen Mills sells a vast range of Irish-made clothing, quality knits, and authentic tweeds, along with Waterford Crystal and fine Irish pottery. The impressive complex incorporates a hotel, restaurant, coffee shop, and a relaxing bar where you can try out your newly acquired gift of the gab with the locals. ∎

IN THE KNOW: JOHNNY'S BAR, BLARNEY CASTLE HOTEL

Every traveler in Ireland dreams of that cozy bar, where garrulous locals welcome you warmly with *caint, ceoíl,* and *craic* (conversation, music, and good-humored fun). If you pick the right night (usually Tuesdays, Thursdays, or Sundays), Johnny's Bar at the Blarney Castle Hotel is just such an Irish idyll. The turf fire warms your bones, even in the depths of winter; the Guinness flows freely alongside the Beamish and the Murphy's (Cork's slightly coffee-flavored local stouts); and the locals gradually gather at the working day's end to discuss their GAA teams' latest exploits or maybe reminisce about some of the legends whose photographs grace the walls, heroes who have worn the Blarney colors or the "blood and bandages" for the county team of Cork. The smooth murmur of Cork-undulated conversation crests inevitably toward a breakpoint of collective laughter, and then . . . then the sound of musical instruments being tuned fills this long bar and lounge—*"Give us a G there, boy"*—and slowly the session begins. A night of musical magic unfurls with the jigs and the reels and the hornpipes and the polkas, and soon every foot in the room is tapping happily.

The main musical mover in these parts is a woman whose feet move as fast on the dance floor as her fingers do on the neck of her famous fiddle. Margaret "Mags" McCarthy is a spellbinding vocalist, dancer, and multi-instrumentalist who has toured the world. McCarthy has a master's degree in ethnomusicology from University College Cork, where she currently teaches Irish dance. If you're lucky enough to catch her at Johnny's Bar, you won't be the first (nor the last) visitor to Blarney to be rendered speechless at her talents.

Another notable local talent is the singer and songwriter Mick Flannery. The Blarney native wrote his debut album *Evening Train,* including songs that won awards at the International Songwriting Competition in Nashville, Tennessee, while studying music and management at Coláiste Stiofáin Naofa in Cork. ∎

Mags McCarthy and friends get Johnny's Bar jumping with a lively session.

Special Places

Cobh: A Town of Sad Farewells

The port of Cobh—once known as Queenstown after an 1849 visit by Queen Victoria—hosted an Admiralty station in Napoleonic times and was the point of departure for British soldiers sailing off to the Crimean and Boer Wars. For many prisoners, such as the United Irishmen sentenced to penal servitude after the 1798 Rebellion, Cobh marked the start of six months chained in the dark, dank hold of a convict ship, bound for Van Diemen's Land (Tasmania) or some other Australian penal colony. Cobh was also the last sight of the homeland for millions of Irish emigrants to America, Canada, England, or Australia in the wake of the Great Famine of the 1840s. And for 79 of the 123 passengers ferried out to the "unsinkable" new transatlantic liner *Titanic* on April 11, 1912, Cobh was their last ever contact with land.

The **Titanic Experience,** just past Cobh's promenade, tells the stories of these travelers. It is in the same building that housed the White Star Line ticket office, where *Titanic*'s passengers bought tickets and queued for the tender to take them out to the waiting ship at Roche's Point. The **Titanic Trail Tour** takes in the streets and piers of Cobh, including the White Star Line's "Heartbreak Pier," the setting of one of Ireland's best known images, taken by Father Frank Browne. A keen photographer, the priest used his two-day trip aboard the doomed liner (from Southampton to Cobh) to document its crew and passengers before being ordered to "get off that ship" by his superior.

The **Cobh Heritage Centre,** situated in the restored Victorian railway station, is where you'll find the "Queenstown Story" exhibit, which tells the tale of Ireland's exiles who passed through here over the last two centuries. The exhibit is a fascinating mix of model ships, photographs, letters, and personal effects, such as locks of loved ones' hair, rosaries, and pocket watches. Among the most poignant artifacts is 19-year-old Jeremiah Burke's message in a bottle, washed up in his native Cork in 1913, which reads, "From Titanic, Goodbye All, Burke of Glanmire."

The museum includes exhibits on the *Titanic* and the *Lusitania,* a passenger liner sunk by a German torpedo in 1917. It also relates the 19th-century phenomenon of "American wakes," whereby heartbroken emigrants bade farewell to friends and family knowing they would never see Ireland again. Individual tales abound, such as that of young Annie Moore, the first emigrant to be processed at New York's Ellis Island. Statues of Annie and her brothers stand on the pier both here and on Ellis Island, their transatlantic voyage immortalized in bronze. Between 1815 and 1970, about three million emigrants sailed from Cobh to seek a better future. The Heritage Centre also enlists a genealogist for those making the reverse voyage wishing to trace Irish roots. ∎

The port of Cobh was renamed Queenstown after an 1849 royal visit. OPPOSITE: Visitors attired in *Titanic*-era dress commemorate the ship's final stop off Cobh on April 11, 1912.

The massive, star-shaped Charles Fort—or Dún Chathail in Irish—faces its twin bastion of James Fort across Kinsale Bay.

Insider's Guide

Kinsale

The first destination for most visitors to County Cork, after Cork City, is the picturesque town of Kinsale. Historically this was a key strategic harbor protected by two military forts built by the British, ever wary of seaborne invasion from continental foes such as Catholic Spain and Napoleonic France.

These days, the only European boats docking here are yachts dispensing discerning diners, keen to sample the delights of Ireland's "Cuisine Capital." Gourmets flock to Kinsale to sample the finest produce of Munster's rich pasturelands and the fruits of the abundant Celtic Sea.

Charles Fort—or Dún Chathail to use its Irish name—is the easier accessed of the twin bastions that face each other across Kinsale Bay. Built by the British in 1682, Charles Fort formed a twin defense of the harbor of Kinsale along with the older **James Fort.** In 1690, the Duke of Marlborough laid siege to Cork and recaptured Kinsale from the Jacobite army of King James of Scotland. Charles Fort served as a British Army barracks for the next 200 years, up to the signing of the Anglo-Irish Treaty of 1921.

Visitors can take an hour-long tour of the site, but a word to the wise: Wear good walking shoes—this place wasn't built for armies who marched in sandals or flip-flops. As you wander through this star-shaped bastion of empire, imagine the life of the common foot soldier stationed in this self-contained citadel on the western edge of Europe. How many generations of young men from places like London, Lincoln, Lancashire, Lanarkshire, and even Llanfairpwllgwyngyll (in Wales) found themselves staring out to sea, day after day, longing for home as they stood guard for a king or queen few of them would ever meet?

Wherever you eat in Kinsale, you can sharpen your appetite (or work off a fish supper) by taking a coastal walk out to **Charles Fort** from the town. Follow the Lower Road around the inlet until you get to the **Spaniard Inn** (a Kinsale institution worth a stop), and then take a left on Scilly to cut down to the Terrace. From there, follow the Scilly Walk to its endpoint and turn left up the walkway onto High Road, where you'll turn right. The **Bulman Bar** at the base of the hill is a perfect stopover for refreshments, before continuing on up to the famous fort. ∎

IN THE KNOW: EATING OUT IN KINSALE

Kinsale is known far and wide as the culinary capital of Ireland, offering a wealth of great restaurants, pubs, and cafés for adventurous gourmands. October is the month to visit for the **Kinsale Gourmet Festival,** or February during **Kinsale Restaurant Week,** but there are also year-round food tours and cooking courses for the culinarily committed.

Bastion Restaurant on Main Street is run by Glaswegian Paul McDonald, whose poached trout is matchless; Bastion also offers a renowned vegetarian tasting menu. The **Black Pig,** on Lower O'Connell Street, has convivial warmth with a burning stove and a lively courtyard. Pair the Sherkin Island oysters and shallot vinegar with a vintage white from their extensive wine bar and you'll understand why owners Siobhan Waldron and Gavin Ryan have won so many awards. For a big foodie night out, **Fishy Fishy** on Crowley's Quay is *the* place to go in Kinsale. Here, Martin and Marie Shanahan serve up wonderfully fresh-off-the-boat catch. Their Surf & Turf dish of pan-fried scallops with Rosscarbery black pudding is a decadent delight.

If you're looking for great seafood at affordable prices, **High Tide** is a family-friendly restaurant in a cozy room fronting Main Street. Classic favorites such as scampi, calamari, and mussels and fries always satisfy, while the monkfish curry provides an unusual surprise. The service is friendly, and there's a wine to pair perfectly with any catch of the day.

If you're fond of fresh air, follow the Scilly Walk to the **Spaniard Inn** for great seafood or pub grub, served on the terrace overlooking Scilly Park. This atmospheric pub was celebrated in verse by the Limerick poet and "Wandering Celt" Desmond O'Grady, who lived his last years in Kinsale after a lifetime of globe-trotting. Farther along the Scilly Walk, the **Bulman Bar and Toddie's Restaurant** prides itself on its global cuisine. The menus change seasonally but the fare always tastes fabulous, especially on a summer's evening when the sun is setting over Kinsale Harbour and the outside tables resound with tall tales, languid laughter, and that celebratory sound of clinking glasses. ∎

Toddie's Restaurant prides itself on its global cuisine.

The tables outside the Bulman Bar resound with tall tales and laughter.

Three Castle Head

Filmmaker Jim Sheridan called this the loneliest place he'd ever been. Located on a storm-lashed headland at the tip of the Mizen Peninsula, Three Castle Head is one of the most haunting (and some say haunted) sites in Ireland.

The ruins here consist of the three dilapidated ramparts of the castle Dun Locha ("fort of the lough"), set atop a 350-foot (106 m) cliff face beside a dramatically perched *corrie loch* (mountain lake). The original fort is believed to have been constructed by the Irish lord Donagh na Aimrice O'Mahoney ("Donagh the Migratory," due to his scholarly pilgrim-

ages to the Holy Land) in 1207. The castle was further fortified in the 15th century. The three lookout towers seen today are linked by a 20-foot (6 m) rampart wall, which extends to the edge of the cliff. One of the multistory towers even leads down to the sea via a series of natural crevices.

Who knows what declarations of undying love, invocations of religious faith, or whisperings of betrayal might have been uttered upon the towers' spiral staircases within this gale-blasted bastion? But there is little doubt among locals that Three Castle Head is now what is known among Celts as a "thin space": a place where the

veil between this world and the next is gossamer thin.

On stormy days, the force of the wind coming in off the Atlantic Ocean raises a froth on the lake that can appear in the shape of what local legend calls the "White Lady." As the story goes, when the White Lady walks across the lake at Three Castle Head, those who see her are not long for this world.

Another old Irish superstition? Maybe. Maybe not. Frenchwoman Sophie Toscan du Plantier told an aunt that she had seen the White Lady here on Christmas week in 1996, the day before she was brutally murdered at her holiday home in nearby Toormore. ∎

At the tip of the Mizen Peninsula, Three Castle Head is one of the most haunting (and some say haunted) sites in Ireland.

GREAT IRISH DRIVES: THE PENINSULAS OF WEST CORK

West Cork offers visitors some of most spectacular driving routes in Ireland. From Kinsale, the Coast Road to Skibbereen is a long and winding windfall of scenic delights and fascinating detours. Stop at the village of **Timoleague** to view the 14th-century Franciscan friary, its shell of lichen green stone still standing despite the ravages of Oliver Cromwell's army in 1642. As you wander through fragments of medieval cloisters, the cooing of pigeons resounds through this sacred place, and the friary's lancet windows, tomb niches, and tall arched nave combine to transport you to an ancient age of prayer and sacrifice.

Take a detour through Courtmacsherry and along the lanes that crisscross the **Seven Heads Peninsula.** Just south of the lively town of Clonakilty is the causeway to **Inchydoney Island,** known for its beautiful beaches. The southern bays and coastlines of Cork and Kerry are dotted with hundreds of islands, many of which can be reached from various points along these coastlines (see Part 5). At Ballinascarthy, near Clonakilty, a stainless steel Model T monument honors Henry Ford, whose father was born here.

History beckons three miles (5 km) west of Clonakilty, where the **Four Alls Bar** and the village of Sam's Cross are signposted off the N71. The cozy Four Alls, set among the rolling green hills of West Cork, is where the commander in chief of the Free State Army, Michael Collins, stopped on August 22, 1922, for his last drink before he died in an IRA ambush. The **birthplace of Michael Collins** stands nearby at Woodfield, where a bronze bust is usually adorned with floral tributes to the fallen Irish hero. Watch for a signpost for the **Drombeg Stone Circle** off the Glandore Road. This is a ring of 17 thin, man-size stones constructed alongside an ancient cooking pit with a boiling oven, dating to around 1500 B.C. Two millennia later, the area around Skibbereen suffered inordinately during the Great Famine, and the **Skibbereen Heritage Centre** commemorates the dead through various exhibits. The center also directs visitors to such tragic but historically significant local sites as workhouses and mass graves.

At Skibbereen, you're at the starting point of three of the five great peninsulas of the southwest: Mizen, Sheep's Head, and Beara (from south to north). Each has its own appeal, and you can lose yourself quite easily here, if you take the time. Indeed, the variety of non-Irish accents you'll encounter among the locals speaks to the fact that so many visitors have ended up settling in wonderful, wild West Cork.

Skibbereen, starting point of three of Munster's five great peninsulas

Meandering through the **Mizen Peninsula** clockwise from Ballydehob, you're spirited into a Beckettian landscape of gorse-covered bogs, rock outcrops, and saltwater inlets. Stop for lunch in the sleepy bayside villages of Schull and Goleen or continue to the end of the Mizen at Crookhaven.

Just outside Schull, look for a bay island with the terracotta splendor of **Kilcoe Castle** rising majestically from ancient gray ramparts. Actor Jeremy Irons accurately restored this medieval fortification, which was one of the last Celtic bastions to fall in Elizabethan England's conquest of Gaelic Ireland. Moving on, wilderness swimmers should make time for **Barleycove,** a beautiful series of beaches backed by grassy dunes and mounds of *machair* (shell-sand turf). High atop impressive cliffs at the end of the peninsula sits **Mizen Head,** the southernmost point of mainland Ireland. Walk beyond the visitors center and cross a bridge over a rocky sea chasm to study an exhibit of charts and signal flags in the old fog station. The intermittent beam of the **Mizen Lighthouse** guides your way at twilight, and a sighting of dolphins or whales might be your reward for a walk to the end of Éire.

After heading north from Mizen Head, turn left at the village of Durrus for the **Sheep's Head Peninsula,** another clockwise drive. You won't find any tourist attractions here, just magical, gently rolling, rocky hills, and a scattering of tiny villages. At the tip, the **Tooreen Visitor Centre** will guide you through the natural wonders of these windswept wilds. The drive back to Bantry along the north side is aptly named the Goats Path. (For the Beara Peninsula drive, see page 118.) ∎

IRISH GARDENS: THE BOUNTY OF WEST CORK

Among the pleasures of driving through West Cork, in addition to the hedgerows lining the roads, are the region's many luxuriant gardens. The **West Cork Garden Trail** links 27 of these, dotted along the peninsulas. Stop and stroll through tall trees and lush, unusual plants and you'll be continually reminded of the blessings of the Gulf Stream, the transatlantic currents that wash this southwest corner of Ireland with warming waters, allowing plants, birds, and insects from southern Europe to thrive here.

At Glengarriff, **Bamboo Park** boasts 30 different species of *Bambusoideae*, surrounded by palms and tropical plants. This garden was created in 1999 by a French couple, Serge and Claudine de Thibault. Bamboo also grows across Killmackillogue Bay in Kenmare, in the subtropical **Derreen Garden,** established by Lord Landsdowne with plants brought home from stints as viceroy of India and governor general of Canada. In this most global of gardens, paths meander past enormous rhododendrons and through primeval-looking forests of giant conifers, swamp cypresses, and North American redwoods, while Australian tree ferns compete with hemlocks from China.

Another garden within easy reach of Glengarriff is **Ilnacullin**, also called Garinish Island, just a 10-minute boat ride across the bay. The island's 37 acres (15 ha) were planted as a wild garden with an enchanting Italian-style centerpiece by Annan Bryce, who bought the gorse-covered island in 1910. The pavilion and sunken Italian garden, inspired by the courts of Pompeii, were designed by architect Harold Peto. The Happy Valley leads from a Grecian temple to a bog garden before climbing to a Martello tower, which affords views of the bay, Seal Island, and the wooded shores of Glengarriff. At the **Liss Ard Estate** in Skibbereen, the bowl-shaped structure of the mini, stadium-like **Sky Garden** offers a unique experience, obliterating all earthly surrounds to leave visitors focused on the sky.

For a very different, must-see garden view, ascend the Stairway to the Sky at **Bantry House.** The garden here was initially laid out by Richard White, the first viscount of Berehaven, between the 1820s and 1850s, after he traveled widely in Europe, absorbing its burgeoning horticulture. He transformed the land rising steeply from Bantry Bay up to the family's magnificent 18th-century residence, employing hundreds in the process. The garden has seven terraces, with the manor on the third level. The formal garden's contrast to the wild expanse of the bay and its islands projects a perfect yin and yang within this Edenic West Cork haven. ∎

The Italian garden at Garinish Island OPPOSITE: Visitors descend some 100 steps to an Italian box-delineated parterre set before Bantry House.

Beara is best navigated in an open-ended figure eight, starting from Glengarriff and crossing the Healy Pass (pictured).

GREAT IRISH DRIVES: **BEARA PENINSULA**

From Glengarriff, the Beara Peninsula drive is a daylong loop, providing photo opportunities around every corner of the long and winding roads of West Cork. This route is a hidden gem, a scenic secret the Irish like to keep to themselves that is every bit as bucolic and beautiful as the Ring of Kerry.

A long, ragged realm of dramatic peaks and valleys, running 30 miles (50 km) east to west, Beara is split between the counties of Cork and Kerry—with Cork edging it on possession. As you drive, watch for the delightful plays of sunshine and shadow on the low sandstone sides of the Caha Mountains that form the peninsula's spine. The highest of these, Hungry Hill, rises to 2,251 feet (685 m).

Be alert: Cars stop often along the heavily indented shoreline, their drivers arrested by the endlessly picturesque vistas. To the south, you'll see Bantry Bay and its islands (see page 294), and to the north gleams the Kenmare River, with a multitude of smaller islands all framed by the dramatic backdrop of Kerry's mountainous Iveragh Peninsula.

Beara is best navigated in an open-ended figure eight, starting from the Victorian health resort of **Glengarriff** ("rugged glen"). Tucked in the shelter of a valley facing Bantry Bay and backed by wooded mountains, this town of 19th-century villas is adorned with hydrangeas and palm trees. At **Eccles Hotel,** take a look around the literary-themed lobby, with its paintings of Tolstoy and W. B. Yeats, who stayed here in the 1920s. George Bernard Shaw was another regular guest.

Traveling west along the southern coast road, you reach the right turn for the **Healy Pass.** A clear day is best for the narrow mountain ascent to the pass. The road snakes along "S" hooks, switchback scissors, and horseshoe bends up to the summit, which marks the Cork-Kerry border. Your reward is a stunning view from a Crucifixion shrine (a wayside Calvary) at the top, almost 1,100 feet (334 m) above sea level.

Descending to the northern foot of the pass, you'll come to the delightful **Derreen Garden** (see page 117), flourishing with subtropical flora thanks to the warm Gulf Stream winds. Continue west along a narrow, winding road over the end of Slieve Miskish.

Heading toward the village of Ardgroom, you'll see signs for various megalithic monuments, including the **Cashelkeelty Stone Circles.** About a mile (1.6 km) east of the town is the **Ardgroom Stone Circle,** known locally as Canfea.

Continuing east, you arrive at the town of Allihies on the black cliffs of west-facing Ballydonegan Bay. This was a copper-mining center in the 19th century, its history shared at the **Allihies Copper Mine Museum & Café,** located in the old Methodist church built for immigrant Cornish miners. The museum offers a historical overview of mining in Allihies from the Bronze Age to the 1960s. The Copper Café has a sensory garden at the back of the building with outdoor seating offering sweeping views of the bay.

Reaching the very tip of Beara feels like arriving at the end of the world. But there's more land to explore, if you can brave the swaying cable car ride to **Dursey Island** (see page 294). Watch out for whales, dolphins, and other marine life attracted by the nutrient-rich waters around Dursey. As you return along the south coast, take a short detour before Castletownbere for the extraordinary ruin of **Dunboy Castle,** the stronghold of O'Sullivan Bere, the last chieftain of Gaelic Ireland. This was the site of the Siege of Dunboy in the summer of 1602, one of the last stands of the Celtic clans against the forces of Elizabeth I. A 5,000-strong English force suppressed the Irish rebels, eventually executing all 58 survivors in the local market square.

As you drive the narrow lanes to the ruins, look to the right (behind the security fencing) into the Gothic gloom of **Puxley Mansion.** This imposing 19th-century manor was torched by the IRA in 1921 as a new generation of insurgents fought crown forces during Ireland's War of Independence. The Puxleys of Cornwall came to Ireland in Cromwellian times, and three centuries later, English novelist Daphne du Maurier, a close friend of Christopher Puxley, re-created their world in her 1943 novel *Hungry Hill.*

A conglomerate of local owners began lavish restoration work in the 2000s, but the Celtic Tiger's roar was silenced in the financial crash of 2008 and plans to reopen the mansion as a luxury hotel stalled. Today, Puxley's well-guarded interior of huge vaults, blank windows, and grand empty rooms remains the stuff of Gothic novels, filled with the ghosts of modern Ireland's dashed expectations.

When you reach the fishing port of Castletownbere, stop into **MacCarthy's Bar** to learn the story of Dr. Aidan MacCarthy and his Japanese sword, which he received from the commandant of a Nagasaki prison camp whom the good doctor saved from a lynching by prisoners after the atomic bomb fell in 1945. There's every chance you'll also find a raconteur willing to share the many myths of Beara among MacCarthy's clientele. Ask about the Hag of Beara, the faction fights of Drimoleague Fair, and Mac-Deichet Uí Thorna, the name carved on Ballycrovane Ogham Stone in the ancient Celtic language, near Eyeries. Buy a round, make yourself comfortable, and the stories will flow long into the night. ∎

The Ardgroom Stone Circle, thought by some to be a Neolithic monument to an unknown Beara ruler

Special Places

Gougane Barra Forest Park

There are several ancient religious sites in Ireland where the medieval imperative of the "green martyrdom" (see page 36) makes perfect sense. The sacred ground at Gougane Barra in County Cork is one such place where those of a spiritual disposition came to get closer to God through the beauty of nature.

Gougane Barra Forest Park is located west of Macroom and is run by Coillte, the Irish state forestry service. This small park—half a square mile (1.4 sq km) in area—sits deep in a rocky bowl of cliffs surrounding the peaceful waters of Gougane Barra Lake. The source of the River Lee rises in the nearby hills and flows into the lake. Remote but accessible, the park has six miles (10 km) of hiking trails of varying degrees of difficulty. The **Waterfall Trail,** the **Lee Trail,** the **Mountain Trail,** and others lead you deep into the wilderness of coniferous and broad-leaved trees, rushing streams and waterfalls, and spectacular lookouts. The forests were planted on virtually treeless land in 1938, and Gougane Barra is now home to 20 tree species, mainly Sitka spruce, Japanese larch, Scotch pine, and lodgepole pine. The **Gougane Barra Hotel** and **Cronin's Bar & Café** offer rest and repast for weary walkers.

Gougane Barra is the anglicized form of the Irish Guagán Barra, meaning "rock of Barra." The name comes from St. Finbarr, who built a small church on the island in the lake here during the sixth century. Finbarr (Fionnbharra—or Fair Head—often abbreviated to Barra) lived from about A.D. 550 to 623 and was bishop of Cork and abbot of a monastery. He also formed several schools and today is the patron saint of Cork, where the French Gothic-style cathedral is named for him, as are several schools worldwide in locations as far afield as San Francisco and Lagos, Nigeria.

Finbarr's Holy Well, topped by a large flat stone and a mound of grassy earth, is a square stone tribute to the saint set on the lakeside at Gougane Barra. Local legend has it that Finbarr's first act on arrival here was to cast a giant serpent from the waters of the lake. As the snake fled, its enormous mass carved a channel in the earth all the way to the sea, thus creating the River Lee.

Gougane Barra's ruins date from around 1700, when a priest named Denis O'Mahony retreated to the island. During the era of the Penal Laws, when Catholicism was outlawed, the church's insular remoteness proved a safe place for the celebration of the Roman Catholic Mass. In the silence of this remote green retreat, you can almost hear the whispered prayers of a congregation that worshipped despite persistent persecution. Standing near the original monastery, 19th-century **St. Finbarr's Oratory** is celebrated for its richly decorated interior. It is the final stop along **St. Finbarr's Pilgrim Path,** which starts 22 miles (35 km) away in Drimoleague, one of five pilgrim paths in Ireland. If you take the path on the saint's feast day of September 25, scores of Corkonians will accompany you to this beautiful sacred site. ∎

St. Finbarr's Oratory sits serenely on an island on Gougane Barra Lake. OPPOSITE: Trees reach heavenward in the soft green light of Gougane Barra Forest Park.

IRISH VOICES: EXPLORING IRELAND'S HOLY WELLS

Historian Shane Lordan studies early Hiberno-Latin literature and insular saints' cults, so when he talks to visitors at St. Gobnait's Holy Well in Ballyvourney—one of two sacred sources that attract the faithful to the monastic site south of the town—he's more knowledgeable than most about saints and scholars. Along with Professor Celeste Ray of the University of the South in Tennessee, Lordan has helped create the first full database and analysis of Ireland's some 3,000 holy wells.

"The holy wells long predate Christianity in Ireland," says Lordan. "When the astute St. Patrick arrived to convert the Irish in the fifth century, he probably identified the emotional and spiritual meaning that the Irish invested in these pagan wells. The early church no doubt saw them as an opportunity to encourage worship of Christ and his saints in ancient places held sacred among the native Irish."

The adaptation of these sacred sites would have been an easy transition, given Ireland's pagan beliefs in pantheism and animism. The Celts imbued the natural world with spiritual qualities: In parts of Cork to this day, farmers will look up at dark clouds and remark that "the Druids are passing." Water was a feminine element, so many ancient wells were dedicated to pagan goddesses. These would have been reinvented as holy wells honoring the likes of St. Dymphna and St. Brigid. St. Patrick used the power of otherworldly water in the pagan Irish mind to reinforce the power of baptism and baptized many converts in holy wells.

Locals have long visited holy wells seeking cures for headaches, bad backs, tooth trouble, failing eyesight, and other ailments. The written prayers and votives left at holy wells might also plead for luck in love, healthy childbirth, or success in exams. Certain wells attracted pilgrims from afar, their reputation for cures spread by word of mouth. Each Christian saint's feast day is an occasion for celebration at his or her holy well, when devotees perform the *turas*, or patterns, a practice of circling the well a set number of times, always in a clockwise direction.

> "Our ancestors recognized water as the essence of life and revered its deities, so the wells represented the flow of life from the spirit world to ours."
>
> — *Shane Lordan*

St. Brigid was known for her love of nature and her care for the earth and the animal kingdom. Modern-day visitors to her many wells leave votives asking for her intercession on matters of pollution, climate change, and animal abuse. "St. Brigid has holy wells dedicated to her all over Ireland," Lordan observes. "Brigid's Well near Liscannor in Clare may be Ireland's best known holy well." Believed to have healing powers, this well is enclosed in an open stone grotto that serves as a gateway to the ancient cemetery on the hill above it. The sound of the running water is audible, and the well epitomizes a Celtic "thin space," where the veil between this world and the next is easy to slip through. When the Celts sought help from their pagan gods, they came to these portals to make their pleas. The fluidity of water was the manifestation of the plane of the gods and the dead ancestors. Later, the pagan belief that the wells served as portals to the Otherworld was replaced by Christian belief in the afterlife.

In Irish folklore, the pagan Brigid and her sisters represented a triple goddess, incorporating "higher ground," higher learning, and higher consciousness. Many pilgrims still celebrate Brigid's pagan roots with the holiday of Lughnasadh. Unable to eradicate Brigid's popularity among native Celts, Christendom reinvented her as the foster mother of Jesus and canonized her in the fifth century. The pagan Brigid was also the patron goddess of the Druids, and signs of druidic language can still be spotted in her well, among hundreds of trinkets, rosary beads, prayer notes, and clothes.

"The faithful leave offerings around the wells, and tie prayers and ribbons on sacred trees that we often find at these sites," says Lordan. "The pagan Druids revered trees such as rowan, hawthorn, willow, hazel, and oak for their sacred properties." Holy wells were especially effective in the curing of eye ailments, sight loss, and warts. Certain well names also reflect their curative reputations: Tobar na Súl ("well of the eye") or Tobar na Plá ("well of the plague"). Here, pilgrims would immerse their bodies or wash the afflicted body part with a cloth. The cloth was then attached to a tree as a votive offering. As the rag rotted away, supposedly so did the disease or illness. ∎

St. Brigid's Well, near Liscannor in County Clare

IN THE KNOW: WHERE TO STAY IN CORK

Your first stop after Cork City has to be the **Blarney Castle Hotel,** a very "country Irish" hotel located right on the village green and a short walk from its namesake medieval strong-hold. The hotel's friendly owners, Ian and Una Forrest, are always around to greet you with a smile, a beverage, and a helping hand with any plans for the day. If you just want to hear some melodious Cork banter, wander into **Johnny's Bar** (see page 109) and follow the flow of opinion, high praise, low criticism, and endless witticism on the footballers and hurlers of Blarney and "de county," and a few curious Cork inquiries about wherever you're from yourself. The hotel menu caters for all-comers, and the portions are always filling in this most homey of Blarney hotels.

You'll find an abundance of accommodation while touring West Cork, but if you want to experience an old-world Victorian resort hotel with modern amenities such as a spa offering seaweed baths, stay at **Eccles,** a traditional family hotel right on Bantry Bay in Glengarriff. This is where Dublin and Cork families come to play in the bay, to tour the gardens and islands of West Cork, and to relax with good food and drink, far from the worries of the modern world. You, too, can sit on the terrace overlooking the bay and the Bamboo Gardens, while you sip a Glengarriff Gin cocktail and wait for something creative from the kitchen: maybe a main course of John Dory fish with prawns, wild mushrooms, confit lemon, and an herb cream?

Should you seek modern luxury in another Victorian land-mark, stay just over the border in County Kerry at the **Park Hotel** in Kenmare. This five-star haven on Kenmare Bay is run with renowned attention to *every* detail by Francis Brennan and his brother John. For those who prefer the quiet life, the **Gougane Barra Hotel,** inside the Forest Park, is the perfect retreat. The bucolic views from most rooms are inspiring, and the restaurant overlooks the lake and St. Finbarr's Oratory. The food is sourced fresh from local suppliers and from the hotel's own herb garden. Before you wander the park paths, fill up on grilled Clonakilty black pudding, potato cake, smoked lardons, and stewed apple. Happy trails! ∎

Eccles, a traditional family hotel, is located right on Bantry Bay in Glengarriff. OPPOSITE: Kenmare's Park Hotel is a modern luxury landmark.

KERRY

Kerry people inhabit the Kingdom. These are vigorous folk, full of "devilment." And like many mountain-dwelling peoples, they choose their words well. Living in the shadows of geological giants such as the Macgillycuddys Reeks, Kerry people know that small talk is for flatlanders from the midlands and cities like Cork and Dublin.

The lively souls of the Kingdom inhabit one of Earth's most beautiful realms. These mountain people have long considered themselves closer to the gods than their fellow Celts. Kerrymen capture a mountain goat each summer and crown him King Puck, to preside over Ireland's oldest country fair, in Killorglin. In neighboring Killarney, travelers flock from around the world to a town filled with musicians, dancers, and storytellers. The town is also the gateway to the crown jewel of Ireland's national parks, Killarney National Park, with its famous lakes, waterfalls, and the ancient residences of Ross Castle and Muckross House.

The locals are well traveled, too. Kerry people have criss-crossed the globe since St. Brendan the Navigator set out with his fellow monks to sail the Atlantic in the sixth century. Another Kerryman, Tom Crean, was at the heart of several Antarctic voyages during the golden age of exploration.

All travelers to the Kingdom embrace the majestic Ring of Kerry. The lesser traveled Dingle Peninsula is equally spectacular, and a visit to the fishing village of Dingle is imperative. Here pubs pulsate with music sessions, floors vibrate with Irish dance, trawlers deliver the freshest of seafood, and the artisan Dingle Distillery offers delicious tastings of gin and whiskey. While there, raise a toast toward Kerry's offshore treasures, the storied islands of the Skelligs and the Blaskets, just a short boat ride away (see Part 5).

Kerry is a kingdom filled with such natural jewels. As playwright John B. Keane observed, "In belonging to Kerry, you belong to the elements. You belong to the spheres spinning in the heavens." ∎

Hikers rest atop lofty Carrauntoohil, the highest mountain in Ireland, towering over Kerry at 3,407 feet (1,039 m).

Magnificent scenery composed of sea views, island sightings, clifftop drives, and the odd bovine or ovine greets travelers along the Ring of Kerry.

GREAT IRISH DRIVES: RING OF KERRY

The Ring of Kerry lingers long in the memories of most visitors to Ireland. This looping route around the coast of the Iveragh Peninsula is one of the great scenic drives anywhere in the world. Passing through Killorglin, site of Puck Fair, the road sweeps down to Valentia Island, taking travelers within sight of the Skellig Islands, and out through historic Caherdaniel, home of the forefather of Irish independence, Daniel O'Connell (1775–1847). The rugged coastal scenery is breathtaking, as the road snakes around the Kerry cliffs before cutting inland to Killarney National Park. On a clear day, the famous lakes shimmer in the distance as you descend toward Kerry's liveliest town.

Start early, especially in summer, to avoid the crowds and to explore the occasional diversion along the backroads. Leaving Killarney along the N72, great views stretch to your left down the wide, mountain-framed expanse of Lough Leane. In 12 miles (19 km), you will reach **Killorglin,** a delightful small town where each August a wild goat is crowned king of the three-day revel known as Puck Fair (see page 134). Cross into town via the bridge, then veer right to follow the main N70 Ring of Kerry route. Before the village of Glenbeigh, a left detours to **Lough Caragh,** a good place to picnic.

Back on the N70, you will soon reach Glenbeigh, where a right turn just before the end of the village leads you to **Rossbehy Strand** (also called Rossbeigh). This popular beach offers water sports and horseback riding, along with an expansive view of a giant spit of shaggy dunes stretching north across Dingle Bay toward the mountainous spine of the Dingle Peninsula. The narrow road continues in a loop back to the N70, but beware—the hedgerows are thick in summer and many corners are blind, with cars having to utilize the occasional shallow pullouts to make way.

Rejoin the N70 and proceed down the northern coast of the **Iveragh Peninsula** through glorious hilly scenery. Just before crossing the bridge into the village of Cahersiveen, a glance to your left reveals the ruins of the birthplace of Daniel O'Connell, champion of Ireland's poor and the first Irish Catholic ever elected to Parliament in London.

Turn right in the village to pass the **Barracks Heritage Centre,** styled as a Bavarian castle, with exhibitions and displays of local interest. Photographers will find a fine photo op by framing the castle from the opposite shores of the river. To find **Cahergal** and **Leacanabuaile stone forts,** cross the bridge and veer left at the top of the hill, following the brown "Stone Houses" signs about 1.5 miles (2 km) down the road. Especially impressive is Leacanabuaile, inhabited during the Bronze Age and perhaps dating back more than 4,000 years. Perched on a rock outcrop, this reconstruction is a great stone-built enclosure, 80 feet (25 m) across, with a square building in the center and the remains of three beehive huts, all inside a circular six-foot (2 m) wall.

Backtrack to Cahersiveen and turn right onto the N70. In three miles (5 km), take a right at the side road (R565) toward Portmagee. Here you can drive across the causeway onto magical **Valentia Island** (see page 296), especially colorful in high summer.

Back on the N70, turn right to continue your Ring of Kerry circuit. The seaside resort of **Waterville,** favored by golfers, stands on sandy Ballinskelligs Bay. From here the road climbs to the classic viewpoint from **Coomakesta Pass,** offering very fine vistas of the Skelligs, as well as Scariff and Deenish Islands. The views continue to improve as you come in sight of the mighty, islet-fringed Kenmare River, far more like a great bay than an estuary. Turn right at Caherdaniel, signposted "Derrynane House," stopping for refreshments, should the mood take you, at the **Blind Piper,** an excellent pub.

Return to the N70 and in four miles (6 km) bear left in Castlecove to find the magnificent **Staigue Fort.** Set in a beautiful, lonely valley, this wonderfully preserved ring fort dates from 1500 B.C. and is more than 100 feet (30 m) in diameter. Within its thick walls, steps lead to some fine sea and mountain views. Back on the N70, turn left and continue as far as Sneem village, where the road forks left on the R568 for a wild 30-mile (50 km) mountain run, eventually taking you past the lakes of Killarney, stretching below to usher you back to the town and a night of Kerry hospitality. ■

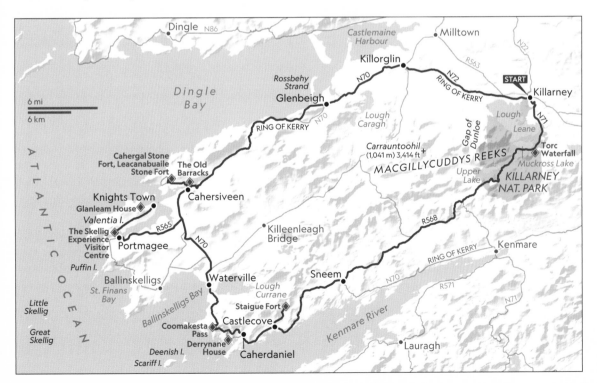

The Ring of Kerry: one of the world's great scenic drives

IRISH VOICES: MASTER MUSICIAN & SEANCHAÍ

His hands are always poised, deft, and sure-fingered, like a typist's or a sculptor's. The illusion of instinct conceals decades of practice.

He changes instruments—piano, guitar, uilleann (elbow) pipes—the way a carpenter might pick up a chisel, a screwdriver, or a wood planer. Keyboards for a chord structure, maybe; guitar to pick out a melody; and pipes to add some "heart and soul." The pipes are "a soul instrument," says Thomas O'Sullivan. "When I play them, they become a part of me, physically, and I'm part of them. It's like breathing ancient Irish air. The uilleann pipes are to me the sound of the Celtic soul."

Thomas O'Sullivan is a craftsman, but a master musician must also infuse the song or the piece with a *feel* that convinces the audience of his or her honesty in the performance. "You have to convey the story within the music," he explains. And storytelling is another skill at which this very personable Kerryman excels.

Take the story of his first music teacher: "Her name was Mother Brendan of the Presentation order of nuns in Milltown. She was a temperamental soul, and, I must admit, I tried her patience sorely. The piece was 'Daffodil Dell' in the student's book *Roland's Piano Tutor*. I learned the piece by ear and when asked to point to a particular phrase on the sheet, I'd just wing it, as my sight-reading was, to say the least, inaccurate. Then, heaven help us, but all hell would break loose. For a nun, Mother Brendan was a fierce woman altogether." O'Sullivan smiles, then adds, "But she gave me the start, as they say in the trade, and that's kept me in good stead for the rest of my life. God bless her.

"She died soon after, and some might say my playing sent her to an early grave," he jokes. "But she gave me a real appreciation for music at the age of 12. As I had piano theory very young, it was easy to learn other instruments, like the guitar, uilleann pipes, flutes, and whistles. The piano is very visual in the music spectrum, so master that and it's very easy to understand the mechanics of other instruments."

His Saturday afternoons were spent indoors being tutored by Mother Brendan, at a time when most young Kerry lads were out playing football, dreaming of Croke Park. "I can still

walk down that convent hallway in my mind," says O'Sullivan now. "It had an atmosphere all its own . . . creaking wooden floorboards and a richly toned bell to call the nuns to prayer . . . the loud ticktock of the big wall clock, slowing time to a steady, metronomic beat. Looking back on it now, it was all very *graaand* for a young lad from Church Street, Milltown."

So, away from the lessons, what excited this young, nun-haunted musician? "Actually, we didn't have a radio or record player at home back in the '60s, so the only music experience was church music, heard via benediction and the High Mass for the dead," says O'Sullivan. The boy soaked it all up. "I was an astute Catholic eavesdropping on religious music played on an old harmonium," he recalls. "My uncle had a radio, so I'd hear English music hall songs of the '20s and '30s on the BBC, but the strong Latin hymn melodies were the first live music I heard and their influence stayed with me."

The story was all-important though: "As an old musical friend, fiddler Donie O'Neill, had a habit of saying: 'That's a great tune altogether, it has a good plot to it.' And so we'll play it and discuss the tune afterward."

> "Music is a universal language that has many accents, a language that's understood and felt by people all around the world. Songs and music connect us all."
>
> — *Thomas O'Sullivan*

There were no TVs in most Kerry homes in those days, which made the *seanchaí* (storyteller) a most valued member of rural society. Young Thomas, with his musical ear for cadence and variations on a theme, soon mastered this art form too, listening to Kerry storytellers entertain their neighbors by the fire deep into the long winter nights. The O'Sullivan home was a lodging house, so there was always an audience, and plenty of source material, thanks to an ever changing and colorful cast of characters.

The real skill of the *seanchaí* was to tell the old stories in entertainingly new ways, inventing slight departures from the standard plots to keep the listeners hooked. O'Sullivan would later spend five years studying the folklore of Kerry's mountain region to write *Kerry Dreamtime—Legend and Lore of the Magillicuddy Reeks*.

"My hero was the late Eamon Kelly, the legendary Kerry *seanchaí*: He devised a style of storytelling all his own and his 'Stories from Ireland' are well worth watching on YouTube. He was a master of the entertaining diversion, but he

Thomas O'Sullivan beats the bodhran (a goatskin, handheld Irish drum) at O'Sullivan's Cascade in Tomies Wood, Killarney.

always circled back to the main theme of the story, like a jazz maestro improvising around the main chord progression."

Growing up in the Kingdom, where the Kerry accent makes even the most mundane conversation sound like a melodic improv contest, the budding musician developed a lifelong love of jazz. "I'm really inspired by jazz improvisation. I could listen to players like Chick Corea and Keith Jarrett all day long," he enthuses. "In my teens I played with some local musicians and some had that improvisatory style, which was very freeing, very liberating, and it applies to traditional Irish music, too. Uilleann pipers that inspired me, such as Seamus Ennis, and fiddlers like Tommy Potts were great innovators and improvisers."

"Music is a universal language that has many accents, a language that is understood and felt by people all around the world," says O'Sullivan. His favorite piece of music is "Jupiter" from *The Planets,* the orchestral suite by composer Gustav Holst. He has tried to record it at home using uilleann pipes for the melody line—an intriguing musical experiment suffusing Celtic soul through an Englishman's early 1900s astronomical fantasia. But Irish music is adaptable to most genres, even an 18th-century sinfonia, as anyone who has heard De Dannan's "trad" take on Handel's "Arrival of the Queen of Sheeba (in Galway)" can attest.

If you're lucky enough to catch O'Sullivan's show "Anamchiar/Spirit of Kerry," you'll hear beautiful Irish poetry in song version, such as his takes on W. B. Yeats's "Song of Wandering Aengus" or Patrick Kavanagh's "On Raglan Road." But a master musician is never limited by geography or genre: You may also hear O'Sullivan play songs of Americana written by Bob Dylan or Tom Waits.

O'Sullivan recalls that the great Kerry playwright John B. Keane once asked a Limerick fiddler where the enchanting music he was playing originated. The musician insisted *he* wasn't playing the music, but rather the music was *playing him.* Those bewitching notes from his instrument were handed down many generations of his Gaelic forebears, according to the fiddler. What John B. Keane was hearing was the "music of all humanity." ∎

Killarney's pubs pulsate with traditional music sessions and Irish dancing shows.

Insider's Guide

Killarney & Killarney National Park

Killarney is the heart of County Kerry. Here, traditional music swirls late into the night and pubs heave happily with both locals and globals. In this lively town, all classes of hotels and eateries welcome travelers to the scenic sweet spot of southern Ireland. Street musicians, pub storytellers, and Irish dancing revues compete for your attention as you wander down High Street, while jarveys (horse-drawn carriage guides) vie to take you on a spin around Killarney's famous lakes.

Killarney has three main lakes— **Lough Leane, Muckross Lake** (or Middle Lake), and **Upper Lake**—and several smaller loughs with names such as Doo and Ardagh. These provide a spacious waterway around the crowded town.

The magnificent Macgillycuddys Reeks are a brooding backdrop to this romantic wilderness, all protected under the designation of **Killarney National Park.** The park is a wild expanse of 25,000 acres (10,000 ha), where lush, moss-carpeted woodlands sweep down to steely gray lakes that mirror the ever shifting Kerry skies. These landscapes were praised by Victorian and Edwardian visitors as the "Mecca of every pilgrim in search of the sublime and beautiful in Nature—the mountain paradise of the west."

Killarney's blanket boglands burst into color each summer with purple heather and yellow gorse splashed across sun-brightened vistas. Ancient oak and yew woods offer shady green relief for the parkland's fauna. Sika deer and native red deer roam the park, and the reintroduced white-tailed eagle now soars above Killarney's lovely lakes. Anglers are urged to catch and release any Killarney shad, a critically endangered fish endemic to Lough Leane. This freshwater member of the herring family, known locally as the goureen, was trapped in the lake some 16,000 years ago.

The lakes of Killarney are best observed from **Ladies' View,** an overlook pointing north over the narrow Gap of Dunloe and the gorgeous Upper Lake. The **Torc Waterfall,** beside Middle Lake, is another must-see. It cascades 60 feet (18 m) down a staircase of rock shaded by sycamore and mountain ash.

In the seventh century, St. Finian founded a leper colony and monastery on Leane's **Innisfallen Island.** Generations of holy men continued to thrive there for 850 years. Today Ireland's only herd of native red deer can be seen swimming across the water to the island to graze among the ancient ruins.

Majestic residences dot the lakeshores. Imposing **Ross Castle,** built in the 15th century by the O'Donoghues, still graces the banks of Lough Leane. The castle's bawn, or walled tower, has been restored, and the castle is open to the public in summer. The heart of the park is the elegant **Muckross House** and estate. This Tudor-style mansion has hosted many of the park's preeminent visitors, from Queen Victoria in 1861 to George Bernard Shaw. Muckross House is now a fine hotel with beautifully kept gardens of rhododendrons and azaleas. Both the house and estate were presented to the young Irish state in 1932, facilitating the establishment of Ireland's first national park at Killarney. ∎

A Killarney jarvey conveys visitors on a jaunting car ride around Lough Leane.

TASTE OF IRELAND: CROMANE OYSTERS

Sean Doyle, head chef at Killarney Park Hotel (see page 144), has many signature dishes from his culinary travels abroad, yet his passion is for local seasonal produce. Here's Sean's tantalizing twist on Kerry oysters.

INGREDIENTS

- ⅔ cup (50 g) white wine vinegar
- 1 cup (80 g) cucumber flesh, peeled and shredded
- ½ cup (60 g) shallots, sliced
- ¾ cup (177 mL) Chardonnay
- ⅔ cup (50 g) cream
- 12 tablespoons (170 g) unsalted butter
- 1 cup (70 g) cucumber skin
- 5 fl oz (147 mL) water
- 10–12 oysters
- 1½ tablespoons (20 g) wasabi paste
- 1 teaspoon lemon juice
- Salt and cayenne to taste

DIRECTIONS

- In a saucepan over medium heat, reduce vinegar, cucumber flesh, and shallots in wine until all the liquid is gone. Stir in the wasabi paste and lemon juice.
- Add cream and bring to a boil before gradually adding the butter.
- Add cucumber skin and water and put through a blender until the mixture forms a liquid. Pass through a sieve to strain; discard seeds and skin left behind. Season to taste.
- Open your oysters, and place oyster juice in a small pan. Add oysters and gently heat.
- Place oysters back in the shell and spoon wasabi sauce over each. Serves 3 to 4 oyster lovers. *Bon appétit!*

Irish Heritage

Ireland's Last High King

Ask any Kerryman (or woman) about the origins of Puck Fair and its famous sovereign goat, King Puck, and you'll rarely get the same answer twice. "Arra…" they'll all start, before offering one of many local creation myths for the three days of livestock trading, goat-crowning, parading, epic partying, and music- and mischief-making that detonate around the town of Killorglin every August. ("Arra" is the dismissive, delaying opening gambit of many a Kerry conversationalist, implying that the person inquiring is somewhat lacking in gray matter for even asking such a thing. The rest of the answer will give a creative—if not entirely trustworthy—account of why many have flocked to this small north Kerry hill town to trade cattle, horses, and country gossip for the past 400-odd years.)

Puck Fair, or Aonach an Phoic ("fair of the billy goat"), is a storyteller's dream, and Kerry people love a good yarn. In high summer in Killorglin, the age-old challenge of adding new twists to ancient tales, while multiplying and muddling the existing myths, is all part of the bacchanalian fun of the fair. Somewhere along the way the townsfolk began capturing a wild billy goat—the word "puck" is an Anglicized version of the Irish word *puc*, for a male, or "billy," goat—from the majestic Macgillycuddys Reeks mountains around the town, hoisting him high on a scaffold platform and declaring him their king.

Of course, every beast should be tempered by beauty, so a young girl from the village is chosen each year

Puck Fair is not all about the billy goat; the Queen of the Fair and her court also receive acclaim.

as Puck's queen. One such previous royal was Rebecca Coffey, who comes from a long line of local musicians. As with many a Killorglinite, she confided that home is where her heart is: "I've never missed a Puck Fair and I love this town to bits."

This odd coronation of King Puck and the Queen of the Fair occurs in what is probably the most republican region of the Republic of Ireland. But then the county of Kerry, otherwise known as the Kingdom, has always been a place apart. And for the three days of its wild festivities, Puck Fair becomes a kingdom within the Kingdom.

The capture of King Puck from the wild is the first act of the annual drama. A pair of townsmen, John McGrath and Pat Cahill, rise early on the day before the fair to venture into the highlands of north Kerry to capture and return with the monarch in waiting, the goat who would be king.

The most popular of the many colorful legends surrounding the origin of the tradition is that a wild billy goat ran into the streets of Killorglin in 1652 to warn the townsfolk that the British were coming (in the form of Oliver Cromwell's notorious New Model Army). If that story sounds suspiciously familiar to American ears, the only ascertainable truth is that the goat has been revered at Puck Fair for as long as anyone can remember.

When we asked Kerry *seanchaí* (storyteller) Thomas O'Sullivan (see page 130) about the truth behind the myths, his indecision was final: "Arra, the only certainty about Puck is that there is the truth, the whole

Killorglin's famous sovereign goat, King Puck, presides over three days of festivities.

truth, and then there is the Kerry truth, which is nothing like the truth. And there's the truth for you."

Whatever the truth about the goat, the importance of other livestock at the agricultural fair has lessened in recent decades. The advent of large-scale agricultural marts throughout Ireland has reduced the need for farmers in the highlands to drive their cattle to Killorglin for a profitable sale each August. The horse fair still thrives though, driven largely by the cash-only, bargaining economy of Ireland's Traveler community (see page 149).

In the pre-internet age, locals often got their news from beyond the neighborhood at Puck Fair, and this included news from abroad. The fair has long been an irresistible draw for returning emigrants from the locale, many of whom must make the impossible choice between

an annual visit home "for Puck or for Christmas."

In the isolated hills of deepest Kerry, bachelor farmers often sought a wife at fairs such as Puck or County Clare's Lisdoonvarna Matchmaking Festival (see page 180). While the internet is the more likely means to that end these days, the sociability around horse racing, games of chance, singing, dancing, and drinking are still enjoyed with gusto at Ireland's oldest fair.

Even in our age of mass communication, the words of playwright J. M. Synge still ring true: "A crowd is as exciting as champagne to these lonely people, who live in the long glens among the mountains." For the three days of Puck Fair, the people of Kerry ignore time's relentless march to stop and crown their king and queen, and to dance to their own ancient drumbeat. ∎

Ireland On Screen

Ryan's Daughter

In 1969, at the height of a hugely successful career making Oscar-winning epics such as *Doctor Zhivago* and *Laurence of Arabia,* the great English filmmaker David Lean decamped to the wilds of Kerry. There he would spend a torturous year filming the controversial *Ryan's Daughter,* a tragic story of forbidden love and betrayal. Lean's forgotten masterpiece transplants the story of Gustave Flaubert's *Madame Bovary* to the tense period in the aftermath of Ireland's Easter Rising of 1916.

Buoyed by a huge Hollywood budget, Lean's extensive crew took over the remote fishing village of Dingle, renting hotels and private houses to accommodate stars such as Robert Mitchum and Sarah Miles for prolonged periods. Local laborers, drivers, and fishermen were employed —and retained—at inflated rates for months, and stories of legendary parties, bad behavior, and riotous bacchanalia still swirl around the town from the time of "Mr. Lean's fillum."

The narrative of *Ryan's Daughter* revolves around Kirrary, a fictional Irish village set high atop a heather-clad hill at the tip of the Dingle Peninsula. Astonishingly, Lean decided that his make-believe village would be no two-dimensional film set. It would be built with the very same materials that had protected Kerry residents from the elements for centuries: stone, slate, tar, and thatching. The fictional town of Kirrary would stand firm against the harsh reality of Atlantic gales for the duration of the shoot. Alas, the entire town, complete with houses, pubs, shops, feeder roads, and a wide main street, was razed as soon as the production ended. Thus, the Dingle Peninsula lost a major tourist attraction that could have been marketed around the film for decades, in the same way that the Mayo village of Cong still attracts fans of *The Quiet Man.*

While John Mills won a supporting actor Oscar for his caricature of the village idiot, the film's real star was cinematographer Freddie Young, who was rightly awarded a statue by the academy for his stunning rendering of the Kerry landscapes in their many moods.

Lean and Young would wait for weeks for the ever shifting Atlantic light to be just right for filming along Inch Strand or the sheltered coves of Dunquin and Ballyferriter. The pair would wait a year before the central storm scene could finally be filmed. By then, they had moved the dangerous shoot to the flat, limestone plateaus along the coast of south Clare. So constant was the sea spray along the wild Atlantic shore that the image had to be kept clear thanks to the invention of a glass disk spinning in front of the lens, known as a Clear View screen. An earlier boat landing filmed in Kerry had ended with actor John Mills being knocked unconscious and almost drowned.

Ryan's Daughter seemed cursed from the start, yet the film survives today as a cinematic testimony to the beauty of the Kerry landscape, which, perhaps unsurprisingly, is not much changed since the heady days when Hollywood came to Dingle. ∎

A fictional village, Kirrary, was built for the film *Ryan's Daughter.*

IN THE KNOW: IRELAND'S SMALLEST RECORD SHOP

Halfway up Dingle's Green Street—its door tucked away at a right angle to the street—nestles the Dingle Record Shop. This tiny space must be the most musical 10 square feet (3 sq m) in Ireland, in terms of both the merchandise on offer and the encyclopedic knowledge of the staff. Mazz O'Flaherty, the singer, songwriter, and musician who can be found behind the turntable/till most days and owner Bryan Lee both know their stuff. You can discuss anything from Robert Johnson's deal with the devil to the Gregorian chants of the Monks of Glenstal Abbey in this broad musical church.

The tiny Dingle Record Shop, on Green Street, is probably the most musical 10 square feet (3 sq m) in Ireland.

If you're from the U.S., you might end up hearing a lively and educational dissertation on the Pogues' best loved song "Fairytale of New York," for example. The song dramatizes emigrant life in that city, and with his tale of star-crossed lovers arguing on Christmas Eve, Shane MacGowan cemented his legacy as one of Ireland's great songwriters. The song was the result of a wager with Elvis Costello (a son of the musical McManus family from Liverpool), who bet MacGowan he couldn't write a Christmas hit. No yuletide in Ireland is now complete without a sing-along to the rousing chorus of "Fairytale."

Linger in the shop and you may hear another ancient lament for exiled Gaels, the hauntingly beautiful "Marble Halls," originally scored by composer Michael William Balfe for his 1843 opera *The Bohemian Girl*. The ethereal, almost angelic voice of Enya has revitalized this timeless lullaby, sung by generations of Irish mothers at children's bedtime.

Or you might hear a great story of one of the most widely performed odes to the Emerald Isle, written by an American visiting his ancestral home in 1959. Johnny Cash's "Forty Shades of Green" became such a standard that an elderly Irishman once thanked him for playing "one of the old traditional songs." Cash's daughter, Rosanne, performed an incomparable version with uilleann pipes, fiddles, and backing vocals by Karen Matheson and Kate Rusby.

Mazz has welcomed scores of musicians into the shop over the years, and her musical podcasts were legendary far beyond the Kingdom. When she hung up her microphone, she collected the finest moments onto a two-CD set called *Fare Thee Well: Sessions From the Shop*. The collection is a fine introduction to the eclecticism of Ireland's musical mindset, mixing reels, sea shanties, *sean-nós* singing, fife-and-drum bands, and laments such as the wistful "City of Chicago" by Luka Bloom (brother of Ireland's singer-songwriter laureate, Christy Moore; see page 45). There are also contributions from the likes of singer-songwriter Johnny Duhan and Irish-language folk/world music band Kila.

The O'Flahertys are a well-known musical clan in the Kingdom, and the *Fare Thee Well* album includes "St. James Reel," written by Mazz's brother Fergus and recorded along with Rory, another sibling, in nearby St. James Church. Mazz's granddaughter Ide Keough sings angelically on "Dá Bhraigheann Mo Rogha do Thúir Acu." Another vocal highlight is Dingle singer Bernie Pháid's lilting rendition of "Nead na Lachain" ("Duck's Nest"). *Fare Thee Well* is a perfect soundtrack for driving the Dingle Peninsula—or anywhere around Ireland. Another musical treasure to take with you is *Ar an Slí (On the Way)*, Mazz's joint CD with Con Durham, the late, lamented Dublin uilleann piper.

One of O'Flaherty's best loved songs is "Eist Eist" ("Listen Listen"). An hour spent in Dingle Record Shop is an escape from today's world of ceaseless noise and distraction into an older, wiser, more melodious realm, where musicians and music lovers still take the time to open their ears and minds and to listen, really listen. ∎

GREAT IRISH DRIVES: THE DINGLE PENINSULA

The loop drive around the Dingle Peninsula is not as well traveled as the more famous Ring of Kerry route to the south. Yet as everyone who takes the time to pursue its full circuit knows, it is every bit as spectacular, and a day spent along the winding coast here will linger long in the mind's travel-highlights reel.

Driving from Killarney, take the N72 to Killorglin and turn north onto the N70 for Castlemaine. From here the smaller R561 takes you along the coast, past **Inch Strand,** where much of the film *Ryan's Daughter* was shot (see page 136). The climb toward Annascaul is a foretaste of the stunning scenery of the Dingle Peninsula, one of Earth's great beauty spots, and one of Ireland's best loved Gaeltachts (Irish-speaking regions).

Stop at the **South Pole Inn** in Annascaul to learn of the heroic life of its former owner, Tom Crean (see page 140). From here, the N86 leads you to the lively fishing village of **Dingle.** Bustling in summertime, enchantingly wistful in winter, Dingle is a town filled with spirit and vim. Small wonder that a stray dolphin showed up here in 1983 and for more than three decades made the harbor his home. A statue on the waterfront, next to Dingle's Tourism Centre, com-memorates the beloved (and much missed) Fungi.

The town's streets are filled with cafés, craft shops, knit-wear, fashion outlets, and warm, inviting pubs and restau-rants. As you stroll, try a taste of Dingle from **Murphy's Ice Cream.** Their Dingle Gin or Bailey's Soda Bread flavors are decadently delicious.

Walk up Green Street (toward Main Street at the top of the hill) and you'll come to an easily bypassed creative hub in a town that attracts the artistic and the artisan. The **Díseart Center of Irish Spirituality and Culture** is located in the former Presentation Sisters' convent. Stop in here and, for a small fee, you can view the 12 stained-glass lancet windows designed by Irish artist Harry Clarke in 1922. These magnificent artworks, in the neo-Gothic Chapel of the Sacred Heart, depict scenes from the life of Christ. Art lovers will also want to view the Nano Nagle Mural, which tells the story of the nun who founded the Presentation Sisters in Ireland. The mural's artist, Eleanor E. Yates, is now working on a fresco of the Last Supper in the Cenacolo, the convent's former dining room. Before you leave, walk through the Díseart's gardens, where a labyrinth invites prayerful contemplation and two ancient Irish Yew trees (*Taxus baccata 'Fastgiata'*) offer their green shade. All shades of musical taste are satisfied in the **Dingle Record Shop,** opposite the Díseart (see page 137). If you love music, try to spend at least one night in the pubs of Dingle (see page 145).

As you head west from town, pause for a 45-minute tour of the Dingle Distillery with its ever expanding range of whiskeys and gins. The distillery's water source is its own well, drawing pure *uisce* (water) from almost 800 feet (240 m) beneath the Kingdom for the making of Dingle's unique *uisce beatha* (water of life), or whiskey.

From here, the drive becomes a one-way loop along some of Ireland's most breathtaking clifftop roads. Drive through Ventry, out to Dunquin, where the **Blasket Island Centre** might tempt you on a boat trip to the islands (see page 300). The clifftop viewing platform provides an excellent photo op if your time is limited.

Make time, however, to drive back across the spectacular **Conor Pass.** Stop at **Louis Mulcahy's pottery shop** in Bally-ferriter for restorative coffee and an afternoon snack, and then browse the shelves for beautifully crafted earthenware that is made on-site, along with books, jewelry, and other gifts from the unforgettable Dingle Peninsula. ■

A taste of Dingle from Murphy's Ice Cream OPPOSITE: The Dingle Penin-sula's twisting coastal roads offer unforgettable views.

In 1914, Ernest Shackleton's ship, *Endurance*, was trapped in the pack ice of the Weddell Sea; it was abandoned in October 1915 and found in 2022.

The Irish Abroad

Tom Crean, Unsung Hero of Antarctica

In the Kerry village of Annascaul you'll spy a pub named the South Pole Inn. Above its doorway is a plaque: TOM CREAN / ANTARCTIC EXPLORER / 1877–1938. Tom Crean grew up when Britannia ruled the waves. The Royal Navy offered the independent-minded Crean an escape from his family farm; he signed up at age 15 and stepped straight into the heroic age of Antarctic exploration. The gregarious Kerryman gained a reputation for reliability, bravery, and seamanship.

In 1901, Capt. Robert Scott set out to conquer Antarctica, Earth's last unexplored continent. At Lyttelton Harbour, New Zealand, Crean and his shipmates from H.M.S. *Ringarooma* were helping Scott's *Discovery* prepare for its historic expedition when a dispute left Scott with a vacancy and Crean volunteered.

On January 3, 1902, *Discovery* crossed the Antarctic Circle with a small crew that included another Irishman, Officer Ernest Shackleton, born in County Kildare. *Discovery* became icebound at McMurdo Sound, where it remained trapped for three years.

Crean and the crew made exploratory runs inland by man-hauling their sledges across treacherous icescapes, instead of utilizing skis and dogsleds, as Norwegian explorers had done in the past. They reached the Farthest South mark at 82°17'S, where they toiled in conditions of minus 70°F (-57°C). In 1904, they freed their ship from the ice and returned to London.

Crean's next adventure was as coxswain on Scott's quest to reach the South Pole before Norwegian Roald Amundsen. *Terra Nova* left London in June 1910 with 60 men, 30 dogs, and 19 ponies. A full-force gale in the South Seas nearly sunk the overladen "floating farmyard." Having set up camp at Cape Evans, Crean led a three-man team that ended up stranded on breaking ice after Scott sent out parties of men to lay supplies along a line to the pole. Crean returned to get help by jumping across ice floes surrounded by killer whales and scaling an icy cliff.

Scott's polar attempt involved a round-trip of 1,800 miles (2,900 km) across crevasse-filled ice fields, and 10,000-foot-high (3,050 m) glaciers, dragging supplies in ferociously low temperatures. In October 1911, 16 men set out for the pole. Crean, not among the five chosen for the final leg, wept bitterly while bidding farewell to Captain Scott.

Crean's trio faced a race for survival as food dwindled on their return journey to Cape Evans, risking a terrifying sled ride down a crevasse-riddled glacier to hasten their journey. Crean's injured friend, "Taff" Evans, had to be hauled over the last leg, and at a camp 35 miles (56 km) from base, Crean volunteered to finish the frigid trek alone and return with help. Roald Amundsen reached the South Pole, Scott and his team perished, and Crean's comrades somehow survived. He was awarded the Albert Medal for his courage.

Crean's third voyage south was alongside Sir Ernest Shackleton, who planned to walk across Antarctica. In 1914, Shackleton's ship, *Endurance,* was trapped in the pack ice of the Weddell Sea, and finally abandoned in October 1915.

The crew of 28 hauled three lifeboats to the edge of the ice, after which their small boats took them over rolling, frigid seas for seven days to the uninhabited wasteland of Elephant Island. The men's struggle to stay alive became part of Antarctic legend. In April 1916, Crean set out with Shackleton and four others on an epic 800-mile (1,290 km) voyage across the stormy Southern Sea to fetch help on South Georgia. Crean, Shackleton, and Frank Worsley then had to cross the mountainous South Georgia interior clad in rags, with little food or water, arriving at salvation "a terrible looking trio of scarecrows."

Tom Crean returned to Kerry in 1920 to run the South Pole Inn. His story is immortalized in the book *An Unsung Hero* by Michael Smith. Shackleton's sunken ship was found on the Weddell seabed in 2022. ■

Kerryman Tom Crean, in Antarctica (1914)

Crean and Edgar "Taff" Evans, mending sleeping bags, Antarctica (1911)

Irish Heritage

The Castleisland Raconteur

The north Kerry town of Castleisland was described by its best loved citizen, journalist and raconteur Con Houlihan, as "not so much a town as a street between two fields." Castleisland was the humble origin of this immensely gifted Irish writer, who confounded the notion of no one being a prophet in their own land. Con Houlihan is not a name well known outside of Ireland, but it's highly likely that more Irish eyes have read *his* words than those of Joyce, Beckett, Yeats, or Heaney.

"Now read on . . ."

Those three words were Houlihan's catchphrase, used as a literary lure to bait readers of his daily sports column in the *Evening Press* and later the *Evening Herald*. For decades, lovers of GAA games,

rugby, soccer, and literature would eagerly await the arrival of the evening edition in their town to read pearls of wisdom, wit, and acute observation in his "Tributaries" column or in the back page "Con Houlihan" column.

Con's columns were great rivers of words, their currents swollen with side stories, tributaries that flowed with an unhurried fluidity that reflected the man. Here was a literary rambler, who would not only stop to smell the flowers, but paint them for you, too.

The fields and rivers around the town of Castleisland shaped Houlihan's vibrant mind. He spent his youth in the rhythms of the family farm, before becoming a teacher. Then, in his mid-40s, his talent was spotted, and he left the Kingdom for

the streets of the capital and a long second career in journalism.

Yet his heart remained in Kerry, usually by a river. A typical piece called "Gone Fishing" contained the following insight: "You meet a better class of rogue on the riverbank. I rarely met an angler who is all bad." Incidentally, the first line of that piece most probably contained Con Houlihan's credo: "Daydreaming is good for you . . ."

Though he died in 2012, stories of the great man are still legion in Kerry, Dublin, and beyond. A bear of a man (he was from mountain stock), he carried his shyness lightly, confiding quietly from behind a huge hand. He knew every barman in town—a great source for news and good gossip— and never watched a game from the press box, preferring the viewpoint of the masses. One keen young writer at the *Irish Press* found himself beckoned into the back room of Mulligans' Pub early one morning, when Con's working day was done but the rookie's just beginning. Now read on . . .

As he sipped his own favored nectar of brandy and milk, the legendary Kerry writer proffered a pint of plain to the startled novice, along with the following advice: "Be careful not to spend too much of your life in offices. Nothing interesting ever happens in offices."

It is advice that this writer took very much to heart.

Thanks, Con! ∎

Stories to tell: Con Houlihan watches the action with the Irish crowd.

TASTE OF IRELAND: THE ULTIMATE BEEF STEW WITH GUINNESS

Con Houlihan grew up in the Kerry farmlands, and legend has it that he rose promptly at 4 a.m., out of habit, in his Portobello home in Dublin. His first task was not to milk cows, as in youth, but to write 1,000 words for the back page of the *Irish Press.* While recording his daily musings on sport, literature, geography, and life's lingering mysteries, Houlihan would cook a beef stew, which he would eat around 7 a.m., before delivering the day's masterpiece to the *Press* offices at Burgh Quay. Once the copy was cleared—it rarely needed editing—the great man was free to ramble the streets of Dublin (or farther afield, if an Irish team or athlete was competing abroad) in search of a good story.

This is one take on a classic Irish beef stew, the food that fueled a thousand great Con Houlihan columns.

Irish stew with Guinness is the quintessential Irish comfort food.

INGREDIENTS

- 2½ pounds (1.13 kg) chuck roast, cut into small cubes
- Salt and black pepper
- 10 tablespoons (78 g) all-purpose flour, divided
- 5 red onions
- 2 celery sticks, cut into half-inch sections
- 4 carrots, peeled and chopped into half-inch sections
- 3 cloves garlic, crushed
- 8 ounces (227 g) button mushrooms
- 2 to 3 tablespoons vegetable oil, divided
- 3 or 4 sprigs fresh thyme
- 6 waxy potatoes, peeled and cut in half
- 1 quart (32 oz) beef or chicken stock (using chicken stock gives it more of a Guinness flavor)
- 1 can (15 oz) Guinness draught stout
- 4 tablespoons Worcestershire sauce or tomato paste
- 2 bay leaves
- 11 tablespoons (150 g) Kerrygold Irish butter
- 2 tablespoons parsley, finely chopped

DIRECTIONS

- Preheat the oven to 300°F (150°C).
- Coat the meat chunks in salt and pepper. Roll in about 6 tablespoons of the flour. The beef, not you. (This was a joke that Con Houlihan liked to crack whenever a recipe appeared in his sports column.)
- Lightly sauté the onions, celery, carrots, garlic, and mushrooms in half of the oil for 5 to 7 minutes; season with salt and pepper. Transfer vegetables to a casserole dish.
- Heat more of the oil in a pan and sauté the meat in batches until evenly browned; transfer the meat to the dish, making a second layer on top of the vegetables.
- Remove thyme leaves, discarding the stems, and sprinkle over the meat. Layer the potatoes on top.
- Pour the beef stock and the Guinness over these layers, and then add Worcestershire sauce or tomato paste and the bay leaves.
- Place the casserole in the oven or simmer on a stove for 1½ hours. A plug-in slow cooker set on low works well, too, and is good for reheating. (While you wait, try knocking out a 1,000-word column by 7 a.m., in memory of the great man!)
- Make a roux by melting the butter in a pan and slowly whisking in 4 tablespoons of flour, tablespoon by tablespoon, to form a paste that can be added to the stew about 15 minutes before serving. This will thicken the stew beautifully. At this point, also add the parsley.
- Remove bay leaves and serve.

TIP: This will feed four hungry Kerry footballers at one sitting, or one sportswriter for about three days.

Step into the Kerry dreamscape at Muckross Park Hotel & Spa, which includes Queen Victoria and Prince Albert on its guest roster.

IN THE KNOW: WHERE TO STAY, EAT & DRINK IN KERRY

Exploring the rugged landscapes of the Kingdom demands a restful bed, a full stomach, and the promise of a relaxing hour or two spent among Kerry people making merry at night. But rest easy. No matter if you stay in the bustling towns of Killarney or Dingle, or in a rural mountain village, or on the very extremities of Valentia Island, this most hospitable county will never let you down.

HOTELS

The family-run **Killarney Park Hotel** is situated in the center of town, just a minute's walk from the national park and with an attentive, friendly staff to make you feel right at home. The pool and spa are particularly relaxing options after a day's hiking (or shopping!). The **Park Restaurant** is a resplendent room in which to sample Chef Sean Doyle's creative delights, be it oysters (see page 133) or a fine local cut such as Kerry lamb loin with peas, mint, and sheep's yogurt. Extensive vegetarian and vegan menus include hearty delights such as potato gnocchi with wild mushroom, leeks, and truffle. Sean's training in the kitchens of Europe com-

bines with his creative use of native Irish produce to produce a menu that never fails to delight the discerning diner.

If you seek peace and quiet with magnificent views of the Kingdom, **Cahernane House** is an excellent four-star option. This beautiful manor on the Muckross Road just outside Killarney overlooks the national park and a relaxing walk is always at your doorstep. Head Chef Eric Kavanagh offers an extensive menu with the great tastes of Munster featured: Dingle crabs are a local delicacy, as are Farranfore strawberries. For the royal treatment, stay in the style of historic guests such as Queen Victoria and Prince Albert at **Muckross Park Hotel & Spa.** The hotel's lakeside location and luxury are matchless, and you'll enjoy the sleep of the carefree traveler with spectacular views awaiting you as the new day dawns.

In Dingle, the traditional charm of **Benner's Hotel** on Main Street is hard to beat. Benner's makes an ideal base for touring the Dingle Peninsula and for a good night out along the town's string of music-filled pubs. The hotel's own lounge and bar areas are warm and inviting, and there are few better places to read the Sunday papers with a cocktail or a hot whiskey.

RESTAURANTS

The **Moorings** in Portmagee is one of Kerry's most intimate settings for a fine seafood meal. With views of the pier where the fishing boats dock, the Moorings' candlelit interior and old stone walls are an invitation to linger long into the hospitable Kerry night. The catch of the day is always fresh and fabulous: Seafood chowder with the Moorings brown bread is a perennial favorite. Another superb spot for chowder—and a perfect lunch stop for Ring of Kerry motorists—is the **Fishery** by the bridge in Killorglin. Polish couple Katarzyna Kalinowska and Jacek Sobala run the Fishery, offering an appetizing array of comfort foods, such as salmon boats in puff pastry. This great eatery, with outdoor tables by the River Laune, is located beside **KRD Fishery Smokehouse,** where you can buy smoked salmon and other seafood delights to go. For a surprisingly authentic taste of Spain in the southwest of Ireland, visit the award-winning **10 Bridge Street** in the beautifully converted Church of Ireland in Killorglin.

O'Neill's Seafood Bar at the Point in Reenard is another surefire destination for those angling for fine seafood. This cozy pub-restaurant is the perfect place for a quiet pint and has a consistently popular seafood menu. O'Neill's also enjoys an enviable pierside location with wonderful views across to Valentia Island (see page 296), especially at sunset.

PUBS

Any night out in Dingle includes the obligatory stop at **Dick Mack's** fabulous drinking emporium, one side an old-style country pub and the other a leathermaking shop. Travelers mix easily with colorful local clientele, and a trad music session is usually in full flow or soon to begin.

Paul Geaney's, on Main Street, is another great Dingle pub. On many a night, you'll be treated to David Geaney's world-class Irish dancing. Paul's own dancing feet have graced many a Kerry senior football team since 2011 and won him an All-Ireland medal in 2014. This is also *the* place in town to watch the footballers of Kerry take on all-comers on their yearly quest for another Sam Maguire Cup. Just speak easy if you're at a table with any Dubliners.

O'Connor's Bar & Guesthouse in Cloghane is a very old pub with great music and wild *craic*. "It's what you'd imagine pubs were like 200 years ago," says Ciaran O'Farrell, a cyclist and history teacher from County Wicklow who regularly stops here. O'Connor's holds an annual sheep-shearing event on the premises. Stop here for a great pint, ample portions, and, like in olden times, accommodations for the weary wayfarer. Another pub that hearkens to 1800s Kerry is **Ashes's Pub** in Camp. This historical inn is a cozy, stonewall oasis from modernity with simple, delicious food and engaging staff.

Every explorer of the Kingdom should pay a stout-handed tribute to Kerry's own hero of the Antarctic at the **South Pole Inn** in Annascaul. When his legendary career in the British Navy was over, Tom Crean (see page 140) returned to Kerry to run this charming pub in the small village of his birth. After Ireland's War of Independence ousted the British military from the Free State, he rarely spoke of his heroic feats. ∎

Awaiting a pint while settled in a quiet snug in a heavenly corner of the Kingdom: Dick Mack's renowned drinking emporium

TIPPERARY

Tipperary is the heartland of Ireland, a rich agricultural county dotted with country towns whose names evoke the bucolic beauty of these hinterlands: Cahir, Cashel, Golden, Finnoe, and, of course, Tipperary town, which even inspired a love song from the Man in Black. Like Johnny Cash in 1959, every visitor to Tipp's lush, mountainous countryside is mesmerized by its 40 shades of green.

The lyricism of the place-names is no surprise, given the deep Celtic history of Tipperary. The Gaelic-speaking Celts valued poetry, and the *filé* (court poet) was held in high esteem in the houses of Irish chieftains, long before the Normans built fortifications such as Ormond Castle. Inland Tipp, far from Viking-threatened shores, was the site of many a monastic settlement in the centuries after the fall of Rome, when the written word held a sacred place in Irish life. Monks toiled by candlelight to keep the flame of Western civilization from extinction.

The elevated ruins of the Rock of Cashel are Ireland's finest remnants of a medieval citadel and early ecclesiastical settlement. It was here, in the fifth century, that St. Patrick converted the king of Munster and changed the course of Irish history. In 1101, another king of Munster, Muirchertach Ua Briain, would donate his fortress on the Rock to the church. The Rock sits high above Cashel as a reminder of the changing ages of Ireland's history, from the Celtic reign of the Munster kings to the Norman invasion and later the Confederate Wars that saw the slaughter of Catholic clergy. Tipperary also played a sad part in another tragic episode of Irish history, as the GAA football team that faced Dublin in Croke Park on Bloody Sunday in 1920. A fierce patriotism animates Tipp's citizens to this day.

The modern-day bard of Tipperary, Shane MacGowan, captured the wistful spirit of all who are born in this beautiful county. His ballad "The Broad Majestic Shannon" celebrates the Tipp men returning from a fair at Shinrone in neighboring County Offaly, whose hearts never stray from their beloved Tipperary. ∎

The elevated ruins of the Rock of Cashel rise above Tipperary's green fields.

Special Places

The Rock of Cashel

To the modern-day traveler speeding south along the M8, the Rock of Cashel appears as a medieval citadel looming high above a busy highway. Especially when illuminated at night, this once sacred site seems to transcend time, suspended on some elevated spiritual plane, the "higher ground" sought out by ancient Ireland's monks and mystics.

Once the seat of the kings of Munster, this extensive religious complex consists of a 90-foot-tall (30 m) round tower dating from A.D. 1100, the Romanesque chapel of King Cormac Mac Carthaigh, a 13th-century Gothic cathedral built circa 1250, a spectacular Celtic high cross honoring St. Patrick, a 15th-century castle, and the exquisitely restored Hall of the Vicars Choral.

Local legend has it that the Rock of Cashel originated in the Devil's Bit, a mountain 20 miles (30 km) north of Cashel. When St. Patrick banished Lucifer from a cave, the devil took a bite out of the mountain, spitting the Rock out to land in Cashel. Cashel is also said to be where St. Patrick converted the king of Munster in the fifth century. The Normans arrived in the 12th century, and most of the buildings date from this later period.

Today the traffic zips by below, disappearing into darkness like the generations of holy men and armies who have passed through here. In 1647, English Parliamentarian troops ransacked Cashel and slaughtered Irish Confederate troops before stripping the site of many religious artifacts. The singer Bono described the common fate suffered by sacred ground worldwide when he noted that "no one can own Jerusalem, but everybody wants to put flags in it."

Today, these ruins of the old citadel of Christianity hover above a multicultural Ireland. Below in Cashel, the Ruen Mying Thai Restaurant hands out *A Guide to the Study of Practical Buddhism* with your pad Thai or Massaman curry. Our earthly aim, it claims, is "deliverance from suffering." Where better to meditate on such things than within sight of where St. Patrick was said to have banished the devil himself? ∎

The Rock of Cashel: once seat of the kings of Munster and a medieval holy citadel with a somewhat satanic origin story

IRISH VOICES: THE TRAVELING LIFE

Every summer, Helen Riley harnesses her family's painted wagon to her blinkered horse and takes to the highways and byways of Ireland. Mostly the byways. Helen Riley is a Traveler, a member of Ireland's tribe of nomads who roam freely across the four provinces of Ireland and the neighboring island of Britain. They are thought of as Irish, but in truth Travelers belong to no country, observing only their people's own codes, handed down through generations via a centuries-old storytelling tradition.

Helen Riley and her granddaughter on their horse-drawn, painted caravan during the summer months, when they take to the roads

Helen Riley is based around the Tipperary townlands of Cashel, Thurles, Cahir, and Golden. Her only address is a mailbox in a small village post office, where she stops intermittently. The closing of many post offices greatly affected her generation of Travelers, who relied on their poste restante service to keep packages for them. These days, however, the distances between members of Ireland's tight-knit Traveler community have been bridged by the connective web of the cell phone, a device almost tailor-made for a people whose traditions have historically been transmitted through the spoken rather than the written word. Helen Riley and her clanspeople will leave you a lovely, warm voicemail in a soft-spoken accent, but rarely, if ever, a text message.

The Travelers of Ireland speak Cant, their own Celtic Indo-European language, which is closest to Old Irish. It is officially called Shelta, a name believed to have derived from the Irish verb *siúl*, meaning "to walk," this being the language of *siúladh*, the moving or "walking people." De Gammon is an ancient indigenous dialect formed using the ogham script, an early medieval alphabet used primarily to write the early Irish language in the fourth to sixth centuries and later the Old Irish language (scholastic ogham, from the sixth to the ninth centuries).

Travelers are often wary around "settled folk," and will adopt a low, conspiratorial tone amongst themselves. The distrust is often reciprocated on the part of settled folk, and Travelers often find themselves unwelcome in pubs, hotels, and shops.

In 2016, the Irish census recorded 32,302 Travelers, representing 0.7 percent of the overall population of the Republic. The numbers of those with Traveler ancestry are unknown, however. Britain is thought to be home to up to 300,000 Traveler people, one of whom, at the time of writing, is the world heavyweight boxing champion. Tyson Fury is of Irish Traveler descent. His father's people came from Tuam, County Galway, and his mother's family from County Tipperary.

Although the Travelers have historically lived largely outside of Irish law and society, government policies in recent decades have aimed at settlement in either public housing or a series of "halting sites" set up near major roadways with electricity, running water, and, more recently, access to Wi-Fi. But for Travelers, the future is always open, and the open road stirs something deep in the soul of the *siúladh*. Helen Riley's family sit out the cold Irish winters in their stove-heated caravan, longing for spring and the chance to take to the road again.

"*Solk us away from the taddy*—Deliver us from evil," laughs a Wicklow Traveler when asked if he'd ever consider taking a house and living the settled life. ∎

"Bug a gushach weed?"
(Will you take a cup of tea?)

—*A hospitable Travelers' welcome*

Clonmel & Environs

Clonmel is blessed by location. The **River Suir** runs through the town, which nestles in a valley, overshadowed by the **Comeragh Mountains** and **Slievenamon.** The rich hinterlands of Ireland's Golden Vale surround Clonmel. Just outside the town you'll see the orchards around the **Bulmers Irish Cider** plant, where the delicious amber nectar is brewed. The town is also home to the **Tipperary Museum of Hidden History.**

Clonmel comes alive in summer, starting with the **Clonmel Junction Festival,** running for nine days beginning the first weekend in July. The festival mixes street theater with rock, traditional, and world music. In addition, the **Clonmel Busking Festival** entertains locals and visitors alike with street music for four days every August.

The name Clonmel comes from the anglicization of the Irish name Cluain Meala, meaning "honey meadow." The fertile soils of south Tipperary would certainly have encouraged apiculture (beekeeping) in these parts for centuries before the early Irish Christians imitated the industrious hive with their monastic settlements.

But while the townlands around Clonmel may have buzzed with bees, the Gaels of this proud town fiercely resisted colonization. Clonmel's citizens cannily avoided the all too common massacre and sacking at the hands of the Cromwellian army in 1650—the fate of the towns of Drogheda and Wexford. Clonmel's town walls were eventually breached, but Hugh Dubh O'Neill, the garrison commander, inflicted heavy losses on the New Model Army. That night, O'Neill led his soldiers out of the town under cover of darkness but Cromwell, wary of their return, accepted the town's surrender without civilian slaughter.

Clonmel's maverick and defiant nature resurfaced centuries later with the formation of Ireland's Labour Party in 1912. Among the founders was James Connolly, who was later executed for his part in the Easter Rising of 1916. In 2015, Clonmel was the location of the country's first marriage between two men.

Clonmel (meaning "honey meadow") sits in a sweet spot between the Comeragh Mountains and Slievenamon.

The quiet market town of **Carrick-on-Suir** lies 13 miles (21 km) east of Clonmel. The journey is worth making for the superb Anglo-Irish estate of **Ormond Castle** and its satellite mansion, the finest Tudor domestic building in Ireland. The castle was constructed in 1309, and its two 15th-century fortified towers testify to turbulent times in medieval Ireland. Black Tom Butler, 10th Earl of Ormond, built a new mansion onto his ancestral castle in 1568.

The castle is lit by an impressive run of mullioned windows situated under the gables. Inside, the Butler family warmed themselves at a beautiful carved fireplace in the Long Gallery, where the fine ceiling and frieze of Elizabethan plasterwork are worth straining one's neck to see. ■

Day and night, the weeklong Clonmel Junction Festival celebrates music from around the globe.

A TASTE OF IRELAND: CASHEL BLUE CHEESE SALAD

Tipperary is orchard country, as anyone who enjoys a fine cider soon discovers. Clonmel is the home of deliciously crisp Bulmers Irish Cider, made from 17 varieties of Irish apples. Their pear and dark fruit varieties are equally tasty. As fruit growers, Bulmers are committed to the health of *Apis mellifera* (the western, or European, honeybee) and have set up a series of "bee hotels" across Ireland. Bee hotels are artificial nesting structures, designed to attract pollinators by providing small cavities for egg-laying. The idea has been adopted by many garden centers and nature reserves around the country.

This delicious apple and nut salad is a light treat in summer, and its star ingredient is Cashel blue cheese, a traditional taste of Tipp.

INGREDIENTS
SALAD
- 1 tablespoon Kerrygold unsalted Irish butter
- 2 tablespoons caster sugar
- 2 red apples, cored and cut into thin wedges
- 3 ounces (75 g) walnut pieces
- 1 head frisée lettuce, thinly sliced
- 2 celery sticks, finely chopped
- 6 ounces (170 g) Cashel blue cheese

DRESSING
- 2 tablespoons walnut oil
- 2 tablespoons olive oil
- 2 tablespoons balsamic vinegar
- Salt and pepper to taste

DIRECTIONS
- Melt butter in a frying pan, add sugar, and stir over low heat until dissolved.
- Add apples and cook for 3 to 4 minutes on each side or until they begin to caramelize. Stir in the walnuts and cook for 1 minute. Remove from stove and allow to cool.
- Place the red cabbage and celery in a bowl. Add the cooled apple and walnut mixture.
- To mix the dressing, place ingredients in a screw-top jar and shake well.
- Drizzle the dressing over the salad in the bowl and toss well. Serve without delay, with blue cheese crumbled on top.

TIP: If you like Irish beef, top off this salad with thin slices of seared prime Munster steak, cut diagonally against the grain. Either way, this salad is perfect for a summer's day.

Irish Heritage

Conflict, Colonization & the Healing Powers of St. Patrick's Well

Whereas the Anglo-Normans and other colonizers left a legacy of castles and conflict, St. Patrick made his mark on the landscape in churches and holy wells. Many of these wells originated as pagan places of worship. St. Patrick's Well at Toberpatrick in Wicklow is a fine example of the holy man blessing a well-visited pagan site and claiming it thereafter as a place of pilgrimage for Christians—St. Patrick was a canny politician. His best known well is in Downpatrick, Armagh (see page 286), and there is even a St. Patrick's Well in Orvieto, Italy. But for quiet contemplation of the holy man's life, head for St. Patrick's Well just outside Clonmel.

Here, below a limestone cliff, a natural spring bubbles into a tear-shaped pool. These waters overflow through flumes into a pond where a sandstone Celtic cross sits on a tiny island. Nearby, the late-medieval ruins of St. Patrick's Church hold the altar-tomb of the White family, residents of nearby Clonmel. The church and the well belonged to the Cistercian Abbey at Inishlounaght. The site was remodeled in 1956, a statue added, and extensive stonework around the waters completed. Sam Yorty, mayor of Los Angeles from 1961 to 1973, provided much of the funding to honor his mother, Johanna Egan, who had emigrated to the U.S. from Clonmel.

Ireland's best loved saint was also an immigrant. A Welshman who arrived in Ireland as a slave, St. Patrick was the first public figure in history to condemn the practice. He was also Ireland's first recorded storyteller; nearly all we know of him comes from his *Confessio.*

Born circa A.D. 385, Patrick was kidnapped from Britain as a young boy, and worked for six lonesome years as a shepherd on Slemish Mountain in Antrim. Told in a dream that "your ship awaits," he escaped to walk the length of Ireland and begged passage home on a ship bound for Europe and eventually back to his parents. He later studied for the priesthood in France before answering another calling delivered in a dream: This vision was of Victorius, an Irishman who beseeched Patrick to "walk amongst us once more."

Patrick honored his calling. He came. He saw. He converted.

Using all his skills as a storyteller and dealmaker, Patrick cleverly adapted many of the old Irish ways to spread his Christian message to this last outpost of pagan Europe, becoming the first Christian missionary to convert souls beyond the Roman Empire. His powers of persuasion were key to converting chieftains and kings and to quelling intrigue and conflict amidst poets and Druids.

Conflict, influence, and intrigue have brooded around Cahir Castle since 1142, when construction began on an island in the River Suir. The Anglo-Norman Butler family took possession in 1375, and it's been captured three times since: The castle fell to Devereux, Earl of Essex, in 1599; it was surrendered to the Baron of Inchiquin in 1647; and Oliver Cromwell seized it in 1650.

Tipperary has a long history of conquest and bloodshed, but if all this left locals battle-weary, they could take the waters at St. Patrick's Well, renowned for curing sore lips, sore eyes and scrofula (tuberculosis of the neck). ■

St. Patrick's Well, a pilgrims' place of healing
OPPOSITE: The imposing walls of Cahir Castle

Peter Barry, with sons Sam (left) and Tom (right), works the slopes of the Armagh vineyard in Australia's Clare Valley.

The Irish Abroad

The Diaspora in Australia

Since the First Fleet landed in 1788, Ireland has left an indelible mark on Australian society and forged one of the most influential immigrant communities in the world. Much of the history of the first Irish settlers in Australia has been mythologized in the story of Ned Kelly.

Ned's father, John "Red" Kelly, from Moyglass, County Tipperary, was exiled to Van Diemen's Land (Tasmania) in 1842 for stealing pigs. Kelly regained his freedom and moved to Victoria on the Australian mainland, where he married Ellen Quinn. Their third child, Edward "Ned" Kelly, came to define Australia's "outback" mentality with his defiance of English colonial law.

Convicted of horse theft and assault at a young age, Ned Kelly became embroiled in a feud with Constable Alexander Fitzpatrick—another Irish Australian—and went on the run. Kelly and his gang became "bushrangers," outlaws living wild in the outback. They evaded capture with help from a sympathetic populace, many of whom resented what they considered an oppressive police force. Several skirmishes left a trail of death until the gang was surrounded at Glenrowan, where a siege ensued. Kelly shot at police from within an improvised suit of armor; bewildered witnesses believed this supernatural vision to be a bunyip, a diabolical creature from Aboriginal mythology, or even Old Nick (the devil) himself. Kelly was captured and hanged. Author Peter Carey reimagined the saga in his 2001 Booker Prize–winning novel *True History of the Kelly Gang*.

Before the Kelly gang roamed the outback, another Tipperary man, John O'Shanassy from Thurles, became premier of Victoria. Later, a Monaghan man, Charles Gavan Duffy, would hold the Australian state's highest office.

Working-class Catholics of Irish origin have long dominated the Australian Labor Party. James Scullin became Australia's first Catholic prime minister in 1929. Later Labor prime ministers John Curtin, Ben Chifley, and Paul Keating were also of Irish Catholic descent. And Scott Morrison was the latest Irish Australian to lead the country. One of Australia's most respected journalists was the "quintessential independent thinker" Paddy McGuinness, named after 1916 Easter Rising leader Padraic Pearse by his father, Australian newspaper editor Frank McGuinness.

Irish engineer Charles Yelverton (CY) O'Connor, a Meath man, is best known for the construction of Fremantle Harbour in Western Australia. And the Irish continue to fly high "down under": Alan Joyce, the current CEO of Qantas, grew up in Tallaght, Dublin, and emigrated to Australia in 1996.

Today, one in three Australians claims Irish origins, and it shows in the national character. The Australians and the Irish share an irreverent sense of humor, along with a sharp distaste for pomp and bombast. Both cultures celebrate the underdog and the notion of fair play. Indeed, much of modern-day Aussie society seems to suggest an alternate Great Britain and Ireland painted on a far broader canvas. ∎

IRISH VOICES: IRISH WINE DOWN UNDER

Australia's ambassador to Ireland, Gary Gray, is an Officer of the Order of Australia. He left his native Yorkshire with his family at age eight to make a new life down under, a voyage that countless Irish have taken through the centuries. Gray went on to marry into an Irish Australian family; his wife's grandfather was Robert "Pop" Walsh, the patriarch of a clan whose political influence sprang from humble Irish roots. "Pop's father grew up in Carrick-on-Suir in Tipperary," says Gray.

The ambassador experienced the Irish influence on Australia's national character firsthand. "The Irish are fiercely independent, resourceful, creative, and persistent," he says, "and family and community have always been central to their lives in their new land." He explains another little-known consequence of the Irish influence on Australian life: "Following Ireland's Jacobite War in the late 17th century, the Wine Geese, as they became known, were a group of ousted gentry and merchants exiled from Ireland, who, over time, came to have an almost singular importance in the French, Spanish, and Australian wine industries."

Australia now has 65 wine regions, each with its own unique topography, geography, climate, and soils, with more than 100 grape varieties planted.

Within this rich history of viticultural success lies the well-known Clare Valley wine region in South Australia, which takes its name from County Clare. The O'Shea family of Hunter Valley, the Horgans of the Leeuwin Estate, and Aussie viticultural names such as O'Leary-Walker, O'Dwyer, McWilliams, and Taylor all indicate deep Irish ancestral roots. "The hidden truth about many of our best Australian wines is that they are, in fact, Irish wines too—cultivated by generations of Irish hands.

"This is a *great* story that needs to be told," says the ambassador. "We often hear of the Irish diaspora and their remarkable influence on art, politics, and culture around the world. We know the Irish contribution to both stout and whiskey distilling as well. Yet despite this, their integral influence on the development of extraordinary Australian wine remains an untold gem in the middle of Ireland's diaspora story." ∎

"The Irish work hard, and, of course, they like a good time, and they brought that spirit to Australia."

—*Ambassador Gary Gray*

A knight's final resting place: the Piers Fitz Oge Butler Tomb in Kilcooley Abbey, carved by master sculptor Rory O'Tunney

Irish Heritage

How Irish Monks Saved European Culture

In the early medieval period, as the Roman Empire crumbled, hordes of invaders—Visigoths and Huns among them—descended on European cities to loot libraries and burn books. Great swaths of learning, much of it biblical, were endangered, and literature, the repository of Western thought, was in danger of being wiped out. As the early Middle Ages eclipsed Europe, the continent's newest readers vowed to copy and save the canon: These were the Irish monastic scholars whom St. Patrick had recently converted just before the last West-

ern emperor, Romulus Augustulus, was deposed in A.D. 476.

The end of the Pax Romana shattered the Christian world. Ironically, the loosening of Roman protection along Britain's shorelines had allowed the Celts to conduct raids for strong, young people to enslave, such as the future saint, Patrick. St. Patrick died circa 461, as Rome descended into chaos, but his legacy transformed a country of fierce pagan warriors into a unified tribe of steadfast Christians. He also bequeathed a love of learning, and lively imaginations found the storytelling genius of the Gospels.

The Celts, a creative race, combined their love of symbols (seen in the swirling letters of the *Book of Kells*) with the words of Jesus and other philosophers. Thus, on rocky western outposts of Europe, including the bleak beehive-huts of Skellig Michael (see page 299), Irish monks kept learning alive for future generations. Their ceaseless efforts often resulted in a sacrifice of their health, a blearing of their eyesight through candlelit toil, and a chronic neglect of sleep. The monks worked defiantly to safeguard the ancient ideas and memories of a continent awash with turmoil. Eventually, their stored knowledge would be injected back into European minds via the continent's monastic network, when Irish monks visited brotherhoods in abbeys such as Luxeuil in Burgundy and Italy's Monte Cassino.

Irish abbeys would be more adept at protecting valuable works when the next existential threat arrived on their shores in the eighth and ninth centuries. The Viking raiders of northern Europe coveted the jewel-encrusted bindings of works such as the *Book of Kells* (see page 56), but the monks always managed to keep this great work one step ahead of the Norsemen, whether it passed through Iona or Northumberland before reaching Kells and then Trinity College, another great repository of Irish learning.

The monks prevailed. The Gospels survived. Amen. ∎

IN THE KNOW: THE ABBEYS & MONASTERIES OF TIPP

St. Patrick is believed to have baptized countless pagans at the well now named after him in Clonmel. So it is no great surprise that County Tipperary, which in medieval times was split between the old north and south Munster kingdoms Thomond and Desmond, would become a hotbed of religion. The **Rock of Cashel** (see page 148) was the original seat of the kings of Munster, and according to legend, it was here that St. Patrick came to convert King Aenghus to Christianity. In 1101, the Rock was granted to the church and Cashel swiftly became a great center of ecclesiastical power.

All around this axis sprang great abbeys and monastic centers of learning. The ruins of several of these can be visited in Tipperary today. In the medieval period, Celtic Christians studied for the priesthood at such sites and embraced the monastic life of penury and penance. Most crucially, their monasteries became repositories for many Western works of art and liturgical literature.

The monastic ruins of **Monaincha,** which was built on an island, can now be reached on foot as the lake has long since been drained. Founded in the eighth century by St. Elair, this was the most famous pilgrimage site in Munster, a place described in the 10th century as the 31st wonder of the world. The Augustinians established a small monastery here dedicated to St. Mary in the 12th to 15th centuries. Note the fine Romanesque doorway, which once welcomed the faithful who came to pray at the high cross; it is made from fragments of other crosses, with carved horsemen, the Crucifixion, and Celtic designs forming a decorative collage.

Near Gortnahoe you'll find **Kilcooley Abbey,** which dates back to 1182, when Donal Mór O'Brien, King of Thomond, granted the land to the Cistercians. Rebuilt in 1445, the abbey is famed for a fine east window and two medieval tombs.

One is for the knight Piers Fitz Oge Butler, who died in 1526. The carved effigy of the knight with a dog at his feet signifies a happy death at home. **Holy Cross Abbey,** founded in 1169 near Thurles, was a Cistercian site named for its a relic of the True Cross, or Holy Rood, which attracted medieval pilgrims. The abbey was restored in 1969, and the Vatican bestowed a new Holy Rood relic, which was stolen in 2011, only to be retrieved a year later.

Ireland's largest medieval priory, **Athassel Priory,** dates from the late 12th century, when it became an Augustinian retreat under William de Burgh's patronage. Nothing remains of the bustling town that surrounded the priory, which was dissolved by Henry VIII in 1537. This was the ruinous fate of monasteries throughout Britain and Ireland as the much married monarch cemented his power as head of the new Protestant faith. The golden age of monastic Ireland was over. The Gregorian chants were silenced, and only the haunting caws of nesting jackdaws now echo around these ancient ruins of Tipperary. ∎

Holy Cross Abbey, founded in 1169, was a site of medieval pilgrimage.

LIMERICK

Irish people are known for an adept ability to tap into a Celtic otherworld—the realm of creativity, the dreamworld of the imagination. In Ireland this is called the Fifth Province, the esoteric sphere of the arts, ideas, and ideals. Though located in Munster, Limerick might well be the capital of this Fifth Province.

Limerick people, despite their birthright of a city plagued by earthly problems, seem able to reinvent the world to their liking. By sheer power of the imagination and force of will, they prevail. It's telling that when the Cranberries, a Limerick rock band, plotted world domination in the 1990s, the key to their success was a song called "Dreams."

The people of Limerick thus have a strange knack of turning desolation and despair into gold. *Angela's Ashes,* Frank McCourt's moving account of his bleak Limerick childhood, made him a literary sensation in his adopted U.S. homeland. The county's sportspeople, too, make a habit of achieving the impossible. The Munster rugby team humbled the mighty All-Blacks of New Zealand here in 1978, a giant-killing feat still talked about with reverence in Limerick pubs. Limerick hurlers have in recent years produced some of the finest performances the ancient game has ever seen. One stunned observer described their record-setting defeat of Cork in a recent All-Ireland final as "almost supernatural!"

There could be something in that: Limerick is a city cursed by St. Mainchín, and St. Mary's Cathedral hosts extraordinary 15th-century misericord carvings of demonic beasts. So, is Limerick some mythical crossroads, where Celtic souls go to make their deal with the devil and achieve their heart's desires?

Interestingly, Pope John Paul II chose Limerick as the place from which to cast the devil out of Ireland in 1979. But then, the pontiff probably didn't stick around long enough to talk to the locals. If he had, he'd have shared a laugh with people whose stoicism and easy charm mean that the angels are usually on their side. ∎

Limerick: a creative wellspring of the arts, ideas, and ideals

The storied battlements of St. John's Castle—also known as Limerick Castle—on the River Shannon

Limerick: City of Satire by the Shannon

Limerick is rarely top of travelers' must-see lists. Yet spend a day there, soak up its history, read some of its literature, listen to the rich rhythms and dark humor of Limerick speech, and you'll understand a lot about satire in Ireland.

Satire is how Irish people coped with the grim realities of life and the feeling that fate had dealt them a losing hand. In Limerick, a city where misfortune rained down relentlessly, many blamed that fate on a late sixth-century curse. As St. Mainchín (or St. Munchin in English) built his church, he requested the help of locals to lift heavy stones. They refused and the irate saint got the job done with the help of strangers. Mainchín fervently thanked these outsiders and prayed that strangers would always prosper in Limerick while natives suffered only failure. The curse became the stuff of legend—and poetry.

One verse of an epic poem by Michael Hogan tells the story: "And the devil will send ye a pest, / In shape of a thief-corporation; / Who from striking big rates will not rest, / Till they murdher ye dead with taxation. / No other good works will they do, / But robbery, ruction, and jobbery; / Pandemonium can't show such a crew / For base, brutal bombast and snobbery, / To damn ye're unfortunate town."

Limerick people still speculate on the "thief corporation" sent to damn their town—many claim it to be the government "above up in Dublin." For centuries, it was believed to be the occupants of St. John's Castle, aka Limerick Castle. Norman occupiers completed the castle on the orders of King John in 1210. In 1176, Donal Mór O'Brien, King of Thomond, had driven the Normans from Limerick, but this led only to the new Shannonside city—rich on river tariffs—being divided into the prosperous English Town and impoverished Irish Town. The outsiders prospering again. The castle was badly damaged in the Siege of

Limerick, when it was occupied by Protestants fleeing the Irish Rebellion of 1641. A massive redevelopment in 2013 restored it to its medieval glory. Satirists noted that the government was now spending $6.1 million (€5.7 m) to improve visitor facilities in a castle whose historical raison d'être was to keep people out.

Once colonized by the Normans and the English, the Irish honed the secret weapon of satire. Satire originally referred to a type of gypsy curse, and it has been long cherished by Gaels as a means of mocking those in power. The Irish are adept at the doublethink of recognizing the "official" Ireland while mercilessly ridiculing its pomposity in literature, song, or art. Everybody recognizes this "unofficial" reality as being merely an expression of what most people are thinking.

In 1729, Dean Jonathan Swift—the founding father of Irish satire—published "A Modest Proposal," an essay that mocked the English government's neglect by positing that the Irish poor, in overcrowded cities such as Limerick, should avert famine by eating their babies. Swift spawned an army of satirical disciples, and his spirit of irreverence for authority permeates the work of Limerick's best known writer, Frank McCourt, who detailed the city's deprivations in his best seller *Angela's Ashes*.

That spirit lives on in 21st-century Limerick in the surreal world of writer and artist Blindboy, a multimedia star in Ireland whose greatest feat may be his total anonymity. He appears in public with a plastic bag over his head. This is Limerick satire to a tee: provocative, contrarian, satirical, whip-smart, yet literally self-effacing. ∎

IRISH GARDENS: GLIN CASTLE

The landscape around the Shannon Estuary is a flat expanse, a caesura between the mighty mountain ranges of Kerry to the south and the barren highlands of the Burren to the north. The terrain here is ideal for garden walks, and the gardens at Glin Castle provide an inviting and slightly surreal Limerick adventure. These gardens incorporate elements of a fantastical imagination at work, and at times it feels like you're walking through a satirical gardener's inside joke.

Located on the southern shores of the estuary, the gardens look out onto soothing Shannon waters and are presided over by a fine Georgian house that was grandiosely enhanced with mullion windows and battlements in the early 19th century. The owner at that time, John Frraunceis Fitzgerald, was the 25th Knight of Glin. He clearly felt that no knight should reside in a humble abode, so Glin House became Glin Castle and was suitably adorned. Gothic gates were installed and even the stable yard got the battlement treatment. Fitzgerald also built a Gothic hermitage and a bathing lodge in the guise of a fortress on the banks of the great river.

All these lavish adornments make for a fun-filled walk through the grounds of what feels like the Victorian-era estate of an eccentric. The last Knight of Glin, Desmond Fitzgerald (1937–2011), added a 20th-century stone circle of lichen-covered limestone boulders in front of the hermitage. This final folly completed the gardens' appeal for walkers who like to daydream with a sense of transcending all bounds of time.

Desmond and his wife, Olda, also restored Glin's beautiful Walled Garden. Wander the garden in springtime, when carpets of flowers and native wild garlic light up the meadows. Gnarled old Irish oaks shade the walkways from the low northerly sunshine, and mosses cover the grounds, along with profusions of ferns, all adding to the ancient feel. You may even be willingly tricked into believing that the huge limestone boulder in the middle of the stone circle sits at the center of an energy field within this mythic demesne of a benign knight of old. ∎

Glin Castle gardens: a green oasis close to Limerick City

Foynes was the takeoff and landing point for transatlantic flying boats in the 1930s and 1940s.

Irish Heritage

Hollywood on the Shannon & Old Lough Gur

The longest waterway in the British Isles, the broad, majestic River Shannon runs through Limerick City. Named for the Celtic fluvial goddess Sionna, Shannon has a central place in Irish history and mythology. Twenty-three miles (37 km) west along the southern banks of the river lies the small town of Foynes, an estuary port that was once an exclusive European gateway to the U.S. Long before Shannon Airport existed, the River Shannon was a runway for transcontinental flights. Foynes was the takeoff and landing point for flying boats, large amphibious aircraft patronized by Hollywood stars, wealthy adventurers, and interwar politicians during the 1930s and 1940s.

Foynes Flying Boat and Maritime Museum is located at the original terminal building. From here, these magnificent machines pulled out before they skimmed the Shannon waters and built up the speed for takeoff to New York. The museum recalls the era from 1939 to 1945, when Foynes was the center of the aviation world. Exhibits describe the flying boats' luxurious interiors, which held passengers such as Maureen O'Hara, John F. Kennedy, Bob Hope, and Eleanor Roosevelt, whisking them to and from Europe.

It was not just dignitaries, millionaires, and movie stars who passed through this town of just 500 inhabitants. During World War II, Foynes was a safe harbor for refugees, who would await paperwork allowing them to pass through Ireland before heading west to new lives in the United States. Foynes thus became an Irish Casablanca. In the mood of that era, the museum's documentary video is run in a 1940s-style cinema. The World War II exhibits take visitors into the strange world of neutral Ireland during "The Emergency" (as the war was called in Ireland), and visitors can then board a life-size replica of a Boeing 314 flying boat. The Maritime Museum focuses on the River Shannon

A fantastic 3-D holographic show re-creates the night in 1943 when Irish coffee was first served to a group of exhausted passengers at Foynes. After this, you can of course sample a tasty Irish coffee where the drink was invented. You can also peruse the maritime collection in the reinstated control tower, where panoramic views of the River Shannon let you imagine when Foynes represented, for many, a passage to a fresh start in the new world.

The loose stone circle around **Lough Gur,** 13 miles (21 km) south of Limerick, on the other hand, lures you away from the glitz of Hollywood and technology into an ancient world. The many stone structures around the small C-shaped lake represent a 5,000-year-old human footprint. The 4,000-year-old **Grange** **Stone Circle** is the largest and most impressive such structure in Ireland, consisting of some 100 boulders. It is believed to have been the site of Bronze Age spiritual rituals.

The **Hunt Museum** in Limerick now hosts many treasures revealed by Lough Gur when water levels fell in the 19th century, and the bronze Lough Gur shield is housed in the National Museum in Dublin. Two nearby battlements worth visiting are **Bourchier's Castle** and **Black Castle,** while **Giant's Grave,** a megalithic wedge tomb, is just a short drive away. ■

TASTE OF IRELAND: A CELTIC COFFEE

Every exile loves Irish coffee, a real taste of home. It was invented in 1947 by Joe Sheridan, a chef at Foynes terminal on the River Shannon, from where flying boats left for the U.S. in the 1930s and '40s. Word of his delicious creation spread, and in 1952, Sheridan accepted a job in San Francisco's Buena Vista Hotel, where Irish coffee became a globally celebrated libation.

Now one such exile, Helen O'Brien, makes her own twist on this classic for wintertime guests in Malta using Coole Swan Irish cream liqueur. She also offers a frappé version on the long, hot days of a Mediterranean summer (simply cool the coffee before making and add crushed ice).

INGREDIENTS
- 1 tablespoon Irish whiskey (Jameson works well)
- Desired amount of brewed coffee
- 1 teaspoon sugar syrup or brown sugar
- 1 tablespoon Coole Swan Irish cream liqueur
- 4 ounces (100 mL) heavy cream
- Chocolate or cinnamon for garnish

DIRECTIONS
- Pour one tablespoon of Irish whiskey into a long, thin glass. Add coffee, hot or cold (with crushed ice, if cold).

- Stir in brown sugar; sugar syrup is even better, as it thickens the coffee so the cream sits more easily on top.
- Whisk heavy cream to almost stiff. Add in a generous measure of Coole Swan Irish cream liqueur.
- Spoon the cream mixture gently over the coffee; the cream shouldn't sink.

TIP: Sprinkle some chocolate over the cream; a chocolate cigarillo (for the cold drink) or a cinnamon stick (for hot Irish coffee) makes a nice finishing touch.

A Coole Swan Celtic coffee capped with the perfect layer of heavy cream

Limerick's "higher ground": Darby's Bed, a Neolithic passage tomb dating back to around 3000 B.C.

Irish Heritage

Darby's Bed & the Celtic Otherworld

Just outside the small village of Galbally, you can ascend a hill that provides not only fine vistas of the Limerick hinterlands, but also insight into prehistoric Ireland and the Celtic Otherworld of Irish myths and legends.

Signs point you to **Duntryleague Hill** (Dun Tri Leach, or "fort of the three rocks"), and it's a steep climb of about 275 feet (275 m). Bring good hiking shoes—and an active imagination—for this visit to the "higher ground" of ancient Ireland. At the summit, you'll find **Darby's Bed,** a Neolithic passage tomb dating back to around 3,000 B.C. This burial chamber was constructed in a place where its pagan occupants would be closest to the sky. The site, also known as Duntryleague Passage Tomb, was once covered over by a rock cairn or earthen mound. The orthostats (large boulders) that still stand upright nearby once lined a passageway to the capped chamber housing the dead.

Nobody knows who was buried here, although many believe it to be the resting place of Oilill Olum, once famed as the king of Munster. Whoever it was, their spirit may have divined a midsummer sunset salute each year, as the tomb's entrance faces directly northwest.

In addition to its archaeological interest, the tomb is also part of Irish myth and legend. The doomed lovers Diarmuid and Gráinne were said to have sheltered here for a night in their flight from the cuckolded Fionn MacCumhaill and his Fianna band of warriors. "The Pursuit of Diarmuid and Gráinne" is a story from the Fenian Cycle of Irish mythology.

Fadó, fadó (long, long ago), the aging warrior Fionn, leader of the Fianna, grieves the loss of his wife, Maigneis. His men arrange a new bride for their leader, the Princess Gráinne, daughter of High King Cormac mac Airt. Every good Irish wedding includes a smattering of scandal and drama, and at this ancient feast, Gráinne is alarmed that Fionn is older than her father, and so she casts a glad eye on Fionn's handsome warrior Diarmuid.

Gráinne slips a sleeping potion to the guests and persuades Diarmuid to elope with her. The would-be lovers hide in a forest across the River Shannon, then make their way to Dun Tri Leach (Darby's Bed), relentlessly pursued by Fionn and the Fianna.

After several evasions as the chase hastens northward, the couple finally make love in a natural chamber fit for such a saga: The cave at Gleniff Horseshoe in County Sligo is a massive rock arch 40 feet (12 m) high and 60 feet (18 m) wide. It was here on Benbulben that Fionn's warriors drove a savage boar toward Diarmuid and Fionn twice refused to bring healing water to his gored former comrade. By the time he relented, Diarmuid was dead. The fate of the grief-stricken Gráinne varies in subsequent retellings.

Like every Irish story, the legend of Diarmuid and Gráinne is constantly being retold by new generations who add their own twist. Playwright and screenwriter Paul Mercier reimagined the legend as a gangland crime thriller in his 2015 film *Pursuit*. ■

IRISH HISTORY: CELTIC MYTHS & LEGENDS

The Irish love to tell stories. The oral tradition honors the *seanchaí* (storyteller) who can mesmerize listeners by telling a story over many nights, always embellishing, always adding to the tale. Ireland's very first TV broadcast was a performance by the Kerry *seanchaí* Eamon Kelly. The media may change, but the Irish continue to retell the same beloved tales.

The myth of the **Children of Lir** might be the best loved story, one continually celebrated and re-created in the Irish arts. The tale recounts how Aoife, the wife of Lir and jealous stepmother, turns Lir's children into swans who retain the power of song but are eventually reborn in human form. Oisín Kelly's statue in Dublin's Garden of Remembrance symbolizes the rebirth of the nation after 900 years of oppression, the same time span as Aoife's spell.

The **Ulster Cycle** recounts legends from the first century A.D., a time of warfare. The heroes from the Ulaid province include Conchobar mac Nessa, King of Ulster, and the warrior Cúchulainn, the boy who slays a dog with his *camán* (stick) and *sliotar* (ball) and becomes Ireland's first hurling all-star. The **Cycle of the Kings,** written between 200 and 475, reflects Ireland's conversion to Christianity and is more historical, most of it involving medieval Irish royalty. The **Fenian Cycle** dates from the third century and recalls deeds of hunting, fighting, and daring done in Munster and Leinster. Most of these stories include the legendary Fionn Mac-Cumhaill and his Fianna warriors.

The legend of **Tír na nÓg** resonates most with the Irish. It recounts how Niamh tempted Oisín to the Land of Eternal Youth across the sea on a magic horse, only for him to return home to an utterly changed Ireland centuries later. The tale is often used as a metaphor by returning emigrants. Jim Sheridan's film *Into the West,* starring Gabriel Byrne, features a horse called Tír na nÓg and shows the power ancient storytelling still wields in modern Ireland. ■

Malcolm Robertson's "Children of Lir" sculpture in Ballycastle

Part Three

The Wild Atlantic Way

The County Clare town of Doolin is
renowned for traditional Irish music.

A Donegal surfer OPPOSITE: Dunguaire Castle, built near Kinvara in 1520 by Rory Mór O'Shaughnessy

A coastal-road odyssey

The Wild Atlantic Way stitches together some 1,550 miles (2,500 km) of highways, byways, and remote coastal *bohereens* (narrow roads) along Ireland's western seaboard. This wonderful route is both snake and ladder: You can take it from the Old Head of Kinsale, Cork, in the south all the way up to the Inishowen Peninsula in northerly Donegal. Or you can slip south down the coastline, breaking your odyssey into a series of fascinating chapters.

Starting out in Cork, the Wild Atlantic wayfarer follows the drives of Part Two through Counties Cork and Kerry before heading to Limerick. Prior to crossing the River Shannon, take in Foynes for a flying visit. Next, Clare beckons with its barren Burren landscapes, the steep Cliffs of Moher, and Doolin's traditional Irish music.

Galway City makes a great midway stopover for a blast of wild Atlantic culture. Pubs pulsate with music and stout-fueled fun, and if you time your visit accordingly, you can partake in one of Europe's wildest arts parties, take a punt on the ponies, or indulge a love of oysters (see Special Events listing on this page).

The wilderness of Connemara provides some of the Wild Atlantic Way's most scenic stretches before Sligo takes you deep into the homeland of poet W. B. Yeats. Stop at the churchyard "Under bare Ben Bulben's head," where "In Drumcliff churchyard Yeats is laid." His gravestone implores the traveler to "Cast a cold eye on life, on death, horseman, pass by."

To give your driver a rest from narrow cliffside roads, take a day to head inland and explore Ireland's past at the National Famine Museum at Strokestown House, County Roscommon. Passing Leitrim's tiny shoreline (just 2.9 miles/4.7 km long), head next to experience the spectacular views from the Slieve League Cliffs—Donegal's best kept secret—taller than Moher and well worth the mountain climb. Then drive to Killybegs for seafood fresh off an Atlantic trawler before the road to Malin Head takes you to Ireland's northernmost point. ∎

GREAT IRISH DRIVES: WILD ATLANTIC WAY—THE SOUTHWEST

This southwestern half of the Wild Atlantic Way begins inland in Cork before snaking its way up Ireland's sea-sculpted coastline. Starting in Blarney, the route takes in Ireland's southernmost point, **Mizen Head,** the five beautiful peninsulas of Cork and West Kerry, the mighty estuary of the **River Shannon,** and the limestone landscapes of the **Burren** in Clare. The myriad towns along the way include the Kerry fishing village of Dingle, the traditional Irish music mecca of Doolin, and Galway City, where the **Galway City Museum** (see page 188) has fine exhibits on the city's maritime history. The drive ends in convivial Clifden, the most westerly town on the gorgeous coastline of Connemara.

Begin your drive early in **Blarney,** where a visit to the castle and its famous stone will give you plenty to talk about with your newfound loquaciousness. From here, head south from Cork and west after Kinsale; at Skibbereen and Bantry peel off onto the main road to loop around the scenic **Beara Peninsula** (see page 118) before stopping in Kenmare. The center can get gridlocked at lunchtime, so park a little way out and walk into town for your choice of fine eateries. The Purple Heather Bistro & Pub or the Lime Tree are always excellent choices if you're there a little later in the day, but book ahead.

From here, it's on to the **Ring of Kerry** (see page 128), picking up the N70 out of Kenmare. This dramatic mountain loop takes you through the country towns of Sneem, Cahersiveen, and Glenbeigh. If the weather is good, consider stopping off at the **Skellig Experience Visitor Centre** for a Star Wars–inspired boat trip to the otherworldly Skellig Islands (see page 299), but check ahead for availability and a weather forecast. The N86 takes you around the **Dingle Peninsula** (see page 139), culminating in the town of Dingle, a lively, welcoming place to stop overnight.

Next morning, after circling the peninsula, take the smaller coast roads (N86, N68, N67) that bring you north into Counties Limerick and Clare and past the towns of Ennis and Kilkee, stopping to gaze in awe at the **Cliffs of Moher.** Just down the winding coast road sits the tiny village of **Doolin** (see page 178), spiritual home of traditional Irish music. Doolin has just a handful of pubs, but it's always worth a stopover for good food, a pint or two, and a chance to relish the jigs and reels of a good trad music session. Locals and legends will roll up spontaneously with instruments in hand to entertain all-comers long into the night.

Leaving Doolin, take the N67 all the way to **Galway** (see page 185), the city of the tribes, with its mesmeric maze of enticing streets and alleyways packed with buskers, dancers, craft shops, music pubs, and fine restaurants and cafés. (For a list of recommendations, see page 200). Whenever you can drag yourself away from these heady delights, head due west along Connemara's coastal roads via Spiddal and Roundstone. The R341 takes you into **Clifden,** Galway's westernmost town. This is the halfway point on your road-trip adventure up Ireland's western coastline, the Wild Atlantic Way. See page 192 for directions on navigating the northwestern half of this memorable drive. ∎

Wild Atlantic Way, South Drive OPPOSITE: **The Cliffs of Moher offer a cross section of the Burren's ancient geology.**

CLARE

Windswept and bewitching, the west of Ireland is charged with a wild Atlantic energy that attracts dreamers and schemers, romancers and dancers. Southern Clare welcomes the visitor with a green, undulating change of scenery, a lowland leveling out after the dramatic highs of the Kerry mountains.

Once you leave the town of Ennis, however, you traverse a topography unlike anywhere else on the diverse island of Ireland. The Burren is a maze of subterranean karst caverns, topped with a limestone lunar landscape aboveground. Sheets of striated stone stretch away into the rocky distance, the limestone showing the scratch-marks of the glacier that tore across Ice Age Ireland. Delicately decorating the moonlike surface are splashes of colorful Mediterranean, alpine, and arctic flora that thrive amidst the divots of this porous rock. This is the view close-up. The wide-angle shot comes out on the Atlantic: From there, the Cliffs of Moher show a cross section of the Burren revealed as layers of rock accumulated beneath the Ice Age–shaped landscape.

This is the Wild Atlantic Way for geology geeks. The beautifully bleak inland topography, stripped of trees centuries ago, competes with gloriously rugged and rocky coastline drives. The timeless nature of life in Clare tempts the traveler to linger ever longer in villages where the seafood is fresh, the pubs crackle with conversation, and the traditional music is always on the lively side. You can watch the sun go down on Galway Bay in Ballyvaghan, find a partner the (very) old-fashioned way in Lisdoonvarna, or dance to Ireland's oldest *céilí* band in Kilfenora.

Yet just when you think you've time-traveled back 100 years, Clare surprises with a twist of 21st-century delight. You might spend a morning exploring holy wells then break for lunch on a chocolate farm that offers a history of humankind's most seductive edible vice. Then follow your nose to a perfumery, miles from nowhere, inhale deeply, and take in a sensual smattering of Clare's wondrous olfactory notes. ∎

Clare welcomes all to a wild landscape of geographic and geological wonders.

The rocky Burren limestone landscape hosts Ireland's greatest diversity of wildflowers, an extraordinary mix of arctic, alpine, and Mediterranean plants.

Special Places

The Burren

The Irish word *boireann* means "rocky land," and at first glance the Burren looks like a dead lunar landscape. Yet a closer look reveals that this bleak limestone wilderness hosts Ireland's greatest diversity of wildflowers, an extraordinary mix of arctic, alpine, and Mediterranean plants. Dig into its history, and you'll find a human-made landscape, a once dense woodland deforested by settlers and invaders. Along the sparse gray hills lie ancient tombs and dwellings, the ruins of churches, ring forts, and sacred holy wells. To delve deeper into the karst geology of the Burren,

visit Aillwee Cave to see stalactites and stalagmites, underground rivers and waterfalls, and a section of the region's labyrinth of caves.

The Burren is a striated landscape of cracked limestone formed beneath ancient oceans and pushed above sea level by a great geological upheaval. The surface of the limestone is split into deep, narrow channels (grykes), with long strips of rock (clints) between them.

Gen. Edmund Ludlow reported to Oliver Cromwell in 1651 that the Burren "had not any tree to hang a man, nor enough water to drown a man, nor enough earth to bury him." Yet

he also noted: "Their cattle are very fat, for the grass growing in tufts of earth . . . is very nourishing."

Indeed, the Burren's nutrient-rich soil and plentiful rainwater gather in the grykes, finding a nurturing space, a nature-made hothouse between the rocks. The result is the extraordinarily varied range of plants: Some 75 percent of Ireland's native wildflowers flourish here, including 24 species of orchids. The creatures in this limestone landscape are rare for Ireland: Multiple species of butterflies feast on the flora, while pine martens (weasels), badgers, and stoats (ermines) all thrive in these rocky parts. ∎

IRISH VOICES: THE LIVING LANDSCAPE

Despite its robust appearance, the Burren is a fragile landscape, needing careful stewardship. Although it is the result of human interference—clearance for farming in the Burren began more than 5,000 years ago—this ecological oasis of biodiversity cannot be sustainably protected and conserved by farmers alone. A desire to help the wider community take informed pride in the landscape and feel empowered to care for it led to the foundation of the Burrenbeo Trust (*beo* is Irish for "alive") in 2001 by Brendan Dunford and his late wife, Ann O'Connor.

What began as a website about the living Burren and the role of local community in its care has evolved into a thriving, inclusive organization that runs more than 25 programs annually, all with the aim of connecting people to the natural and cultural heritage of the Burren.

Kate Lavender began working for Burrenbeo in 2012, when it expanded from a one-woman show to three part-timers (it now has a staff of nine). Her favorite part of the job? Interactions that "involve local school children, exploring their places and working as a team. Children are bursting with ideas and creativity, making exploring the landscapes with them an adventure. Their connections to their places become noticeably strengthened throughout the program, and their action plans never cease to amaze me. They are the future of these places and, given the right opportunities and encouragement, the world will be a very different place when it's eventually in their capable hands," she says.

In addition to the annual Burren in Bloom and Winterage Weekend festivals welcoming the summer and winter seasons, adult programs likewise inspire and promote pride of place through the sharing of knowledge, stories, and insights. Burrenbeo runs a popular walk series guided by an array of local farmers, landowners, and residents. There are also monthly "tea talks" in a local hall that "bring people together by the fire to share Burren stories over a cup of tea—a simple yet effective way to create pride in place and community spirit," says Lavender.

Lavender also coordinates the Burrenbeo Conservation Volunteers program. "A day out volunteering in the Burren, working with great company, leaves you with such a sense of satisfaction of not only a good day's work but also of being part of a friendly community of welcoming and inspiring people making a difference on the ground.

"Our Burren in Bloom and Winterage Weekend festivals celebrate the Burren and its farming traditions," Lavender explains. "Nothing lifts spirits more than seeing spring flowers herald the arrival of spring after a long, cold, damp winter, and following a herd of cattle up onto their winterage pasture in the Burren uplands is an exhilarating experience and a timeless tradition."

Burrenbeo now plans to expand their agenda. "The Burren is a special place, yet *every* place is unique and deserves protection and care. Our programs are applicable across Ireland, so we strive to connect communities across Ireland to their places and to create a vast army of stewards to care for local environments into the future." ∎

The Poulnabrone Dolmen is one of Ireland's most iconic monuments, and one of several remnants of Neolithic life—and death—on the Burren.

"Following a herd of cattle up onto their winterage pasture in the Burren uplands is an exhilarating experience and a timeless tradition."

— *Kate Lavender*

Kerry (green and gold) and Dublin (blue), GAA Football's fiercest rivals, contest another All-Ireland final.

Irish Heritage

The Gaelic Athletic Association: Social Pulse of Ireland's Heartland

The small Burren town of Carran is the birthplace of Michael Cusack, founder of the Gaelic Athletic Association (GAA). The center bearing his name tells his story in the thatched cottage where Cusack was born in 1847.

Founded in 1884 in Thurles, County Tipperary, the GAA is an amateur organization. Two sports dominate its calendar, with local and national championships held for men's and women's teams. The first,

Gaelic football, is a thrilling and passionately supported game in which the 15 players of each team run with the ball in hand or at foot.

In hurling, the oldest team sport in Europe, the *sliotar*, or ball, travels at ferocious speeds, propelled by a thwack of the *camán*, or hurley, a stick carved of ash wood. Women's hurling is known as camogie. Players of both games, all amateurs, must be extremely brave, quick, and agile. Crowds are noisy, knowledgeable,

and ready to cheer (and sometimes jeer) their local heroes. The banter, even at a big match attended by tens of thousands, can be richly personal, as workmates, family, or even students of the players voice their feelings. The Dublin captain who regularly lifted the Sam Maguire Cup (the All-Ireland Men's Football Championship trophy) in front of 82,000 in recent years was back teaching schoolboys on the following Monday morning.

The genesis of the GAA aligned with the late 19th-century spirit of the Celtic Revival, a renaissance in Irish culture, history, and language. On a British-occupied island, the games became popular both as a healthy pastime and as an expression of nationalism and self-determination. Soon nearly every parish in Ireland had its own club, and county teams called on players from these to compete at "All-Ireland" level. These clubs also served as the social glue in remote rural areas and provided a cultural bridge for the island's many exiles: Teams representing New York and London also compete in the national championships, and the 1947 All-Ireland Football Final was contested in Manhattan's Polo Grounds.

From 1913 onward, most finals were played at Croke Park in north Dublin, the headquarters of the GAA. The stadium, which was redeveloped in the 1990s and 2000s, holds more than 80,000 spectators and is home to the GAA Museum. Croke Park's field is considered sacred ground due to the Bloody Sunday massacre of 13 spectators and a Tipperary player, Michael Hogan, by the Royal Ireland Constabulary in 1920, during Ireland's War of Independence.

If you can somehow score a ticket for either the All-Ireland football or hurling final in September, when the champions from the island's 32 counties are crowned, you'll witness the ultimate spectacle of Irish sport. ▪

IRISH HISTORY: SUPERSTITION & THE CURSE OF THE MAYO FOOTBALL TEAM

In Gaelic games, superstition runs maybe a little deeper than in other sports. The Irish are, after all, a people who believe in the thin veil between this world and the land of the *aos sí*, or the fairies, and the importance of having those otherworldly creatures on your side at all times. Croke Park is thought by many to be what is known in the Celtic realm as a "thin space" where this Otherworld is always near, perhaps because 14 people died there in the 1920 Bloody Sunday massacre during Ireland's War of Independence.

In 1985, the great Kerry footballer, Páidí Ó Sé, enlisted the car of the Taoiseach (prime minister of Ireland), no less, to transport his talismanic "lucky underpants" to Croke Park in time for the All-Ireland final. He had left them at home, and felt Kerry were doomed without them. The talismanic garment was duly delivered, and that afternoon Ó Sé lifted the Sam Maguire Cup as Kerry defeated their archrivals Dublin.

The last time Mayo won the trophy was in 1951. Legend has it that on their victorious bus ride home, so joyous was the party that they failed to stop and pay proper respect to a funeral cortege passing through the Mayo village of Foxford. A local priest, enraged by this insult to the dead, stepped forward and placed a curse on the county footballers that would haunt them for decades: No Mayo team would ever win an All-Ireland final while any member of the team of '51 still lived. In the next 70 years, eight different senior Mayo men's sides made it back to Croke Park, only to suffer failure in the final. In 2019, Padraig Carney died in California, leaving just one member of the team still alive when Mayo reached yet another final in 2021: The 95-year-old Paddy Prendergast watched from his home in Kerry as the Mayo side that had ended Dublin's six-year reign as champions in the semifinal *somehow* contrived to fall at the final hurdle. Again.

Then, just two weeks later, Paddy Prendergast died.

All Gaeldom now wonders: With every member of the '51 team now deceased, will the curse of the Mayo footballers finally be lifted? ▪

For fans of Mayo's senior football team, superstition and dread have haunted every All-Ireland final since 1951.

Songlines

Traditional Irish Music

Trad music is sacred to the Irish, so when the Cobblestone, a Dublin pub beloved for its traditional Irish music sessions, was recently threatened by the march of development, hundreds stepped lightly toward Dublin City offices. Their ultimately successful protest against the Cobblestone's extinction took the form of a mass musical session aimed at annoying the bureaucrats inside.

While visiting musicians, including banjo-playing actor Steve Martin, have dropped into the Cobblestone, most are likely to head to the Clare village of Doolin, spiritual home of the music that resonates worldwide via Ireland's diaspora. This music was historically the legacy of the Irish peasantry. In Celtic times, a harpist would be part of a chieftain's court alongside *filés* (poets) and *brehons* (lawmakers). He or she would be judged on their ability to conjure music's otherworldly powers, demonstrating proficiency in *geantraí,* the music of happiness; *goltraí,* the music of sadness; and *suantraí,* the meditative music of sleep.

The end of the Celtic world saw the outlawing of Gaelic culture by the English overlords via the Penal Laws. Itinerant musicians of the 17th and 18th centuries would instead memorize up to 500 songs to pass along to the next generation. The legend of Turlough O'Carolan, the blind harpist, still echoes through modern Ireland in tunes such as "O'Carolan's Draught."

In Jacobite times, folk songs criticized the English occupation in code, and music became a dangerous, subversive weapon of the oppressed. Not until the Celtic Revival of the 1890s could *céilís* (dances) be overtly enjoyed again. Many were organized by the Gaelic League and the GAA. By the 1930s, the Kilfenora Céilí Band, originally trained as a fife-and-drum outfit by the British Army, entertained at dances in Clare and Galway. (The band, perpetually regenerated by family and friends, is now well into its second century.)

Irish trad has distinctive regional styles: Fiddlers, for example, become known for performing in a Clare or Donegal style, distinguished by the slide of a note or the speed of a progression. Dancing styles are similarly defined. Predominant dance tunes are jigs, reels, slides, hornpipes, polkas, and mazurkas. The *sean-nós* dancing of Galway and Connemara is more flat-footed than elsewhere. Although the extensive arm waving of many styles of Irish dance was suppressed by priests in the newly independent Catholic Ireland of the mid-20th century, it made a spectacular comeback in the 1990s, thanks to Michael Flatley, an Irish American Riverdancer from Chicago.

Sean-nós also denotes the a cappella style of storytelling through songs that are sometimes performed as slow airs on uilleann (elbow) pipes, as well as fiddle, flute, or tin whistle. Sinéad O'Connor released a fine collection of traditional songs in 2013 titled *Sean-Nós Nua (New Old-Style).*

Pipers are especially revered in Clare: The Willie Clancy Summer School attracts uilleann players to Miltown Malbay each year, including many Irish Americans. Following the Great Famine of the 1840s and the great scattering, generations of musicians brought their jigs, reels, and folk ballads across the globe. In America, the music of the Scots-Irish evolved into Appalachian old-time music and eventually into bluegrass and country and western forms. Paddy Moloney of the Chieftains tellingly observed that "for me, to go to Nashville was like going to another part of Ireland."

The great Clare fiddler Martin Hayes, who spent years working in Chicago, completed this musical circle by forming the Irish and American ensemble the Gloaming. His legacy is the regional style of fiddling from the mountains of west Clare, which Hayes attributes to what traditional Irish musicians call *dríocht,* a supernatural magic or enchanted wizardry. Hayes also regularly plays with the Tulla Céilí Band, of which his late father was a founding member. ∎

A bodhran player (second from left) brings the beat to an Irish music session, a scene replicated in pubs across Ireland.

The small, Clare-based Burren Perfumery creates cosmetics and perfumes from local plants and herbs.

The Chemistry of Love

In pagan Ireland, the pursuit of love was a key element of many Gaelic festivities—even one that celebrated the dead. The festival of Samhain was an ancient celebration of the Otherworld, a night of the spirits that became Halloween and spread worldwide. Across the centuries in Ireland, bonfires were lit, ghost stories shared, and those with "the gift" told fortunes, chief among them one's prospects in love. The feast of Oíche Shamhna (Halloween) traditionally includes a light fruitcake bread into which the baker adds a pea, a stick, a piece of cloth, a coin, and a

ring. Whomever is served the slice with the pea won't marry that year, the stick foretells an unhappy marriage, and the unlucky person whose cake includes the cloth is in for bad luck or poverty. The coin, however, indicates coming wealth, and the ring that you'll be wed within the year.

In Clare, the hopeful single person can head to **Doolin** and dance the night away as the entrancing rhythms and heady swirl of traditional Irish music propel hearts to beat faster, hands to grip tighter, and prospective partners' eyes to catch across the dance floor.

Or, you can head to the nearby town of **Lisdoonvarna** in September and have a quiet word with Willie Daly at his office in the **Matchmaker Bar.** Lisdoonvarna hosts Europe's biggest matchmaking festival, a monthlong celebration of love and the quest to find one's other half. This event has attracted the lonesome and the love-struck for more than 160 years, and Willie Daly is the current keeper of the *Book of Love,* which holds thousands of details in the matchmaker's quest to make perfect matches. Local legend says that if you touch this storied tome with both hands, you'll be wed in six months.

If the airs of Clare put you in an amorous mood, two destinations deserve your attention. Deep in the heart of the wildflower-dotted limestone landscape is the **Burren Perfumery,** an olfactory oasis of sensual delights. The owners produce handmade perfumes and cosmetics using organic ingredients inspired by the Clare landscapes.

Their process is explained as you spend time in the Soap Room, the Blending Room, and the Herb Garden before heading to the tempting shop and welcoming tearoom.

From the town of Ballyvaghan, signs point the way to **Hazel Mountain Chocolate Factory & Café,** close to the ruins of **Corcomroe Abbey.** Even 12th-century Cistercians may not have resisted the array of chocolate and fudge temptations that

now courts gourmands at this remote country spot. Relaxing with a hot chocolate at an outdoor café table at this reinvented Irish dairy farm makes for a romantic interlude between the botanical and archaeological attractions of the Burren. Hazel Mountain provides fascinating tours and has a shop full of sweet delights. One of the chocolatiers, G. P. Hillson, has also written a wonderful book, *For the Love of Chocolate.* ∎

IN THE KNOW: WHERE TO STAY, EAT & DRINK IN CLARE

After a day exploring the gorgeous Clare countryside and coastlines, your reward will be an unforgettable night in pubs where every knee jumps and every foot taps (or dances) to the mesmerizing rhythms of traditional Irish music played late into the night.

For sheer luxury, it's hard to beat **Dromoland Castle** on the 400-acre (162 ha) estate in Newmarket-on-Fergus. Stepping outside to a restful lake vista, you can take a boat ride, an archery lesson, a falconry class, a long hike, or enjoy a round of golf, then retire to the cocktail bar for a well-earned libation before dining in the excellent Earl of Thomond restaurant.

If you want to feel like a guest in Clare's most private 18th-century manor house, spend a night at **Gregans Castle Hotel,** nestled in one of the Burren's most beautiful valleys. The garden walks with their views of the Burren's unusual landscape, the fine culinary creations of Chef Robbie McCauley, and the cozy Corkscrew Bar are all conducive to a restful country retreat. A surreal Clare experience awaits at **Ballyportry Castle,** where the 15th-century tower house has been modernized to accommodate up to eight guests. Turf fires, stone walls, and a stone bathtub will make you feel like an ancient Irish chieftain, albeit with modern conveniences.

Sheedy's Country House Hotel in Lisdoonvarna situates you in the heart of the Burren, a short drive from the pubs of Doolin and the Cliffs of Moher. Owners John and Martina always extend the warmest of Clare welcomes to their family hotel and restaurant. Another option in town is the **Wild Honey Inn,** the first Irish pub to achieve a Michelin star, thanks to Chef Aidan McGrath's "wild food from the land and sea."

All of Doolin's four pubs have regular music sessions to beat the other's band; in addition, **McDermott's, Gus O'Connor's, McGann's,** and **Fitzpatrick's** offer pub grub with extensive menus to fuel your tapping feet. ∎

The downstairs kitchen at Ballyportry Castle's Gaelic tower house

GALWAY

County Galway is the heartland of the west of Ireland. The first sighting of stone walls stretched across green fields heralds the traveler's entry into the hardscrabble Celtic realm, where every living thing seems to exist between a rock and a hard place.

The university town of Galway, tucked in the innermost crook of the famous bay, is a creative hub that celebrates the mythical, the fantastic, and the linguistically elastic. Its location at the gateway to Ireland's largest Gaeltacht (Irish-speaking region) means that people here switch easily between the language of their ancient ancestors and the tongue of the Sasanaigh, the English colonizers.

Visit in summer and you'll enjoy some of the most spectacular festivities anywhere in Europe. The Galway International Arts Festival in July brings dramatic parades along with music, theater, and other events. August heralds a celebration of the sport of kings as the Galway Races generate glamor and glitz, and some serious wagering on the horses. This season of sensual stimulation culminates in September's International Oyster and Seafood Festival, as Galwegians enjoy one last bacchanalian blowout before winter descends.

Traveling into the hinterlands of Connemara, listen carefully and you'll detect the Irish mindset in richly lyrical rhythms of speech, as native Irish speakers think in Gaelic before speaking in English. The visitor, however, may be rendered completely speechless by the beauty of Connemara. Scattered across this scenic splendor is evidence of the entire history of the Celtic race and their conquerors: From the prehistoric clifftop fort of Dun Aengus on the Aran island of Inis Mór to the 12th-century Norman battlement at Ashford Castle; from Victorian Kylemore Abbey and its English walled gardens to Coole Park, Lady Gregory's western domain with its list of literary guests from the Celtic Revival inscribed on the Autograph Tree—the sweep of Irish civilization is written large across Galway's western wilderness. ∎

Pine Island on Derryclare Lake in the fabled region of Connemara

Insider's Guide

Galway & Connemara

Nestled in a bay that gives scant shelter from North Atlantic winds and rain, Galway is Ireland's westernmost city and one of Europe's liveliest places. From spring through September, a string of festivals turns Galway into a dizzying celebration of life.

Each April, a poetry *cúirt* (court or gathering) celebrates a rich lyrical heritage—Ireland's current president is a Galwegian poet, and a statue of another Galway bard beatifies the town's Eyre Square. The Galway International Arts Festival dazzles with performers and parades every July, and princes, paupers, and punters mix easily at the Galway Races in early August. September brings the Galway International Oyster and Seafood Festival, when the local delicacy is washed down with plentiful pints of creamy Guinness.

Lively Galway is also a city full of ghosts. The first you'll meet is that of Christopher Columbus. The Italian was recorded in the annals of **St. Nicholas's Collegiate Church** in 1477 as he passed through a few years before he set off on his voyage to the Americas. Perhaps he offered up a prayer to Nicholas, patron saint of mariners. The church was founded in 1320, funded by the Tribes of Galway (the medieval city's 14 merchant families). It has switched from Catholic to Protestant and back through the ages, reflecting Ireland's conflicted history, yet its peaceful interior remains a haven in this cosmopolitan port.

Wander next down the **Spanish Parade** beside the sun-dappled waters of the River Corrib gushing from the salmon-leap weir upstream near Galway Cathedral. Galway was likely named for a girl drowned here some 3,000 years ago. Named

Galway is Ireland's westernmost city, and its labyrinth of streets thrums with music, dance, and song.

Gaillimhe or Galvia, she was a princess of the Fir Bolg, a mythical race of Greek origin. The Spanish Arch, a gate in the walls of the medieval city, leads you to the **Galway City Museum** (see page 188). Then cross the River Corrib to **Claddagh,** an old fishing village along the briny quay. The romance of the Claddagh ring still resonates here: After jeweler Richard Joyce was captured by Algerians and sold into slavery to a Moorish goldsmith in the 18th century, he returned to Claddagh with a new ring design, featuring a heart topped with a crown. Those wearing it in exile pointed the heart facing outward to signify single status, or inward to show their heart was "spoken for" back home. Exile, separation, and heartbreak are large parts of the story of the west.

For a gut-burning Redbreast Irish whiskey, stop off in **Garavan's** or any Galway pub where you can relish the joys of a music session by an open fire. Inhale the quintessential west of Ireland aroma of burning turf and lose yourself in the mad swirl of a reel with fiddles, tin whistles, bodhrans (goatskin drums), and uilleann (elbow) pipes all mixed into a mesmerizing musical stew. Then, a hush is called, silence descends, and a plaintive female voice bleats a multiversed tale of emigration and absence in the unaccompanied, *sean-nós* (old form) style.

In **Eyre Square,** you'll hear the ghost of John F. Kennedy, echoing his famous speech made here in 1963: *"If the day was clear, and you went down to the bay, and you looked west . . . you'd see Boston, Massachu-*

A string of festivals—from spring to Halloween—turns Galway into a dizzying celebration of life.

setts. And you'd see there, working on the docks, Dohertys, Flahertys, and Ryans, and cousins of yours who've made good." Here, too, stands the statue of Irish-language poet Pádraic Ó Conaire. Yet if you want to hear *real* Irish, go to **Connemara.**

The region of Connemara offers the quintessential Irish dreamscape of cliffs, bogs, and wild Atlantic weather. Ask most residents to define its boundaries and few will know where it begins or ends: It's neither a county nor a province. Connemara is more a state of mind. Or, given how many Connemarans operate in two languages, and straddle two continents as exiles in America, maybe it's a state *between* mindsets.

Set on the very westerly edge of Europe, Connemara sweeps scenically across the western realms of County Galway. The rugged countryside is framed by the magnificent **Maumturk Mountains.** Mist rolls inland over rugged Atlantic coastlines and shrouds loughs teeming with salmon and trout; Connemara's lake and river fishing are among Europe's best.

Twisted hawthorn trees pointing eastward at 90-degree angles testify to the force of the gales that blast the elevated boglands. Connemara, which long defied English colonization, has also faced down history's winds and retains the essence of Irish identity. ∎

The Gaeltacht, where Gaelic is the main language spoken, is home to nearly 100,000 Irish speakers; bilingualism breathes new life into the ancient culture.

Irish Heritage

The Gaeltacht

Spend time in the Gaeltacht, or Irish-speaking areas, of the west of Ireland and you'll get to know the rich, resonant sounds of the native language. The term "Gaeltacht" refers to any or all of these districts where Irish Gaelic is the main language spoken. The Gaeltacht had 96,090 inhabitants in 2016, with most living in the western counties of Donegal, Mayo, Galway, and Kerry, as well as smaller communities in Cork, Waterford, and Meath.

Learning a couple of words (*"cúpla focail"*), even just good morning (*"Dia duit ar maidin"*) or thank you (*"Go raibh maith agat"*), is easy and will garner you an extra smile. Most Gaeltachts offer summer schools for children, akin to American summer camps but with predominant linguistic and cultural aspects.

Every Irish child who spends a summer in the Gaeltacht retains lifelong memories of active days in rural Irish towns, playing hurling or cycling the boglands. The nights are even better, with lively *céilís* (dances) where the swirl of jigs and reels sends teenagers spinning into each other's arms atop a sprung dance floor made of Irish oak to add mighty spring to one's step.

The one rule of the Gaeltacht school is that no English is spoken. Irish is Ireland's official language and serves as a "periscope into our psyche and our souls," according to writer and documentary filmmaker Manchán Magan.

Listening to the sound of the Gaelic language is a way of seeing the world through Irish eyes. Ireland's western waters, for example, may well have churned up the Gaelic noun *farraige* (sea); like many a poetic Irish word, it resounds with its own meaning and its pronunciation—*fffffarrrrra gaaaaa*—is the sound of waves breaking on these timeless rocky shores.

The Irish are a people who for centuries thought in one language (Gaelic) yet spoke in another (English). This agile duality within the Irish mind may be the reason so much of Irish literature has such poetic textures. As Magan notes, Irish is a language richly descriptive of the land, yet it acknowledges the existence of other realms. So as you drive in the west of Ireland, tune your radio to RTÉ Raidió na Gaeltachta (RnaG at FM: 92 MHz-94 MHz) and take a linguistic trip into the sounds of the unknown. ■

IRISH VOICES: THE POET PRESIDENT OF IRELAND

Born in 1941, Michael D. Higgins has spent a lifetime leading the people of Galway, Connemara, and the Aran Islands. A lecturer of sociology at the city's university, he was twice mayor of Galway and served as Ireland's minister for arts, culture, and the Gaeltacht (Irish-speaking region) and as senator for the region before becoming the most popular president in the history of the Irish Republic. This dynamic Irishman would surely have reigned justly as a great chieftain in ancient times. In another age, he would certainly have been a *filé* (an Irish court poet), having published several volumes of poetry that evoke the quiet forces of life in rural Ireland.

Higgins grew up in the west of Ireland, and when asked why poetry is such an expressive force in Irish life and why the Irish hold proponents of the art form in such high regard, he explains: "Poetry is a pure art form. It's a pure distillation of language, with no excess, no words wasted, which allows language to be parsed for the purest expression."

While he now ponders his poetry in Áras an Uachtaráin, the official home of the president of Ireland in Dublin, it's clear that his heart belongs to the Galway and Connemara region that he long represented. He has followed in the footsteps of Ireland's other poet-senator, W. B. Yeats.

In addition to his way with words, President Higgins is beloved by his compatriots for his warm and ever present smile. When Michael D., as he's affectionately known hereabouts, is asked what makes Galway, Connemara, and the Aran Islands so special, the poet-president responds, "Galway is a place that exists on the periphery, a place between realms. Between the Gaelic and English languages. Between the traditions of literature and the spoken word. Between island life and mainland life. Between ancient Ireland and our future vision.

"The west is a place dominated by the elements, the whole region lives between the river and the lake and the sea, and, in the case of Aran, between the islands and the sea," he adds.

And, given its proclivity for poets and artists, maybe we should add between the heavens and earth. The opening lines of the president's poem "Stardust" beautifully capture the elemental creativity that seems to glimmer potently amidst all who are drawn to Galway's western dreamscapes:

It is of stardust we are
Moulded by vapours and fragments
From the making and breaking of galaxies.
We are the broken bits of our cosmos
Moved by traces of embedded memory,
Of hopes unrealised and fading.
The promise of our as yet uncreated wholeness remains . . . ■

Michael D. Higgins personifies a vivacious joy common among Galwegians.

"Connemara is a place that seduces, a place where people can renew their spirit, where the creative artist in particular can find new rhythms of complexity."
—*Michael D. Higgins*

Traditional wooden Galway hookers, with their distinctive red sails, compete in a west-of-Ireland regatta.

Maritime History

Every visitor to Galway should spend time absorbing some local history in the Galway City Museum. Located behind the Spanish Arch, an apt landmark in a port city, the museum occupies a building that affords fine views of Claddagh fishing village, the River Corrib, and Galway Bay. Among its iconic offerings are a beautifully crafted Galway hooker (traditional fishing vessel long known as the workhorse of coastal Connemara and North Clare) and a collection of curraghs (rowboats made of a framework of laths covered with tarred canvas).

The hooker on view here, *Máirtín Oliver,* was crafted especially for the museum. These boats got their name from "hook and line" fishing, or long-lining, which used long lines of baited hooks to catch fish individually. Although hookers are traditional fishing boats, the larger of their four classes, the *bád mór* (big boat) and *leathbhád* (half boat) were also used for the transport of cargo. These would haul up to eight tons (7.25 metric tonnes) of turf, livestock, general supplies, lime, *poitín* (illegal whiskey), and seaweed (a valuable fertilizer) to and from Ireland's western islands. The smaller *gleoiteog* (neat vessel) and *púcán* (open boat) are more nimble boats, used by lobster and small-catch fishermen.

Sails were made of unbleached calico, a heavy textile that was soaked in a protective solution made from tree bark or from a tar-and-butter mix. This annual tradition of "barking the sails" gave the sails of Galway hookers their distinctive red or rusty brown hue.

Once you've studied the craftsmanship of the *Máirtín Oliver* up close, try to catch sight of a hooker in full flight on Galway Bay. All classes use three red sails—mainsail, foresail, and jib—to fully harness the wild Atlantic winds. To watch these sleek vessels under full sail is to witness Irish maritime history in motion.

The advent of the engine-powered boat made sail and oars all but redundant by the mid-20th century, but in recent decades, Galway hookers and curraghs have enjoyed a remarkable revival. Their legacy is now celebrated at the three-day Gathering of the Boats festival (called Cruinniú na mBád in Irish) at Kinvara in mid-August. Up to 100 Galway hookers are the stars in a weekend of racing and festivities.

If you're up for a long walk westward from the city, you can admire many hookers at Nimmo's Pier and the Claddagh. Continue out to Salthill and you might spot more on the waters of Galway Bay, perhaps the red-sailed splendor of *Lovely Anne, Star of the West,* or *Croí an Cladaig (Heart of Claddagh)*. The Galway Hooker Sailing Club has helped restore many of these vessels, employing the skilled craftsmanship of contemporary boatbuilders such as Ciaran Oliver and Cóilín Hernon. This and other sailing clubs now pass along the skills and traditions of the hookers to the next generation of Galwegians. ∎

TASTE OF IRELAND: GUINNESS & OYSTERS

What could be more appetizing than a plate of succulent oysters, raised along the west coast, washed down with a creamy glass of Guinness? This salty delicacy of the Atlantic mixed with certain freshwaters is perfectly cleansed by the stout's smooth flavors brewed from the harvests of this temperate island: Ireland's favorite drink is a rich blend of roasted barley, malted barley, hops, and yeast, but the key ingredient, it is widely believed, is the freshwater found in such abundance throughout Ireland. Ask any homesick Gael from Austin to Adelaide, and they'll tell you the "pint of plain" brewed along foreign riverbanks is just not the same.

Guinness and oysters is such a celebrated pairing that it's now the toast of several Irish festivals. The oldest is Galway's International Oyster & Seafood Festival, which originated as the Clarinbridge Oyster Festival, established in the County Galway village of the same name in 1954. (The festival proved so popular that it has long since moved to the city of Galway.) Over the course of a raucous three days and nights in late September, more than 100,000 oysters are washed down with countless pints of stout. The Irish and World Oyster Opening—or "shucking"—Championships are a highlight, with concerts, street parades, and seafood trails keeping crowds happy and well fed.

The festival oysters are nurtured west of Clarinbridge at Dunbulcan Bay, which affords shelter from wild Atlantic storms. Some 700 acres (285 ha) of beds ensure these oysters flourish in a perfect confluence of freshwater and seawater, in which they mature in three to five years.

For many gourmands, there are only two ways of eating oysters: either raw, with a squeeze of lemon or a little cayenne pepper, or else deviled on the half shell. When opening an oyster with a strong, sharp knife, hold it firmly in a thick cloth and ensure that none of the oyster liquor (juices) are lost. This seafood tastes great with wheaten bread and butter. And, of course, always with a Guinness.

Same again please! ∎

Fishing for oysters and mussels, a time-honored coastal Irish profession

IRISH VOICES: THE STONEWALLER

Seen from above, the west of Ireland looks like a rugged landscape of green fields with a vast net of crochet lace spread across it. "My grandfather said we lived between a rock and a hard place," says Rory O'Shaughnessy, an affable Galwegian who works as a heritage specialist, tour guide, and local historian of his south Galway homeland.

This latticed web consists of stone walls erected over centuries, mainly to delineate land ownership; in the medieval period before the Norman conquest, they were built to keep cattle corralled. "In the old Celtic world," says O'Shaughnessy, "cattle was king."

He continues: "The stone walls were always a part of our life. When you knocked a wall, you built a wall," he recalls. "In fact, building and repairing walls paid for my beer in college." While O'Shaughnessy studied archaeology and history at NUI Galway, it was the stone walls of the Burren and Connemara that taught him much regarding both disciplines. Like many here, he inherited the stonemasonry skills of his forefathers.

Ireland has more walls than any other country in Europe, some 248,000 miles (400,000 km) of drystone walls and 130,500 miles (210,000 km) of stone-earthen banks. The lines of the stone walls uncovered from the bogs around the Céide Fields of north Mayo are early indications of Stone Age farming in Ireland. O'Shaughnessy explains that the same masonry skills were later used to build Christian monastic settlements and Norman estates. In the 19th century, when land ownership reverted to Irish farmers, the walls kept cattle out of crop fields. An area dense with stone walls tells many historical tales: One is of a land repeatedly subdivided among generations of sons.

"You build with the stones you have available. Connemara is mostly granite and quartz, and the Burren yields limestone," says O'Shaughnessy. "There are two basic types of walls: the single and the double stone wall." In the higher grounds of the Burren, where livestock were brought in winter (contrary to most European practices), the single wall predominates. "This is a single stone deep," he says, "and it's dry, meaning no mortar is used to bond it. The single stone has larger rocks at the base and tapers toward the top with smaller stones, and friction alone holds it up.

"Look at these walls from the east around sunset and you'll see the sunlight through them," says O'Shaughnessy. "These spaces are key, because the wind blows through them. They act like a net, not a sail, so on higher, exposed ground, they won't blow down. You'll also see places where larger gaps were left for sheep to pass through: These were called sheep's creeps, puickets, poteens, or hoggs." (The Irish have 32 words for field, according to author Manchán Magan.)

The Burren varies in landscape, with karst limestone uplands and fertile lowland pastures. "You see all kinds of mixed walls there as different generations have worked on them. They get more eccentric with age, like us all," O'Shaughnessy laughs. "But we find stacked or wedge walls everywhere, dating from medieval times to late last week."

On lower lands, the double wall prevails. "This type has two faces of stone, one on each side, and the core is filled with small stones, O'Shaughnessy says. "They're both pointed—built with cement or lime mortar—and dry. Two stones are stacked on top of a single stone, in an alternating pattern that tapers upward. They have a base stone and a through stone halfway up—this is a single stone running through the entire width of the two faces and the core. These often protrude from the face and provide stability. Double walls are topped with a capstone or coping stone.

"For me, the king of all walls is the Feidín wall," says O'Shaughnessy. This is a hybrid with a double stone base and a single stone top. These walls are often bolstered by

The Double Stone Wall
Very strong and durable, the double stone wall is constructed with two faces of stone housing an inner core of smaller stones. They can be pointed (built with mortar) or dry (with no mortar).

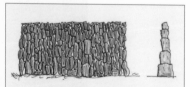

The Stacked Style
Built using the long angler stone typical of areas of exposed limestone pavement, these walls are quite strong (despite appearances), relying on friction to stand up.

The Stacked Style With Feidín
A very strong wall commonly found in fertile upland areas close to exposed limestone pavement; these walls may have protected tillage fields from roaming stock.

Ireland has some 248,000 miles (400,000 km) of dry-stone walls, more than any other country in Europe. Those seen here are at O'Brien's Castle on the Aran island of Inisheer, constructed in the stacked style with local limestone rocks.

"uprights," or "mother" stones. Feidín walls are found in both uplands, where angular stone is picked straight off the bedrock, and lowlands, where stones that have been rounded by glaciers are chosen. The deeper glacial soils of south Galway and the fertile Burren valleys yield such rounded boulders.

The ancient craft of wallbuilding originated in the Neolithic period (circa 3800–3200 B.C.), when Ireland's first farmers erected walls alongside burial chambers, such as Poulnabrone in the Burren. Cahers, or forts of the early Christian and early medieval periods, were also built surrounded by double stone walls. The Céide Fields and the burial chambers at Ireland's UNESCO World Heritage sites at Newgrange, as well as the beehive huts on the Skellig Islands, all have dry-stone constructions.

In the 18th and 19th centuries, the walled garden format became popular to protect plants within an artificial environment. Ashlar walls (held together with lime mortar) also appeared. "My first job was working in the walled garden of the Tullira Castle in County Galway with John Fuery, the great stonemason," O'Shaughnessy says, "and we must have mixed enough lime mortar on that job to build the hanging gardens of Babylon.

"Ireland has become the mecca of stonewalling," he says proudly. "You'll see these various types of walls as you drive through the Burren and Connemara; or, to see them all together, the Dry Stone Wall Association of Ireland has a monument with all styles at the Gathering of Stones in Lough Boora Discovery Park, County Offaly." ∎

"Stonewalling is a wonderful tradition, a satisfying job where you get to see the end product, where you work in a team breathing fresh west-of-Ireland air, and where you are literally restoring history."

—Rory O'Shaughnessy

Malin Head, at the tip of County Donegal, the northernmost point on the Wild Atlantic Way

GREAT IRISH DRIVES: WILD ATLANTIC WAY—THE NORTHWEST

The northwestern part of Ireland's Wild Atlantic Way takes you on an odyssey into the lesser traveled regions of the country, from Clifden through the wild expanses of Connemara and northward up the western coastlines to the rugged mountain landscapes of Donegal. (For the southwestern part of this drive, see page 170.)

Trying to keep to a tight schedule here is completely at odds with the local Irish approach to life, where shoppers happily stand in line for half an hour to buy groceries as Biddy Lynch fills shopkeeper Philomena O'Malley in on the news from the next town over. Why rush them? After all, won't it be something to discuss later when there's a lull in the conversation at Danagher's Bar? Switch off the GPS too, as it'll only distract you from the scenery, and in any case, getting lost is a great excuse to stop and talk. And Irish people *love* to talk and share a good story. Take time to enjoy their company; doing otherwise is to bypass one of the Wild Atlantic Way's major entertainments.

On leaving Clifden, head north on the N59, stopping to view spectacular **Kylemore Abbey and gardens** (see page 198). Stop for lunch or supper in Westport, Mayo's liveliest town, where you are guaranteed to find a good traditional Irish music session in full swing.

The rugged north Mayo coastline offers many delights, distractions, and worthwhile detours, including **Achill Island** (see page 309), linked by bridge to the mainland. Once you reach Achill and the glorious, island-dotted seascape of Clew Bay, you have entered the realm of Grace O'Malley, the Pirate Queen and Gaelic Ireland's last great female leader. Take time on your drive to explore the many castles from which the adventurous Grace and the greater O'Malley clan ruled the seas off the west of Ireland in the 16th century (see page 312).

Just inland from Achill and Clew Bay, you will enter the Atlantic boglands of **Wild Nephin National Park** (see page 217), which can be traversed on wooden walkways. A long walk here is a good way to stretch car-weary muscles and to examine up close the variety of plant, animal, and insect life that thrives in the nurturing habitats of these raised boglands.

Farther north in County Mayo, the **Céide Fields** are Ireland's most extensive Neolithic sites, with a Stone Age fort and fascinating exhibits on the first farmers' field systems. These are thought to be the oldest known field systems found anywhere in the world. The site's modern visitors center, perched high on a hilltop overlooking the Atlantic, also provides a welcome break in the journey for lunch or refreshments. A viewing platform on the edge of the 360-foot-high (100 m) cliff is a fine place to pause for reflection along the Wild Atlantic Way. If you decide to hike around the site, don sturdy hiking boots and rainwear, as the terrain and the weather can be unforgiving.

Rosses Point, just outside Sligo, is a picturesque village and peninsula where the tabletop mountain of **Benbulben** lurches into view. You are now in Yeats Country; stop to pay your respects to Ireland's finest poet and Nobel laureate and enjoy the artifacts that tell the story of a literary life in Sligo's **Yeats Memorial Building.**

Continuing north, the landscapes of Donegal soon surround you with their own epic works of creation, none more astounding than **Slieve League Cliffs** (see page 232). Time your arrival well before dusk and drive to the parking lot halfway up the steep mountainside, where a viewing plat-

form faces the sheer cliffs that soar some 1,955 feet (596 m) above the ocean breakers. Energetic hikers can climb to the summit for sensational views of the Atlantic at its wildest.

From Ardara, just to the north, the N56 takes you along a scenic string of remote towns on the Donegal coastline and just inland, including An Clochán Liath (Dunglow) and Gweedore. Stop at the Victorian castle domain of **Glenveagh National Park** (see page 236) and savor Donegal's daunting natural drama at ground level on a long walk. Wear that warm woolen sweater that you've bought on your Irish travels, and a good raincoat, as the bracing winds of the north are often laden with moisture accumulated over the Atlantic and unleashed in a sudden downpour. To experience the region's changeable climate from a somewhat drier, warmer vantage point, and to *really* immerse yourself in the wild Atlantic experience, spend a night or two in a lighthouse keeper's cottage at Fanad Head (see page 321).

The desolate wilderness of this long drive north runs out at **Malin Head,** the stunning northernmost point in Ireland. From here, the Wild Atlantic Way ends in a wistful spin down to Derry—via a stop into the revived Celtic Rainforest at **Wild Ireland** (see page 240)—and a return to the creature comforts of city life. ∎

Wild Atlantic Way, North Drive

A bog oak dominates the Céide Fields Visitor Centre in County Mayo.

Guests can enjoy a traditional afternoon tea in the Connaught Room, with fine views of the castle's gardens and Lough Corrib.

Special Places

Ashford Castle

Step inside Ashford Castle and you're instantly charmed by an old-world elegance and steeped in timeless Irish hospitality. This 800-year-old castle, built by Normans and once the hunting retreat of the Guinness brewing dynasty, sits majestically on the banks of Lough Corrib and is now one of National Geographic's Unique Lodges of the World.

You're welcomed by staff eager to make you feel like a lady or a lord. You also find yourself among the ghosts of history. Legends linger here about the Irish Pirate Queen Grace O'Malley, Princess Grace of Monaco, and Ronald Reagan, all guests once lulled by the peaceful ease of this stately retreat.

The castle's location is idyllically Irish. To the west, across the Maumturk Mountains, rugged Connemara landscapes sweep wildly to the Atlantic. Take any trail down a leafy lane on the Ashford estate and you'll hear lake breezes sough through exotic trees, many planted by Guinnesses, who commanded ship captains to bring back saplings from global voyages. A discerning eye will find the forests here filled with sequoias, cork trees, bamboo, and palm trees, nurtured by fertile soils and Ireland's temperate island climate. The castle also has a history of absorbing foreign transplants hospitably. An invading Norman family built the first castle tower in 1228 to keep out the fearsome O'Flahertys, one of Connacht's wilder tribes. Once ensconced, the de Burgos would, over centuries, become "more Irish than the Irish themselves," coming to be known locally as de Burcas (in Gaelic) or the Burkes.

The Guinness family owned Ashford Castle between 1852 and 1932. This was their summer home; in winter they returned with aristocratic peers to shoot woodcock, snipe, and pheasant. George V, Prince of Wales, was guest of honor at the 1905 hunt. In 2013, Ashford Castle was bought by the Tollmans, South African hoteliers who set about restoring the building under the guidance of a conservation architect and reviving its distinguished cultural heritage.

The estate offers gourmands a choice of three restaurants, as well as Mrs. Bee's tea shop, which sells local produce and crafts. After a day spent outdoors, guests can relax at the Prince of Wales Bar, enjoy a single malt in the billiards room, or catch a classic movie in the on-site cinema. Or descend for a wine tasting in a 19th-century tunnel or luxuriate in a state-of-the-art spa. Whatever you do here, you'll leave modern life far behind and step back into a world of timeless elegance. ■

IN THE KNOW: THE SPORTING LIFE

The Ashford estate has a proud tradition of entertaining guests with activities beyond the castle walls. Through the hotel, guests can hire a local expert for fly-fishing on Lough Corrib, book a round of golf on the nine-hole course, or get maps for walks around the estate and beyond. The hotel also offers Pashley British Army bikes to the intrepid. Located on-site, Ireland's School of Falconry offers Hawk Walks, where you can experience an active hunt with a Harris's hawk (*Parabuteo unicinctus*) on the estate. You'll also encounter peregrine falcons and a Eurasian eagle-owl, and learn of the swift boxes installed on the castle's bell tower to house birds that regulate the number of vermin and midges around the lake. For guests who fancy a birds-eye view of the forests, tree-climbing and zip-lining are also on offer. Lough Corrib stretches 40 miles (64 km) south to Galway and affords some of Europe's finest fishing, with the Corrib and its tributaries teeming with northern pike, perch, roach, trout, and salmon.

In addition, guests and nonguests alike can take a boat cruise to the monastic ruins of Inchagoill Island for a quiet moment at St. Patrick's Church. Or riders can trek through the estate's lush woodlands on an Irish Draught horse via the Ashford Equestrian Centre. The school here caters to English- and Western-style riders of every level; children will thrill to a ride on a tiny Connemara pony. For the competitive, there are also lessons in archery and clay pigeon shooting, perhaps accompanied by a sporting bet to be settled later at the George V Bar. Whatever activities you pursue, the fresh west-of-Ireland air is a real tonic for body and soul. ■

The beautiful grounds of the Ashford estate have several trails through gardens and wilderness that make for memorable horseback riding.

Lough Corrib is believed to have some 365 islands ("one for every day of the year," as locals say), depending on water levels.

Insider's Guide

Lough Corrib & Its Islands

Lough Corrib is an angler's paradise that shimmers across the low-lying karst landscape of Galway and Mayo. The lake supposedly has some 365 islands, depending on water levels.

Corrib Cruises runs one- and two-hour trips daily from Ashford Castle, Oughterard, and Lisloughrey Pier. Patrick and David Luskin, brothers whose family has plied these waters for generations, provide a rich historical and cultural commentary. In summer, the boats stop at Inchagoill ("island of the devout stranger"), site of two ancient churches. The older church is believed to have been built by Lugnaedon, a hermit and nephew of St. Patrick. The upright stone of Lugnaedon here dates back to the sixth century. This pillar's original ogham (early medieval alphabet) script, deemed pagan, was covered over with crosses probably around the seventh century, but records remain. Nearby is Teampall na Naoimb, or "church of the saints," a Hiberno-Romanesque church with a 12th-century arched doorway.

The many religious sites around Lough Corrib suggest this was a sacred lake in ancient times. The recent discovery of multiple wooden boats on the lake bed, some dating from the Iron Age, has fortified this belief. The find was made by a mariner, Captain Trevor Northage, while mapping the lake floor for the fishing fraternity. Hollowed-out log boats showed up on his scanner, some retaining evidence of fire in their centers, suggesting sacrificial offerings —perhaps to the pagan sun god Belenus, or to Manannán mac Lir, the Son of the Sea. ∎

GREAT IRISH DRIVES: THE SHORES OF LOUGH CORRIB

The savvy Wild Atlantic wayfarer should allow a full day to drive along the shores of Ireland's second largest lough, seeking out the tales and treasures that lead locals to believe that this is Ireland's sacred lake.

Start out of Galway on the N59 Clifden Road. When you reach Moycullen, turn right between stone-walled fields and thick hedges for a few miles to Carrowmoreknock, where there is a peaceful jetty with boats and a view over Lough Corrib to the mountains. At the next T-junction, turn left to the N59, then right to resume your drive. In two miles (3 km), a sign on the right leads to **Aughnanure Castle,** the six-story abode of the "ferocious O'Flahertys" bristling with murder holes, secret rooms, and bartizan side turrets, enclosed in a walled ward with its own picturesque lookout tower.

Back on the N59, continue to the little town of Oughterard. Keep an eye out for the sign on the right that points to the Lakeshore Road 3, a meandering five-mile (8 km) drive through intensely green and lush backcountry to the shores of the lake at Currain. Return to Oughterard by the same route and follow the N59 northwest to Maam Cross, a meeting point that lies bleak and exposed in the bogland. Here a signed turning on the right leads over wild moors to Maam (aka Maum), where you turn right on the R345 for Cong.

Soon Lough Corrib appears, offering superb views and opportunities for bird-watching. Along this road you can spy **Hen's Island** (see page 312), the Corrib castle of Grace O'Malley, Ireland's Pirate Queen. Continue along the R345 to Cong, a beautifully kept village. At the far end, you'll come to the ruins of **Cong Abbey,** a handsome gray-stone monastery founded in 1128. Carved flowers, leaves, and tendrils still decorate the pillar capitals, with tiny staring stone heads peeping out among the leaves. From here, a walk along the River Corrib rewards with the Monk's Fishing House and, across the bridge, a National Geographic-

sponsored Fishers of Men memorial. Ashford Castle guests will start their loop drive of the lake from here.

From Cong, follow the R346 to Cross, then the R334 southeast to Headford, where you'll see signs to the glorious monastic ensemble of **Ross Errilly Friary** set out in the fields by the sullen Black River. Under the slim church tower, the 14th- and 15th-century buildings stand simple and perfect—the best preserved Franciscan friary in Ireland. Elaborate and evocative tombs abound here, such as that of Hugh O'Flaherty under the east window. Huge fireplaces, spouts, chutes, and bread ovens give an eerie feeling of monkish presence.

Five miles (8 km) south of Headford, another detour from the N84 brings you into the lakeside townland of Annaghdown. Turn right immediately past the graveyard (following the "Annaghdown Pier" sign) to find the blunt and undecorated ruins of **Annaghdown Priory,** which makes for a complete contrast to the architectural elegance of Ross Errilly Friary. St. Brendan the Navigator died here in A.D. 577 after an adventurous life on land and at sea, nursed by his sister Brigid in the nunnery he had founded. Return to the N84 and turn right for your journey back to Galway. ∎

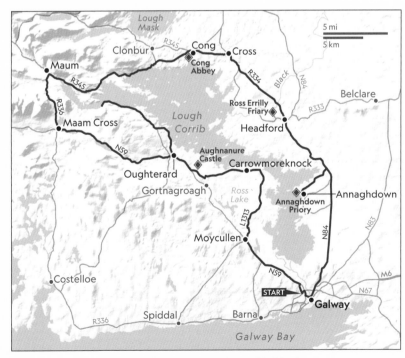

Lough Corrib and Islands Drive: Start out from Galway or from Ashford Castle.

Nestled in the heart of Connemara, along the Wild Atlantic Way, Kylemore Abbey is a haven of history, beauty, and serenity.

Special Places

Kylemore Abbey

About three miles (5 km) north of Letterfrack on the N59 awaits one of Ireland's most photographed houses, the mock-Tudor Kylemore Abbey.

Sitting dramatically on Polla-cappul Lough, which mirrors the abbey and the ever changing Connemara skies, the gleaming structure is faced with Kingstown granite shipped from the quarry at Dalkey on Ireland's east coast. The stories behind this magnificent edifice—now a convent—contain an opera's worth of drama and tragedy.

Kylemore House was originally built in the 1860s by Mitchell Henry, a wealthy businessman and liberal Member of Parliament in London, as a gift for his beloved wife, Margaret. The magnificent baronial castle and 15,000-acre (6,000 ha) estate of bogs, mountains, and lakes later passed through the hands of several owners after Henry sold Kylemore in 1902—the Earl of Manchester, an inveterate gambler, proved a predictably short-term proprietor. Eventually Kylemore was bought by the Belgian nuns of the Benedictine Order in 1920. The nuns, fleeing war-ravaged Ypres, found a peaceful sanctuary here in Connemara.

Tours of the house run regularly, mainly taking in the ground-floor rooms where guests were entertained; visitors seeking a quiet corner for spiritual contemplation can head for the church in a nearby garden. This miniature cathedral is a neo-Gothic delight, constructed by Henry as a memorial for his wife after Margaret died of dysentery while traveling in Egypt. The couple now lie together in the nearby mausoleum.

The name Kylemore comes from An Choill Mór, meaning "large

woodland." Henry planted more than 300,000 trees on his new estate, mainly oak, ash, sycamore, and conifers. Today these woods form an elegant green curtain behind the abbey, a steep wilderness that provides sharp contrast to the estate's six acres (2.4 ha) of formal Victorian walled gardens, which form an oasis of order under the unruly ruggedness of the Connemara Mountains. The gardens, designed by Henry's French gardener, James Garnier, included some 21 centrally heated greenhouses (fired by lime kiln) erected to grow bananas and grapes; several have now been restored.

On-site, Mitchell's Café serves warming soups and stews on cold days, as well as the usual teas, coffees, and snacks, and sells baked and cooked products made by the Benedictine sisters themselves. Lead us not into temptation, but the nuns make a wicked line of irresistible handmade chocolates. ∎

IRISH HISTORY: THE CELTIC REVIVAL AT COOLE PARK

At the turn of the 20th century, Irish land reform and rising nationalism threatened to end the power of the Anglo-Irish aristocracy. Many residents of Ireland's country manors were Irish culture's greatest champions, even as the Victorian era of the "big house" drew to a close. A leading light in the literary and artistic movement called the Celtic Revival (also known as the Celtic Twilight) was Lady Augusta Gregory, whose Coole Park estate in Galway is now open to the public as a nature reserve of approximately 1,000 acres (4 sq km) located west of Gort. Several miles of signposted trails and a formal 18th-century walled garden await the intrepid visitor.

In addition to establishing societies for the promotion of the Irish language, Lady Gregory also welcomed many distinguished artists and writers to Coole Park, among them playwright George Bernard Shaw and Ireland's greatest poet, W. B. Yeats, whose Hiberno-Norman 14th-century tower house at Thoor Ballylee was just three miles (5 km) away. Yeats composed "Coole Park, 1929" as a paean to Lady Gregory's home and its role in the revival of Irish literature. At the apex of World War I, he wrote one of his best loved poems, "The Wild Swans at Coole," using the birds at Coole Park and their lakeside domain as a metaphor for a changing world. The death of Lady Gregory's only son, Robert, a pilot killed in the Great War, inspired the Yeats poem "An Irish Airman Foresees His Death."

Despite all the changes wrought in Yeats's Ireland throughout the 20th century, Coole Park retains a fascinating natural monument to the Celtic Revival in the Autograph Tree, where guests of the estate inscribed their names into the bark of a towering copper beech tree. The result reads like a who's who of the Celtic Revival: Aside from those of Shaw and Yeats, the bark still bears the autographs of playwrights Sean O'Casey and J. M. Synge, mystic poet/novelist George William Russell, and novelist George Moore. The tree also shows the mark of Douglas Hyde, the first president of Ireland, incised when independence was but a distant dream.

Twenty-first century ecological changes in the west of Ireland might prove more damaging for Coole Park than the previous century's political upheavals. In 2014, disease forced the felling of many trees. Climate change has brought disastrous flooding to farms in the region, including to Yeats's tower at Thoor Ballylee, forcing what Seamus Heaney called the "most important building in Ireland" to close until funds are secured for permanent restoration.

The idea of towers as safe creative spaces, hideaways of artists, and repositories of great art stretches back to the early Irish monks, who crafted their masterpieces by beeswax candlelight in the early Middle Ages. ∎

Coole Park has several miles of signposted trails.

Ballynahinch Castle Hotel is set within 700 acres (283 ha) of woodland below the inspiring backdrop of the Twelve Bens mountain range.

IN THE KNOW: WHERE TO STAY, EAT & DRINK IN GALWAY

Galway is the heart of the welcoming west of Ireland, and the city is an idyllic place to wander, taste the best of Irish food and drink, enjoy the arts, and sleep in late next morning. Book well ahead if you're visiting during one of the major festivals, or stay outside the city and travel in for the events. Treat yourself to some fresh west-of-Ireland air at one of Connemara's many fine hotels.

HOTELS

Abbeyglen Castle Hotel *(Sky Road, Clifden)* The Abbeyglen overlooks the town of Clifden. Let the sound of wild Atlantic waves soothe you to sleep after a fresh seafood supper or a dinner of Connemara lamb in the hotel's restaurant.

    Ballynahinch Castle Hotel *(Sky Road, Clifden)* is an elegant manor house overlooking a private lake against a backdrop of the Twelve Bens mountains. Fishing, woodland walking, and cycling will give you an appetite for the fine fare in the hotel's Owenmore Restaurant overlooking a salmon-filled river. Or try the delicious Killary prawns, organic venison, or woodcock at the Fisherman's Pub & Ranji Room.

    The Connemara Coast *(Connemara)* Located right on Galway Bay, this remote retreat is just a 10-minute drive from Galway City. The swimming pool and gym are excellent ways to work up an appetite for the choice of superb restaurants on-site here. **Renvyle House** *(Connemara Loop, Renvyle)* A historic estate house in the wilds of Connemara, Renvyle House offers extensive grounds with a private freshwater lake for fishing and boating and an outdoor heated swimming pool. The Rusheenduff Restaurant has an excellent locally inspired menu supervised by award-winning chef Tim O'Sullivan.

RESTAURANTS

Aniar (*53 Lower Dominick Street, Galway*) In this cutting-edge restaurant, chef-owner J. P. McMahon presents a wonderfully creative take on the best of west-of-Ireland produce. The tasting menu is a spectacular spectrum of local flavors, including pear, tarragon, cucumber, yogurt, oyster, mackerel, arrow grass, elderberry, kelp, and sea buckthorn.

Ard Bia at Nimmos (*Long Walk, Galway*) Situated beside the Spanish Arch, Ard Bia is a perfect prelude, or conclusion, to a ramble around Galway's Long Walk. Harissa-steamed mussels with Gubeen chorizo, orange, and coriander followed by the Irish cheeseboard with Crozier Blue, Durrus, and St. Tola make for perfect marching orders.

Pizza and Pasta Napoli (*15 Cross Street, Galway*) Situated next to Tigh Neachtain's friendly pub in Galway's Latin Quarter (see below), this delightfully intimate Italian eatery serves up generous slices of pizza or whole pies.

Upstairs@West (*The Twelve Hotel, Barna Village*) West Restaurant presents contemporary dishes with a knowing nod to the finest Irish culinary traditions. All dishes are prepared in season and cooked to order using the best of the region's local produce. The low lighting, champagne bar, cozy booths, and dark wood decor give West the elegant feel of a hip club restaurant right in the heart of Connemara.

WA Café (*13 New Dock Street, Galway*) This Japanese eatery owned by master chef Yoshimi Hayakawa offers some of the best sushi anywhere in Ireland.

PUBS

The Crane Bar (*2 Sea Road, Galway*) Don't miss this legendary establishment, where musicians entertain seven nights a week. It's a grand place to enjoy an Irish whiskey and sit listening to the lovely lilt of Galwegian accents murmuring mellifluously all around you.

The Dáil (*corner of Cross Street & Middle Street, Galway*) is a fine spot to catch a GAA or soccer or rugby game, especially if the local Tribesmen or Tribeswomen (Galway county teams) are in action. The cocktails are great, the menu will please all-comers, and—as long you're not wearing a Kerry or Dublin shirt—the Dáil will always extend the warmest of Galway welcomes.

Garavan's (*46 William Street, Galway*) has the city's best whiskey selection and, with its cozy fireplaces and warm atmosphere, there are few more restful places to spend a wild, wet evening when those Atlantic winds are doing their worst. The building dates back to medieval Galway. A tip for the morning after a long Galway night out: Garavan's serves one of the best Irish coffees anywhere in Ireland.

The Quays (*11 Quay Street, Galway*) is one of the city's great music venues, with an elevated stage and a vibrant party atmosphere. For almost 400 years, taverns such as this on Quay Street have attracted revelers from all corners of the globe who found themselves in the City of the Tribes with brass in pocket and shore leave to enjoy. The Quays' music hall is open seven nights a week during the summer, showcasing both local and international bands.

Tigh Neachtain (*17 Cross Street, Galway*) With a delightful all-wooden interior, Tigh Neachtain is located across the road from the famous Druid Theatre. With an excellent restaurant upstairs (the Kasbah Kitchen), an outdoor seating area, and frequent trad music sessions, there's always drama aplenty here in one of Galway's favorite pubs. ∎

Tigh Neachtain: a favored watering hole among Galwegians

MAYO

The traveler with a taste for history seeking places where prehistoric Ireland and the ancient Celtic world still resonate should be sure to head to the ruggedly scenic county of Mayo. The Gaelic world's greatest adventuress, Grace O'Malley (aka Granuaile) made coastal Mayo and Galway her wild Atlantic realm at the turn of the 16th century, when Elizabethan England ruled the waves.

From her battlements in Clew Bay and down the coastline, Ireland's Pirate Queen set sail to plunder the shipping lanes between colonial Europe and the Americas. A new Granuaile Trail celebrates this legendary seawoman. The village of Killala in the northwest of the county was the site of a French invasion in 1798, another part of Mayo's rich history of maritime adventure.

The farming and building methods of Ireland's first settlers can be explored in the Céide Fields museum and archaeological site. The story of recent rural life in Ireland—from the 1850s to the 1950s—is told in a series of exhibits in the Museum of Country Life just outside Castlebar. Towns such as Ballina, Foxford, and Swinford tell their own stories of a countryside with a parallel history in emigrant cities such as Boston, San Francisco, and Sydney. (U.S. president Joe Biden's emigrant story began with Edward Blewitt leaving Ballina in 1850.)

Today lovers of traditional Irish music flock to the cozy pubs of Westport, Mayo's party town. Beyond here, the Mayo boglands stretch westward to the ocean, encompassing extensive Gaeltachts (Irish-speaking regions). The raised Atlantic boglands and mountains make for great hiking and bird- and wildlife-watching in Wild Nephin National Park.

Another peak, Croagh Patrick, is Ireland's holy mountain and as such is a place of pilgrimage for souls devoted to the patron saint. The sacred peak overlooks Clew Bay and the islands of Mayo, which offer unrivaled beaches and opportunities for adventure sports. ∎

Clew Bay as seen from the slopes of Croagh Patrick: County Mayo offers unrivaled hiking, biking, and adventure sports.

The Museum of Country Life in Turlough Park, near Castlebar, presents a stunning architectural juxtaposition of old and new.

Special Places

The Museum of Country Life

Between the towns of Westport and Ballina lies Mayo's county seat, Castlebar. While not on the Wild Atlantic Way's marked driving route, it's worth taking an inland detour here to visit one of Ireland's most attractive and culturally revealing museums. The Museum of Country Life in Turlough Park, some five miles (8 km) outside Castlebar, is the only branch of the National Museum of Ireland outside Dublin; the museums of Archaeology, Decorative Arts and History, and Natural History are all in the capital.

All four branches of the National Museum of Ireland illuminate their subject matter in their own unique way—from bog bodies (Archaeology) to Ice Age mammals (Natural History) to historical Irish fashion (Decorative Arts and History). One of the Museum of Country Life's central exhibits tells the story of rural Ireland between 1850 and 1950, and thus its artifacts and stories still resonate richly with emigrants who left in the latter half of the 20th century. An early Aer Lingus shoulder bag, for example, would have carried many a

keepsake across the Atlantic in the 1950s and '60s, and would evoke very mixed emotions in Irish hearts.

The Museum of Country Life perches on a hill in the bucolic grounds of Turlough Park House, a High Victorian Gothic edifice dating back to the 1860s that was the ancestral home to the Fitzgerald family of Turlough. Some rooms—including the estate's impressive library, where tenant farmers came to pay their quarterly rent—are now open to the public, offering a glimpse into the lives of the 19th-century gentry in

Ireland. The extensive gardens include a vinery (a special type of greenhouse for grapevines and other fruiting plants), along with several gentle walks, terraces, and a sunken garden. The ruins of the original house (occupied from 1722 to 1786) can still be seen, and a section of the Castlebar River runs through here. Views are further enhanced by an artificial lake with islands that are often adorned with a bevy of swans.

The museum is in a sleek modern building, constructed on the hill above this lake. The rotating exhibitions draw from the National Folklife Collection, an extensive treasury of some 37,000 items. Popular attractions have included the Cross of Cong, from the County Mayo monastic settlement of Cong, a 12th-century processional cross that purportedly contains a piece of the True Cross of Christ; trades and crafts, including online exhibits on building a curragh (a traditional west-of-Ireland fishing boat); and "The Times," a historical exhibit documenting the seismic political upheavals and agricultural changes in Ireland before and after the establishment of the Free State in 1922.

Permanent exhibits at the museum tell fascinating stories about all aspects of rural life, from the story of the humble potato, introduced by Sir Walter Raleigh in late 16th century, to the knitted clothes and woven linens of the peasantry to the tin and metal trades long practiced by Irish Travelers (see page 149). Talks and events are held here regularly to educate the young and old on Irish traditions and ancient ways. For example, a lecture on Samhain, the ancient Celtic winter festival, might explain the culture and history of Irish death traditions, while a children's arts-and-crafts class provides creative instruction on the making of Halloween masks.

The excellent museum shop sells an extensive range of informative books and maps on a variety of local and national subjects, as well as gifts. A great range of tasty fare is available at the on-site café in a charming courtyard setting. Time your visit around midday and you can enjoy a nutritious lunch (or a sticky toffee cake) followed by a leisurely stroll around the exhibits or the gardens of Turlough Park.

Across the road from the museum, the ninth-century Turlough Round Tower stands high on a hill beside the ruins of an 18th-century church. This mysterious lookout has no entrance at its base, and only a single window way up high on the side facing Turlough Park. Who knows what monastic ghosts stare down from its cold core at night upon the moonlit lake of the Fitzgerald estate in the distance—and who knows what other fellow spirits inhabit the sleek building that houses the flotsam of so many bygone Irish lives?

The route of the Castlebar to Turlough Greenway means that museum visitors can start their day off with a gentle cycle or a vigorous walk from Lough Lannagh in Castlebar along a six-mile (10 km), mainly off-road, riverside route that will take them all the way to the Museum of Country Life, passing through some beautiful Mayo countryside and woodlands and taking in many sites of interest along the way. The Greenway is classed as easy to moderate for leisure walkers, and the route is waymarked using fingerpost signage with blue text and symbols on a white background. Visitors wishing to walk from Castlebar to the museum should allow at least two hours. Cycling will take you about an hour from Castlebar. ∎

A vintage photo shows Aran islanders gathering armfuls of seaweed. When mixed with sand, seaweed made soil in which to grow crops atop the limestone bedrock.

Flower-bedecked Westport Bridge spans the Carrowbeg River in the planned 18th-century town of Westport.

Westport & Ballina

Of all the towns along the Wild Atlantic Way, there are few more quintessentially Irish than the Mayo hot spots of Westport and Ballina. These are special places filled with life, even on a dark winter's night, always crackling with traditional Irish music and keen country talk about everything from imminent Atlantic storms to the eternal Mayo quest for the Sam Maguire Cup, the All-Ireland Football title that has accursedly eluded the boys in red and green since 1951 (see page 177).

Visiting Americans might also be engaged in lively conversations about Washington politics. The town of Ballina claims a famous son: President Joe Biden's roots lie in Mayo. In the wake of the Great Famine of the 1840s, Edward Blewitt (1795–1872) and his family were among the million-plus Irish men and women forced to undertake the perilous voyage to the United States.

In 2016, thousands of Coveys (Ballina residents) lined the streets to welcome Edward Blewitt's great-great-great-grandson, then vice president Biden, back to his ancestral home.

Laid out in 1780 by English architect James Wyatt (1746–1813), Westport is one of the rare planned towns in Ireland (most developed in haphazard increments according to historical happenstance). Westport's design was commissioned in the 1780s by John Browne of Westport House. The center followed the Georgian architectural style and incorporated the Carrowbeg River.

Today, Westport retains a certain Georgian-era elegance, especially along the tree-shaded mall that runs along the river. From here, Westport's two parallel main streets run uphill—Bridge Street to the Clock Tower and James Street to the Octagon, with its tall column crowned by a statue of St. Patrick.

One of the town's must-sees is **Westport House,** the stately home of the Marquess of Sligo. The house was built in the 18th century near the site of the original O'Malley Castle. Grace O'Malley was believed to have been born here sometime around 1530, and a bronze statue in the grounds now honors the Pirate Queen. Westport House is located in a lush parkland setting with a lake, terraces, gardens, and views of Clew Bay, the wild Atlantic, and Ireland's holy mountain, Croagh Patrick.

Westport's shops and bars are invariably warm and welcoming. Many pubs have lively traditional music in the evenings, with terrific sessions to be found in the **Porter House, Hoban's,** and **McHale's,** especially during the Westport Music & Arts Festival in October.

The Mayo mecca of music is **Matt Molloy's** on Bridge Street. Here the owner and veteran flautist of the Bothy Band, Planxty, and the Chieftains is just one of any number of master musicians who might show up for a session on any given night.

Another great pub for music, good food, and Mayo-flavored *craic* is the **Quays Bar** on Westport Quay, located about two miles (3 km,) west of town among handsome 18th-century stone warehouses.

From here Westport opens up onto Clew Bay, one of the most beautiful and storied inlets in all of Ireland. This is a wild, windswept seascape, one sprinkled with some 365 islands, including many containing secrets of one of the most piratic and charmingly erratic parts of Ireland. ■

Westport is one of the great Wild Atlantic Way destinations offering a myriad of lively pubs with trad music and good food.

GREAT IRISH DRIVES: GALWAY CITY TO WESTPORT

If you only have a day or two to spend on west coast roads, this spectacular drive through Galway and Mayo is richly rewarding. The road trip from Galway City to the town of Westport constitutes a C-shaped half loop that takes you the length of Galway Bay, along Connemara's coastline, and on up past Killary Fjord. You'll pass through the idyllic village of Leenane and the beauty spots of Mayo, including the breathtaking Doo Lough Pass.

Leaving the city of Galway, take the R336 west, stopping for coffee at **Spiddal Craft Village and Café,** where local artisans sell fine gifts of cloth, glasswork, jewelry, and basketry. Stay on the R336 until you reach Maam Cross, then turn left (west) onto the N59 for Clifden. **Aughnanure Castle,** a well-preserved Norman battlement just past Rosscahill, is worth a look. The fearsome O'Flaherty family ruled west Connacht for 300 years from this six-story tower on the shores of Lough Corrib. In 1546, the O'Flahertys joined forces with the Mayo O'Malleys when Donal an Chogaidh O'Flaherty married Grace O'Malley, the Pirate Queen.

Four miles (7 km) before Clifden, **Dan O'Hara's Homestead Farm** has a terrific tour of a restored pre-famine cottage. The charismatic host, raconteur Martin Walsh, tells the story of Connemara in a vividly entertaining way using poetry, song, and even a sip of "the rare old mountain dew" (*poitín,* or Irish moonshine). The heritage center has an excellent café, or you can stop for lunch in Clifden, where **Mannion's Bar** serves local seafood (the steamed mussels are delicious) and traditional Irish cuisine, including Connemara lamb stew. As you leave Clifden heading north on the N59, a fine detour is the Sky Road, a scenic seven-mile (11 km) loop that takes you to the **Discovery Point** with spectacular views of Clifden Bay, Streamstown Bay, and the Atlantic Ocean. Take the upper road for the best vistas.

Just before Letterfrack, turn right into **Connemara National Park,** a protected area of 7,307 acres (2,957 hectares). The park encompasses the Twelve Bens, a range of mountains that offers a variety of hikes and climbs to suit all-comers. Diamond Hill, accessible from the visitors center in Letterfrack, is the focus of the most popular loop (4.3 miles/7 km). Hikers might spot mountain hares, red deer, and stoats.

Just north of Letterfrack, you'll pass **Kylemore Abbey** (see page 198). From here the landscape becomes mountainous and sweeps you down to one of Ireland's two fjords, Killary,

carved out between the Maumturk Mountains to the south and the Mweelrea Mountains to the north. Look for the extensive fish farms that supply most of the blue-shell mussels served in area restaurants; their distinctive sweet taste comes from the inlet's mix of fresh- and saltwater.

The village of Leenane nestles in one of Connemara's most striking valleys, sheltered by towering mountains. The **Sheep and Wool Centre** here has excellent knits. For a deeper dive into the sheep-rearing process, take the 30-minute drive through the glens inland to **Joyce Country Sheep Farm.** Once there, Joe, the genial owner, directs a thrilling demonstration of the herding skills of his beloved border collies.

Returning to the N59, head north and then turn left onto the smaller R335 toward Louisburgh. The scenery from here just gets more awe-inspiring, especially along the **Doo Lough Pass,** one of the west's best kept secrets. There are numerous pull-off points where photographers like to watch in wonder as they try to capture the shifting shadows and lights of the west of Ireland. In the small town of Louisburgh, the **Granuaile Visitor Centre** tells the story of Ireland's Pirate Queen (see page 310) and the adventurous O'Malley clan.

As you travel east along the R335 toward Westport, the important role that religion has played in this part of Ireland becomes clear. You'll see signs for Kilgeever and Murrisk Abbeys, and between these ancient monasteries looms Ireland's most sacred mountain, **Croagh Patrick.** When you finally reach Westport, stop in for a well-earned pint at **Matt Molloy's** pub on Bridge Street. Sit long enough, and you'll hear the strains of a trad music session starting up. Sip a pint, enjoy the rhythms, and your cares are soon forgotten. ∎

Mayo's green wilderness OPPOSITE: O'Dufaigh's Bar, Louisburgh

Ireland On Screen

The West in Film

The west of Ireland has for decades provided stunning settings for Hollywood movies. In recent years, the Irish film industry has increasingly told its own stories, often set along the Wild Atlantic Way. The filming of John Ford's *The Quiet Man* began in 1951 in the Mayo village of Cong and paired a Hollywood legend, John Wayne, with a Dublin actress, Maureen O'Hara. This story of a boxer returning to his homeland was shot throughout Connemara.

Another Oscar-winning film, *The Field,* adapted from John B. Keane's play, tells the story of land and its importance in Irish life. Shot in and around the beautiful Connemara village of Leenane, the film starred Irish actor Richard Harris as the domineering patriarch Bull McCabe.

The region's spectacular scenery was shown in a darker historical light in the 2018 film *Black '47.* Shot in the style of a Western, the narrative revolves around an Irish Ranger who returns from fighting for the British Army abroad to find his homeland devastated by the Great Famine.

Stories of modern Ireland have been told in several movies starring Brendan Gleeson. In *The Guard,* Gleeson portrays an unconventional Irish policeman forced to work alongside an uptight FBI agent (Don Cheadle) as they track a drug-trafficking operation. Although a comedy, the film tackles issues of 21st-century Ireland, including immigration, racism, and politics.

Gleeson's Irish priest is another nuanced character caught in the cross fire of modern Irish life in *Calvary.* The film begins with a sinner in the confession box admitting to a murder—but the killing isn't due to happen until next "Sunday week." And the victim is Father James himself—"because you're innocent." This surreal take on the Passion of Christ was mostly filmed in the scenic wilds of Sligo's Yeats Country. Both *The Guard* and *Calvary* were written by John Michael McDonagh.

One of the most moving films to emerge from Ireland is Jim Sheridan's *Into the West.* The magic-realist narrative starts amidst the squalor of a Dublin slum, where "Papa" Reilly (Gabriel Byrne) grieves the death of his wife and tries to raise two young sons. The "King of Irish Travelers" is a broken man, but the children's grandfather is a *seanchaí*, a storyteller, who regales them with Irish legends.

He is followed one day from the Irish sea by a white horse called Tír na nÓg ("land of eternal youth"). The animal is stolen and thus begins a journey of rediscovery, as the boys are drawn back into their Traveler culture, escaping the oppressions of settled life. The mythical Tír na nÓg takes them into the west, all the way to the Atlantic coastline, where a dramatic denouement ensues. ∎

Gabriel Byrne and Ellen Barkin star in *Into the West,* a story of Irish Travelers.

IRISH VOICES: THE WHISKEY HISTORIAN

Born in San Francisco, Fionnán O'Connor was studying medieval literature at UC Berkeley when he started a whiskey club in a bar called Beckett's. Another Irishman abroad, Brian Sheehy, who ran several West Coast bars, employed the young enthusiast to proselytize the elixir known in Ireland as *uiscé beatha* (water of life). O'Connor later lectured at Berkeley on the history and appreciation of whiskey while working for Bushmills. He now lives in Dublin.

Discussing whiskey is best done in one of O'Connor's favorite Dublin pubs—the Palace or Bowes—with a pint of Guinness at hand to cleanse the palate of the oily coating that, say, a Powers John's Lane Single Pot Still Whiskey leaves behind.

O'Connor's book, *A Glass Apart,* traces the revival of Irish single-pot still whiskey. This unique Irish taste is "something almost spicy, almost gingery, almost liquoricey, almost like spry grass and with an aroma similar to Christmas pudding," says O'Connor. This whiskey historian also unearthed and re-created several long-lost Irish whiskey recipes using grain mixes called mash bills that date back to the 1800s. "We're talking to ghosts by distilling these again."

O'Connor traces the invention of whiskey to the class of apothecaries called *ollamhí,* who acted as medics in Gaelic chieftains' courts. The *ollamhí* distilled potions to keep the clan in good health. Eventually, they distilled liquor. Interestingly, these spirits were prevalent in the Celtic fringes of Scotland (where it's "whisky," spelled without the e) and Ireland long before they were widely drunk in England.

Whiskey was offered by a host as a booster to one's health, and thus the toast became an expression of Irish hospitality: *Sláinte!* (Good health!). "The *ollamhí* discovered that distilling is really the art of crafting magical tastes from vapors," says O'Connor. The monks later continued this wonderful tradition of sensual apothecary.

Fionnán O'Connor, whiskey historian and bon viveur, hard at work

The homemade version of whiskey was *poitín,* a smoky drink made on small stills, but not, as myth often claims, from potatoes. "There is little sugar in potatoes," O'Connor explains. "Most *poitín* was made from malt grain, barley, or oats, just like moonshine was made from maize. The raw barley, which gives a marzipan taste, malt, and wheat combine to give Irish whiskey that lovely oily viscosity that coats your tongue." The English eventually taxed these homemade spirits, and, starting in 1661, made *poitín* illegal. Of course, small-still distilleries persisted in the highlands of Scotland and along the remote west coast and islands off Ireland.

And, what, according to O'Connor, is the best Irish whiskey today? "It's hard to beat that oily taste of Redbreast or the unfathomable delights of Green Spot," he says. "Actually, that's an impossible question," he laughs. "But I'll keep working on an answer for you!" ∎

"Guinness and whiskey are the yin and yang of the Irish taste buds."

—Fionnán O'Connor

A hawthorn fairy tree and fence near Killary Harbour are festooned with strips of cloth, offerings by those seeking favors from the *aos sí* (fairies).

Irish Heritage

Irish Ways & Irish Laws

The story of every island is one of invasion. In Ireland, conquest was followed by absorption, as a charm offensive kicked in to seduce the invader into adopting Irish ways, if not always Irish laws. The Norman settlers of the 12th century were not the first to find themselves becoming "more Irish than the Irish themselves."

According to the *Leabhar Gabhála*—Ireland's earliest book—the first inhabitants here traveled from Greece, led by Parthalon, 300 years after the Deluge. The next settlers were Nemed and his sons, who soon scattered. However, one group settled to worship the sun, the rain, and the land. The Fir Bolg, or Bag Men, carried small bags of rich earth to make lands fertile for farming.

The Tuatha Dé Danann were the legendary People of Danu, the earth goddess. They ousted the Fir Bolg and brought druidism, philosophy, and magic to Ireland. Irish life became imbued with their love of poetry, music, and song. These feminine graces were counterbalanced with the masculine traits of the warriorlike Celts, who invaded from Spain to claim their island of destiny, Inisfáil. The Tuatha Dé Danann went into the earth, the enchanted forests, and the "thin places" of Celtic mysticism, where their Otherworld can be reached from our reality. Chief among these sacred places are holy wells, where pagan gods were worshipped, and, later, Christian saints. The fluidity of water—a feminine element—meant the veil between worlds was thin here.

The Tuatha still inhabit the land of the *aos sí,* or the fairies. Irish people hang votive ribbons on a fairy tree (usually a rowan or mountain ash) to request their help. The *sí* might trap a gifted musician in a fairy ring (a circle of mushrooms) for days, as they spirit them to play at a wedding in the Otherworld. Yeats's poem "The Stolen Child" recounts the common experience of a child taken by fairies "to the waters and the wild" who returns as a "changeling." To this day, the Irish fear invoking the ire of the *sí:* A motorway in Galway was rerouted recently as builders refused to cut down a fairy tree.

The earliest traces of human construction and agriculture in Ireland are found at Mayo's archaeological site of the Céide Fields (see page 193). In the 1930s, schoolteacher Patrick Caulfield investigated the ancient stone walls unearthed by turf-cutters in the boglands of Ballycastle. In the 1970s, his son, Dr. Seamus Caulfield, traced the patterns of a 5,000-year-old farming landscape buried in the bog.

With these boundaries came laws of the land, formalized into the Brehon Law of medieval Ireland. Brehon Law gave women many notable rights. Ownership of property continued after marriage, and a woman could divorce after a year and a day of wedlock. Women could also rise to positions of power.

The last great Gaelic female leader was the remarkable Grace O'Malley (1530-1603; see page 310), aka Granuaile, who saw the Irish aristocracy and their language forced west, given the choice of going "to hell or to Connacht." The Flight of the Earls for mainland Europe in 1607, led by Hugh O'Neill and Rory O'Donnell, marked the end of the old Gaelic order.

The Elizabethans swept aside Irish laws that had withstood four centuries of Norman invasions. The 1366 Statutes of Kilkenny, for example, sought to curtail Irish cultural influence, but failed. Instead, the Norman newcomers took on the Irish language, along with many Gaelic names and customs. It helped too that both natives and settlers were Christian.

This process of easy adaptation had prevailed 1,000 years previously with the coming of Christianity to Ireland. Tolerance and a disgust at injustice run deep in Irish DNA, so Christianity proved an easy sell. The tenets of Celtic society were loyalty, courage, and generosity. St. Patrick applied the Christian virtues of faith, hope, and charity to appeal to these native values.

The pillaging Vikings, the scourge of monastic Ireland, were similarly absorbed, many eventually settling as traders in Dublin, Wexford, and Waterford. All of the invaders—Scandinavians, French, and English alike—encountered the Irish mindset of demanding justice for injury suffered, embedded in Brehon Law: A wolf bite required restitution from the beast's owner; a family whose patriarch was killed then became the financial responsibility of the murderer.

The Penal Laws of the 17th and 18th centuries, another attempt to suppress Irish ways, merely drove native culture and the Catholic religion underground. The Irish used sacred pagan places to celebrate "rock masses" and educated their children in "hedge schools." Although English replaced Gaelic as the language of Ireland, the Celtic Revival (also called the Celtic Twilight) of the late 19th century sparked a resurgence that led to independence in the 20th century, and Irish children still attend Gaeltacht schools (see page 186) each summer.

De Valera's constitution of 1937, which once more formalized Irish laws for Irish people, has since evolved to meet the social demands of an ever changing Ireland. Granuaile would approve of one change in 21st-century Ireland: An Irishwoman's right to divorce has been restored. The woman who sailed to Greenwich, London, for an audience with Queen Elizabeth I might also have smiled when Queen Elizabeth II visited Ireland.

The Irish have withstood multiple invasions, not only with a Celtic warrior mentality of resistance but also via an Irish adeptness for diplomacy in the form of storytelling and hospitality. The Irish stance seems to be "So you're invading? Well, you're welcome anyway, leave your weapons at the door, and sit and drink by the fire. We have a good story for you. Our story." ∎

Mayo's sacred mountain of Croagh Patrick is Ireland's oldest pilgrimage destination, its paths well worn by thousands of Irish Christians.

Ireland's Sacred Mountain

The Egyptians have Mount Sinai. The Japanese have Mount Fuji. For the Irish, the summit to reach to get closer to God is **Croagh Patrick.** This sacred Mayo mountain is renowned as the site of Ireland's oldest pilgrimage, a destination of deep spiritual meaning for Irish Christians. The well-worn trails on its rocky sides are dotted with the devout no matter when you visit.

Many climb Croagh Patrick on Reek Sunday, the last Sunday in July, a tradition originating with the Celtic festival of Lughnasadh. This harvest thanksgiving to Lugh, pagan god of the Tuatha Dé Danann (a divine Irish race), was celebrated on various high grounds, and Saint Patrick probably recognized the Mayo mountain as the most sacred among the pagan natives he sought to convert.

Ireland's patron saint fasted here for 40 days and nights in A.D. 441. Today the climb is a communal experience for the Irish faithful, and the most visceral way for visitors to experience the psychic pull of this sacred place. The conical Croagh Patrick is about six miles (10 km) west of Westport and rises 2,510 feet (765 m) above Clew Bay. Below, multiple islands dot the bay, "like so many dolphins and whales basking there," in the words of the Victorian British traveler W. M. Thackeray.

From the mountaintop church, called **St. Patrick's Oratory,** Nephin Mountain is visible, with the bulk of Achill Island and Blacksod Bay completing the spectacular panorama.

Starting at medieval **Murrisk**

Abbey, pilgrims follow a stony pathway along the foothills. Vendors sell walking sticks, particularly useful for the stony descents. The path takes you past the **National Famine Memorial** (see page 227), a huge sculpture of a "coffin ship," and on toward the iconic statue of St. Patrick. The trail then leads to a series of stations, where believers stop to pray and often to circle seven times. The **First Station,** Leacht Benáin, is a circular cairn, where Benáin (St. Benignus) is believed to be buried.

Pilgrims walking along the Cosán Phádraig ("Patrick's way") from Ballintubber Abbey often join the climb here. On this well-trod pathway, you'll see Lough Nacorra below, where the saint supposedly banished the demon Corra. North of this is Log na nDeamhan ("hollow of the demons"), where Patrick banished all snakes from Ireland. According to legend, the cacodemons (marvelously named malevolent reptiles) attacked at the summit of the reek, but the snake banishing saint drove them underground, throwing his black bell after them.

The **Second Station,** at the mountain's summit, is the church and Leaba Phádraig ("Patrick's bed"), a layer of rocks on which the saint slept during his 40-day stay.

The final **Third Station** is Rellig Mhuire, a triangle of stone cairns dedicated to Mary, which may have once been the burial site of a pagan goddess. The cairns are located on the descent along the western Lecanvey slope.

While the climb is its own spiritual reward, many relieved revenants celebrate their return at **Campbell's Bar** in nearby Murrisk with a sincere thanksgiving toast to Ireland's favorite saint and deliverer from evil. ▪

IRISH HISTORY: STATION ISLAND & IRISH PILGRIMAGES

The Irish psyche was receptive to the Christian notion of pilgrimage when St. Patrick set out to convert the island's fifth-century pagans. The Celts were a seafaring people, long used to great quests, and the animism of their pagan faith meant that sun worship, for example, could easily be transferred to a practice of sacrifice in anticipation of a new dawn. Such may have been the thinking behind the long-observed tradition of climbing Croagh Patrick by night, a trek echoed on sacred mountains worldwide.

Patrick also left a legacy of sacrificial struggles in dark, subterranean places, the most infamous being **St. Patrick's Purgatory,** an ancient pilgrimage site on Lough Derg, County Donegal. According to legend, Christ showed Patrick purgatory, whose entryway was a cave on Station Island. The island became the endpoint of a medieval pilgrimage route from Drogheda to Kells along the Boyne River, most likely stopping at Mellifont, Slane, and Donaghmore. Pilgrims probably headed northwest toward Enniskillen before sailing up Lough Erne and then on to Lough Derg.

Today, Lough Derg is host to a three-day pilgrimage. Pilgrims fast starting at midnight and are ferried out to Station Island early the next day. There they are assigned a dormitory room and, barefoot, begin a continuous cycle of prayer and liturgies. They pass the first night praying in the island's basilica and only sleep on the second night. Pilgrims have one meal a day of dry toast, oatcakes, and black tea or coffee. On the third morning, they return to the mainland, continuing their fast until midnight. In the last century, the Mayo town of **Knock** became Ireland's prime pilgrim destination, due largely to its international airport, opened in 1986 after years of lobbying by a local priest, Father James Horan. The faithful believe Our Lady, St. Joseph, and St. John the Evangelist appeared to Knock villagers in 1879. Today, 1.5 million pilgrims visit the shrine at Knock each year. ▪

Pilgrims descend after climbing Croagh Patrick.

On board the International Space Station, NASA astronaut Catherine Coleman plays a flute on loan from the Chieftains' Matt Molloy.

The Irish Abroad

The Irish in Space

As Oscar Wilde, that master of the bon mot, proclaimed: "We are all in the gutter, but some of us are looking at the stars." Wilde himself epitomized the star-crossed lover who sought solace in nature's beauty, trusting his fate to the heavens above. Indeed, the Irish are a fiercely superstitious and fatalistic race, so it's small wonder that they've long been entranced by all things astrological and, more recently, astronomical.

The Neolithic designers of Newgrange had an eye on the sky when they designed tombs with entryways sited to fill with the sun's rays on the winter solstice. Celtic Druids practiced an astrology based on the 13 cycles of the moon, with each phase linked to a sacred tree. The early Irish were also sun worshippers, burning votive boats that would carry the sunken sun back to the surface by dawn.

The Victorian age brought out a desire to study the stars up close. In the early 1840s, the third Earl of Rosse designed and built the world's largest telescope, known as the Levi-athan of Parsonstown, at Birr Castle in County Offaly. In the 21st century, the fate of partitioned Ireland became a subject for America's favorite science fiction show, *Star Trek: The Next Generation.* In "The High Ground," Lieutenant Commander Data cites the reunification of Ireland in 2024 as an example of terrorism effecting political change. The episode was banned by the BBC.

A more harmonic cultural exchange came in 2011, when NASA astronaut Catherine "Cady" Coleman played a flute belonging to the Chieftains'

Matt Molloy and a tin whistle belonging to Paddy Moloney while aboard the International Space Station (ISS). The American in orbit accompanied the band as they recorded a traditional arrangement in Dublin for a track titled "The Chieftains in Orbit." Another Irish musical crew, U2, used the spacecraft-shaped "claw" stage of their 360° Tour to televise live images of nightly conversations with ISS astronauts. Bono's dreams of changing the world had finally gone stratospheric.

The Irish imagination still reaches heavenward and the Irish still gaze at the stars. But they do so now via space-age technology, such as Ireland's first satellite, the Educational Irish Research Satellite, EIRSAT-1, built at the UCD Centre for Space Research. Perhaps the finest Irish gift to gutterbound stargazers was the filmmaker Emer Reynolds's awe-inspiring documentary on the Voyager program, *The Farthest*.

We'll leave the last word, as ever, to Oscar Wilde: "We shall not die, / The Universe itself shall be our Immortality." ■

IN THE KNOW: WILD NEPHIN NATIONAL PARK

Stargazers in Ireland regularly head to northwest Mayo, where the light pollution of Irish cities fades to black. Here in Ballycroy, Ireland's newest national park extends wooden walkways over an expansive Atlantic blanket bog for walkers, and campers sleep beneath the deep, dark galactic dome of an unspoiled night sky. Wild Nephin is Ireland's first International Dark Sky Park.

Ballycroy's isolated setting to the west of Mayo's mountains allows visitors to feel they've escaped the modern world. With the peaks at your back, you can gaze westward toward the Atlantic waters beyond the western seaboard and Achill Island. Nephin Mountain comes from the Gaelic *néifinn,* meaning "heavenly," "sanctuary," or "Finn's Heaven."

Wild Nephin's walkways are a great way to experience the park's 27,000 acres (11,000 ha) of Atlantic blanket bog at ground level without getting your feet wet. An elevated peak, a short hike from the visitors center, has labeled illustrations of the vista before you.

Hosting a wealth of wildlife, the park's habitats include alpine heath on Slieve Carr, as well as upland grassland, lakes, and the fluvial catchments of the Owenduff and Tarsaghaun Rivers. The Owenduff bog is one of the last intact, active blanket bog systems in western Europe, enriched by up to 80 inches (2,000 mm) of rainfall per year. Many plants thrive within this wet habitat, painting the landscape seasonally from nature's rich palette. Myriad shades make up the grassy green background of black bog-rush, purple moor grass, deer grass, lichens, and sphagnum mosses. This multi-hued canvas is liberally dotted with the brighter lights of orchids, lousewort, bog cotton, and bog asphodel, and the composition is completed with the vibrant pinks and purples of bell heather, milkwort, and butterwort.

Wild Nephin also supports many bird species, as well as mammals, some nocturnal by nature. Elusive otters feed on eels and salmon and occasionally appear in the pools of the blanket bog within this naturalist's paradise. And when darkness descends, heaven's above. ■

Wild Nephin National Park, Ireland's first International Dark Sky Park

IN THE KNOW: WHERE TO STAY, EAT & DRINK IN MAYO

Much of the landscape of County Mayo consists of remote, mountainous bogland, but when you finally arrive in the towns of Castlebar, Ballina, or Westport, you're sure to find a warm Connacht welcome with a turf fire, a nightcap, and a hearty west-of-Ireland meal.

The notion of hospitality has been revered throughout Irish history, no matter who held power. Renovated and restored Norman castles and Anglo-Irish manor houses still deliver on the promise of a sumptuous stay, with spas, swimming pools, and fine dining options often included. Yet local bed-and-breakfast guesthouses can be equally inviting.

The large Ashford Castle Estate (see page 194) straddles two counties, with the imposing castle itself in Galway and the northerly estate grounds lying in Mayo. Here, a night at the **Lodge at Ashford Castle** is an affordable option for families and groups wanting to avail themselves of the many adventure activities and fine dining options. **Wilde's at the Lodge,** for example, offers creative cuisine from Jonathan Keane, a Connemara native recently named the best chef in Ireland. Both Wilde's and the **Quay Bar & Brasserie** afford diners great views of Lough Corrib and Cong Harbour. The Quay offers a lot of fun cocktails too, perhaps enjoyed on the hotel patio, overlooking the waters of Ireland's sacred lake. On a cold Connacht night, a fireside seat in the Quay Bar is the perfect spot to treat yourself to a very rare Willie Napier

1945, a whiskey aged for 44 years from the long-closed Tullamore Distillery. The warmth in your belly will confirm why the Irish call whiskey *uiscé beatha*, the water of life.

You don't have to be a hotel guest to dine like royalty at the castle's **George V Dining Room** or enjoy the many delights of the more casual **Cullen's at the Cottage,** such as the catch of the day, Killary Fjord mussels, or the always appetizing Dooncastle oysters. The **Dungeon** in the castle is also more informal, good for a fun group dinner surrounded by heraldry (and hilarity). Also in the castle basement is **Stanley's,** an American-style diner for coffee, burgers, and great comfort food such as the Elvis sandwich.

Another old-world welcome awaits travelers to north Mayo at **Belleek Castle,** just north of Ballina. Belleek was the dream medieval castle—finished in 1831—of Sir Arthur Francis Knox-Gore. This magnificent manor house was designed by architect John Benjamin Keanes for Knox-Gore in the neo-Gothic style. Belleek's dining room is a medieval fantasy, created with the wood of a Spanish galleon. **Jack Fenn's Café & Bistro** is the hotel's award-winning restaurant, housed in the restored 19th-century coach house with extensive courtyard seating. Here the Dún Briste seafood stack is presented as "a symphony of seafood," with steamed mussels, smoked salmon, Achill oysters, prawns, Marie Rose sauce, and homemade brown bread to soak up all those tastes of the sea.

For a delightful seafront stay on nearby Achill Island (see page 309), the **Bervie** offers a haven of home comforts with terrific views of the cliffs and the ocean. Owners Elizabeth and John Barrett make any stay restful and relaxing, and the fare here is exceptional.

The many bars of Mayo would easily fill another book, but a must-stop for traditional Irish music lovers is **Matt Molloy's** on Bridge Street in Westport, where the sessions start early and the guests "giving a song" might include anyone from a trad legend to an international rock star. Westport is abuzz with great hostelries, especially in summer, so be sure to also try some of the venues mentioned on page 207. ∎

Elizabeth Barrett welcomes guests to the Bervie guesthouse, a former Coast Guard station with ocean views. OPPOSITE: Cullen's at the Cottage, Ashford Castle

SLIGO

The northwestern county of Sligo is often referred to as Yeats Country for its influence on the work of Ireland's greatest poet. Sligo's dramatic countryside includes the limestone mountain of Benbulben, under which W. B. Yeats is buried, and where the final act in the Irish mythological legend of Diarmuid and Gráinne played out. Drama is deeply imbued in the memorable landscapes and the culture of this ruggedly beautiful county.

William Butler Yeats spent much of his childhood in northern Sligo, and landscapes such as the Isle of Innisfree in Lough Gill, Knocknarea Mountain, and Rosses Point Peninsula inspired much of his earlier poetry. While it was W. B. Yeats who articulated the dramatically changing Ireland of the late 19th and early 20th centuries in verse, his brother Jack Butler Yeats was the one who painted Ireland in that era. The family's Sligo home would color Jack's artistic vision just as it informed his brother's poetry.

The Yeats brothers grew up in a county resonant with the echoes of Celtic myth and history: The megalithic cemetery of Carrowmore is part of a massive complex of Stone Age remains connecting Carrowkeel to the Ox Mountains and the Cuil Irra Peninsula, where the passage tomb of Miosgán Médhbh is named for the legendary Queen Maeve of the Ulster Cycle of Irish mythology.

Sligo, the county town, is a sheltered port on the Wild Atlantic Way. Irish drama lovers from all over the west flock to dramatic, musical, and comedic acts at the Hawk's Well Theatre here, the first purpose-built theater in rural Ireland. Also in Sligo Town is the Yeats Memorial Building, a stopping point for many a poetry pilgrim on the way to pay their respects to Ireland's Nobel laureate at his resting place in Drumcliffe Graveyard farther north. The town of Sligo also has many fine culinary attractions, and no "horseman" should pass by (as Yeats's gravestone implores) without spending at least a night here. ∎

Classiebawn Castle is dwarfed by Benbulben, County Sligo's dramatic and iconic tabletop mountain.

Irish Heritage

Ireland's Poetic Imperative

The worried Tory Islander wanted to know: "Is it a smitten sheep, and will I get the rose, Doctor?" What the farmer was asking—in his lyrical Irish way—was whether his livestock had a contagious disease and, if so, might his skin break out in a rash. His medical inquiry typifies how the poetic rhythms of the Gaelic language shape the way English is spoken in Ireland, even by a poor, uneducated farmer on a remote Atlantic island. The Irish think in Irish and so their English often emerges in their native language's expressive turns of phrase.

Ireland's greatest poet, William Butler Yeats, recognized the power of both languages spoken in the west of his homeland. Yeats, educated in London, promoted the spoken Gaelic language of the Irish peasantry as a means of reconnecting with ancient Ireland. The poetic landscapes of Sligo also inspired him: The shadows and light alternating on the surface of Lough Gill, the twilight cloaking Knocknarea Mountain, and the play of cascading water at Glencar were all imbued with a timeless magic for Yeats, a mystic who connected psychically with the Otherworld of Ireland's *aos sí,* the supernatural race of fairy people who are both revered and feared by the Gaels.

Yeats also tapped into the medieval Gaelic tradition of the *filé,* or court poet, in the house of Irish chieftains. He spent hours visiting the sisters Constance and Eva Gore-Booth—one a revolutionary, the other a suffragist poet—at their country home of Lissadell House, near Drumcliff. The house's Irish name, Lios an Doill Uí Dálaigh, translates to "O'Daly's Court of the Blind," referring to the 13th-century O'Daly school of poetry.

The court poet in Irish antiquity was allowed to criticize the chieftain, even satirize him, and Yeats pulled no punches on the politics of his own volatile age: "Easter 1916" describes the "terrible beauty" midwifed by Ireland's revolution; "A Meditation in Time of War" ponders Ireland's participation in the First World War; and "The Second Coming" foresees a world where "things fall apart, the centre cannot hold."

Yet it is mostly for evocative images of life's fragile beauty that Yeats is celebrated. Who can resist his plea to "tread softly for you tread on my dreams" (from "He Wishes for the Cloths of Heaven")? What mortal can resolve the eternal mystery of the creative arts, as conveyed in his poem "Among School Children": "O body swayed to music, O brightening glance, How can we know the dancer from the dance?"

As you wander Yeats Country, keep an edition of his collected works handy to identify poems with Sligo place-names such as "The Lake Isle of Innisfree" (on Lough Gill) or "Sleuth Wood in the Lake" (Slish Wood on Rosses Point Peninsula). Two excellent recordings to take on your drives around Sligo are the Waterboys' *An Appointment with Mr. Yeats* and a selection of Yeats's poems interpreted by various musicians, *Now and in Time to Be.*

In Sligo, the Yeats Memorial Museum on Hyde Bridge has manuscripts, letters, photos of W. B., and his 1923 Nobel Prize citation: "for his always inspired poetry, which in a highly artistic form gives expression to the spirit of a whole nation." On nearby Stephen Street you'll find contemporary sculptor Rowan Gillespie's impressionistic statue of the poet, his spindly legs and billowing cloak imprinted with verse. Poetic pilgrims also venture to stand under the shadow of the flat-top mountain of Benbulben, a fine place to, as the poet's famous self-penned epitaph on his tombstone implores, "Cast a cold Eye / on Life, on Death."

Yet take heart, as Yeats's poetic legacy thrives in the 21st century. Aosdána, the association of Irish artists, honors the spiritual descendants of Ireland's creative gods, the Tuatha Dé Danann. Since Yeats was honored, the nation has produced another Nobel Prize–winning poet, Seamus Heaney, and the current president of the Republic, Michael D. Higgins, is himself a poet. ∎

William Butler Yeats (1865-1939), Irish poet, playwright, and Nobel Prize winner

The Irish Hunger Memorial, a chapter of Ireland's history made manifest in Battery Park, in lower Manhattan

The Irish Abroad

The New York Diaspora

Irish emigration to New York City began in earnest during the 1840s, when the Great Famine ravaged the homeland. The city became a mecca of hope for desperate exiles, whose passage was a trial by storm and pestilence aboard the infamous "coffin ships." Disease and hunger killed many long before the Statue of Liberty heralded their arrival to the United States. Even then, ships would stall in New York Bay while authorities checked for contagion aboard. This torturous ordeal is graphically reimagined in Joseph O'Connor's novel *Star of the Sea*.

Many Irish found accommodation in the slums of southern Manhattan, where today the Tenement Museum vividly re-creates the crowded living conditions endured in New York City by immigrants from more than 20 countries. Another Manhattan marker from the time is the Irish Hunger Memorial in Battery Park City, a 19th-century Irish cottage donated by the Slack family from Carradoogan, County Mayo. The half-acre (0.2 ha) site is landscaped with soil and native vegetation transported from Ireland's west, and with stones from every Irish county.

A number of immigrant Irish women worked as domestic servants or nannies for the city's wealthy, and the men found work as laborers in a city continually reconstructed. Irish novelist Colum McCann found inspiration in the story of the "sandhogs," the men who dug the tunnels of New York City subways and the foundations for the Brooklyn Bridge, among other projects. The narrative of his book *This Side of Brightness* weaves between generations of New Yorkers, taking readers into the lives of the construction workers and eventually deep into the world of the city's homeless subterranean dwellers as he illuminates both the bright and dark sides of the immigrant's American Dream. The Martin Scorsese blockbuster film *Gangs of New York* (2002) dramatized the fierce, ghettoized rivalries of late 19th-century Manhattan with a cast of thousands and a standout performance by one of Ireland's greatest actors, Daniel Day-Lewis.

The plight of a young Irish family of 20th-century immigrants drives the narrative of Jim Sheridan's autobiographical film *In America*. In it, a couple and their two young children try to fit in at a Hell's Kitchen tenement building occupied by drug addicts, cross-dressers, and a reclusive Nigerian artist/photographer. Still grieving the loss of a child, the parents also struggle to find work on a temporary visa, a quandary shared by thousands of Irish who arrived in the United States in the 1980s.

The story of *Brooklyn*, the 2015 film adaptation of Colm Tóibín's award-winning novel of the same name, turns this culture shock around and examines what happens when the emigrant returns to Ireland as a changed person. Set in 1951, the plot follows Eilis Lacey, a young Irishwoman who starts a new life in Brooklyn, where she marries Tony, an Italian plumber. A family tragedy brings Eilis back to her hometown of Enniscorthy, where she is forced to choose between her new American life and the comforting rut of her familial home. The long arm of the Catholic Church stretches across the Atlantic to both help and hinder the young woman as she reconciles her old and new identities. The

claustrophobic social mores of 1950s Ireland and the liberating opportunities of the United States are finely contrasted in this tale of divided loyalties.

The closing of such opportunities is the topic of 2017's *Emerald City,* a film which dramatizes the end of an era for a crew of hardworking, hard-partying Irish American construction workers in the Big Apple. The message of the movie, according to director Colin Broderick, is that the Celtic Tiger (the Irish economic boom of the 1990s and 2000s) and repressive U.S. immigration laws have ended the 200-year reign of the Irish construction workers who helped build New York.

Today, Irish immigrants work everywhere from white-collar jobs in Times Square to the offices of the city's construction firms. In the decades after the early arrivals, the Irish gained positions of political power through the Tammany Hall machine of the early 20th century,

whereby power brokers such as William M. "Boss" Tweed came to prominence. Many Irish immigrants ended up joining the city's police and fire departments, and any list of NYPD or NYFD employees will illustrate just how many Irish descendants continue this tradition of service.

The Irish have, of course, served the wider United States as well. Half of all American presidents can trace their heritage back to the Irish village from whence their forebearers set out for a new life: President Biden is a descendant of the Blewitts of County Mayo and the Finnegans from County Louth. His great-great-grandfather Patrick Blewitt was born in Ballina in County Mayo in 1832. President Obama paid a visit to Moneygall, his ancestral homeplace, in 2011, and now has a motorway plaza named in his honor in County Tipperary. Chicago, New York, and other American cities may be a long, long way from Tipperary, but the ties that bind the two nations remain strong. ∎

Irish, American, and papal flags flutter in a St. Patrick's Day parade along 5th Avenue in New York.

IRISH HISTORY: THE GREAT FAMINE

The Great Famine of the 1840s is seared into the Irish consciousness and commemorated at several sites around the country. The haunting **Famine Memorial** along Dublin's quays evokes the streams of desperate, skeletal humanity that traversed Ireland to board disease-ridden ships bound for Britain and America. **Doagh Famine Village** in Donegal tells the story of Irish life from the famine era to the present day. Pilgrims to Croagh Patrick pass the **National Famine Memorial**, John Behan's bleak, bronze "coffin ship" with skeletal bodies in the rigging, in Murrisk. The **Cobh Heritage Centre** in Cork and the **Famine Museum** in Louisburgh in County Mayo also tell stories of this cataclysmic event that left a million Irish dead.

One of the most evocative places to learn about this tragic chapter in history is at **Strokestown House** in County Roscommon. The short detour off the Wild Atlantic Way—Strokestown is 45 miles (72 km) from Sligo—is well worth making. Strokestown House and the **National Famine Museum** take visitors inside an afflicted estate that suffered the worst ravages of Ireland's Great Famine of 1847–1850, when a potato blight (Phytophthora infestans) brought from America wiped out the Irish peasantry's main source of nutrition.

Strokestown House is a Palladian villa set on about 300 acres (120 ha) that was the family home of the Pakenham Mahons from the 1600s until 1979. By the early 18th century, the estate spanned 11,000 acres (4,500 ha). When famine followed the repeated failure of the potato crop, landlords took the opportunity to clear their land of poor tenant farmers and use it for more lucrative produce, mainly sheep, for export to Britain. The Mahon family alone evicted some 3,000 people in 1847. Many were forced into emigration, on transatlantic ships overloaded with other refugees, who often slept above a cargo of food. A visit to Strokestown House's huge kitchen is an insight into the class-divided society of 19th-century rural Ireland.

The exhibits and stories told at the National Famine Museum are deeply moving. The memories kindled here resonate in our present-day world of displacement and war, as evidenced by an exhibit juxtaposing an image of a poor peasant's hovel from 1840s Ireland with a modern-day photo of a scene in a starving Eritrean farmer's dwelling. The museum also invites Syrian refugees, many of whom have been settled locally, to come and share their stories of exile and loss.

Stories of exile, loss, heartbreak, and revenge at the Strokestown Estate include the killing of Maj. Denis Mahon, the master of the house, on November 2, 1847. This was an act of revenge for the deaths of local Roscommon refugees aboard two "coffin ships" to Canada (starvation and typhoid took a huge toll on the 1,490 emigrants on the Virginius and the Naomi). Mahon was shot in the chest returning from a meeting of the Roscommon Board of Guardians, where he had gone to seek relief for his tenants. News of the assassination spread quickly through the surrounding townlands of Roscommon and Mayo and was widely celebrated by an angry populace: Bonfires were lit on many hills. Several suspects were arrested and executed for the murder, but the most likely culprit, Andrew Connor, escaped to Canada. Major Mahon was buried hastily in the middle of the night of November 4, and his remains lie now in the ruined mausoleum on the avenue leading to Strokestown House. His only daughter, Grace Catherine, was on her honeymoon at the time of the murder and vowed never to return to the ancestral seat. Her husband, Henry Sandford Pakenham, ran the estate as an absentee landlord. The murder weapon is still kept at Strokestown House. ∎

Strokestown House, former home of the landlord Pakenham Mahon family, is now a museum detailing the trauma of the Great Famine. OPPOSITE: The National Famine Memorial at Murrisk

DONEGAL

To venture to Donegal, in Ireland's northwesternmost corner, is to take a leap of faith that many travelers don't make. This is the only county in Ireland with no rail services, and access from the Republic is limited to one main highway. Yet richly rewarded is the adventurous soul who regardless motors on. The landscapes here are wild and windswept, constantly recast in a series of ever changing light. Donegal is the great Irish stage for nature's atmospherics, a spectacle of shifting sunshine and shadow that lures artists to the shores of the Bloody Foreland (so named for the sunset's red light here) and the far-flung islands of Arranmore and Tory. Here in this northerly county, you'll find warm, welcoming people who invite you "in out the bitter cold" into their hearts and homes. Small wonder the best known song from this cradle of old Irish culture is the wistful ballad "The Homes of Donegal."

Singers and musicians from these parts are celebrated worldwide. A family of local musicians conquered the world with an eclectic mix of folk, traditional Irish, and new-age music, which even incorporates jazz and Gregorian chant. Their name, Clann as Dobhar ("family from Gweedore") was shortened to Clannad. One sister, Enya, went on to woo the world with her own blend of ethereal Celtic music.

The region's music is surely inspired by the drama of landscapes such as Lough Derg and the austere Station Island, known as St. Patrick's Purgatory. Also here is Glenveagh, perhaps Ireland's most spectacular national park. Donegal's dark history incorporates famine hardships and the Poisoned Glen, which legend suggests was contaminated by toxins from the eye of Balor, the slain one-eyed giant king of Tory.

Donegal has hidden gems too: What rambler through this bogland wilderness would expect to find wolves, bears, and wild boars in Burnfoot, near the city of Derry, or a peace garden overlooking a city split in two? Finally, there are the Slieve League Cliffs, a seascape that takes the breath away in every sense. ∎

Slieve League towers over the Atlantic coastlines of Donegal.

IRISH GARDENS: THE GARDENS OF DONEGAL

The epic wilderness surrounding **Glenveagh Castle,** set within the exposed granite mountains of central Donegal, is an unrivaled stage for any horticultural production. The castle's gardens, the legacy of American-born Cornelia Adair, Glenveagh's best-known lady of the castle, are now among the many alluring attractions of Glenveagh National Park (see page 236). Cornelia's labor of love started in 1869 and included the Pleasure Gardens and the Walled Garden, today complemented with the Gothic Orangery, the Italian Terrace, and the Tuscan Garden.

Salthill House has a more rebellious Irish garden. This is the residence of the Temple family, owners of the Magee clothing company. The riotous meadows become rich carpets of wildflowers in spring, leading into fern- and moss-cloaked woodlands, and on into the rose-scented walled gardens. Look out for the lollipop-like globe thistles (*Echinops*) and the Japanese hornbeam (*Carpinus japonica*) trees.

Mowed lawns sweep down to a human-made lake from the Georgian **Oakfield House,** a mansion built in 1739 for the Anglican dean of Raphoe. Lebanon cedar, lime, and chestnut trees punctuate the grounds, and a small temple, the Nymphaeum, sits by the lake. Visitors can stroll along leafy avenues, under recently replanted oaks, toward a miniature castle. Well-kept wooden walkways facilitate strolls across wetlands and water, and the Difflin Lake Railway provides a fun, 2.5-mile (4 km) ride.

In Muff, hidden away on the quiet backroads near Burnfoot, you'll find one of Donegal's best kept secrets: the **IOSAS (Islands of Saints and Scholars) Celtic Peace Garden.** The inspiration of Father Neal Carlin (see page 235), this garden was conceived as a meditative oasis in a troubled world. Any tormented soul would find spiritual sanctuary on its peaceful pathways, and many have. The looped main path leads visitors along a series of individual homages to Irish saints from the golden age of Celtic spirituality (A.D. 400–1100). The artist Maurice Harron's arresting sculptures depicting the crucified and the risen Christ are placed throughout the grounds, setting the mood of faith and hope.

Several of the saints' tributes take the form of buildings, giving visitors the chance to physically enter the history of Celtic spirituality at home and abroad. Here a round tower honors St. Enda; a wooded bird sanctuary commemorates St. Ciarán. Look, too, for the whale-shaped mini-lake, a salute to St. Brendan the Navigator. Nearby, a holy well represents the healing powers of St. Attracta, and a building re-creates the shape of St. Killian's reliquary at Wurtzburg, representing the evangelization of Europe. St. Gall's hermitage, which became a library, reflects how the Irish saved civilization in the early Middle Ages.

The power of the written word comes even more alive in St. Columbanus's cave, where his words "appear" on the walls as your eyes adjust to the dark: The written word illuminates the blackness. The focal point of the peace garden is the oratory dedicated to St. Canice, used for masses and meditation. All of the golden age saints are honored here in stained-glass windows. ∎

A train leads to Oakfield Park's lower gardens. OPPOSITE: Glenveagh Castle and gardens

Close to heaven: The cliffs of Slieve League are the highest sea cliffs in Europe, looming over the Atlantic at 1,972 feet (601 m).

Special Places

The Slieve League Cliffs

Almost all first-time visitors to Ireland view the Cliffs of Moher, yet most travelers don't know that 200 miles (325 km) up the coast stand giants that dwarf their counterparts in Clare.

At 1,972 feet (601 m), the precipices of Slieve League are the highest sea cliffs in Europe—and may be the closest place to heaven in Ireland. If you have the courage and the stamina to climb to the top of the mountain of the same name (Sliabh Liag in Irish), you'll be blessed with divine views of the Atlantic Ocean, Donegal Bay, and the Sligo Mountains to the south. This holy mountain was a site of Christian pilgrimage for more than 1,000 years, although it was likely a sacred place from pagan times.

The **Sliabh Liag Visitor Centre** here offers local food as well as stories and folklore about the cliffs; it also shares vital safety advice and weather warnings for hikers. After disembarking at the parking lot, look out for the word "Éire" (Ireland), along with the number 71, written in large stones on the headland ground.

These rock signs, dotted along the northern coast, acted as navigational aids to Allied pilots in World War II who flew along the "Donegal Corridor," where the quick and thick Atlantic mists must have made discombobulation a regular hazard.

The view ashore is different, however. When the Atlantic clouds shroud these soaring cliffs, you can't help but be enraptured by the twilight swirl of mists on this ancient mountain. As you start to climb, you'll see sheep drift through the mist, dancing daintily past terrifying drops, and wonder how much good wool goes south each year.

Donegal's heavenly mists make mystics of us all, but one man with his feet firmly on the ground is Martin Doherty, whom you'll often meet at the parking lot halfway up Slieve League. Doherty began his working life in local woolen mills. That was the 1980s, before globalization gave the world cheap sweaters and shamrock hats started to be made in China. Now he spins woolens at home, selling his products from his trailer at this and other popular spots around Donegal.

Doherty is a great man for the football—both soccer and Gaelic. He'll talk all day about local prospects, like the one who was spotted by scouts from "o'er beyooond" (meaning the professional soccer clubs in England or Scotland). But the young lad, he says, wants to stay and try to win an All-Ireland with Donegal (the highest honor in Gaelic football). The lure of unimaginable wealth in the English Premier League, or the glory of bringing the Sam Maguire Cup home and being welcomed by a bonfire in every village of the county, lit to honor the conquering heroes on their bus ride back from Dublin: The youth of Ireland have divided dreams, home and away, same as ever.

At Slieve League, it feels like you can touch the sky, and let your wildest dreams take flight. ∎

IN THE KNOW: WRAP YOURSELF IN DONEGAL WOOLS

Donegal has long been known for its wools, knitwear, and tweeds. Despite the mass production of clothing over the last 50 years, and the homogenization of fashions, Donegal products have kept their cachet in a globalized world.

The wools of Donegal are known for their characteristic blend of flecks, many inspired by the county's rugged landscapes: Gorse yellows, heather purples, grass greens, fuchsia pinks, sea blues, and earthy browns all color Donegal wools. Donegal yarn is also distinguished by its high levels of lanolin, a natural water-repellent chemical in wool.

The wool was traditionally spun into yarn and then knitted or woven in local homes. This hard-wearing, coarse fabric was handwoven in Donegal by part-time fishermen-farmers and part-time weavers in the late 1800s and early 1900s. **Donegal Yarns,** located in Kilcar, is one of the last remaining companies producing this indigenous product in Ireland.

Another firm, **Magee 1866,** is a globally renowned business founded on handwoven tweed. Its name touts the year John Magee, a Belfast native, established a tweed wholesale firm in Donegal Town. Robert Temple from Killygordan joined him, and the pair turned Magee into a signature brand in tweed.

Soft yet durable, tweed is an ideal fabric for dissipating the damp, cold weather of northwest Ireland. Magee uses timeless designs such as herringbone—inspired by fish bones—and a speckled pattern they call "salt & pepper." Designs are sent to weavers, who still work in their Donegal homes, with the raw fabric returned to the mill to be washed and finished. This oily fabric is rinsed in the peaty waters of the River Eske for a distinctive, soft finish.

Other places to shop for beautiful fabrics along the Wild Atlantic Way include **John Molloy Woollen Mills,** a family-run business in Ardara; **McNutt of Donegal** in the seaside village of Downings; and **Studio Donegal** in Kilcar.

To experience the simple rural life out of which these knitting and weaving crafts evolved, visit **Glencolmcille Folk Village,** a thatched-roof replica of a rural *clachan* (settlement) overlooking Glen Bay Beach in the Donegal Gaeltacht. The craft shop has a large selection of locally made knitwear, along with tapestries and handcrafts. ∎

Eddie Doherty learned to weave by hand at the age of 16.

A statue of the Donegal abbot and missionary evangelist Columba, also known as Colmcille, stands in the Waterside, Derry.

In the Footsteps of Colmcille

No person, past or present, is as tied to Donegal as St. Columba (521–597), who is known in his native county as Colmcille. Colmcille was born in Gartan on the Leac na Cumha ("stone of sorrows"), a flat slab covered in prehistoric rock art. He slept here before his exile to Scotland, inspiring later emigrants to spend *their* last night in Ireland on the stone, to invoke his blessing on new lives abroad. Close by stands a towering Celtic cross erected in his honor in 1911 by Cornelia Adair of Glenveagh Castle.

The saint was an interesting mix of rebelliousness and reconciliation. His life story is told at the **Colmcille Heritage Centre,** located on the edge of Glenveagh National Park. His main mission was the conversion of Scotland's Picts to Christianity; he is remembered too for his reconciliation of the Scottish and Irish parts of the kingdom of Dalriada, brokering peace between King Aed and King Aidan. Although born into a powerful, warlike family, Colmcille chose a life of poverty and sacrifice.

Colmcille was also a poet. The saint defended the Gaelic poets *(filés)* from the chieftains' criticism of their lifestyle, poetry, and songs, earning him the title Patron of the Bards. He was the central figure in one of the first known copyright wars, when he famously refused to hand over a transcribed psalter belonging to his mentor, Finnian. The conflict resulted in his voluntary exile to Scotland.

The Colmcille Heritage Centre uses artistically designed banners, stained glass, illustrated panels, and a wax model with authentic clothing to convey the life of the saint. His work is set in the context of the medieval monastic tradition, and a step-by-step illustration of ancient manuscript fabrication shows the artisanship of the monks.

Colmcille was responsible for founding many monasteries, from Raphoe and Inishowen in Donegal to Iona in Scotland. **Colmcille's Way** (Slí Cholmcille) is a walking route that has expanded in recent years to take in several Donegal sites associated with the great saint.

Father Neal Carlin walked in the saint's footsteps, both geographically and spiritually, until his death in 2021. Ordained in 1964, he spent years ministering in Scotland. Like Colmcille, he led a simple life, shunning all luxuries. As the 1960s ended, Carlin's nationalist family was drawn into the long conflict that followed the murder of civil rights marchers in Derry on Bloody Sunday.

Throughout the Troubles, Father Neal urged local militants to turn away from the gun and to grasp the ballot paper instead. Sensitive to the prisoners' demands, Father Neal worked tirelessly to negotiate an end to the 1981 hunger strikes in the Maze prison, where friends from Derry served time. In that year, he founded the Columba Community of Prayer and Reconciliation, based on the saint's well-known tenets of peace through forgiveness.

Working in communities blighted with urban decay and addiction, Father Neal took practical action to give young men renewed hope and a sense of purpose. In 2001, he established the White Oaks Addiction Treatment Centre in Muff, where residents work on the organic vegetable farm. At White Oaks, his healing nature—and his dark Derry humor—were valued by all. In 2001, he enlisted the help of his brother, Brendan Carlin, to create the IOSAS Celtic Peace Garden (see page 230).

Brendan Carlin remembers his brother, the visionary priest: "Father Bradley, who eulogized Neal, said it perfectly, citing his initials: 'NC. Non-conformist. Non-compromising. Noble Christian.'"

Sounds a lot like the nomadic Colmcille. ∎

TASTE OF IRELAND: DONEGAL BAY PRAWNS IN GARLIC-BASIL CREAM

No county in Ireland is as tied to its fisheries as Donegal, and no Wild Atlantic Way town has as much salt in its air as Killybegs. This simple recipe for Donegal Bay prawns makes enough to feed six tired fishermen and is a great way to turn a fresh-off-the-boat catch into a sizzling evening treat, soaked up with Irish wheaten bread and washed down with a fine white wine.

INGREDIENTS

- 2 tablespoons Kerrygold Irish butter
- 2¼ pounds (1.1 kg) Donegal Bay prawns, peeled and deveined
- 3 garlic cloves, crushed
- 1½ cups (375 mL) heavy cream
- 14 fresh basil leaves

DIRECTIONS

- Over medium heat, melt butter sufficient to coat the bottom of a large sauté pan.
- Add the prawns and sauté until pink and opaque, about 3 to 4 minutes.
- Stir in the remaining ingredients except the basil, and cook to reduce the liquid.
- Tear basil leaves over the top and serve immediately, while sauce is still hot, with Irish wheaten bread.

Donegal Bay prawns sizzling in garlic-basil cream

Special Places

Glenveagh National Park

The quartzite rock of Errigal Mountain rises to 2,464 feet (751 m) near Gweedore and emits an ethereal pinkish glow at sunset. This tallest of the Seven Sisters peaks glistens like a beacon over Glenveagh National Park, then casts a long shadow as the sun falls into the Atlantic to the west.

Glenveagh is a hiker's paradise with a dark history, stretching across 23,887 densely wooded acres (9,650 ha) in northwestern Donegal. Here, the crystalline waters of Lough Beagh are whipped by the wild winds that whistle across the Derryveagh Mountains.

The park takes its name from the valley of Glenveagh (Gleann Bheatha in Irish), meaning "glen of the birches." Southwest of here rise the ice-carved cliffs of the **Poisoned Glen,** a corruption of another old Gaelic name that also translates to "heavenly glen" (the Irish for heaven is *neamh* and poison is *neimhe*). The poignant history of Glenveagh echoes this strange juxtaposition of evil and Eden, shadow and light.

The focal point of the park is **Glenveagh Castle**, which was started in 1870 and completed in 1873. The fortification was modeled on Balmoral Castle, the Scottish holiday home of the British royals; ironically, Glenveagh was occupied by the Irish Republican Army (IRA) in 1922, during the civil war. This castellated granite mansion, with its neo-Gothic architecture of ramparts, turrets, and a round tower was sited to render its owners the best views of Lough Veagh.

Those original owners, John George Adair and his wife, Cornelia, cast their own shadow and light over Donegal. The landlord gained lasting infamy for the Derryveagh Evictions, when 244 tenants were ousted from his land in the harsh winter of 1861. Many homeless families perished in freezing weather. Cornelia Adair is more fondly remembered: She laid out the rhododendron gardens (see page 230) and introduced to the estate the red deer that later became Ireland's largest herd.

A more recent resident is the golden eagle, reintroduced to the northwest in 2000 after having been hunted to near extinction in the 19th century. Numerous other avian residents also find sustenance in the locale's many lakes, nourished by plentiful populations of brown trout, salmon, and arctic char.

Cornelia's horticultural legacy has taken root, and the castle's informal gardens now host many delicate plants imported from faraway climes, including Chile, Madeira, and Tasmania. These find shelter from Donegal's harsh Atlantic winds by windbreaks of pine trees.

Walking the castle grounds is a joy, as you traverse various terraces, an Italian garden, and the Belgian Walk, constructed by soldiers from Belgium billeted here during World War I. For more ambitious hill-walkers, the Trail Walker Bus takes you from the parking lot to the start of the park's seven walking trails. ∎

Home to herds of red deer, Glenveagh National Park offers wildly romantic paths for rambling.
OPPOSITE: Glenveagh Castle and Gardens, focal point of the national park

Crohy Head, a remote point on the Mullaghmullan Peninsula, is known for its rock formations, including the Breeches sea arch.

Exploring Donegal

Donegal is the perfect destination for lovers of outdoor activities. The county has miles of unspoiled beaches offering some of Europe's best surfing. Horseback riding, biking, and hiking trails crisscross the dramatic landscapes, and numerous wildlife and bird-watching areas lure naturalists to spot everything from whales to willow warblers. While you'll need to don a thick wet suit to hear whale song in Donegal's shipwreck-strewn waters, onshore you'll easily discern the delightful *hu–it* tweet of the willow warbler. In the Donegal Gael-

tacht, this sonorous songbird goes by the Gaelic name of *ceolaire sailí,* or musician of the willow.

For dedicated bird-watchers, the wildlife refuge called **Wild Ireland** (see page 240) is worth visiting for its avian inhabitants alone; these include native rarities such as old Irish game fowl, migrant species such as stork, geese, and woodcock, as well as exotica such as Silkie chickens from Asia. Located nearby is **Inch Wildfowl Reserve,** where, from April to October, you can witness a winged spectacle straight out of ancient Ireland: the sunset

descent of thousands of graylag geese onto Lough Swilly.

Inch Wildfowl Reserve nestles in the shadow of another ancestral gathering place—this one of human origin—and one Donegal's great attractions, the **Grianán of Aileach.** One of Gaelic Ireland's four royal sites and Donegal's most impressive stone fort, the Grianán of Aileach is located near the village of Burt at the summit of Greenan Mountain. The Irish name translates to "stone forts of the sun," suggesting its main purpose was sun worship. This impressively reconstructed fort is believed to have been built in prehistoric times by the Tuatha Dé Danann at the direction of their king, Dagda. The enclosed circle was likely also used to keep livestock safe from ancient predators of the Celtic Rainforest, mainly wolves. St. Patrick, who rarely missed a trick when it came to pagan venues, preached here in A.D. 442. The views of Lough Swilly and Lough Foyle from the fort are stunning, particularly when the red sunsets of Donegal cast their spell.

The timeless lure of wild Atlantic breakers has long attracted surfers to Donegal's many beaches. **Bundoran** has earned a reputation as Ireland's surfing mecca, but be sure to bring your "wettie"—as locals will tell you, it can get "a wee bit chilly" here. But fear not, a warming hot whiskey is never far away. The beach is close to the town's main street, with its string of bars, including the **Kickin Donkey & George's Bar.** National Geographic has recognized Bundoran as one of the "Top 20 Surf Towns" in the world.

Photography enthusiasts should make for **Bád Eddie** (*Eddie's Boat*), a wreck that has sat on Magheraclogher Beach since the 1970s and one of County Donegal's most recognizable landmarks. Donegal's most beautiful church, the ruin at **Dunlewey,** is similarly remote, but equally rewarding photographically. For a bracing end to the day, a long sunset walk along **Port Arthur Beach** in the Gaeltacht of Gweedore is hard to beat. The town of Derrybeg is less than two miles (3 km) away with the promise of cozy pubs and trad music.

Before leaving Donegal, head to **Malin Head,** on the Inishowen Peninsula, where you'll reach Ireland's northernmost point. At low tide north of Trawbreaga Bay, you'll see the wreckage of the *Twilight*, which sank in 1889. Then, hike to **Dúnalderagh** ("Banba's crown") to relish the views and taste the Atlantic winds at their sharpest. ∎

TASTE OF IRELAND: BOXTY

The word "boxty," meaning "poorhouse bread," describes traditional potato pancakes (also known as "stamp"). These originated in the poverty-stricken northwestern counties of Donegal, Cavan, Monaghan, and Leitrim, where no potato scraps were wasted.

INGREDIENTS

- 2 cups leftover mashed potatoes
- 2 cups grated raw potato (a starchy variety, such as russet, works well)
- 2 cups all-purpose flour
- 1 teaspoon baking soda
- Good pinch of salt
- 1½ cups buttermilk (plus more if needed)
- ¼ pint (150 mL) milk
- Donegal rapeseed oil (This also comes in lemon, garlic, and chili flavors.)

DIRECTIONS

- Soak the grated potatoes in a large bowl of cold water. Rinse and repeat, then place in a clean towel and wring out as much liquid as possible.
- Place cold mashed potatoes, prepared grated potatoes, and flour, baking soda, and salt in a large mixing bowl. Add the buttermilk and combine. If the mixture is too thick, add a little more buttermilk until you have a loose batter.
- In a skillet, heat a generous amount of the rapeseed oil over medium heat, then drop in spoonfuls of mixture. Cook for about 5 minutes on each side, or until golden.

Boxty, Ireland's traditional potato pancake

Irish Heritage

Wild Ireland

In a remote forest in Burnfoot, a local lawyer with a passion for animals is re-creating ancient habitats in the hilly boglands and reintroducing long-extinct species to Ireland. Called Wild Ireland, the native animal sanctuary is Killian McLaughlin's vision for a 21st-century Celtic Rainforest, where creatures such as wolves, brown bears, and wild boar roam freely.

Warmed by the Gulf Stream, Ireland enjoys perfect conditions for temperate rainforests, with lush green vegetation encouraged by a moderate climate and plenty of rainfall. McLaughlin's childhood interest in animals, particularly the extinct megafauna of long ago, nurtured in him a deep appreciation of the rainforest habitats of ancient Ireland and a desire to understand their disappearance. He learned how the extinction of bears and wolves led to imbalances in the lushly forested landscapes that our ancestors once shared with such wildlife.

The wild boar is a prime example: Plentiful in medieval Ireland, these porcine foragers were vital eco-regenerators, especially for the Irish oak (*Quercus petraea*). Nature's plow, wild boars churn up the ground beneath the forest undergrowth, leaving a freshly turned seedbed for acorns to fall onto; they also clear bramble that can outcompete baby oak trees for light and nutrition. With the help of his wild boars, McLaughlin has planted more than 300 oaks and other native species, such as Scotch pine (*Pinus sylvestris*), which had previously survived only in County Clare.

Wild Ireland is populated with ancient Irish animals, such as arctic foxes and brown bears. The sanctuary also provides room for nonnative creatures to roam, including Barbary macaques rescued from the streets of Brussels and Paris. ■

Killian McLaughlin's Wild Ireland sanctuary hosts rescued wolves, bears, and lynx, among other native and exotic wildlife.

IRISH VOICES: THE ANIMALS' ADVOCATE

Killian McLaughlin moves through his Wild Ireland sanctuary squawking at many feathered friends; squeaking for Uisce, the otter; and howling loudly with his beloved wolves. He is Donegal's Doctor Dolittle; he talks to the animals. Hilariously, he even takes out his phone and gets one of them to respond to relatives back in Siberia via YouTube, in a neck-folded, transcontinental dialogue between very excited Eurasian cranes. This bird hadn't sung in the Irish wilderness for more than 800 years until now; the ancient Gaels described its song as *corr gaire,* or crane laughter.

"This isn't a business," McLaughlin explains. "The animals are our passion. They aren't caged; they have spaces where they can take themselves away from visitors. The humans are guests in the animals' home, so it's up to us to spot them in the vegetation."

Wild Ireland is a fabulous journey into an ancient Gaelic wilderness that our ancestors once shared with species that include brown bears, old Irish goats, golden eagles, and wild boars. As its founder demonstrates, it's a very aural experience: Besides the crane's long-distance phone calls, listen for the clip-clop sound of the strange-looking western capercaillie, which gave this original angry bird its Gaelic name of "horse of the forest," or the rasping hoot of a snowy owl, or the courting song of whooper swans, so evocative of Ireland's legendary Children of Lir. And, of course, that heart-stopping howl of the wolf. "These are primordial sounds that I think all Irish people remember deep in their subconscious," says McLaughlin. "They're burned into our folk memory."

McLaughlin has always heard the call of the wild. As a child he taught an injured crow named Jack to speak. He believes that a child's bond with wild creatures is innate, but something Irish people have largely lost. "Then I discovered we had wolves, brown bears, lynx, wild boars, and all these creatures called 'megafauna' living right here on this island. And that really captured my imagination. It set me off on a journey to re-create that land in the forest."

His journey heralded the return of the ancient cry of the wolf, which now echoes across Donegal for the first time in almost 400 years. Wolves were native to Ireland up to the 17th century, when Oliver Cromwell—coveting agricultural land—placed a bounty on them in 1653. Hunters got five pounds for a male, six pounds for a female when the pelt was presented to the authorities. The Irish people rejected that bounty, however, because for centuries wolves had been household pets. So it was professional wolf hunters from Europe who took up the call and caused the extinction of the Irish wolf. "Wolves are the epitome of the Irish wilderness," says McLaughlin. "Our ancestors respected them as 'Mac Tír,' or 'son of the land,' which was really a term of royalty." He pauses. "There's something in that that just speaks to my soul," he concludes, tapping his heart twice with a clenched fist.

Old Irish legends also sparked the young McLaughlin's interest. The initiation rite to join the Fianna (the mythical band of Celtic warriors) meant a young boy would set out into the forest, hunt and kill a wild boar, then bring it back as proof of his warrior mettle. "Wild boars are pack animals: If you mess with one, you mess with them all," McLaughlin explains, "so this was a test of intelligence too."

Whether he's talking about the wild boars of legend, his rehabilitation of bears that he rescued from caged captivity in Lithuania, his lynx Naoise (the "original Celtic Tiger"), or his pack of wolves, the animals' advocate speaks from the heart. "These are no longer just wolves. These are Oisin, Fergus, and Finn," he says. "They are part of the family now, and the dream is to expand Wild Ireland to give all these animals more room to roam in larger swaths of the forest. The ultimate goal is to re-create an authentic wild space, to give the visitor a feeling of going into the wilderness to see wildlife as it was in ancient Ireland," says McLaughlin. "And it's good to know that these animals will live a healthy, well-cared-for life in a little patch of reclaimed Celtic Rainforest up here in Donegal." ∎

"I remember growing up, feeling hard done by that Ireland didn't have the big predators of Africa or India. Then I discovered Ireland was once named Wolfland because we had so many in the wilderness, and also as *pets* in Gaelic Ireland."

—*Killian McLaughlin*

IN THE KNOW: WHERE TO STAY, EAT & DRINK IN DONEGAL

Ireland's northernmost county embraces many of the country's most remote reaches, yet no matter the distance traveled, the welcome is always warm in Donegal.

One place that feels like home yet wraps guests in an old-world cocoon of elegant ease is **Castle Grove Country House and Restaurant.** Castle Grove has been run by Caroline Sweeney's family since 1989. Located just north of Letterkenny, this 17th-century manor house sits serenely near the banks of Lough Swilly on an estate of 250 acres (100 ha), with farmland and gardens to supply fresh produce for the kitchen. Afternoon tea is served daily (with champagne if you're feeling celebratory), and the dining room serves local delights such as ginger soy-cured salmon with lemon dressing. The Irish beef roasts and Donegal lamb dishes are sumptuous feasts when paired with a Malbec or Merlot from the choice house wine list.

Rathmullan House is another gorgeous country house on Lough Swilly, run by the Wheeler Family for more than 50 years. This 18th-century Georgian manor, set amid seven acres (3 ha) of wooded gardens, offers elegant accommodations and fine fare, including fresh fruit and vegetables from their own walled garden and locally caught seafood.

Travelers to the Grianán of Aileach and Wild Ireland are welcomed with special rates (and hot chocolate!) at the **Grianán Hotel** in Burt, below the famous fort (see page 238) and next to the Old Church Visitor Centre, which has an interactive exhibit on the Tuatha Dé Dannan.

After scaling the heights of Slieve League, reward yourself with a stop at **Sliabh Liag Distillers** in Ardara to sample their An Dúlamán Irish Maritime Gin. This savory spirit uses five locally harvested seaweeds to capture *draíocht na farraige* (the magic of the sea). Their Legendary Silkie Irish Whiskeys are blended with a hint of the rich smoky styles of traditional Donegal whiskey. If the taste of the sea is what tingles your taste buds, head to **Kealy's Seafood Bar** at the harbor in Greencastle. Here you'll relish the Foylemore oysters, Greencastle crab dishes, monkfish, hake, and chowder that simmers with seafood flavor.

The **Lemon Tree,** in the heart of Letterkenny, has been attracting foodies since 1999. This family-run restaurant offers contemporary, seasonal dishes, using locally sourced ingredients that highlight the rich bounty of County Donegal and its maritime surrounds. Gourmands on the Wild Atlantic Way should also check out Donegal's **Food Coast Experiences** calendar and the **WAW Seafood Trail.**

The pubs of County Donegal are legion and legendary. Many host trad music nights, and the music lovers' pub of pilgrimage is **Leo's Tavern** in Gweedore. Owner Leo Brennan was the father of Enya and Moya, Pól, and Ciarán of the band Clannad. And if you fancy airing your own pipes, head for the **Singing Pub** in Meenaleck.

Other great Donegal pubs include **McCafferty's,** called Harry's by locals, wonderfully situated at the area called Mountain Top in Letterkenny. It offers fine views across the tranquil valley of Muckish, Donegal's tabletop mountain, and Errigal, the county's highest peak. Another option, **McGinley's,** is more centrally situated on Lower Main Street in Letterkenny. A gastropub, the **Drift Inn,** now occupies the old railway station in Buncrana. For a traditional-style pub in Donegal Town, try the **Forge.** A great mix of past, present, and future is **Dicey Reilly's** in Ballyshannon, not just a pub but an off-license (liquor store) and microbrewery, too. ∎

The Lemon Tree offers contemporary Irish cooking using locally sourced ingredients.
OPPOSITE: A warm welcome is assured at Castle Grove Country House and Restaurant.

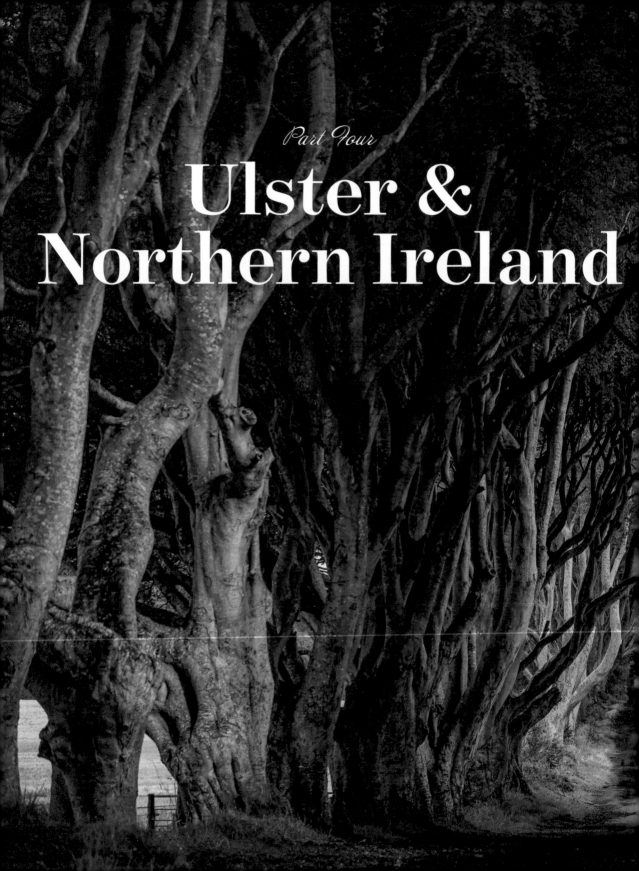

Part Four

Ulster &
Northern Ireland

The Dark Hedges, an avenue of beech trees between Armoy and Stranocum in County Antrim and a location for the *Game of Thrones* TV series

BEST TIME TO VISIT: The weather along the north-facing headlands is predictably severe in winter, and the daylight hours limited, making spring and summer best to drive the Causeway Coast. May and early summer are prime for anglers at the northern lakes.

SPECIAL EVENTS: Derry Halloween, a spooky, four-day event (near October 31); Summer Jamm, a multiday musical extravaganza in Derry City and Strabane (June); Belfast International Arts Festival (October–November); St. Patrick's Day at Down Cathedral, Downpatrick (March 17)

GETTING THERE: George Best Airport (named after the Manchester United legend) lands you in the outskirts of Belfast. Remember you're outside the EU while in Northern Ireland, and the currency is sterling, not euros. Dublin is just a 90-minute drive away and many visitors start there and take a day trip north, or rent a car for a multiday road trip.

"The Turf Man" bronze statue, in Bellaghy, was inspired by the Seamus Heaney poem "Digging." OPPOSITE: Mussenden Temple stands on the cliffs near Castlerock.

Soak in the poetry of the Causeway Coast

The six counties of Northern Ireland stretch eastward from Donegal and embrace one of the island's finest drives, the storied Causeway Coast. Here, the moody northern climes have inspired some of Ireland's finest poets, and today the homes of Seamus Heaney in Derry and Patrick Kavanagh in Monaghan host visitors centers where poetry lovers can linger and listen at these writers' inspirational wellsprings. Derry itself is a lively city with fine culinary venues and pubs. The old town is walkable, with its historic walls and the Peace Bridge stretching over the River Foyle, seeking to unite this town with two names (historically, "Derry" was favored by Nationalists, "Londonderry" by Unionists).

Beginning the route from Donegal, drivers along the edges of Counties Derry, Antrim, and Down find coastlines strewn with the wrecks of ships and ancient clifftop castles. The main event, of course, is the geological wonder of the Giant's Causeway, where mammoth hexagonal blocks rise from the sea. Nearby, at the Old Bushmills Distillery, in the village of the same name, the traditions of the past are strictly observed to create one of the world's great single malt whiskeys.

Trapped in its own past for much of the 20th century, Belfast looks to a brighter future as a reimagined, innovative 21st-century city. History is now seen through a prism of educational enlightenment in this long-troubled town, as evidenced by one of Europe's finest museums, the Titanic Experience in Belfast's docklands.

Counties Down and Tyrone offer bucolic outings, including three of Northern Ireland's great gardens: Blessingbourne House, Mount Stewart, and Rowallane. Here too are the Castle Ward Estate, recognizable as Winterfell to fans of *Game of Thrones,* and the Ulster American Folk Park, which traces the province's profound influence on American life through Scots-Irish emigration of the last three centuries. Finally, no trip to Northern Ireland is complete without a visit to Downpatrick, where the life of the island's patron saint is celebrated at his burial place. ∎

DERRY

Derry City (aka Londonderry) is the first stop in Northern Ireland for those completing the Wild Atlantic Way in Donegal and continuing on toward the Causeway Coast route. A layover of at least one night—and the bulk of two days—is necessary to take in the divided nature of this lively city.

Once you cross the River Foyle, the road east takes you along the southern banks of Lough Foyle and through a string of low-key country villages that includes Campsey, Greysteel, Ballykelly, and Limavady, the latter known for its agricultural market. One of Ireland's great archaeological treasures, the Broighter Hoard, was found in Limavady in 1896. The hoard of Celtic gold included a magnificent torc (neck ring) and a miniature boat with delicate oars. (The collection is now displayed in the National Museum in Dublin.) Limavady is also the source of the "Londonderry Air," the traditional tune used for the evergreen "Danny Boy" (see page 45). Jane Ross, a folk song collector, heard and transcribed the classic fiddle aria here in the 19th century.

County Derry's scenery becomes beautifully rustic as you near Binevenagh Forest, and the Causeway Coast proper starts when you reach Magilligan Strand. Horses and cars share this long and wide expanse of sand, marked by the twin 18th-century remains of Downhill Palace and Mussenden Temple. Beyond the town of Coleraine, Portstewart Strand is the next Blue Flag beach along the Causeway Coast. The town was a Victorian beach destination, and its harbor and scenic coastal paths form an inviting Atlantic promenade.

The neighboring popular resort town of Portrush has two pristine beaches, West Strand and Whiterocks Beach; the latter boasts limestone cliffs stretching from Curran Strand to Dunluce Castle in the neighboring county of Antrim.

Travelers who also want to visit the Seamus Heaney Home-Place (see page 257) in Bellaghy, located in County Derry's far south, are better off taking the roads west from Belfast later in their journey. ∎

The Peace Bridge connects long-divided communities in Derry.

Insider's Guide

Derry: East & West of the River

The River Foyle divides Derry, a town that grew around a sixth-century monastery founded by St. Colmcille (Columba) within a deep valley cloaked in oak forests. Walking the present-day city that sprawls across the Foyle's east and west banks is a challenging workout of steep streets but ultimately rewarding vistas.

The original walled city lies on a hill on the river's west bank. Its high walls were built by English settlers sent by London guilds in the 17th century as part of King James I's colonization of the region, the Ulster plantations. These fortifications defended repeated attacks from Irish rebels opposed to the crown. The walls now form a mile-long (1.6 km) walkway around the inner city. Never breached, they withstood several sieges, including the infamous 105-day Siege of Derry in 1689, giving Derry its nickname: the Maiden City.

In 1613, the city was renamed Londonderry, a move that would cause a sharp schism in Derry's identity. The name Derry was an anglicization of the Gaelic *Daire* or *Doire*, meaning "oak wood." While the city's official name is still Londonderry, Derry has been used in the names of the local government district and council since 1984; most citizens, even Protestants living on the east side, now use the shorter, original name.

Modern Derry, a city of about 110,000, extends considerably north and west of the old city walls and east of the river, but a sense of division persists. The mainly nationalist section of the city to the west of the Foyle is referred to as the **Cityside,** the largely Unionist district to the east as the **Waterside.** Within the Cityside, the low-lying, marshy district on the west bank known as the **Bogside** is remembered for the 1969 street battles that pitched Catholic

inhabitants against the forces of a British state that denied them rights such as equal access to housing and employment. In 1972, at a march against internment, British paratroopers shot 26 people, killing 14, on the Bogside. This event is commemorated on the district's gable walls at the ends of row houses.

Derry is a city of fine architecture and a walk within the old walled city, encompassed by the Cityside, goes past many late Georgian, Victorian, and Edwardian buildings. The focal point of the city's grid pattern is the central **Diamond,** with its moving War Memorial, erected in 1927 to commemorate citizens who died during World War I. Nearby **St. Columb's Cathedral** was built in 1633 as the first post-Reformation cathedral built for the Anglican Church. The 19th-century Catholic **St. Eugene's Cathedral** stands as its counterpart on the Bogside.

As Derry tries to heal its sectarian divisions, one secular edifice acts as a suture across the divide: the soaring **Peace Bridge.** Opened in 2011, this cycle and pedestrian pathway was purpose-built to foster links and strengthen peaceful coexistence between communities in the Waterside and the Cityside. The curved, asymmetrical bridge symbolizes flexibility and stretches 770 feet (235 m) across the Foyle. Farther up the river, the statue **"Hands Across the Divide"** imagines a brighter future. ■

Maurice Harron's bronze statue "Hands Across the Divide" OPPOSITE: Derry's Peace Bridge

At Free Derry Corner in the Bogside, a gable wall mural commemorates the autonomous nationalist area declared between 1969 and 1972.

Insider's Guide

The Best of Derry

Derry is too often defined by its troubled recent history, rather than by the warmth of its citizens and their darkly humorous wit and wisdom. To surround yourself with this conversational gift, go to a GAA match in **Celtic Park** or head for the **Brandywell,** home of Derry City F.C. (the city's soccer club). The Candystripes—so named for their red-and-white striped shirts—suffered pariah status during the Troubles, exiled from the Irish League (Northern Ireland's professional league),

before joining the Republic's League of Ireland in 1985.

Some key local linguistics to prepare you: If City are "jammy" (lucky), fans around you will be "lured" (delighted); if they lose, they'll be in a "gunk" (funk); and if they lose heavily, they'll be "dead broke" (highly mortified) and it might be best to "keep yer bake shut" (stay silent). A defiant freedom of expression, however, is the theme of **Free Derry Corner** on the Bogside. Here a gable wall mural commemorates Free Derry, the autonomous nation-

alist area declared between 1969 and 1972. A memorial to the 1981 hunger strikers, another to the IRA's Derry Brigade, and other nearby murals on the gable walls on the end of city streets, can be explained by local guides for hire.

For a deeper dive into the Troubles, the **Museum of Free Derry**—also on the Bogside—tells the story of the Free Derry Irish nationalist movement of the 1970s.

The rich history of Derry unfolds around the city center. A good start is the beautiful neo-Gothic **Guild-**

hall, built in 1887. Look out for its stained-glass windows, donated by London guilds, showing exponents of many trades, from fishmongers to musicians. To fully explore the old city, buy a **Visit Derry Pass,** an official sightseeing ticket for the Walled City that also allows access to 10 handpicked attractions over two days, including the **Tower Museum** and **St. Columb's Cathedral,** as well as the **Chapter House Museum,** located on the cathedral grounds, and the **Saint Columba Heritage Centre,** next to the Long Tower Church. The latter offers insight into the life of Columba (Colmcille) and the city's monastic sites.

The **Siege Museum** has a permanent display on the Siege of Derry and the Associated Clubs of the Apprentice Boys of Derry, the network that keeps Unionist traditions alive. The **Foyle Valley Railway Museum,** located on the site of the Foyle Road Station, tells the story of the golden age of steam on the northern railways in the early 20th century. Also of interest is the **Amelia Earhart Centre,** which celebrates the 1932 landing of aviator Amelia Earhart in a pasture in Ballyarnett, Derry. The 34-year-old American, who had left Newfoundland 14 hours and 56 minutes earlier, became the first woman to fly solo across the Atlantic. ∎

IN THE KNOW: WHERE TO SHOP, STAY, EAT & DRINK IN DERRY

Derry is a wonderfully convivial city for a night out, especially if you're just off the last leg of the Wild Atlantic Way going south to north, or the Causeway Coast trail traveling east to west. A welcome stop is Derry's **Craft Village,** an eclectic mix of artisan craft shops, enticing eateries, and coffee shops set within a Victorian-style village complete with reconstructed 18th-century streets and a Dickensian English square.

An excellent place to stay in Derry is the boutique **Shipquay Hotel,** within an Italianate building overlooking the city walls and the Guildhall. The hotel restaurant serves fine food with plenty of choice from a good wine list. Try the house boxty dish, which combines homemade chive and spring onion boxty, Clonakilty black pudding, pancetta, caramelized onion, and poached egg.

Many people say **Harry's Shack** on Strand Street has Ireland's best fish-and-chips (haddock in buttermilk batter, served with mushy peas). Their Mulroy Bay mussels are worth a try, too. To eat with the locals, head for **Soda & Starch Pantry & Grill** in Derry's Craft Village, where Chef Raymond Moran serves great steaks and burgers with his secret-recipe house sauce. His hearty boxty with cabbage and bacon is a northwest traditional delight.

Derry is filled with welcoming hostelries, but no matter where you socialize in Ulster, it's best to avoid talk of religion. The visitor who finds themselves in an awkward situation may appreciate the local joke describing a relentless interrogation by an Ulsterman that culminates in the question: "Ooh aye, but are ye a Catholic atheist or a Protestant atheist?"

The **Blackbird Bar** is everything you want in a Victorian-style drinking emporium, with leather-seated booths, soothingly low lights, and a cordial atmosphere for chat and great food. Musicians perform some nights, making the Blackbird even livelier.

The place for pre- or post-theater drinks and eats in Derry is **Badgers Bar,** located near Derry's best drama venues. The **Grand Central Bar** offers good pub food, a great beer range, and mighty traditional music sessions. Trad music is also found in **Peadar O'Donnell's Bar,** where, when the polished performers take a breather, the locals are likely to break into a verse or two of "The Parting Glass" or "The Town I Loved So Well" (a song about Derry) just to amuse themselves until the players return. ∎

The Soda & Starch patio: an alfresco feel, without the Derry rain

The Irish Abroad

The Diaspora in Britain

For 800 years, the Irish looked to London, not Dublin, as the source of their laws. For much of that time, London was the capital of an empire that the Irish were part of, if never willingly.

But despite that centuries-long marriage of inconvenience, and an inevitably prolonged divorce, many Irish retain a special affinity for London. The British capital provided an outlet of escape and opportunity for many emigrants who tired of the economic, cultural, and parochial constraints of a largely rural homeland.

The imaginative Irish, being creatively inclined, have always thrived amid Britain's artistic and literary scenes. The darling of London's late 1800s literary circle was Dublin-born playwright Oscar Wilde. A man who imagined a world where one's two-dimensional image could hide all your faults and keep you forever young, Wilde's outlook was at least a century ahead of his time. Few modern-day Twitter users could articulate so well his many witticisms, including the truism that the "only thing worse than being talked about is not being talked about."

Another Irish playwright, George Bernard Shaw, won the Nobel Prize in Literature in 1925. The judges noted his "stimulating satire . . . infused with a singular poetic beauty." Two years earlier, Irishman W. B. Yeats, who was educated in London, had won the Nobel for "his always inspired poetry, which . . . gives expression to the spirit of a whole nation."

A pattern was set: The inspiration was Ireland, but the global stage was London. Later literary exiles included Edna O'Brien in the 1960s and Joseph O'Connor in the '80s. O'Brien's novel *The Country Girls* (1960) was banned in her conservative homeland, where the Catholic Church determined what the Irish read—or tried to. The ban boosted sales hugely in Britain, where many Irish sought work in the postwar

Visiting Glasgow Rangers fans wave Union Jacks to defy their cross-city soccer rivals at Celtic Park, Glasgow.

boom years, while their newly independent state stagnated.

As the new medium of television took off, garrulous Irish presenters such as Eamonn Andrews and Terry Wogan became stars of the British small screen. Their success elevated the standing of a generation of immigrants who had arrived in 1950s Britain to signs declaring: "No Irish. No blacks. No dogs."

That landlords' obscenity was appropriated by an English-born son of Irish immigrants, John Lydon, as the title of his autobiography. Better known by his stage name of Johnny Rotten (of the Sex Pistols), Lydon was one of a remarkable number of successful British rock stars with Irish roots: John Lennon's grandparents were from Dublin, while Boy George, the Gallagher brothers (Oasis), Morrissey and Johnny Marr (the Smiths), and Shane MacGowan (the Pogues) were all the children of Irish exiles.

MacGowan in particular captured the wild spirit of the Gael disoriented by dislocation in England. This often humorous clash of cultures is witnessed every March, when tens of thousands of Irish horse racing fans decamp for a week of Dionysian debauchery at the Cheltenham Festival, just northwest of London.

Each weekend from September to May, the Irish also travel en masse across the Irish Sea to cheer on soccer clubs in Liverpool, Manchester, and especially Glasgow. Irish players, such as Donegal man Seamus Coleman, carve out lucrative careers "over beyond." Another Donegal player, Packie Bonner from Burton-

The Irish writer in exile: novelist Edna O'Brien at her home in London

port, became a national hero in 1990 when his penalty save in Turin paved the way for Ireland's first appearance in a World Cup quarterfinal. The manager who plotted this success was an Englishman, Jack Charlton, who had won the trophy as a player in 1966. Charlton's squad comprised many second-generation Irish, whom he recruited throughout Britain. As these sons and grandsons of emigrants now wore the green, they brought a renewed pride to a homeland still wracked with unemployment and emigration.

Packie Bonner played his entire senior career with Glasgow Celtic, a club founded in 1887 by a Marist clergyman, Brother Walfrid, from Ireland. Brother Walfrid's aim was to alleviate poverty among the immigrant Irish in Glasgow, many of whom were from Donegal. This spiritually Irish club produced the first British team to win the European

Cup in 1967, doing so with a team of local recruits all born within 30 miles (50 km) of the city. Celtic built a fierce rivalry with crosstown counterparts the Glasgow Rangers; the intensity of their "Old Firm" battles was compounded by sectarian undertones, as Celtic identified as the "Catholic Irish" team, while Rangers maintained a Protestant-only team policy until 1989.

In 1892, the first turf in Celtic's new stadium in Scotland was transported from County Donegal and laid by Irish patriot and poet Michael Davitt, then planted with shamrocks. The Irish community viewed this as their small patch of Britain that would be forever Ireland.

Such is Glasgow Celtic's long standing as *the* Irish team in Britain that the government of the embryonic Irish Free State presented the club with an Irish Tricolor to fly over Celtic Park in 1922. ∎

Irish Heritage

The Seamus Heaney HomePlace

Located in Bellaghy, close to the poet's birthplace, the Seamus Heaney HomePlace celebrates the life and work of the Derry man who became Ireland's fourth Nobel laureate in 1995.

The exhibition is housed in a modern building that allows for quiet, unhurried contemplation of the poet's work. The HomePlace consists of two floors filled with artifacts, personal stories, family photos, and books, many donated by the Heaney family. Multimedia exhibits include video recordings from friends, neighbors, and world leaders. We also hear the soothing voice of the poet himself. A re-creation of Heaney's Dublin study takes you into his creative world.

Heaney and his family were among many Derry and Belfast families who sought refuge in the Republic as the Troubles ignited in the early 1970s. Their crossing to "the south," and the plight of relatives left behind, including a murdered cousin, were explored in *North,* one of his best known works.

He famously identified how Ulster's sectarian divisions silenced speech itself in the poem, "Whatever You Say, Say Nothing." Heaney also used the rural language of his Derry homeland to convey the archaeological and anthropological digging that his life's work entailed. In the dark days of the 1970s and 1980s, the poet declared the purpose of his poetry in "Personal Helicon"—to see himself and to hear what resounded in the darkness around him. Visitors to Dublin's National Museum (see page 28) who have seen Ireland's bog bodies will appreciate the deep divination and precise descriptive power of Heaney's craft in his lines on pagan sacrifices from European bogs in poems such as "The Bog Queen" and "The Grauballe Man."

Heaney was the carrier of a torch that has passed from the ancient *filés* (poets) of the Gaelic courts to the wandering bards of the Penal Laws era, such as Antoine Ó Raifteirí, to W. B. Yeats and successors such as Patrick Kavanagh (see page 262). Poets in Ireland have long had a cultural license to comment on—even criticize—their leaders. Speaking truth to power can also act as inspiration for the powerful: On Heaney's death in 2013, U.S. president Clinton paid tribute to his "good friend" when he said, "His uniquely Irish gift for language made him our finest poet of the rhythms of ordinary lives and a powerful voice for peace."

Another admirer, U.S. president Biden, often quotes the poet's vision of peace in troubled times from "The Cure at Troy." In this verse adaptation of Sophocles' play *Philoctetes,* Heaney celebrates the rare points in the human saga when "hope and history rhyme." Among the most quoted in modern Irish poetry, this line was also referenced in the 2000 U2 song "Peace on Earth."

Seamus Heaney is buried in the cemetery of St. Mary's Church, Bellaghy. His epitaph reads, "Walk on air against your better judgement" (from "The Gravel Walks"). ∎

The Seamus Heaney HomePlace OPPOSITE: Seamus Heaney (1939–2013)

MONAGHAN

L et us arise and go now, not, as Yeats called, to the Lake Isle of Innisfree, but into the lake-strewn heartland of another great 20th-century Irish poet, Patrick Kavanagh. Kavanagh made the stony gray soil of Monaghan resonate to a wider world with his rustic verse. Although part of Ulster, his native county remains in the Republic. What attracts most visitors to Monaghan today are the region's wondrous waterways, teeming with trout, salmon, and pike. This multitude of lakes and rivers makes Monaghan—and the surrounding wetlands of Counties Fermanagh (in Northern Ireland) and Leitrim and Cavan (in the Republic)—a veritable Eden for anglers.

Kavanagh often wrote of his "beatific wonder" at the natural world and the mysteries of its creation. Fishermen who take to the lakes before dawn and find themselves seemingly afloat on the early morning Monaghan mists will certainly empathize. The literary works of this rural dreamer and visionary are celebrated at the Patrick Kavanagh Centre in his native village of Inishkeen (see page 262). There you can learn of the poet's early years in the Mucker townlands around Inishkeen and of his later literary and journalistic career in London and Dublin.

The town of Monaghan is worth visiting for its interesting architecture and layout. Although County Monaghan has been in the Republic since 1921, it formed part of the ancient kingdom of Ulster and was planted and colonized by non-Catholic Scottish settlers in the early 17th century. The wealth generated by Ulster's thriving linen industry is reflected in the county town's fine buildings, three squares, Victorian drinking fountain, and the huge St. Macartan's Cathedral, which was constructed between 1861 and 1891. The cathedral's 250-foot (76 m) spire dominates the town. Some 5,000 years of rich archaeological and social history are covered in the Monaghan County Museum. The highlight is the 14th-century Cross of Clogher, a wonderful altar crucifix of bronze from the ancient bishopric a few miles northwest of the town. ∎

Castle Leslie Estate, on the outskirts of the village of Glaslough

The waterways of Monaghan and neighboring Cavan, Fermanagh, and Leitrim are an angler's delight.

Insider's Guide

The Lakelands of Monaghan

Your day might start before dawn here, assembling the right tackle for pike, perch, bream, roach, or carp. Monaghan's lakes—along with those in the neighboring counties of Leitrim, Cavan, and Fermanagh—promise some of Europe's best coarse fishing.

Your heart might start racing as you pull on your Wellies (boots named, incidentally, after Dublin-born Arthur Wellesley, first Duke of Wellington, hero of Waterloo in 1815, and a son of the Protestant Ascendancy).

Trout might be in the ascendancy if it's spring and the mayflies are dappling on the surface. There are few more thrilling sounds for the aficionado than that *plash* breaking the still silence of an early morning lakeshore or riverbank. Especially when you're lucky enough to glimpse the muscular, meaty leap of the brown trout, a creature from the murky underworld tempted to break the water's surface by insects in the air above. The Celtic mystics and Druids believed that certain fish had otherworldly qualities and

saw them as sacred creatures from another realm.

For serious fishermen, **Glaslough Lake,** located on the grounds of Castle Leslie Estate, is worth seeking out. Permission must be obtained from the owners and a fee paid. The lake, stocked with coarse fish, is one of the most beautiful fishing spots anywhere in Ireland. Boat rental and gillie (guide) services can be arranged via the estate.

There are no license or permit requirements on many waters in

Monaghan, and generally the fishing is free. However, always check with the local authorities. Staff in Monaghan's many fishing shops—such as **Gormley's** in Emyvale—will advise on license requirements and on the renting of boats. They'll also refer you to local gillies who are knowledgeable on the region's labyrinth of lakes and rivers. Many of these waterways are bisected by the border with Northern Ireland, so remember that anglers who cross over for coarse fishing will need a coarse rod license and, in certain places, a permit.

Across Ireland north and south, a catch-and-release policy is promoted, meaning all fish should be returned to the water. This doesn't stop you from enjoying a piscine taste of Monaghan at day's end; the county has many eateries with extensive menu choices featuring local fare caught by licensed commercial fishers. The **Courthouse Restaurant** in Carrickmacross offers excellent tapas. A perfect end to a day on the lakes is an evening at **Andy's Bar,** an old-style, wood-paneled gastropub in Monaghan Town. The food is excellent, there are 101 gins to choose from, and the tall tales of fishermen are always indulged by friendly barmen. ∎

TASTE OF IRELAND: FRIED TROUT WITH TOASTED HAZELNUTS & HERBS

Monaghan and Cavan are lake country, and any angler lucky enough to hook a trout in Ireland knows that this meaty fish is one of the finest tastes you can fry up in the open air.

This recipe has echoes of the legend of Fionn MacCumhaill, who accidentally tasted the Salmon of Knowledge. This great fish had ingested the nine hazelnuts that fell into the Well of Wisdom. The poet Finn Eces (or Finegas) had spent seven years fishing for this prized catch, which would bestow great wisdom on whoever ate it. However, the bard let young Fionn cook the salmon, and when the boy burned his finger in the sizzling fish fat, then licked it, he gained a taste of the coveted knowledge. The poet then made the boy eat the whole of the fish to ingest its full wisdom. You'll probably be wiser to share your trout.

INGREDIENTS

- 4 fresh trout, about 10 oz. each, gutted, washed, and dried, complete with heads and tails
- Salt and pepper
- ¾ cup (4 oz) plain flour
- 2 sticks (8 oz) Kerrygold Irish butter
- ¾ cup (4 oz) hazelnuts, shelled
- 2 tablespoons lemon juice
- 2 tablespoons finely chopped chives
- 2 tablespoons finely chopped tarragon
- 1 lemon, cut into 4 wedges
- Sprigs of watercress

DIRECTIONS

- Season the fish inside and out with salt and pepper and toss in the flour.
- Fry in half the butter until golden brown, about 5 minutes on each side. Turn with care, just once, to avoid the skin breaking.
- Toast the hazelnuts lightly under a broiler, turning frequently. Remove the skins, then chop the nuts.
- Transfer the fish to four warmed plates and sprinkle the nuts over the trout. Keep warm.
- Melt the remaining butter in a small saucepan until golden brown and foaming. Add the lemon juice, then pour the butter mixture over the trout, sprinkle the herbs on top, and garnish with the lemon wedges and watercress. Serve with boiled potatoes and green vegetables. Feeds four hungry anglers.

Fried trout enhanced by toasted hazelnuts and herbs

Irish Heritage

The Monaghan Mystic

On the eastern border of County Monaghan lies the hardscrabble farmland around Inishkeen, where small farmers eke out a living from the steep sides of drumlins and reedy valleys. Patrick Kavanagh (1904–1967) eulogized and excoriated this landscape in wondrous poems that could shine with an animistic belief one moment then turn as black as the northern soil the next.

Kavanagh was a small-scale Inishkeen farmer until he left in his early 30s to work as a writer, first in London, then in Dublin just as "The Emergency" (World War II) brought austerity to neutral Ireland. His epic poem "The Great Hunger" (1942) poignantly captures the privations, hopelessness, and hardships of rural life at the time.

Writing columns and reviews for newspapers made Kavanagh one of the best known faces in Dublin pubs in the 1940s and '50s. During this era, the censorious shadow of the Catholic Church loomed over all published works. His fictional account of rural life, the semiautobiographical novel *Tarry Flynn*, was banned in 1948.

Kavanagh suffered a severe loss in a litigation case he took against *The Leader* magazine for an anonymously written profile of him as an alcoholic letch. He would battle alcoholism and lung cancer for many years prior to his death at 63. His Dublin poems, including "Canal Bank Walk" and "On Raglan Road," glorified the grandeur of God's creation in everyday places. This latter poem, set to the tune of "The Dawning of the Day,"

would become Ireland's favorite folk song (see page 45).

Inishkeen remained the prime wellspring of his talent, from lyrical works, such as the autobiographical novel *The Green Fool* (1938), to bitterly realistic poems such as "Stony Grey Soil" (1940), in which Kavanagh bemoans peasant life and the work that restricted his artistic potential. Today, Inishkeen's old village church now hosts the Patrick Kavanagh Centre. It features a fascinating exhibition on the poet and his oeuvre, and his influence on poets such as Seamus Heaney.

Kavanagh's grave lies outside, marked with a simple wooden cross and the words: "And pray for him who walked apart on the hills, loving life's miracles." He remained a devout Catholic throughout his life, and his work used many religious allusions, such as his admonition to a simple plowman to "drive your horses in the creed / Of God the Father as a stook . . . For you are driving your horses through / The mist where Genesis begins" (from "To the Man After the Harrow"). The center offers a tour of Kavanagh Country, including the family farm of Shancoduff.

Patrick Kavanagh's poetry spanned the rural and urban world of Ireland in the mid-20th century. A statue of the poet now graces the Grand Canal bank walk in Dublin, near Leeson Bridge. His spirit, however, lingers in Inishkeen. ∎

The Patrick Kavanagh Centre welcomes visitors. OPPOSITE: Patrick Kavanagh in a favored snug

ANTRIM

As you enter County Antrim, the Causeway Coast takes on a magical air. The mystique stems from ancient Irish legend: This is the land of the Giant's Causeway, the steps across the Irish Sea to Scotland laid down by that titan of Irish myth, Fionn MacCumhaill himself. The hero of Ireland's epics supposedly built this bridge to his lover on the Hebridean island of Staffa. The columns of cooled basalt are a geological wonder, and this is Northern Ireland's most visited site. Yet humankind's insignificance amid such magnificence is aptly reflected in the visitors center's invisibility: Its stone facade is largely absorbed into its coastal surrounds.

The scars of human conflict are all too visible on the so-called peace walls and in sectarian divides of Belfast, however. A taxi tour of sites of the Troubles is a fascinating, if frightening, glimpse into the hearts of darkness produced by Ulster's history of conquest and colonization.

A more life-affirming product of the past can be enjoyed at the Old Bushmills Distillery in the village of the same name. The ancient Gaelic term *uiscé beatha* (water of life) makes perfect sense when you take a tour and inhale the sweet whiskey vapors from stacked wooden barrels, an invigorating breath of the liquid gold as it matures to 10-, 21-, or even 30-year-old peaks of perfection. This evaporation is called the "angels' share."

Elsewhere in Antrim, other legends lure you to sweet spots throughout this historic county. Just along the coast from the Giant's Causeway, the clifftop ruins of Dunluce Castle perch precariously over the swells of a wind-whipped northerly sea, as they have since medieval times. A more recently created legend is evoked at the Dark Hedges in Ballymoney, where visitors transition into the dreamlike realm of *Game of Thrones* via an often mist-shrouded avenue of beseeching beech trees. Carrick-a-Rede Rope Bridge near Ballintoy dares you to make a more audacious crossing, this one to the sea stack that anadromous salmon pass through in the thousands each year. ∎

The Tall Ships Race comes to Belfast Harbour, County Antrim.

GREAT IRISH DRIVES: THE CAUSEWAY COAST & BEYOND

Starting out from the lively city of Derry, this diverse drive takes you west to east along Ireland's north and northeast coastlines. If you're coming from Dublin, you can start at Strangford and travel east to west.

From Derry, you'll pass several small towns along the south shores of Lough Foyle before reaching **Limavady.** Here the appealing **Sculpture Trail** is worth a stop, to wander among depictions of several Celtic myths and legends, such as Manannán mac Lir, the mighty Celtic god of the sea. Portstewart Strand offers a wide beach and the remains of the 18th-century **Mussenden Temple** and the **Downhill Demense.** The nearby resort town of **Portrush** is another Derry destination worth seeking out.

The historic and geologic wonders of the county of Antrim come thick and fast along this rugged coastline. **Dunluce Castle** is steeped in storybook adventure, not least of which is its daring recapture from English occupiers by the bloody-handed Sorley Boy MacDonnell in 1584. The town of **Bushmills** is known throughout the world for its whiskey, and a brisk "stiffener" is recommended before you set out onto the windswept **Giant's Causeway.** The volcanic basalt columns that jut out into the sea like organ pipes can be explored from every angle. It's especially evocative around dusk.

In picturesque Ballintoy, the next town to the east, you can take sustenance and steel your nerve before walking across the **Carrick-a-Rede Rope Bridge,** swinging some 100 feet (30 m) above the ocean. The nearby town of Ballycastle is notable for the 16th-century **Bonamargy Friary,** the resting place of Sorley Boy MacDonnell, Ulster's fearless warrior chieftain. The towns of Cushenun, Cushendall, Carnlough, and Glenarm will take you past the **Glens of Antrim,** an area known for its natural beauty.

Also worth a detour on your way south are **Glenarm Castle** with its walled garden, and **Carnfunnock Country Park** with its sundials and wooden sculptures. In addition, Carnfunnock also offers a maritime-themed outdoor adventure playground, a golf driving range, an orienteering course, and the fun challenge of a hedge maze in the shape of Northern Ireland. The latter is planted with more than 1,500 mature hornbeam (Carpinus betulus). If there's time, **Carrickfergus Castle** is another picturesque place to enjoy a tour.

Daredevils and adventurous souls step lightly across the Carrick-a-Rede Rope Bridge.

Next stop is **Belfast,** the storied port where so many great ships were built and **Titanic Belfast** (see page 271) now beckons with myriad stories of that dark night on the Atlantic in 1912. Post–Peace Agreement Belfast is a lively, modern city where a night out will probably entice you to stay on for another; it's easy to make gregarious new friends here, once your ear adjusts to the wild accents, hilarious turns of phrase, and razor-sharp wit of entertaining regulars in great gin joints such as the **Crown.**

You can clear your head the next day with a bracing walk up to **Scabo Tower** near Bangor, built as a memorial in 1857 and offering expansive views of the surrounding country-side. Farther east, **Mount Stewart House and Gardens** (see page 285) is a delight for horticulture vultures. The charm-ing coastal towns of Millisle, Ballywalter, and Portavogie take you down to your penultimate stop at Portaferry. Here you can visit the **Exploris Aquarium,** located on the shores of the Strangford Lough European Marine Site. Fans of *Game of Thrones* can make a pilgrimage to tour **Castle Ward House** and its grounds, just west of Strangford, the final stop on your driving odyssey along the Causeway Coast and beyond. ∎

Renowned as the oldest licensed distillery in the world, the internationally acclaimed Bushmills first opened in 1608.

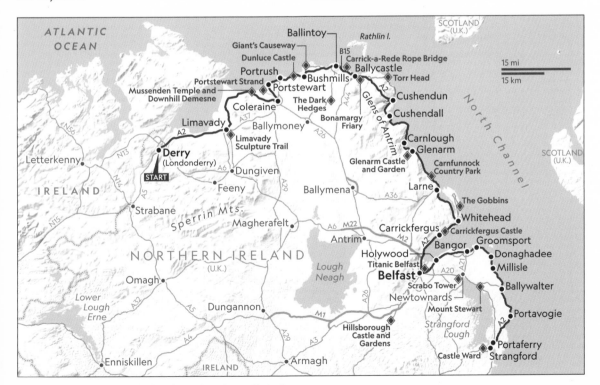

The Causeway Coast Drive winds along the northern shores of Ireland.

Special Places

The Giant's Causeway

Derry, like Belfast, is a city where districts are defined by the Union Jack, St. George's Cross, or the Irish Tricolor flying proudly. Halfway between the two cities, however, you'll find a flag that reminds us that these shorelines have other stories to tell. The Jolly Roger beckons travelers to the **Smugglers Inn,** a charming pub about a mile (1.6 km) from the **Giant's Causeway.**

If you enjoy a salty sea tale, you might hear the legend told at the Smugglers Inn (and elsewhere) that the causeway was formed when the Gaelic warrior Fionn MacCumhaill flung swaths of the Antrim coast into the sea, creating a path to confront the Scottish giant Benandonner and reach his lover on the island of Staffa.

If you're more scientific, you'll learn that the causeway resulted from volcanic flows cooling into 37,000 basalt columns some 60 million years ago. Victorian guides named the most striking of these formations the **Giant's Organ Pipes.** Here, the cooled lava flow is evident in the dark columns that resemble stacked pencils, up to 40 feet (12 m) high, in the face of the 300-foot (92 m) cliffs.

The mythology and geology of the Giant's Causeway is explained in the visitors center nestled into the cliffs, which includes shops and eateries as well as an interpretive center, where interactive exhibits forearm you with useful knowledge of specific rock formations, such as Giant's Boot, the Wishing Chair, the Camel, and Giant's Granny. The center also offers guided tours with rangers and information on four walking trails.

There's no entry fee to the causeway, nor any restrictions to accessing the rocks, all about a 10-minute stroll from the visitors center. Make sure you bring good rainwear and hiking shoes to navigate the wet rocks. Time your visit for after 7 p.m. in summer and you'll have this UNESCO World Heritage site practically to yourself to craft dramatically lit photographs without too many "extras" in your shot. As the light declines, using long exposures (slow shutter speeds) adds great detail to the shadows on these hexagonal basalt rocks and brings out beautiful blues and radiant reds and oranges in the sea and skies.

Once you've captured the magic to share with others, or just enjoyed the timeless wonder of these rocks yourself, return to the visitors center along a cliff path that affords fine views down onto the causeway. Spying all the rocky coves and caves that stretch along the craggy Antrim coastline, it's easy to see why smugglers and pirates are part of the Causeway Coast's rich history alongside giants and geological wonders.

If there's time, make the 20-minute drive to the **Dark Hedges,** the avenue of inward-leaning beech trees featured in the TV series *Game of Thrones.* These are located along Bregagh Road between Armoy and Stranocum, about 12 miles (19 km) southeast of the Giant's Causeway. ∎

The Giant's Causeway is an area of about 40,000 interlocking basalt columns. Visitors can walk across the mostly hexagonal rocks to the edge of the ocean. OPPOSITE: The Giant's Causeway at dusk

Peace walls such as these, separating Catholic and Protestant districts, are sectarian scars on Belfast City and other parts of Ulster.

Insider's Guide

Belfast

In the words of a Belfast native, the capital of Northern Ireland is "a funny wee city, so it is now." Indeed, you'll need to appreciate the dark humor of Belfast people to see the city's funny side: Its main attractions are a museum commemorating the world's greatest maritime disaster and a trip around the Belfast equivalent of the Berlin Wall.

In Belfast, there are at least three sides to every story, but it can be difficult to track down the neutral voice. Take a guided trip by taxi around the so-called peace walls and all drivers will bring you into both the Falls Road (Catholic) and the Shankill Road (Protestant) districts, but the commentary you'll get on the political murals will depend very much on who is behind the wheel. The blame game is enthusiastically pursued on both sides. As Bono once observed: "Choose your enemies wisely, for they will define you."

The peace walls separating the two factions are the geographical scars of the sectarian war that started in 1969 and ended in 1998, referred to in Ireland as the Troubles.

These barbed wire–topped walls have gates used to close off each community from the other. A total of 108 peace walls, or security fences, were built across Northern Ireland, most in Belfast, with others in Derry, Portadown, and Lurgan. The Belfast walls snake around some 21 miles (34 km) of Protestant and Catholic enclaves. The walls are noticeable for their height, which can climb up to 25 feet (8 m) in combative places—to prevent the throwing of petrol bombs or missiles across the divide. Taxi drivers will tell you mirthfully that "our walls here are taller than those in Palestine and the West Bank, so they are." This verbal tic among northerners—adding an affirmation at the end of a sentence—is a preemptive strike against any incredulity on the listener's part.

Belfast in the 21st century, however, has much to savor and is several light-years from the gloom and doom of the Troubles. This is a city where the arts thrive and cafés, restaurants, and bars thrum with conversation and music. Listen out for *the* Belfast melody, the children's street game song "I'll Tell Me Ma." One of the best known versions united musicians from the Protestant and Nationalist traditions: Van Morrison grew up in Protestant Bloomfield; his father, a Belfast shipyard electrician, had a sizable jazz and blues collection from time spent in Detroit. Meanwhile, the Chieftains were a traditional Irish group mainly from the Republic (harpist Derek Bell was from Belfast). Their collaboration on "I'll Tell Me Ma" combined quintessential Celtic instruments—bodhran, uilleann pipes, tin whistle—with a few bars of the Unionist marching song "The Sash My Father Wore." The track appeared on the album *Irish Heartbeat,* and no doubt Van the Man reacted with a wicked Belfast chuckle. ∎

IN THE KNOW: TITANIC BELFAST

The story of R.M.S. *Titanic* has been told many times, first as news, relayed via transatlantic cable, then as history, and finally as myth. Much of the myth was made real again in 1985, when a team led by National Geographic Explorer Bob Ballard located the ship's sunken wreckage on the ocean floor.

Today, the *Titanic* story is told in one of the world's great museums, **Titanic Belfast,** on the site of the Harland & Wolff shipyards on Belfast Lough. The building itself grabs attention, much like the great ocean liners were designed to do: Four sharp, upswept angles represent the symbol of the White Star Line, the company that built the doomed *Titanic* and several sister ships. They also call to mind the magnificent ocean liner's prows and, with a little imagination, you can even perceive the glitter of an iceberg in the reflective silver cladding. The huge *Titanic* sign is cut from the same type of one-inch (2.5 cm) steel plate used to build the ship. Inside, exposed rivets, rusted metal plates, and tiny lights like mid-Atlantic stars further transport you back to that fateful night of April 15, 1912.

Exhibits along a self-guided tour deliver the sights, sounds, and smells of the great ship, and the stories of those who made her. A theater shows fascinating film footage of the passenger liner lying broken in two 12,415 feet (3,784 m) down on the bed of the Atlantic, her rails and hatches, foremast, and anchor chain all visible. The audio tells the tale of *Titanic*'s rediscovery by Ballard's team. ∎

Exhibits at Titanic Belfast evoke the great ship.

S.S. *Nomadic,* a White Star Line tender

Meryl Streep starred in *Dancing at Lughnasa*, the story of five unmarried sisters determined to enjoy their simple rural life in 1930s Ireland.

Ireland On Screen

Northern Ireland in Film

The Troubles in Northern Ireland have presented filmmakers with a rewarding canvas on which to write all-too-human stories of conflict, tragedy, betrayal, and heightened drama.

Neil Jordan, one of Ireland's finest filmmakers, grew up in Sligo, close to the border. Jordan's first feature was *Angel* (1982)—released as *Danny Boy* in the U.S.—about a musician who gets dragged into IRA operations. As an adult, Jordan lived in Bray, a town devastated by the massacre of the Miami Showband on their return from a concert in the

north, which may have sparked his story of a musician's world blown apart by men of violence. Stephen Rea, the guilt-wracked saxophone player, would later play the lead in *The Crying Game* (1992), which won Jordan an Academy Award for best screenplay. Rea's character was an IRA gunman who empathizes with a kidnapped British soldier, with unexpected results.

The emotional toll of living in a divided community, often with divided loyalties, has been the theme of many films out of Northern Ireland. *Cal* (1984), written by

Bernard MacLaverty and directed by Pat O'Connor, tells the story of a young man torn between love and fear in a community pervaded by distrust of neighbors, workmates, and the authorities.

Many of the most affecting Northern Irish films are based on real-life events. *In the Name of the Father* dramatizes the 1970s incarceration of the Guildford Four, Irish émigrés falsely accused of planting deadly pub bombs in the London suburb. Jim Sheridan's drama focuses on the death of Giuseppe Conlon, father of Gerry, who was also incarcerated when he traveled from Belfast to visit his imprisoned son. Giuseppe died in prison.

Daniel Day-Lewis's intense portrayal of Conlon's agonized powerlessness is heartrending. The film's theme song, written by Bono, Gavin Friday, and Maurice Seezer, captured the cloying paranoia of the Troubles and the glamorous escape that London promised for those who felt caged in Belfast. The music was driven by a militaristic tattoo of tribal drumming and included samplings of the Lambeg drum favored by loyalist marchers.

The story of the nationalist marchers killed by British paratroopers in Derry is the subject of *Bloody Sunday* (2002). The film was shot in cinema verité style, with scenes filmed in Guildhall Square and Creggan, both in Derry, on the actual route of the 1972 march.

Despite all the pain and angst that ensnarled Ulster for decades, the province's most acclaimed actor recently portrayed it through a loving lens. Kenneth Branagh's *Belfast* (2021) takes us back to the city via warm memories of childhood. Another film celebrating a sense of hope in Ulster life is *Dancing at Lughnasa* (1998), a story set around the festival of Lughnasadh, the Celtic harvest festival. ∎

TASTE OF IRELAND: AN ULSTER FRY

Ulster is the northernmost of the four Irish provinces, and when you visit the ruins of Dunluce Castle (see page 266) perched on an Antrim coast clifftop, you'll realize that this is no country for cold men or women. A wee Ulster fry is just the meal to keep those bitter northerly winds at bay as you drive the Causeway Coast. This hearty breakfast is sometimes jokingly referred to as "a heart attack on a plate" and can be served for lunch or supper, too.

INGREDIENTS

- 1 or 2 Ulster sausages
- Vegetable oil
- 2 rashers (strips of bacon), back and streaky
- 2 slices of white or black pudding
- 2 potato farls (potato cakes)
- 1 slice soda bread
- 1 potato cake, cut in half
- Kerrygold Irish butter
- Mushrooms
- 1 tomato, sliced
- 1–2 eggs

DIRECTIONS

- Fry the sausages in a small amount of oil until almost cooked, then add the rashers and black or white pudding and fry until cooked. Remove from the pan and drain on paper towels. Keep warm.
- Fry the farls, soda bread, and potato cake until lightly toasted; drain and keep warm.
- Add oil and butter to the pan, fry the mushrooms and tomato, then add these to the plate with the sausages.
- If needed, add more oil and butter, fry the eggs, spooning hot oil over both yolk and white until cooked.
- Serve the whole "fry-up" on a warmed plate with a pot of hot tea. Serves one hungry Ulsterman or woman.

A filling Ulster fry, perfect for a winter's morning in the north

TYRONE

The name Tyrone comes from the county's location in Tír Eoghain, a Gaelic kingdom of the O'Neill dynasty that existed until the 17th century, when Britain's Ulster plantations swept the Irish aristocracy off these northern lands.

While the land deeds went to Elizabethan and later Tudor English lords, it was largely Scottish laborers and small farmers who performed the day-to-day agricultural work. Many had fled their homeland, fueled by a fierce distrust of English authorities, an antiestablishment sentiment that persisted in the face of the native resentment they experienced in Ulster. Many would subsequently seek freedom and autonomy in southern U.S. regions such as Appalachia. Their story is told at the Ulster American Folk Park, where Scots-Irish abodes on both sides of the Atlantic are re-created with period details that illustrate the leap people of faith took between the old world and the new.

A more conventionally Anglo-Irish "big house" is the fine Elizabethan-style Blessingbourne Country Estate, which sits amid woodlands, lakes, and wildlife habitats on the edge of the Clogher Valley. Elsewhere, County Tyrone is ribbed with the Sperrin Mountains, which provide wonderful views across this and neighboring counties of Ulster. In the east, the county abuts Ireland's largest lake, Lough Neagh.

Locals' pronunciation of Tyrone depends largely on their heritage. Tír Eoghain is Irish for "land of Eoghan," pronounced tirr-OWE-ANN by native Gaelic speakers. Historically, this was anglicized as Tyrowen, which British settlers pronounced as TIE-rown. This split diction, common throughout much of Northern Ireland, illustrates why those under suspicion often found it wise to still their tongues. Better to hold one's counsel than reveal one's allegiances linguistically. The name of one of the best books written about the period of Northern Ireland's Troubles took its title from the sage advice given to many an Ulster interrogee: *Whatever You Say, Say Nothing* by Patrick Radden Keefe. ∎

The Gortin Glen Lakes region combines mountain peaks, forests, and valleys.

The Ulster American Folk Park brings home the experience of the Scots-Irish emigrants who made their way to the Americas.

Irish Heritage

The Ulster American Folk Park

More than 27 million Americans can trace their lineage to the Scots. Over centuries of conflict, those bloodlines mingled with English neighbors to the south and, later, in England's contentious settlements of the Ulster plantations in Ireland. The escape valve for these 18th- and 19th-century northern Protestants was America. Unlike other migrations, the Scots-Irish were absorbed straight into the wilderness. While they are often overlooked in historical terms, the Scots-Irish left their mark on American culture through their music, first in Appala-

chian forms such as bluegrass, and later in country music, with its predominance of Scots-Irish writers and musicians. This also explains the huge popularity of country music in Ireland, and particularly Northern Ireland.

The Ulster American Folk Park gives an authentic flavor of Scots-Irish life in bygone rural Ulster, while exploring the insecurity of tenure that forced many to emigrate. Another part of the park shows the types of houses that emigrants constructed in the United States and the lives they made there.

Thomas Mellon was just five

when he emigrated to the U.S. in 1818 with his family from a simple house at Camphill, north of Omagh. His descendants created a memorial to him here, and to the millions like him, who were forced from their native land by poverty and lack of opportunity. The Ulster-American Folk Park has grown around this house since its inauguration in 1976. The young emigrant grew up to be Judge Mellon, whose son Andrew helped found Pittsburgh's steel industry. The main benefactor, Dr. Matthew T. Mellon, attended the opening of the park's visitors center in 1980 and recounted tales told by his great-grandfather, Judge Thomas Mellon, of his 1818 Atlantic crossing, a dreadful three-month voyage.

The Mellon house is typical of 19th-century peasant dwellings—dark and low with smoke-pickled yellow walls and creaky wooden beds, smelling of turf smoke and damp. Another, earlier house stands nearby, the kind lived in by most peasants in the 18th century, a single-room cabin into which parents and their children would have crammed.

Most of the buildings of the old-world collection were rescued from demolition and brought here, including a dark, cobwebby blacksmith's forge, piled with bricks of turf. A weaver's cottage includes one of the big looms from the cottage weaving that sustained Ulster's linen industry until industrialization. Nearby is the Hughes House, birthplace of John Joseph Hughes, who emigrated in 1817 as a child, later to become the first Catholic archbishop of New York and founder of that city's St. Patrick's Cathedral in 1858.

Also within the park is a whole 19th-century street re-created from small-town Ulster shops and businesses. This leads to a dockside with a ticket office, where a cobbled quay hosts a full-size reproduction of the central section of an emigrant ship. You'll pass down a gangway into the hold, with its low beams, tables, and wooden box berths—four feet (1.2 m) wide by five feet (1.5 m) long—where a whole family would sleep.

A re-creation of an American dockside, with dilapidated houses advertising "Cheap Logins," reinforces the struggles most emigrants faced on reaching the United States. The setting also includes log cabins of the type built by settlers who tried their luck in the open spaces of the Midwest.

Among their number were the Ulster forefathers of 17 presidents, including Andrew Jackson, Ronald Reagan, and Bill Clinton. President Clinton, along with Senator George Mitchell, enjoys a special popularity in Ireland for brokering the 1998 Good Friday Agreement. His three presidential visits helped "hope and history rhyme," as Seamus Heaney wrote (see page 257), in Ulster for the first time in centuries. ∎

IRISH GARDENS: BLESSINGBOURNE HOUSE

A visit to the gardens of Blessingbourne will inspire any horticulturalist. Built in the 1870s on bucolic parkland near Fivemiletown, the large Elizabethan-style manor overlooks Lough Fadda and is surrounded by gardens with fine yew and holm oak trees, a gravel terrace, and a rhododendron walk. Visitors can take the 2.5-mile (4 km) woodland trail that leads around the lake or travel the five-mile (8 km) mountain bike trail. The whole estate is a working farm comprising some 550 acres (220 ha).

The **Victorian Rock Garden** dates to the 18th century and was created by Mary and Hugh Montgomery. The huge leaves of gunnera plants from the original garden can still be seen throughout the estate. The **Sunken Garden** was the creation of Angela Lowry and her husband, Capt. R. H. Lowry, along with the estate's farmer Hughie McMahon in the 1980s. A stroll here feels like a return to an enchanted earlier age.

The most recent horticultural attraction at Blessing-bourne, the **Memory Garden** commemorates soldiers of the U.S. Army based at Blessingbourne during World War II. Its focal point is an impressive oak tree from which you can look down toward the private Lough Fadda. Fishing enthusiasts can purchase day licenses for this well-stocked lake.

For little sprites, the high point of a visit here is undoubtedly the **Fairy Tree,** a special place to make a wish and seek the fairies' help in making dreams come true. Fittingly, it is a hawthorn, one of ancient Ireland's sacred tree species. ∎

The enchanting surrounds of Blessingbourne House

GREAT IRISH DRIVES: THE SPERRIN MOUNTAINS

The Sperrin Mountains are a lonesome, enticing wilderness. They rise in a series of waves on the border between Tyrone and Derry, seamed with the parallel east-west valleys of the Owenkillew and Glenelly Rivers. Human presence is limited to a few small villages, and the views are far and wide. This is the haunt of soaring birds of prey, scurrying mountain hares, and the occasional happy hiker.

From Omagh, take the B48 north to the heavily wooded slopes of Gortin Glen, where a marked scenic drive of **Gortin Glen Forest Park** takes you to enchanting corners of this conif-

erous forest. Bucolic vistas lie ahead as the B48 dips into the small, welcoming village of Gortin, where the **Foothills Restaurant** provides great meals for hungry hikers (and drivers).

From here, take the B46 east beyond Drumlea Bridge, bearing left on a twisty mountain road along the south side of the valley. At Monanameal, the road splits, with one direction toward Greencastle; keep straight. After one mile (1.6 km), you'll pass a field on your left with two ancient stones, one a standing stone, the other a pillar known as the **Aghascrebagh Ogham Stone,** with an inscription at least 1,500 years old in the ancient Irish writing of ogham—the only specimen of its kind in County Tyrone. The script reads DOTETTO MAQI MAGLANI, which translates to "Dotetto, son of Maglani."

From Crouck Bridge, return up the Owenkillew Valley on the north side of the river, bearing right at Scotch Town to reach the spectacular viewpoint of **Barnes Gap.** From here, terrific views stretch ahead across the Glenelly Valley to the highest Sperrin peaks: **Sawel Mountain** (2,225 feet/678 m) to the right, with its satellite **Dart Mountain** (2,030 feet/619 m), and the bulge of **Mullaghclogha** (2,080 feet/635 m) straight ahead.

Down in Glenelly, keep to the south side of the valley. After some very snaky miles, turn left to descend and cross the river at Oughtboy Bridge. Bear right on the B47 until Mount Hamilton (Sperrin), where you'll bear left to cross the moorland heart of the hills. This narrow mountain road takes you under the eastern flank of Dart Mountain, and then Sawel Mountain, the highest summit in the Sperrins.

This is a good place to stop, get out of the car, stretch, and spot birds of prey: Big buzzards, little dark peregrine falcons, and large, pale hen harriers ply these skies. On the far side of the hills, the mountain road descends to meet the B44 at Park, but you can choose to return over the Sperrins into the Glenelly Valley. ∎

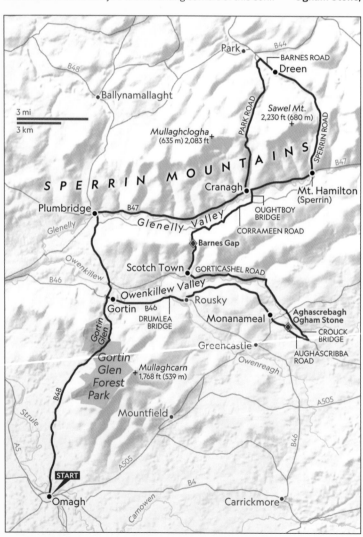

The bucolic Sperrin Mountains Drive is an escape into northern nature. OPPOSITE: The rolling landscape of the Sperrins, cloaked in bright winter sunshine and a dusting of snow

DOWN

Tucked into the northeast corner of Ireland, directly east of Belfast, the county of Down is surrounded to the north and east by the Irish Sea. Cruising its coastline is a delight, taking you through a string of small coastal villages such as Strangford and Portaferry, all punctuated with picturesque seascapes.

A short distance inland, you'll come across some of Northern Ireland's finest gardens, including those at Mount Stewart House, located on the eastern shore of Strangford Lough. This is a fascinating place to visit as much for the history of the neoclassical house as for its supreme horticultural heritage.

Rowallane Garden, just south of Saintfield, is another National Trust property that rewards a long, leisurely visit. The gardens of historic Hillsborough Castle are also worth strolling through. Hikers who like a wide vista should make the climb all the way up to Scrabo Tower atop Scrabo Hill. The surrounding park embraces the beech and hazel woodlands of Killynether. If you relish such elevated experiences, Silent Valley Mountain Park in the Mourne Mountains is one the best hill walks *anywhere* in Ireland. The highest Mourne peak of Slieve Donard looms some 2,790 feet (850 m) over Down; it is particularly alluring to explore in summer months when the hillsides are cloaked in heather mauves and gorse yellows.

A fun family day out is a visit to Castle Ward, where the historic farmyard was the location used for Winterfell in early episodes of the television series *Game of Thrones.* Medieval fun and games such as archery are offered, and the rest of the estate is a rustic treat.

The focal point of Down for many visitors is Downpatrick, where St. Patrick is believed to be buried on Cathedral Hill alongside St. Brigid and St. Colmcille. This serene hill site is also home to Down Cathedral and St. Patrick's Visitors' Centre, where a multimedia exhibition tells the story of Ireland's patron saint. ∎

Cathedral Hill rises above the Down countryside. St. Patrick is believed to be buried on this hill, as are Sts. Brigid and Colmcille.

The ruins of Dunluce Castle sit imposingly above the Antrim seas, an evocative location for TV's *Game of Thrones*.

Insider's Guide

Cloaked in Legend: Winterfell & *Game of Thrones*

Fans of the book and television phenomenon *Game of Thrones* can sign up for tours combining locations featured in the television series. Most leave from Belfast, but some run from Dublin and Derry, too. The Iron Islands and Giant's Causeway tour is particularly wild, taking in locations along the Antrim coast. These include Dragonstone beach, where Melisandre burned the effigies of the Seven Gods, the Carrick-a-Rede Rope Bridge, Renly's camp in the Stormlands, Lordsport's harbor in the Iron Islands, dramatic Dunluce Castle—

the location for Pyke Castle—and the Giant's Causeway. The tour provides participants with fabulously tailored leather Ironborn cloaks, hand-painted banners, and metal swords so you can storm the beach with your fellow Ironborn. The costumes make for memorable photos at the Dark Hedges, the mystical lane taken by Arya Stark as she fled King's Landing disguised as a boy.

The Tollymore Forest Locations Trek takes you deep into the enchanting forest where rangers of the Night's Watch found dismembered bodies in the snow. This walking tour

also takes in Tyrion and Jon's campfire, and the bridge where the Starks found a dead direwolf and her pups. Intrepid trekkers don Northern wool cloaks for photos in the Wolfswood and the Haunted Forest.

For a gentler walk, take the Maritime Mile through Belfast's Titanic Quarter. To celebrate 10 years of filming for the series, six stained-glass windows were created, depicting some of the most iconic scenes from all eight seasons. The trail seeks out these windows, starting at the House Stark window at AC Hotel by Marriott and ending at the House

Lannister window at H.M.S. *Caroline*, next to Titanic Studios, home to many epic *Thrones* sets.

The highlight for most *Thrones* fans, however, will be a pilgrimage to Winterfell itself, aka Old Castle Ward. It was here that King Robert Baratheon came to ask Ned to be Hand of the King. Castle Ward is an 18th-century manor house located near Strangford, notable for its split personality—architecturally speaking—which reflects the divergent tastes of Lord Bangor and his wife, Lady Ann Bligh. The entrance side of the house has a classical Palladian style with columns supporting a triangular pediment; the opposite side is Georgian Gothic with pointed windows, battlements, and finials.

Your *Game of Thrones* tour of Winterfell starts in the courtyard of Old Castle Ward. The extensive grounds of the Castle Ward Estate provide a picturesque workout, taking in locations such as Robb's camp in the Riverlands. Winterfell visitors will be authentically attired in Northern wool and leather cloaks, marching with metal swords and hand-painted Stark banners for the visit to Inch Abbey, the crumbling 12th-century ruin where Robb Stark became King in the North. Finally, the tour takes you into enchanting Tollymore Forest, the Whispering Wood, and the Wolfswood, where the Starks found the direwolf pups, and the Haunted Forest north of the Wall. ∎

IRISH HISTORY: THE IRISH WOLFHOUND

The "direwolves" of *Game of Thrones* are a fictional breed, but wolves and dogs have long played a major part in Irish history. The dogs used on-screen are actually Northern Inuit (Utonagan) dogs, bred to resemble wolves, and the show's writers took the name from a real, but long extinct, species of Pleistocene megafauna that once roamed the earth, the dire wolf (*Aenocyon dirus*).

The Irish wolfhound is a historic sight hound breed that has inspired Irish literature, poetry, and much mythology for centuries. When St. Patrick fled his six years of slavery in Ireland, it is believed that the ship he escaped on was transporting Irish wolfhounds to Rome, where they were hugely popular as hunting dogs. They were also prized as protection from wolves, and thus were they named.

The speed of the Irish wolfhound is a sight to behold, and a huge advantage in its pursuit of game. The breed is exceptional for combining power and swiftness with keen sight. The wolfhound is also distinguished by its remarkably precise and energy-efficient sprint—a double-suspension rotary gallop—whereby all four paws coordinate to touch the ground simultaneously, propelling this hunter with the speed of a lighter greyhound. It was said that the perfect wolfhound will be fast enough to catch a wolf, and strong enough to kill it.

The last wolf in Ireland was killed in County Carlow in 1786, and thereafter, the wolfhound became a status symbol rather than a working dog. By the late 19th century, the original canine type was presumed extinct but had been re-created specifically for the canine fancy, mainly by a Scot, Capt. George A. Graham. The wolfhound soon regained its popularity, particularly on the hunting estates of the Anglo-Irish aristocracy.

At Ashford Castle (see page 194) in the west of Ireland, you can enjoy an early morning ramble through the woods with the resident wolfhounds, Garvan and Cronan. These canine lords of the manor could have stepped out of the Fianna Gaelic legends of old. ∎

Cronan and Garvan, the Irish wolfhounds of Ashford Castle

IRISH GARDENS: PARKLANDS OF NORTHERN IRELAND

Ulster's history naturally lends many of its gardens a distinctly English influence, and the grounds of **Mount Stewart House** hold the jewel in the crown of the province's gardens. The 19th-century ornamental estate consists of a series of formally designed gardens within an ornamental section and several more informal ones around the banks of Strangford Lough. A visit to Mount Stewart is thus a walk through a variety of horticultural styles.

The main gardens here, laid out by Edith, Lady Londonderry, display a whimsical delight in what seasoned gardeners refer to as "painting" in colorful plants: A floral Red Hand of Ulster, for example, is planted in front of a topiary Celtic harp in the Shamrock Garden. Look out for statues of the extinct dodo bird within the spectacularly colorful Italian Garden, carved by local stonemason Thomas Beattie and dedicated to political guests entertained by the Londonderrys at Mount Stewart. These included Prime Ministers Winston Churchill and Harold Macmillan. The estate's Spanish Garden shows more muted colors, with green shades of hostas, various lilies, and hydrangeas. The enclosed Mairi Garden, named for Edith's youngest daughter, exudes the magical character of an enchanted or secret garden. The Londonderry clan are buried next to the garden's Tír na nÓg ("land of eternal youth") towers. At the lakeside, you come across a riot of hydrangeas and water lilies, with swans and the octagonal folly Temple of the Winds, giving these shores a timeless and romantic feel.

If Mount Stewart's largely formalized gardens are fit for an English prime minister, **Rowallane,** near Saintfield, is a parkland more suitable for an Irish mystic. This is a slightly wilder affair, built with rugged rocks and rowan trees (fairy trees) that indicate the presence of mischievous Celtic sprites hereabouts. Since ancient times, the Irish have planted the rowan beside their homes. In Celtic mythology this was the tree of life, symbolizing courage, wisdom, and protection.

Rowallane's Rock Garden, formed by natural outcrops of whinstone, is decorated with ferns, ericas, and various alpine plants. Look out for the strange formation known as the Bishop's Throne and the nearby cairn of stacked, rounded river stones from Bloody Bridge in the Mourne Mountains. These features were created by the Reverend John Moore, who also constructed the garden's centerpiece, the old walled garden. His nephew, Hugh Armitage Moore, created the wild gardens beyond this, and the contrast between the walled and wild outer gardens feels like a journey from cloistered contemplation out onto the winding paths of worldly experiences.

Finally, to a garden fit for a queen. Historic **Hillsborough Castle** boasts Europe's largest rhododendron, Lady Alice's Temple, and the Granville Garden created by Queen Elizabeth II's aunt, Lady Bowes-Lyon, in the mid-20th century. The castle itself was constructed in the 1770s and is today the queen's official residence in Northern Ireland. It has also been the home of the secretary of state since the 1970s. On most days, visitors can also enjoy a guided tour of the castle. ■

Rowallane inspires gardeners with plantings from around the world. OPPOSITE: Mount Stewart House, the jewel in the crown of Ulster gardens

Downpatrick, resting place of Ireland's beloved patron saint and a favored destination for pilgrims from all over the island

Special Places

Downpatrick: Resting Place of Ireland's Patron Saint

St. Patrick's immense influence on the Irish is felt throughout the island, and thousands flock to Downpatrick to pay their respects at his burial grounds, especially around his feast day of March 17.

The evangelizing saint is believed to have been buried in Down in A.D. 461 in the place where some of the remains of St. Brigid and St. Colmcille now also lie. Although the exact burial spot is unknown, a granite memorial stone from the Mountains of Mourne, inscribed "Patric," marks his grave. (The stone was laid over

St. Patrick's grave by the Belfast Naturalists' Field Club in 1901 to stop pilgrims removing the sacred earth.) The 12th-century Norman lord Sir John de Courcy vowed that he had reburied Patrick's bones here, along with those of St. Colmcille, who died on Iona in 597, and St. Brigid, who died in Kildare in 523. The veracity of who really lies under the great rock is probably more a matter of faith than historical record, but then, St. Patrick was known as a great storyteller.

The gravestone stands on the grounds of **Downpatrick Cathedral.**

The cathedral, built on a hillock, is mostly a 19th- and 20th-century construction. Historical records indicate a Celtic monastery at this place from as early as the sixth to seventh centuries. The site was plundered by Vikings and occupied by several armies in the bloody course of Northern Ireland's history. A later monastic settlement was built here in 1888 to house visiting Benedictine monks.

Opposite the cathedral sits the **St. Patrick's Visitors Centre,** sharing the narrative of Patrick's life story via a multimedia exhibition. A compelling IMAX presentation virtually sweeps visitors around Ireland to the sites of Patrick's major achievements in his quest to convert the pagan Irish.

The cathedral and visitors center are located on a hill overlooking the town and surrounding countryside, and you can enjoy the views from the rooftop terrace at the center's café, while indulging in some coffee and calories.

In common with all early Christian missionaries, Patrick was a great mortifier of the flesh. At **Struell Wells,** in a green valley two miles (3 km) south of Saul, the saint tested his own fortitude by immersing himself in freezing water and spending, as recorded in his *Confessio,* "a great part of the night, stark naked, singing psalms and spiritual songs." These wells thereafter became one of the most significant holy water sources in Ireland and gained a widespread reputation for their healing powers. The Struell Wells were developed into a pilgrimage complex in the 18th century. Today you can explore the disused women's and men's bath-houses, with their benches and dark, cold bathing tanks. Look, too, for the well whose water cures eye disease and for the domed drinking well—known colloquially as the Tub—in which St. Patrick spent his prayerful night of immersion. The wells enjoy increased volumes of visitors around midsummer, when the waters are reputed to rise up and become especially curative. ∎

IRISH HISTORY: WHY THE IRISH LOVE ST. PATRICK

Ireland's great love for St. Patrick can be attributed to many of the quirks and qualities that he shared with the pagan people he came to convert. Patrick was an underdog who had endured slavery and exile in his youth, and this played well with the Celtic antipathy toward injustice. The young shepherd of Antrim persevered to escape his life of slavery in Ireland after he followed the message of a dream telling him that "your ship is ready." He walked the length of Ireland to find the ship, then wandered across a "desert" in Europe (probably the icy wastelands of the frozen continent). He returned home to Roman Britain before once more answering the call of a dream to "walk among the Irish again."

The Irish love a good storyteller. They are voyagers and travelers. They are also big dreamers. When Patrick returned to the island the Romans had named Hibernia ("winterland") as an evangelizing missionary, he knew exactly how to charm the Celtic soul.

Ireland's patron saint was, by all accounts, a fine orator, and he possessed a sharp instinct for what moved these pagan people. The Celts were sun worshippers, so Patrick combined the power of the recurring light in the sky with the Christian story of Jesus' Crucifixion and resurrection. The result was the Celtic cross. The Irish danced around Druids' fires, so rather than trying to extinguish their celebrations, Patrick encouraged bonfires in celebration of Christian feast days, especially Easter. To their horror, the Druids learned that Patrick had charmed the Gaelic chieftains into approval of his Christian fire atop Slane Hill, in defiance of their pagan flames on the ancient Hill of Tara. It was then they must have known that the future belonged to the new religion. ∎

St. Patrick journeys to Tara to convert the Irish in the fifth century A.D.

Achill Island in County Mayo is
the largest of the Irish isles.

Part Five

Offshore
Ireland

Puffins nest on the Saltee Islands. OPPOSITE: Shepherds lead the way from Dunquin Pier after a crossing to the Blaskets.

A nation defined by its shorelines

However you arrive, your first sight of Irish soil will likely be an offshore island, or a craggy rock outcrop illuminated by the beacon of a lighthouse. The islands range in size and tone. The Blasket and Aran Islands off the west coast, for example, bestowed a rich literary, linguistic, and folkloric history as the last bastions of the Gaelic world, while islands such as Irelands Eye and Bull Island in the east are playgrounds and picnic sites for day-trippers from Dublin.

Other islands, such as Valentia off Kerry and Tory off Donegal, inhabited for centuries, have served as sites for transatlantic communications and lifeboat rescue stations. Lighthouses dot many Irish coastlines and offshore islands. All were automated in the 20th century, but several now offer overnighters a taste of a lighthouse keeper's life.

Ireland is an island nation, but the Irish mindset has never been insular. The coastlines have always shaped Irish identity and set the Gaels apart from Europe. Yet the oceans also connect us to the world. St. Brendan the Navigator sailed from Dingle in the early 500s, and his fellow Kerryman Tom Crean almost reached the South Pole in the early 1900s. The adventurous Gaels have always been a race of ambitious seafarers.

In the 21st century, the seas around Ireland also bring to the island the global challenges of climate change, rising sea levels, and ocean acidification. Since the turn of the millennium, the nation has been preparing for these sea changes.

Ireland will soon become the first country to systematically map its marine territory, with a mammoth project (Infomar) due for completion by 2026. The nation's ocean territory—339,770 square miles (880,000 sq km)—is about 10 times the island's landmass, one of the largest seabed territories in Europe. The project's first phase used remote sensing equipment to survey vast stretches of offshore waters beyond Ireland's continental shelf, land that extends under the sea to 200 nautical miles from the coastline. ∎

THE ISLANDS

The 80 or so islands off Ireland's mainland vary wildly. Many, such as the Skelligs (County Kerry) and the Saltees (County Wexford), host vast colonies of seabirds. Only 20 are inhabited by humans.

The western islands, particularly Aran and the Blaskets, were bastions of ancient Irish culture. Students of the Irish language still visit Aran to hear the purest (closest to ancient Irish) form of Gaelic. The Aran Islands also produce a globally popular knitwear using traditional stitching designs passed down through generations. Stories, too, survive along the intergenerational grapevine: The Blaskets became a literary hot spot in the 20th century, when Irish academics helped *seanchaí* (storytellers) write down their stories.

The Blaskets were abandoned in the 1950s, and cottage ruins are ghostly reminders of a lost world. Only a café for day-trippers is permanently inhabited. Much older human footprints dominate the Aran Islands, where ancient Celtic forts hover over sheer sea cliffs. In medieval times, religious men sought closeness to God (and sanctuary from Vikings) on the islands, most dramatically in the Skelligs' monastic settlements. Tales from the future are told there too: Skellig Michael starred as Planet Ahch-To in recent Star Wars films.

Many islands, such as Dalkey Island and Irelands Eye off Dublin, host Martello towers, built by the British as lookouts for a Napoleonic invasion. In a very Celtic way, these battlements have transmogrified into icons of Irish art. Chapter one of Joyce's *Ulysses* transpires in Sandycove Tower, and Martello towers are favored subjects, and residences, of Irish artists.

The islands are an eternal lure for those seeking the solitude to imagine. John Lennon bought Dorinish Island in Mayo's Clew Bay in the 1960s. Like the ancient monks, he sought inspiration in the rhythms of the waves, the ever changing skies, and the songs of seabirds. As Irish writer John McGahern observed, "The most elusive island of all, the first person singular." ∎

Wexford's Saltee Islands host vast colonies of gannets and other seabirds.

Islands of West Cork

Many west Cork islands, such as the gardener's mecca of **Garinish Island,** nestle in inlets such as Bantry Bay. On **Whiddy Island,** also in Bantry Bay, you can explore a sixth-century holy well, a church, and an ancient graveyard at Kilmore Lakes. The Bank House, the island's only pub, welcomes many visiting bird-watchers.

Bere Island, just off Castletownbere, is worth a boat ride as you travel along the south side of the Beara Peninsula (see page 118). Ferries arrive on the island at Lawrence Cove, located in the village of Rerrin, a place with a long military history and cozy Murphys pub.

Dursey Island is located off the western tip of the Beara Peninsula. To get there, you must brave Ireland's only cable car, high above the churning swells and treacherous waters of the Dursey Sound. The island is sparse (a coffee-and-sandwich van at the cable car site is the only sustenance on offer) and has just a handful of human residents. However, Dursey hosts a wealth of migrating birdlife, and you might also spot minke whales, Risso's dolphins, and harbor porpoises in its rich surrounding waters.

Sherkin Island, a 10-minute boat ride from the fishing port of Baltimore, is known as Ireland's island of the arts. Writers, musicians, and painters live here alongside fishermen and farmers. Boats from Baltimore also service **Cape Clear,** Ireland's southernmost inhabited Gaeltacht island, eight miles (13 km) off the coast. The 150 or so islanders celebrate their patron saint on March 5 at St. Ciarán's well. Cape Clear is another bird-watchers' haven and wildlife here includes whales, leatherback turtles, dolphins, and sharks.

And finally, sparsely populated **Hare (or Heir) Island,** also called **Inishodriscol,** attracts hikers with its colorful fuchsias, wildflowers, and stunning coastal scenery. ∎

Dursey Island awaits those who brave the cable car ride over dangerous waters. OPPOSITE: The Baltimore Beacon, known locally as Lot's Wife

Special Places

Valentia Island: Kerry's Secret Eden

If Kerry is the Kingdom, Valentia Island, lying off the Iveragh Peninsula, is a Kingdom within a Kingdom. One of Ireland's most accessible islands, continuous ferry service runs from Reenard Point on the mainland to Knightstown from Easter to early October. A bridge also connects the island with the town of Portmagee, continuing the R565 main road onto Valentia.

In Knightstown you'll discover the incredible story of this island of 665 residents, which is about seven miles (11 km) long by almost two miles (3 km) wide. The **Valentia Heritage Centre** gathers all the island's history in the old village schoolhouse.

The island's north coast can verily boast Ireland's oldest archaeological artifact, a rock imprint made by a tetrapod dating from 385 million years ago. Much geological continental drift has occurred since a lizard-like mammal crawled from the sea and left tracks on the lava-like molten rock—akin to canine paw prints on concrete sidewalks—

meaning this stratified rock was probably several hundred miles from the location of modern-day Ireland. The prehistoric creature's feet and tail tracks were exposed by erosion and found here in 1992.

Nearby stands **Valentia Island Lighthouse** at Cromwell Point, named for Henry (not Oliver) Cromwell, a 16th-century Lord Deputy at the time when a fort was built here. The lighthouse has operated since 1828 and now offers lively tours and overnight accommodation.

Valentia Island Lighthouse, at Cromwell Point, guides ships through the northern entrance to Valentia Harbour.

Outdoor dining and drinks at the Royal Valentia Hotel garden are a summer day's delight.

The British influence on the island runs deep. The Knight of Kerry is one of three still active Anglo-Irish hereditary knighthoods. The Fitzgerald family took up residence on the Glanleam Estate in 1780. In 1807, it was bought outright by Maurice, the 18th knight. His successor, Sir Peter Fitzgerald, developed Glanleam into a stunning estate and initiated many developments on Valentia: the building of the seaport, the opening of the slate quarry, and the building of the town of Knightstown.

Sir Peter's influence in London also ensured that the transatlantic cable to the town of Heart's Content in Newfoundland would originate on Valentia. The story of the laying of this undersea cable—off the world's biggest ship, S.S. *Great East-* ern—is told at the Heritage Centre. The line cut the time of a transatlantic message from two weeks to mere hours. The notable second cable message was sent in 1866, from Queen Victoria to U.S. president James Buchanan, hailing "an additional link between the nations whose friendship is founded on their common interest and reciprocal esteem."

The **Slate Quarry** opened on the north-facing slopes of Geokaun Mountain in 1816. The island's high-quality metamorphic rock was exported around the world and used at the Paris Opera House and London's Houses of Parliament. Welsh miners were employed until a rockfall closed the mine in 1910. As elsewhere in Ireland, statues of the Virgin Mary and St. Bernadette were erected high above the quarry entrance in 1954, and a yearly mass is celebrated here. Today the Slate Quarry, visible to passing hikers, is again in operation.

Verdant Valentia Island is particularly spectacular in the months of May and June, when montbretias splash orange hues along the lush hedgerows and dense green shadows are cast by the island's subtropical growth. This is best observed in the knights' old residence of **Glanleam House,** overlooking the beautiful bay that stretches across to Beginish Island, where gardens run riot. The house is now a hotel, and its gregarious German maître d', Meta Kreissig, would give any Kerry storyteller a run for their money. ∎

Special Places

The Skelligs

They rise out of the wild Atlantic Ocean like two sandstone cathedrals, their weather-sharpened spires pointing heavenward. The mystical Skellig Islands have served throughout history as the inhospitable site of a medieval monastery, as a place of penitent religious pilgrimage, and more recently as a Hollywood film location. Bird-watchers also sail to the Skelligs for the massed colonies of gannets, razorbills, puffins, and guillemots.

The **Skellig Experience Visitor Centre** on Valentia is a good starting point, both to book passage and to fully absorb the history and spiritual meaning of this sacred place. Listen carefully to the safety video—there are no guardrails or safety nets on the steep stone stairway up to this medieval site.

Skellig Michael and **Little Skellig** stir something deep in the Celtic soul. Here on these barren rocks, Irish Augustinian monks defied the collapse of Roman Europe, and later the repeated raids by Vikings along Irish shores. Here they kept the faith not only in God, but in civilization itself. In beehive huts made of rocks, these stoic mystics eked out a spiritual existence, keeping their bodies alive on the meat of fish and seabirds, and occasionally eggs stolen from clifftop nests. These monks sought out their "green martyrdom" from the sixth century onward in a place almost entirely devoid of plant life, tending a tiny patch of grass to raise goats or sheep.

Skellig Michael is a small pyramid-shaped rocky outcrop rising 7.5 miles (12 km) off the Kerry coast. Some 700 feet (215 m) above the sea, the monks, led by St. Fionán, built their settlement. They also constructed more than a thousand stone steps up the steep side of Skellig Michael, perhaps to be closer to God. After several Viking raids, the monks deserted the site in the 13th century, retreating to the Augustinian monastery in Ballinskelligs.

In 1996, Skellig Michael was declared a UNESCO World Heritage site. The citation noted the settlement as a "unique artistic achievement" and a place imbued with a "strong sense of spirituality." The Irish spirit is largely driven by the imagination, and Skellig Michael inspired ascetic holy men to imagine their worlds anew.

Skellig Michael has long been said to be "out of this world" and "closer to heaven" by monks, saints, sinners, and day-trippers. Irish playwright George Bernard Shaw observed: "I tell you, the thing does not belong to any world that you and I have lived and worked in: It is part of our dream world." Filmmaker J. J. Abrams used Skellig Michael as the location for the planet Ahch-To in *Star Wars Episode VII—The Force Awakens* (2015) and *Star Wars Episode VIII—The Last Jedi* (2017). Since then, fans of the franchise have flocked to visit this "alien planet," where the monastic ruins represented a Jedi temple. The annual May the Fourth Be With You (May 4) Star Wars–themed celebration centers around Portmagee and Kerry beaches with views of the Skelligs. ∎

High on Skellig Michael, the beehive stone huts of medieval monks remain. OPPOSITE: A cliff-hugging switchback path leads to Skellig Michael's lower lighthouse, built in the 1820s.

Humpback whales are among the multifarious marine life that feed off the coast of the Blasket Islands.

Insider's Guide

The Storied Blasket Islands

Lying off the tip of the Dingle Peninsula, the Blaskets are among the most storied of all Ireland's islands. In April 1947, with storms cutting them off from the mainland, the islanders sent a telegram to Taoiseach (Prime Minister) Eamon de Valera: STORMBOUND DISTRESS. SEND FOOD. NOTHING TO EAT. BLASKETS. Supplies arrived two days later. The remaining 27 residents were evacuated by 1954 when it was decided the government could not guarantee their safety nor pro-

vide adequate health services. But by then the rich history and folklore of these islands had been immortalized in several autobiographical works that are now part of Ireland's literary canon.

Most visitors' first sight of the archipelago is from the viewing platform outside the **Blasket Centre** in Dunquin. From a nearby pier, a ferry takes you nearly 1.5 miles (2 km) across to the **Great Blasket**, a mere 1.6 square miles (4.3 sq km) in area and now mainly

owned by the government. It rises to 958 feet (292 m) at its highest point, An Cró Mór.

Five of the six Blaskets—the Great Blasket, **Inishnabro, Inishvickillane, Inishtooskert,** and **Tearaght**—lie like a school of humpback whales in the Atlantic. The smallest, **Beginish,** is as flat as an eel. In 1974, Inishvickillane was bought by Charles J. Haughey, a three-time Taoiseach of Ireland. Inishtooskert is known as the "dead man" due to the shape of its rocky silhouette—his head to the north, hands on his belly, and upright feet pointing south.

The Great Blasket has one village, built on the east side, facing the mainland, in the early 20th century. Many houses are now ruins, but one hosts a café for day-trippers, and the Great Blasket Island Experience offers rental accommodations during summer. The company recruits two caretakers annually to run the houses and café, where they live without electricity or hot water. These are now two of Ireland's most sought-after jobs.

The islanders of old were multitaskers. These hardy people planted potatoes, raised sheep, gathered seaweed, and made dangerous forays in homemade rowboats called *neamhógs* out into the Atlantic in search of lobster, ling, cod, and mackerel. Isolated from the mainland and at the mercy of the elements on this treeless island, the islanders spent the long winter nights mending nets, crafting furniture and musical instruments such as fiddles, and telling stories. Only Irish was spoken, and the Blaskets are still part of the Gaeltacht. The Irish language's poetic expressionism and flair—there are 32 Irish words for "field"—lend themselves to great storytelling.

The islanders are no longer there, but their history lives on despite the gales of change in the seven decades since the Blaskets went silent. Between 1929 and 1935, three books made the islands known throughout the English-speaking world, thanks to visiting academics who helped to capture the oral tradition on the page: *The Islander,* by fisherman Tomás

O'Crohan, recalls in raw, earthy terms the harsh island life at the turn of the 20th century. Faithfully restored, his house on the Great Blasket opened to visitors in 2018. *Twenty Years A-Growing,* by Maurice O'Sullivan, is a lighter read, perhaps because its young author had decided early to follow hundreds of his island predecessors into emigration. O'Sullivan was persuaded by his editor, the linguist George Thomson, to become a guard (policeman) in Connemara.

A third book, *Peig,* tells of the hardscrabble life on the Great Blasket of Peig Sayers, a mainlander who "married in" to island life. Only six of her 11 children survived, and the perils of the sea, the cliffs, and life-threatening illnesses were ever present.

The book has light moments too, such as stories of matchmaking, and the complications of suitors wooing in a tight-knit community amid a maelstrom of music and drink and watchful eyes. Her story, and those

of her fellow islanders, is told at the excellent Blasket Centre, the visitor facility in Dunquin. Outside the center, you'll encounter "The Islandman," Michael Quane's dramatic sculpture depicting a stoic figure holding onto his hat against whipping wild Atlantic winds.

Fairies and spirits of the dead are still commonly sensed by visitors to the Blasket Islands. The cries of seals might account for some of the "voices" often heard here. One local legend, however, tells of an islander playing his fiddle alone at home one night, when he heard a refrain of voices harmonizing above his roof. This ghostly tune came and went several times—"a wandering air wailing in repeated phrases"—until the fiddler repeated the ephemeral tune note for note. This melody is now known as *port na bpúcaí* (fairy music) by all who play it, including Kerry *seanchaí* (storyteller) Thomas O'Sullivan (see page 130). ■

The strikingly modern Blasket Centre in Dunquin offers fine views of the archipelago.

IRISH HISTORY: LIFE ON THE EDGE

The history of the offshore islands often diverges sharply from that of mainland Ireland. In medieval times, these were hideaways for hermits, offering monks a "green martyrdom" close to exile, and closer to God. As the Celtic world ceded to British rule, the ancient Gaelic culture found refuge in the far-flung western islands of the Blaskets, the Aran Islands, Achill, and Tory. During the Celtic Revival (also known as the Celtic Twilight), W. B. Yeats, J. M. Synge, and others saw them as repositories of romanticism.

The lives lived on these outposts of ancient culture are often more complex and cruel. In his book *On the Edge,* historian Diarmaid Ferriter (see page 26) documents the history of Ireland's offshore islands over the last 180 years. He recounts the islanders' exposure to the elements, their poverty despite intense labors, and the hostility they faced from officials seeking rent while denying basic services. "This was a hard, dangerous life," says Ferriter. "There were about 38,000 residents on 211 inhabited islands in 1841. By 2011, only 8,500 were left on 64 islands." Ferriter's own ancestors were the Hiberno-Norman lords of Ballyferriter on the Dingle Peninsula, the nearest mainland to the Blasket Islands.

As Irish President Higgins (see page 187) has observed, the islands exist between worlds. In Irish myth the Celtic paradise was the island of Hy-Brasil, or Tír na nÓg ("land of eternal youth"). Kerryman St. Brendan set sail from Dingle in search of an earthly Eden, maybe America. In reality, Ireland's islands now exist between the old world and the new: "The Blasket Islanders' westward-looking observation of 'next parish, America' was very real," says Ferriter, "given the numbers that left for the railway town of Springfield in Massachusetts." Faced with a fate of eking out a hard living from the sea and limited sheep farming, many islanders opted for new lives in America and elsewhere. It was said that for many years you could always tell two or more Blasket Islanders out walking together, even on a street in London or New York. The men would still walk in single file—a habit formed on the cliffs of their island homeland.

The slow decline in populations began in the famine era.

Blasket Islanders called this little *clochán,* or cluster of houses, "the Village."

In 1841, the Great Blasket had 153 inhabitants. During the Great Famine (1846–1850) this fell by about a third, a big decrease but not as great as the decline on the mainland. All Irish islands were somewhat inoculated by their isolation—the blight avoided these small patches of land, and their remoteness prevented famine-related diseases such as dysentery and cholera. Plentiful supplies of fresh fish warded off starvation, too.

Another mitigating factor was the presence of Protestant groups such as the Dingle and Ventry Mission that sought to convert Catholics by opening soup kitchens for the hungry. The missions targeted young souls especially. A "soupers" school was opened on the Great Blasket in 1840, similar to the deeply divisive Protestant school on Achill run by the evangelical Edward Walter Nangle. "Allegations at the time and since that the Achill mission was the apotheosis of 'souperism' largely arose from what happened in the famine years," Ferriter explains, "when meals were provided for schoolchildren and conversions increased." The phrase "to take the soup" is still used in Ireland to suggest a betrayal of one's identity.

Many islands had a long history of rent refusal by residents who felt that the governments in London, and later in Dublin, had abandoned them. These communities were dependent on the mainland for the services of the doctor, priest, postman, and policeman. Education was contentious too: The Great Blasket had a national school from about 1860 onward, but gradually children were sent to mainland schools. By 1949, an *Irish Press* journalist found just one child still living on the Great Blasket. The story on Gearóid Cheaist Ó Catháin, headlined "The Loneliest Boy in the World," described a child with "only seagulls as playmates." This brought Gearóid a flood of toys donated by readers worldwide.

Depopulation continued after Irish independence, despite the affection that Ireland's leader had for the islands. "After the stress of the civil war period [1922–23], de Valera briefly sought refuge and rest on the Blaskets and a field is named

Islanders were versatile, crafting everything from lobster pots (as seen here) to fiddles.

after him in Valentia," says Ferriter. "Like many of his contemporaries, Dev believed the islands were outposts of a pure Irish identity."

As Taoiseach, de Valera tried to address islanders' concerns with a 1947 tour of the western islands, but the die was already cast. The last 22 residents left in 1954, dispirited following the death of a young man named Seáinín Ó Ceárna, whose illness went untreated during winter storms. Many islanders who were rehoused in Dunquin and Dingle retained sheep on the islands, which they continued to shepherd. "The islanders' exodus and dispersal onto the mainland and beyond represented an ending, a dying of an old Gaelic community that had kept alive the language, storytelling, and musical heritage of their forebears," says Ferriter. "Some essence of the national identity was lost." ∎

Dun Aengus is the largest of several prehistoric hill forts on the Aran Islands and dates to between 800 B.C. and A.D. 400.

Special Places

The Aran Islands

The three Aran Islands—**Inis Mór** ("big island"), **Inis Meáin** ("middle island"), and **Inis Oírr** ("eastern island")— rise out of the Atlantic Ocean like three limestone afterthoughts of the mainland Burren landscape. These sparse, treeless isles possess their own wind-blasted beauty. They are also sacred outposts of a pagan, Celtic Ireland that has long since been swallowed by the tides of conquest, colonization, and modernity.

It is often said that, because of their isolation, the purest Gaelic is spoken on Aran. Other ancient aspects of Irish culture survive here too: The knots of houses irregularly grouped together, called *clocháns* (farm clusters), were common all over pre-famine Ireland.

A more ancient settlement is the archaeological wonder of Aran: The ruins of the prehistoric fort of **Dun Aengus** on Inis Mór perch on the edge of a 330-foot-high (100 m) cliff. The fort's semicircular drystone wall once protected some of Ireland's earliest inhabitants, and the site has huge cultural significance in the Irish psyche: Its presence marks this as a sacred place, a reminder of a pagan past, when druids may have used it as a temple looking west at the setting sun.

Artists, playwrights, and poets have long come to Aran to tap into this ancient culture. W. B. Yeats followed folklorist and playwright Lady Augusta Gregory to Aran in 1896 to garner the islanders' stories of fairies and Celtic mysticism. There he felt "fired by the sense of a dawning age." This soon blossomed into what became known as the Celtic Revival (or Celtic Twilight), the Gaelic revival that fueled the idealism of the Easter Rising of 1916. Both Lady Gregory and Yeats were also struck by how the islanders casually accepted pagan animism and how vividly they felt the breath of their ancestors in their hardscrabble lives.

The islanders lived by their own moral codes, as English author Arthur Symons related in his story of Aran. According to the islanders he interviewed in the 1890s, "if any gentleman has committed a crime . . . we'll hide him. There was a man killed his father and he came over here and we had him for two months and he got away safe to America."

When J. M. Synge arrived on Inishmaan in 1898, he used this story for *The Playboy of the Western World* (1907), a play that caused uproar on its Dublin opening and later in New York and Philadelphia for its alleged indecencies and realistic portrayal of the previously romanticized islanders. On Inishmaan today, you can step inside Synge's cottage and sit in **Synge's Chair,** a scenic rock lookout at the edge of a limestone cliff. Today's islanders live transatlantic lives in constant touch with friends and family abroad. By 2019, almost half of all Aran households had broadband access.

Most visitors stay in one of the B&Bs on Inis Mór, such as **Kilmurvey House,** an 18th-century manor that once belonged to the "ferocious O'Flahertys," where you might meet the odd ghost. The island also has several hotels, including **Tigh Fitz,** which offers fine sea views. **Inis Meáin Knitting Company,** on the Middle Island, is worth a visit to learn about the islands' local traditions, including the Aran sweater (see page 306). ∎

IN THE KNOW: INIS MEÁIN RESTAURANT & FARMSTAYS

For a travel experience you'll find nowhere else on Earth, head to Inis Meáin Restaurant and Farmstays on Inishmaan. This intimate nature lodge experience offers total seclusion and immersion in an island wilderness on the edge of Europe. Established by Marie-Thérèse and Ruairí de Blacam in 2007, the restaurant wraps guests in a cocoon of opulence with views of the windswept island and the Atlantic all around. Chef Ruairí is a native of Inis Meáin and he takes an elemental approach to creative cuisine, using the freshest island ingredients: lettuces, herbs, fruit, and vegetables grown in the restaurant's garden; fish or shellfish freshly caught in the ocean; or prime homestead-reared meat. A maximum of 16 guests relish a four-course dinner that changes nightly. As you dine, the magnificent vistas of westerly skies, rocky island landscape, and ocean waves are visible through the wraparound windows of the building, which is itself a marvel of Celtic chic.

After Marie-Thérèse collects you off the ferry, many guests don't even spot the restaurant building as they approach: Clad in the limestone of Aran, the low-lying edifice blends into the rugged island stonescapes.

"Everything about this place chimes with the Aran landscapes, from the interior limestone slabs, to the simple yet terrifically tasteful food," says guest Kati Schulz. "The windows are portals out to the island environment, the constantly changing skies, the swooping birds. You completely unwind watching this endlessly evolving wilderness and its wildlife." The farmstays must be reserved well in advance of your arrival at Inis Meáin. ∎

Inis Meáin Restaurant surrounds diners with Aran's natural wonders.

Irish Heritage

Aran Knitwear

The knitwear of Aran, and particularly the famous Aran sweater worn by generations of island fishermen, is recognized globally as an intrinsically Irish product. The bold patterns of Aran knitwear have their origins in age-old traditions of island life, yet they have been adapted by modern-day Irish designers and now grace everything from wedding dresses to beanie hats to designer interior decor.

Traditionally, women on Aran hand-knit sweaters (here called jumpers) for their husbands and sons who worked long days exposed to the elements. The men toiled in all types of weather, hauling baskets of seaweed from the shore and mixing it with sand to produce the fertile soil in which crops could grow on these barren islands. In fishing season, they braved Atlantic storms in their curraghs—wood-framed canoes with tarred skin—to catch cod, ling, or perch, or to set lobster traps. The sea was seen as a place of work, not pleasure, and most Aran fishermen would not learn to swim, reckoning that this would just prolong their passing should they capsize. Their remains, washed ashore, would often be identified by the familial patterns on their sweaters.

In the past, Aran sweaters were knit of undyed cream-colored yarn spun from unwashed wool that still contained natural sheep lanolin, which made the garment more water-repellent, and meant that fishermen could wear them even when wet. Today's Aran knitters tend to use lighter yarns, often mixing imported softer, fine wools such as New Zealand merinos with strong, coarse Irish wools.

Like Irish tweed weavers, Aran knitters use the basic colors of nature to reflect their world aesthetically: the dun brown of the bog, the light blues of the sky, and the yellows and purples of gorse and heather, as well as the traditional cream. Aran sweaters are still handmade in the region through a sprawling cottage industry, and many visitors leave warmly dressed in an example of this craftsmanship. Irish knits may also be found throughout Ireland and beyond, both authentic hand-knits and "Aran-style" interpretations made across the globe. Look for "Made in Ireland" on the label. ∎

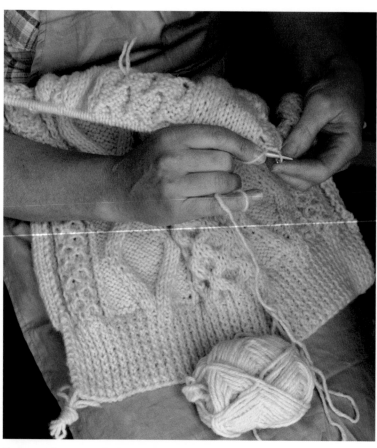

The famous Aran sweater has been hand-knit by islanders for generations.

Diamonds, cables, and the blackberry stitch form a distinctive raised pattern for the back of this heirloom sweater, hand-knit in Donegal.

IN THE KNOW: STORIES IN STITCHES

The people of Aran historically told their stories in the oral tradition, passing on tales by the fireside down through generations of listeners who themselves became *seanchaí* (storytellers). This method of keeping culture alive in an unwritten, unrecorded way applied to their knitting patterns, too. The women who made Aran sweaters and other knitwear didn't follow written patterns but passed on or improvised a sequence of stitches around hundreds of motifs known to the island community. Three basic patterns predominate—cables or twists, diamonds, and honeycombs—arranged among many others as chosen by individual knitters, sometimes specifically for the wearer.

CABLES: Aran patterns include an infinite number of cables, including braided cables, lobster claws, and trellis stitches. Cables and twists are prime examples of the raised stitchwork that gives Aran knitwear its distinctive three-dimensional aesthetic. These cables often represent the ropes used extensively in the islands' fishing communities.

DIAMONDS: Representing worldly wealth, Aran diamonds also project hope for success in physical spaces, such as nets to be filled with fish, or drystone walls to be filled with crops or livestock.

HONEYCOMB: A repeating pattern of stitches is used to create this textured knit, a tribute to the hardworking honeybee and a symbol of plenty.

OTHER STITCHES: The vertical **tree of life** stitch reflects the maker's wish for a healthy family for the wearer, with branches arching outward from a central trunk to indicate the stages of life. The **trellis stitch** is a crisscross pattern symbolizing the Irish landscape of stone-walled fields. The three-dimensional, or raised, nature of this and other ancient Aran stitches reflects the sculpted aesthetic of much Celtic metalwork, jewelry, and stonework. A repeating pattern of bumpy clusters make up the **blackberry stitch** (also called Trinity stitch), celebrating the bounty of nature.

A runged ladder to good health and a long life is implied by the **ladder of life stitch,** which had particularly strong resonance for families of fishermen who made their living on the storm-tossed Atlantic. The **basket stitch** (also called lattice stitch) symbolizes a fisherman's basket and an abundant catch.

In island lore, the **zigzag stitch** represents twisting cliff paths, while double zigzags that intertwine symbolize the coiling together of two lives in marriage and the ups and downs of the path of love, which never runs straight. Used as a blessing stitched into clothes that loved ones would wear daily, this traditional stitch is now popularly integrated into the design of modern Aran wedding dresses.

Also known as carrageen moss, the **Irish moss stitch** is named after the edible seaweed found on the shores of the Aran Islands and used to enrich the soils of the barren fields of Aran to grow crops such as potatoes. Thus carrageen moss served as a symbol of nature's vitality as well as representing the islanders' eternal debt to the sea. ∎

Special Places

Achill Island

The brightest jewel among Ireland's islands may be Achill Island. Connected to Mayo by bridge, Achill is a verdant, mountainous landmass unlike the bleak Aran Islands to the south. Steep cliffs shelter Blue Flag beaches, and sheep wander craggy clifftops—when they're not busy regulating traffic on the island's scenic roads.

Achill is Ireland's largest island, with a population of approximately 2,600 and an area of 57 square miles (148 sq km). The O'Malleys, the hereditary chieftains of this island kingdom, reigned here from A.D. 814, when they repelled a Viking incursion from Clew Bay.

The Anglo-Norman invasion of Connacht in 1235 saw their territory of Umhall ceded to the Butlers and later the de Burgos, lords of Ashford Castle. The adaptable O'Malleys then became kings and queens of the seas, trading widely. The ruin of the clan's 15th-century Kildavnet Castle sits at the mouth of Achill Sound. The legend of Grace O'Malley (1530–1603), also known as Granuaile, the Pirate Queen (see page 310), still swirls around Achill and the islands of Clew Bay.

Capricious Atlantic weather provides the drama hereabouts these days. The sun will shine brightly on the sheltered inlet where the Pirate Queen kept her tower house; then Irish mists will roll down the hill where the ruins of a deserted famine village echo with unbearable emptiness. Next moment, wild winds will whip around the graveyards haunted by Achill's many victims of that Irish apocalypse.

The bulk of **Slievemore** ("big mountain") rises to 2,200 feet (672 m). At its base you'll find the **Deserted Village,** with the ruins of about 80 houses. The settlement provides a snapshot of rural life during the Great Famine, when one-room cottages were built with unmortared stone, and the tracks of "lazy beds" (potato rows) are still visible in the fields. In Achill, as elsewhere, the Rundale system was imposed by landlords: Tenants rented communal grazing land and retained small lots for crops. When the potato failed in 1845, many afflicted families moved to nearby Dooagh to harvest seafood, while others emigrated.

Geographically, Achill is a clenched fist, pointing a defiant finger toward the Atlantic. The ocean responds with violent storms and contrasts of shadow and light. These changing atmospherics are manifest at the cliffs of Croaghaun and in Keem Bay, a popular surfing spot.

The stunning shades that wash over Achill from dawn to dusk have attracted artists to this creative haven for centuries. Among their numbers is landscape painter Paul Henry (1876–1958), who lived on Achill for almost a decade with his wife, artist Grace Henry (1868–1953). His works reflect the austere yet harmonious rural idyll that Eamon de Valera envisioned for Ireland's emerging Free State. ∎

The annual Mayo International Kite Festival is held on Achill. OPPOSITE: The road to Keem Beach

The islands lie like humpback whales in the pirate-plied waters of Clew Bay, providing a safe haven for goods plundered on the high seas.

Irish Heritage

Ireland's Pirate Queen

The lonesome shorelines of Mayo and Galway were the windswept realm of Grace O'Malley, who would become known as Granuaile. After O'Malley's death in 1603, these stunning seascapes would forever be linked with the woman whose legend lives on as Ireland's Pirate Queen.

The wild life of Grace O'Malley (born circa 1530) was the final gasp of the dying Gaelic world defying the great British Empire. This fearsome warrior woman grew up the daughter of a Connacht chieftain, and like him, she would command her own army and fleet of privateers from Clare Island, a remarkable position of power for a woman in the 16th century.

The headstrong O'Malley got her nickname of Granuaile (from the Gaelic Grainné Mhaol, or Bald Grace) as a young girl. Her father, Eóghan Dubhdara Ó Máille (Owen "Black Oak" O'Malley) refused to take his daughter onto the high seas, saying her long red hair would get entangled in the ship's rigging. When he returned from his next voyage, he was met at the quays by his strange-looking daughter who had shorn her own head.

Grace was 16 when she married her first husband, Donal O'Flaherty. In 1566, two years after his murder, she married Anglo-Irish Lord "Iron Dick" Burke on the Brehon Law proviso that either could divorce the other after a year and a day. Grace promptly invoked this Celtic prenup, slamming the door of Rockfleet Castle against him—having first secured all of Iron Dick's castles (see page 312). ∎

IRISH VOICES: THE CALL OF ACHILL

Annette O'Malley is a descendant of Granuaile's brother, the Lord of the Owls. She was a long time living abroad, away from her beloved Achill Island, and it is the Gaels in exile that she remembers now. Her parents were both from Achill, though they met in Luton, England, and she was born in Kent. She is back living in a house on Achill Sound, and plans to renovate the cottage of her great-grandmother on the island. Her two young daughters, Cara and Evie, will be the fifth generation of women to own the dwelling.

As the rambunctious girls clamber around the Pirate Queen's tower at Kildavnet, their mother recalled the gangs of Irish navvies (construction workers) who would stay at her aunt's guesthouse in Luton, where she grew up. "There was always the air of lonesome, displaced men, working abroad without women," she recalls. "They'd have dirty, muddy boots on the floor, and ashtrays overflowing by the end of the night. They'd be working all day on bridges, motorways, or the buildings, but their hearts were always elsewhere."

In summer, the O'Malley clan would return to the island. Achill was Annette's Irish idyll, a wild green retreat from the concrete sprawl of London. "The local kids would hear the accent and to them you were 'the English,'" she says. "But this place has *always* felt like home to me."

When she made her way out into the world, she cast her net farther afield, to another island, less than half the size of Achill and a good deal more crowded: Manhattan. Here, her organizational talents led to a career in construction management. Like her famous ancestor, O'Malley would oversee gangs of men of many nationalities, ensuring work got done on time and everyone got paid. She negotiated between architects and laborers—tamping the inevitable rows that flared in the testosterone-fueled close quarters of a building site. She ran a tight ship, and her career in London, New York, and elsewhere has ensured that her daughters get the education she wants them to have back in the homeland, on Achill.

Coincidentally, Granuaile's place in Irish folklore was secured in London. The Pirate Queen set sail from Clew Bay in 1593 and proceeded up the River Thames to the court of Queen Elizabeth I at Greenwich. To the amazement of royal courtiers, she was granted an audience with the most powerful woman on Earth. A peace was brokered with the English monarch, who held the Pirate Queen in high regard, not least for her defiance of the patriarchal conventions of 16th-century Europe. Famously, Grace refused to curtsy in obeisance before Elizabeth, whom she viewed as a royal equal. She merely bowed her head in respect, and proceeded to amaze all within earshot by addressing the sovereign head of the British Empire in Latin, the language of the educated aristocracy throughout Europe.

"Both Cara and Evie now speak Irish, and play Irish music," says O'Malley of her daughters, "and that does my heart a world of good to hear." The people of Achill are loyal and true to each other, she reflects. "Once you're accepted as one of their own, you won't *ever* be alone in the world."

The girls scamper the broken stairways to the first-floor chamber where ancestral fires once burned and O'Malley family feasts were eaten. They peer across Achill Sound, spying vessels bound for Clare Island and beyond. They shout and holler and playact piratical mimicry with untamed glee. They look for rainbows.

One thing is certain: The hearts of the next generation of O'Malley women will be fearless and brave. ∎

A new generation of O'Malleys gazes abroad from Achill Island.

> "There's a natural wildness that seeps into the soul in Achill, an independent spirit that lets you be your true self."
>
> —*Annette O'Malley*

IN THE KNOW: GRACE O'MALLEY'S COASTAL DOMAIN

The O'Malley clan owned many castles and tower houses in the western realm of Galway and Mayo as they expanded their wealth and influence through trade and piracy in the 16th century. This was an era when England ruled the world's waves and the empire of Elizabeth I pushed the ancient Gaelic world to the western fringes of Europe. The O'Malleys went from landed nobility to rulers of the seas off Ireland's west coast. Granuaile's main castle at Kildavnet, Achill Island, looked out onto Clew Bay, the island-splattered expanse that was perfect for the deeds and deceits of piracy.

Local legend has it that Grace had the mooring ropes of her fleet run through her castle bedroom window and tied to her big toe, so that she would be awoken if anyone tried to steal her ships. The Pirate Queen and her privateers exacted pilotage charges and cargo levies from passing shipping until she dominated the entire sea trade from the west of Ireland to the European continent.

COUNTY MAYO

In County Mayo, where the island-dotted seascape of Clew Bay is guarded at its entrance by Clare Island, **Granuaile's Castle** stands beside the harbor. The Pirate Queen is believed to be buried at **St. Brigid's Abbey,** a former Cistercian monastery on the island's south coast. Clare Island's current population of about 150 includes about 10 branches of the

O'Malley clan. O'Malley's castle here, a tower house, is now a national monument. Built in the 16th century by the Ó Máille (O'Malley) family, kings of Umall, the castle was converted into a police barracks in the 1820s, when Ireland was under British rule. Purple slate flashing was added to the two bartizans—the overhanging turrets—at this time.

On nearby Achill Island, **Kildavnet Castle**—aka Kildownet Tower or Carrickkildavnet Castle—sits at the southeast corner of the island, opposite the Corraun Peninsula. The tower house, built circa 1429, guards the mouth of Achill Sound and the passage connecting Clew Bay with Blacksod Bay to the west. The four-story tower had a machicolation, defensive loops, buttress fortifications, and a bawn wall to protect against intruders.

Castlekirk on Lough Corrib is today a haunting ruin surrounded by the waters of Lough Corrib. The tower house of Castlekirk is also known as Hen's Island, a reference to the feminine realm that Granuaile commanded in the 16th century. This tower house, located on a tiny half-acre (0.2 ha) island, can be seen from the road from Clonbur, approaching Maum. The castle was built in the early 12th century by the sons of Ruaidrí na Saide Buide, King of Connacht. When the 16-year-old Grace O'Malley married Dónal an-Chogaidh O'Flaherty in 1546, she was given the nickname "the Hen" to compliment his moniker of "the Cock." Her vengeful reaction

Once a stronghold of the O'Malley clan, Rockfleet Castle still stands at the entrance to Clew Bay.

to Dónal's murder ensured the tower would forever after be known as Hen's Castle. The island is also thought to be bewitched; the *aos sí* (fairies) are believed to bring their stolen children here on certain nights when strange lights are visible flitting about the castle stones.

Isolated **Doona Castle** on Fahy Strand, Ballycroy, was seized by the heartbroken Pirate Queen from the MacMahon clan as she sought vengeance for the killing of her lover, Hugh de Lacy. Granuaile attacked the castle and killed de Lacy's murderers on Cahir Island. After this daring raid, Grace O'Malley became known as the Dark Lady of Doona.

The Pirate Queen musical ran on Broadway in New York in 2007.

Westport House (see page 206) was built by the Browne family in the 18th century near the site of Grace O'Malley's birthplace (she was born around 1530). Grace's father was Eóghan Dubhdara Ó Máille, or Owen "Black Oak" O'Malley; his family were based in Clew Bay, from where he ruled the seas as lord of the Ó Máille dynasty and ruler of Umall. The O'Malleys built a row of castles facing the sea to protect their territory and taxed fishermen from as far away as England and Wales. A bronze statue of Granuaile now graces the grounds of Westport House.

Rockfleet Castle, also called **Carraigahowley Castle,** is a 16th-century tower house near Newport, County Mayo. This is likely where Grace O'Malley died in 1603. The castle's secondary name of Carraigahowley means "rock of the fleet," indicating the fortification's key strategic location for the O'Malleys' many maritime campaigns. Its four floors stand at almost 60 feet (18 m), giving fine vistas of the many islands of Clew Bay.

Today, the **Granuaile Centre** in Chapel Street, Louisburgh, helps keep the legend of the Pirate Queen alive. Mayo authorities are also planning to create a "Granuaile trail" that will soon link many of the region's historic sites of this great woman's life.

COUNTY GALWAY

Built in the early 1500s, **Bunowen Castle** in County Galway was Grace O'Malley's first home as a married woman, following her union with Donal O'Flaherty, head of the O'Flaherty clan. Like the O'Malleys, the "ferocious O'Flahertys" were seafarers, and Bunowen offered the couple easy access to the Atlantic Ocean. During her 16 years there, Granuaile bore three children—Eóghan (Owen), Méadhbh (Maeve), and Murchadh (Murrough)—until Donal was murdered as he hunted on the hills around Lough Corrib.

COUNTY DUBLIN

The most famous dinner-table setting in Ireland belongs to Grace O'Malley, yet it has never been used. The empty table space is found in **Howth Castle** in County Dublin. In 1576, while returning from an excursion to Dublin, Granuaile paid a courtesy visit to Lord St. Lawrence, the eighth Baron Howth. She was duly informed that the family was at dinner and the castle gates were closed against her. In her disgust at such an un-Irish display of inhospitality, Grace abducted St. Lawrence's grandson, the 10th baron, releasing him only after exacting a promise to keep the Howth gates always ready for opening to unexpected guests, and to set an extra place at every meal. To this day, this pledge is honored. ∎

Ireland On Screen

The Islands in Film

Many Irish myths and legends involve idyllic offshore islands, such as Tír na nÓg ("land of eternal youth"), and mythic sea gods. So it's no surprise that many films about Ireland's offshore islands are steeped in ancient lore. One of the great maritime Gaelic legends is that of the selkie, a seal that sheds its skin to become human. This shape-shifting human can then transform back into a seal to leave behind life on land and answer the irresistible call of the sea.

The Secret of Roan Inish (1994) tells the story of Fiona, a young girl sent to live with her grandparents near Roan Inish ("island of seals"), where selkies are believed to live. Fiona retains a vague memory of an infant brother, who was swept away in a cradle. The film begins with the girl's return home from Glasgow; her father had emigrated there in search of work, a familiar trail for the Donegal diaspora. Each night, her grandfather shares stories about the evacuation from their home on Roan Inish, near Narin, County Donegal, during World War II. Fiona learns of the sanctity of seals in the eyes of her people, and gradually unravels the mystery of her family's bloodlines.

Another cinematic retelling of the selkie story is *Song of the Sea* (2014). In it, 10-year-old Ben discovers that his mute sister, Saoirse, is a selkie who must free the *aos sí* (Irish fairies) from the Celtic goddess Macha.

Beautifully rendered in hand-drawn animation, this is the second installment in Tomm Moore's Irish folklore trilogy, following *The Secret of Kells* (2009; see page 57). The finale is *Wolfwalkers* (2020), a story about Ireland's last wolves.

Ondine (2009), written and directed by Neil Jordan and starring Colin Farrell, hurtles the selkie legend into modern-day Ireland, amid many challenges of 21st-century life—enforced migration, drug-smuggling, and broken families. The narrative begins when a fisherman, Syracuse (aka Circus), nets an unexpected catch while trawling. The barely dressed woman whom he resuscitates identifies herself only as Ondine and says that she is being pursued by evildoers from a threatening otherworld outside of Circus' fishing community. Cork's Castletownbere location provides a scenic backdrop to the ensuing love story between man and selkie. The narrative explores how our ancient human belief in these mythological creatures might be mirrored in the selkies' belief that humankind's better nature might prevail in a world filled with malice and sadness.

Another film that examines coastal and island life in the harsh light of modern life is *Reefer and the Model* (1988), written and directed by Joe Comerford. Reefer, a former IRA man, uses an old trawler to run a ferry between the Galway coast and the Aran Islands. Reefer's friends Spider and Badger and the pregnant Teresa (the model), who has escaped a troubled life in England, involve him in an armed robbery. The film was released toward the end of a decade when Ireland's economic woes had forced thousands—including many from the western islands—into exile in cities such as London, Glasgow, and New York.

A more romanticized version of Aran life brought the newborn Irish Free State into cinemas around the world in 1934. Ethnographer/filmmaker Robert J. Flaherty's *Man of Aran*, a blend of fiction and documentary, showed islanders eking out a living from fishing in dangerous seas and farming potatoes in limestone-laden fields. The film is famed for its spectacular cinematography; however, as George Stoney's 1978 documentary *How the Myth Was Made* exposed, certain scenes were fabricated, including the climactic shark hunt, a practice that islanders had abandoned decades previously.

As for Aran's best known tale, the 1962 film of J. M. Synge's classic *The Playboy of the Western World* (see page 305) was released on DVD in 2021. Filmed in Kerry, this drama featured many contemporaneous actors from Dublin's Abbey Theatre. ∎

Rathlin Island, County Antrim. The legend of the selkie—a seal that takes on human form—endures in Irish film and folklore.

Irish Heritage

Ireland's Culinary Culture

In the 1980s, food lovers venturing outside of Dublin headed mainly for Ireland's culinary capital in Kinsale, County Cork, or for gourmand gems such as Maura O'Connell Foley's Lime Tree in Kenmare, County Kerry. That vanguard restaurant—like the O'Connell Foley family's Purple Heather and Packie's eateries and the Shelburne Lodge—became famous for freshly caught seafood and prime Munster meats.

Today, according to Máirtín Mac Con Iomaire, a lecturer at the School of Culinary Arts and Food Technology at Technological University Dublin, great local food is served across the country. "Traditionally, Ireland exported the best of its agricultural produce," he explains, "but this changed when the Celtic Tiger boom [in the 1990s and 2000s] saw

the mushrooming of quality restaurants across the whole island."

The Irish food revolution has enabled today's hungry traveler to enjoy fine cuisine in as far-flung a location as Inis Meáin, the lesser visited Aran Island. At Inis Meáin Restaurant (see page 305), you're served a gourmet meal made of fresh Aran ingredients prepared by an internationally experienced local chef. Chef Ruairí de Blacam's success story is part of a nationwide blossoming in the culinary arts.

Mac Con Iomaire has witnessed this revolution from within. "Most Irish people probably have little or no knowledge of the richness and variety of their ancestors' diet—which included wild garlic; honey; grouse; game; white meats, or *bán bhia* [literally "white food," meaning

milk, buttermilk, curds, etc.]; eels; wrasse; oats; rye; gruel; pottage; watercress; apples; hazelnuts; bilberries; sorrel; tansy; and edible seaweed." All these were part of a varied Gaelic diet prior to the introduction of the humble potato by Sir Walter Raleigh in 1589. "Yet in recent decades, we've gained a new appreciation of our culinary heritage, and learned to tell ancient narratives anew through our food."

"The Irish have realized the excellence of the produce of their homeland: the rich yellow butters, cheeses, and succulent beef produced by grass-fed cattle, for example, in our temperate island climate. These all gave a uniquely Irish taste." Mac Con Iomaire relates a story of a Cork farmer's underwhelmed reaction to a chef's delight with his dairy produce: "Arra, that field always gave great butter," he dryly concurred.

Another recent innovation in the Irish kitchen is that chefs are now trained to question orthodoxies and to be creative. "'Don't copy, innovate' is the message now," he says. "European kitchens traditionally rang with the words 'Oui, chef!' Now, we Irish are asking, 'Why, chef?'" Watch out for new Dublin restaurants run by young, innovative chefs such as Cúán Greene and Mark Moriarty. According to Mac Con Iomaire: "I'm convinced that we'll soon see Ireland as a major food destination among global travelers." ∎

The Lemon Tree in Letterkenny, County Donegal, is an enduring destination for good food.

Drop scone pancakes, a traditional Irish treat for breakfast or teatime, are beloved in kitchens across Ireland.

TASTE OF IRELAND: DROP SCONE PANCAKES

These old-fashioned pancakes were widely cooked in Irish country farmhouses, mostly because they were both economical and delicious. As chef Maura O'Connell Foley remembers, "They are traditionally eaten with homemade butter and jams, much like how my mother would make them for me. I now serve them in more of a savory way at Shelburne Lodge, with bacon for a welcome saltiness. When cooking bacon, it should always be over high heat, ideally using a hot griddle pan. I serve the pancakes with maple syrup or a homemade apple syrup." The recipe is one of many in Foley's beautiful cookbook, *My Wild Atlantic Kitchen: Recipes and Recollections.*

INGREDIENTS

- ¾ cup (90 g) plain white flour
- A pinch of sea salt
- 2 rounded teaspoons baking powder sieved
- 1 teaspoon demerara sugar
- 2 eggs
- ½ cup (100 mL) milk
- ½ cup (40 g) butter, melted and cooled
- Butter for cooking (preferably use clarified butter)
- Rasher of bacon, if desired
- Apple or maple syrup, to serve

DIRECTIONS

- Add the flour, salt, and baking powder to a bowl and then mix in the sugar and blend thoroughly with a whisk.
- Beat the eggs lightly, add the milk, and beat until blended (about 30 seconds).
- Add the eggs and milk to the dry ingredients and gently mix to combine, being careful not to overmix.
- Lastly, add the cooled melted butter.
- Lightly grease a large heavy-based frying pan with 1 teaspoon butter over medium-high heat until it sizzles (be careful that the butter does not burn).
- Using a dessert spoon, dollop spoonfuls of the mixture into the pan, allowing a little space for the mixture to spread.
- Cook until the pancakes start to rise and bubbles appear on the surface, about 3 to 4 minutes, then quickly flip and cook for 3 minutes more or until the pancakes are cooked through. Add 1 teaspoon butter to the center of the pan again, turn once more briefly, then turn out onto a warmed plate.
- While the pancakes are cooking, heat a griddle pan over high heat and lightly grease with a little oil. When the pan is hot, add rashers of bacon (if desired) and fry for 1 minute on either side until golden brown. Serves 6 to 12 hungry gourmands (making about 12 to 14 pancakes).

TIP: The batter keeps for up to 2 days in the fridge; however, if stored in the fridge the pancakes will be thicker and need longer to cook.

IRISH LIGHTHOUSES

Most of Ireland's 80-plus lighthouses are run by the Commissioners of Irish Lights. This organization promotes these beacons of maritime safety with their Great Lighthouses of Ireland project, working to preserve the lengthy history of Irish lighthouses and honor the heroic but lonely work of their keepers. Since the automation of the lights in the 20th century, the romance of this way of life has largely passed into nautical legend. Several lighthouses have been repurposed as destinations for adventurous dreamers to stay as guests, available to rent by the night or the week. What intrepid traveler hasn't dreamed of waking inside a sturdy oceanside tower during a gale-force storm?

Many Irish lighthouses are magnificent works of architecture. Their construction involved amazing feats of engineering amid seemingly impossible conditions. Consider the five-year construction of the 98-foot (30 m) Fastnet Rock Lighthouse, completed in 1854 on a remote rocky islet off the Cork coast: Each granite block weighed nearly two tons (1.75 metric tonnes) to more than three tons (3 metric tonnes), and the tower is designed to sway up to 10 feet (3 m) during storms. These wonderfully utilitarian buildings are the legacy of great men, such as Belfast-born George Halpin, who directed the construction of more than 50 lighthouses over five decades. The majority of Irish lighthouses were built between 1810 and 1867. Others are much older: The 59-foot (18 m) Maiden Tower at Mornington in Meath was erected during the reign of Queen Elizabeth I.

We read much about dramatic shipwrecks and daring rescues around our shores. But who knows how many lives have been saved by lighthouses that guided storm-tossed ships away from rocky shorelines, dangerous reefs, shoals, and sandbanks? As Ireland's Nobel laureate George Bernard Shaw observed, "I can think of no other edifice constructed by man as altruistic as a lighthouse. They were built only to serve." ∎

Fanad Lighthouse, gleaming in the mists of County Donegal, is one of the Irish coastline's most beautiful beacons.

The Baily Lighthouse at Howth Head, County Dublin, is the latest beacon along a stretch of coastline where Irish lights have shone for sailors since 1667.

Keepers of the Light

The earliest recorded entry into the pharological history of Ireland is probably St. Dúbhan's fire on the headland we know today as **Hook Head,** then called Hy Kinsellagh. This was likely a metal cage of burning wood or turf, set atop a pile of stones, or maybe hung from a mast high on the treacherous Wexford cliffs.

William Marshal, son-in-law of the Norman knight, Strongbow, established a permanent tower here in the 13th century. Monks and priests were Ireland's earliest keepers of the coastal flames, tending these guiding lights. The dissolution of the monasteries under Henry VIII caused a navigation calamity. Elizabeth I restored the care of maritime beacons across the British Isles, however, and enacted strict laws penalizing interference with their functioning. This didn't stop profiteers, known as wreckers, who used decoy beacons to lure ships onto the rocks and provided coastal dwellers with many a bounty.

The Commissioners of Irish Lights was established in 1786 to oversee the building and running of lighthouses. The organization's costs are today paid for by light dues collected from ships arriving in Irish ports, calculated by their tonnage.

From the early fires lit by well-meaning monks, the coastal beacons have evolved in tandem with technological advances. Paraffin lamps were used extensively until gas burners became standard. The electrification of Ireland from 1880 onward revolutionized the shoreline beacons; offshore lighthouses still needed generators, however, which necessitated the transportation of diesel to these rocky outposts. Today, LED technology and solar panels make the powering of high-energy lights much easier and more efficient.

The invention of the helicopter revolutionized the running of off-shore lighthouses and reduced the need for keepers to remain on-site for long periods. With full automation, completed in 1997, the era of the lighthouse keeper ended. Today, the towers around Ireland's shores, many dating from Victorian times, are more than just lighthouses used to guide ships away from danger. They are platforms to host a pleth-ora of technology that can transmit vital information in almost real time to grateful mariners—tidal directions, depths, weather conditions, and more.

This information is now emitted from the lighthouses and their 116 buoys via the global Automatic Identification System (AIS)—a tracking network that uses trans-ceivers on ships—and also via the ubiquitous medium of Twitter.

With automation, the romance of lighthouse life became a thing of the past, but interest is now stoked by initiatives that give visitors access to the beacons' histories and even overnight stays. Irish lighthouses retain their purpose as the sentinels of safe passage for ships, and many are stalwarts of Victorian architecture and engineering. Their extraordinary coastal settings also provide bird-watchers and wildlife lovers with platforms to appreciate maritime Ireland's natural wonders.

The Irish lights shine on, illuminating present dangers, forewarning future perils, and now illuminating their own storied pasts. ∎

IN THE KNOW: STAYING IN A LIGHTHOUSE

Many Irish lighthouses now offer overnight stays and weekly rental deals for those seeking some stormy coastal isolation. In 2015, the Commissioners of Irish Lights initiated the **Lighthouse Trail,** giving visitors the choice of 13 dramatic destinations for maritime adventure. This allows them to reserve accommodations at: **St. John's Point Lighthouse** and **Fanad Head Lighthouse,** County Donegal; **Blackhead Lighthouse,** County Antrim; **St. John's Point Lighthouse,** County Down; **Wicklow Head Lighthouse,** County Wicklow; **Galley Head Lighthouse,** County Cork; **Loop Head Lighthouse,** County Clare; and **Clare Island Lighthouse,** County Mayo.

Elsewhere, the clifftop **Rathlin West Lighthouse,** on Rathlin Island, County Antrim, has one of the largest seabird colonies in Europe with guillemots, razorbills, kittiwakes, fulmars, and puffins all nesting within sight of the "upside-down lighthouse" in summer. **Blacksod Lighthouse** in County Mayo offers stunning scenery around Blacksod Bay, where marine megafauna find sanctuary under the supervision of the Irish Whale & Dolphin Group. **Hook Lighthouse** in County Wexford offers sunrise and sunset tours led by a local guide. These culminate in the watch-room and balcony, where you will be served Irish mead, prosecco, tea, or coffee along with Ballyhack Smokehouse smoked salmon on traditional brown bread and homemade canapés.

Ballycotton Lighthouse in County Cork is another great destination for nature lovers. Ballycotton Sea Adventures runs voyages around the lighthouse, taking you to inlets where you might spot peregrine falcons at dawn and dusk. Seals and dolphins are often seen in the harbor, and whales are visible from the cliffs in December and January. The beach at Ballynamona is part of a wildlife sanctuary, offering protected habitat for herons, oystercatchers, and sand hoppers. **Valentia Island Lighthouse,** located on the site of the 17th-century Fleetwood Fort, is a must for history buffs.

Ireland's Lighthouse Trail is an excellent way to get the measure of the whole island, its wild seas, and the flora, fauna, rock pools, and birdlife of its wondrous shorelines. ∎

Inside Fanad Head Lighthouse in County Donegal, where an overnight stay allows visitors to experience a taste of the lighthouse keeper's life

IN THE KNOW: IRISH LIGHTS

The lighthouses of Ireland illuminate the way for travelers on the waters around this westerly European island: the wild Atlantic Ocean to the west; the Malin Sea off northerly County Donegal; the eastern Irish Sea that separates the British Isles; and, to the south, the Celtic Sea. In the ancient Celtic tradition of the candle left burning for wayfaring strangers in kitchen windows, these giant beams cut through the darkest nights. They are beacons of hospitality, illuminating safe harbor, and welcoming all-comers with a promise of refuge in a storm. Thirteen of these "altruistic edifices," as George Bernard Shaw called them, now make up the Great Lighthouses of Ireland, an initiative by the Commissioners of Irish Lights (aka Irish Lights) that spans the Republic and Northern Ireland. These include the two lighthouses at **Wicklow Head,** erected in 1781. Ship captains used these lights to fix a passage—west by northwest—between the India sandbank and the Arklow bank. Today the disused higher lighthouse on the bluff can be rented overnight; a newer, lower beacon guides vessels from its cliffside perch.

The current tower at **Hook Head** in County Wexford stretches four stories above the peninsula and once housed a monastery. It was later a site for 17th-century money counterfeiting, and the visitors center explains how the phrase "by hook or by crook" originated here. The shipwreck of the *Sirius* led to the 1815 opening of the light at **Ballycotton** in County Cork. It was automated in 1992, and navigational aids are now monitored by telemetry link with Irish Lights in Dun Laoghaire, County Dublin.

When **Galley Head** opened in 1878, high on Dundeady Island in County Cork, it was the world's most powerful lighthouse. The lantern illuminates passage both for sailors and landlubber travelers on the road to Castle Freke. This landward light was allegedly arranged at the suggestion of the sultan of Turkey, a guest of Lord Carbery. Lesser titled guests can now rent the keepers' cottages. **Loop Head** in County Clare must afford the best views of any lighthouse in Ireland. To the far south stretches the coastlines of Kerry; just across from Loop Head Peninsula stand the magnificent Cliffs of Moher. Diarmuid and Gráinne's Rock, a mighty sea stack, sit across the chasm known as Lover's Leap, and a romantic stay in the lighthouse keeper's cottage is an option.

From **Clare Island Lighthouse** in Clew Bay, County Mayo, on the island's northern cliffs, you'll survey Grace O'Malley's castle below in the harbor, with dramatic views of Achill Island across the bay. **Blacksod Lighthouse** on the Mullet Peninsula, County Mayo, was built in 1864. The conical lantern atop this two-story house beams upon the cliffs of Achill Island. In June 1944, an ominous weather report from Blacksod lighthouse keeper Ted Sweeney convinced Gen. Dwight D. Eisenhower to postpone the D-Day invasion for 24 hours.

St. John's Point on the long finger of Dunkineely Peninsula guides trawlers as they navigate Donegal Bay toward **Rotten Island Lighthouse.** These two lights steer weary fishermen into the inner channel shelter of Killybegs and home to welcome beds. The 100-foot (30 m) St. John's Point tower has two adjoining keepers' cottages that can be rented.

Fanad Head at the entrance to Lough Swilly, County Donegal, is a scenic highlight of the Wild Atlantic Way. The lighthouse here dates from 1817 and now offers spectacular accommodation for those with a taste for adventure.

Often called the "upside-down lighthouse," as the light is located beneath the keepers' quarters, **Rathlin West Lighthouse** is set into a cliff at Crockantirrive, County Antrim. Nearby **Blackhead Lighthouse** would have been the first lighthouse seen from *Titanic* as she pulled out of Belfast Lough to complete her sea trials. The octagonal tower stands 52 feet (16m) tall on a dramatic clifftop setting. In County Down, **St. John's Point Lighthouse** is distinguished by yellow and black hoops, applied in the early 1950s by playwright Brendan Behan. **Haulbowline Lighthouse** at the entrance to the glacial fjord of Carlingford Lough, County Down, is one of the most striking of Irish lights. The 112-foot (34 m) tapered tower has a balcony halfway up and stands as a monumental example of Georgian architecture and engineering. The lighthouse was completed in 1824.

Other notable beacons include the **Baily** in Howth, County Dublin, the last Irish lighthouse to be automated, in 1997. The original lighthouse dates from 1667; a later building was used as an illegal distillery, with the thick Howth fog providing a convenient cloak for clandestine dealings. The third, newer lighthouse that stands today was built farther south at Dungriffin in 1814. The light at **Fastnet Rock,** off County Cork, was built in 1904 to replace the Cape Clear Light. This tall tower serves as the midpoint of the famous Fastnet yacht race, which starts from the Isle of Wight and ends at Plymouth, England. ∎

Fastnet Rock is Ireland's tallest and widest rock lighthouse tower.

Clare Island Lighthouse offers overnight stays in Pirate Queen territory.

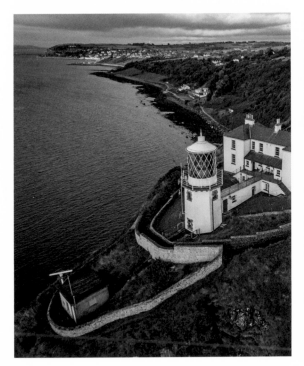

Blackhead Lighthouse shines a beacon on Antrim's perilous coastline.

The vibrant hues of St. John's Point Lighthouse are a recognizable sight.

ILLUSTRATIONS CREDITS

Map data sources: Ordnance Survey Ireland (modified data); National Parks and Wildlife Service, Department of Housing, Local Government and Heritage copyright Government of Ireland. Both licensed under Creative Commons Attribution 4.0 International (CC BY 4.0) Public License, *creativecommons.org/licenses/by/4.0/legalcode;* Contains public sector information licensed under the U.K. Open Government License v3.0.

Cover: (UP LE), StockFood/Jan-Peter Westermann; (UP CTR), Chris Hill/National Geographic Image Collection; (UP RT), STOCKFOLIO®/Alamy Stock Photo; (LO), Andrea Pistolesi/Getty Images; back cover, Brian Morrison; 1, Ashford Castle; 2-3, Trish Punch; 4-5, copyright © Susan Seubert Photography; 6, Jim Richardson/National Geographic Image Collection; 10, Dave Yoder; 11, Patryk Sadowski; 12-3, Jeff Mauritzen; 14, Luca Zanier/Anzenberger/Redux; 15, Eóin Noonan/Sportsfile via Getty Images; 16-7, yktr/Getty Images; 18, Julien Behal/PA Images via Getty Images; 19, chudo2307/Adobe Stock; 20, Jeff Mauritzen/National Geographic Image Collection; 22, TM and © Copyright Fox Searchlight Pictures. All rights reserved./Courtesy Everett Collection; 23, © BBC Archive/Steffan Hill; 24, Colm Henry; 25, Paul Faith/PA Images via Getty Images; 27 (UP), Mike O'Toole/UCD; 27 (LO LE), Bettmann/Getty Images; 27 (LO RT), Kadel & Herbert/FPG/Archive Photos/Getty Images; 28, Sergiu Cozorici/Getty Images; 29, Maxwell Photography; 30-1, Anna Gorin/Getty Images; 32, George Munday Photographic; 33, Jeff Mauritzen; 34, Trish Punch; 35, Goran Peuc; 36, Chris Hill/National Geographic Image Collection; 38, Freddie Stevens; 39, Nick Bradshaw; 40-1, Brian Morrison; 42, Sam Abell/National Geographic Image Collection; 43, Julien Behal/PA Images via Getty Images; 44, Ebet Roberts/Redferns/Getty Images; 45, Simone Joyner/Redferns/Getty Images; 46-7, Ken Williams/Shadows and Stone; 48, Ken Williams/Shadows and Stone; 49, Brian Morrison; 50, Anthony Murphy/Mythical Ireland; 52, Anthony Murphy/Mythical Ireland; 53, The Print Collector/Getty Images; 54, Anthony Murphy/Mythical Ireland; 55, Danny Clinch; 56, Hulton Archive/Getty Images; 57, Courtesy of Cartoon Saloon; 58, Anthony Murphy/Mythical Ireland; 59 (LE), learpiximages/Alamy Stock Photo; 59 (RT), Julien Behal/PA Images/Alamy Stock Photo; 60, Gareth McCormack/Alamy Stock Photo; 61, Coole Swan; 62, Jeff Mauritzen; 63, Album/Alamy Stock Photo; 64-5, Luis Alberto Cañizares; 66, Chris Hill/Getty Images; 67, scenicireland/Christopher Hill Photographic/Alamy Stock Photo; 68, Piaras Ó Mídheach/

Sportsfile via Getty Images; 69, Jeff Mauritzen; 70-1, Colm Hogan; 72, Jeff Mauritzen; 73, Brian Morrison; 74, Hugh Rooney/Eye Ubiquitous/Universal Images Group via Getty Images; 75, Dylan Vaughan for Kilkenny County Council; 76, Gunnar Knechtel/laif/Redux; 77, Rive Gauche; 78-9, Dylan Vaughan; 80, Timothy Seren/ullstein bild via Getty Images; 81, George Munday Photographic; 82-3, Chris Hill/National Geographic Image Collection; 84, Clive Barda/ArenaPAL; 85, © Loupe Images/Photo by Peter Cassidy, Recipe by Brontë Aurell; 86, Chris Hill/National Geographic Image Collection; 87, Brian Morrison; 88, Corbis via Getty Images; 89, Dunbrody Country House; 90-1, Berthold Steinhilber/laif/Redux; 92, House of Waterford; 93, Flavio Vallenari/Getty Images; 94, Andrea Pistolesi/Getty Images; 95, Liam Murphy; 96, Jeff Moore via Getty Images; 97, Ami Vitale; 98, Irimaxim/Dreamstime; 99, Anita Murphy Photography; 100-1, Blarney Castle & Gardens; 102, Nigel Hicks/Alamy Stock Photo; 103, Jeff Mauritzen; 104-5, Fabiano's_Photo/Shutterstock; 106, Irish Government - Pool/Getty Images; 108, Barbara Norman/Getty Images; 109, Courtesy of Blarney Castle Hotel; 110, Karl-Heinz Raach/laif/Redux; 111, Liam Murphy; 112, Jeff Mauritzen; 113 (LE), Ingolf Pompe 29/Alamy Stock Photo; 113 (RT), Richard Cummins/Alamy Stock Photo; 114, Paul Stack/Getty Images; 115, imagespace/Alamy Stock Photo; 116, Fiona Naughton; 117, Chris Hill/scenicirelandgallery; 118-20, Jeff Mauritzen; 121, Trish Punch; 122, Richard Cummins/robertharding/Alamy Stock Photo; 124, Simon Lazewski; 125, Park Hotel Kenmare; 126-7, Dave Yoder; 128, Chris Hill/National Geographic Image Collection; 131, Jeff Mauritzen; 132, Dave Yoder; 133-5, Jeff Mauritzen; 136, Padraig & Joan Kennelly/Kennelly Archive; 137, Patrick Comerford; 138, © Marco Bottigelli/Getty Images; 139, Catherine Karnow; 140, Bettmann/Getty Images; 141 (LE), Frank Hurley/Royal Geographical Society via Getty Images; 141 (RT), Herbert Ponting/Royal Geographical Society via Getty Images; 142, David Maher/SPORTSFILE; 143, Alida Ryder; 144, Muckross Park Hotel & Spa; 145, Dave Yoder; 146-7, Brian Morrison; 148, Chris Hill/National Geographic Image Collection; 149, Jeff Mauritzen; 150, Artur Bogacki/Alamy Stock Photo; 151, John D. Kelly Photography; 152, Universal Images Group via Getty Images; 153, Artur Bogacki/Shutterstock; 154, Jim Barry Wines; 156, The Irish Image Collection/Design Pics Inc/Alamy Stock Photo; 157, Hugh Rooney/Eye Ubiquitous/Universal Images Group via Getty Images; 158-9, mikroman6/Getty Images; 160, Brian Morrison; 161, © Andrea Jones/Garden Exposures Photo Library; 162, Fox Photos/Getty Images; 163, Rafa Elias/Getty Images; 164, Neil Jackman/Tuatha by Abarta Heritage; 165, David Morrison/Getty Images; 166-7, Jeff Mauritzen;

INDEX

ACKNOWLEDGMENTS

For Helen and David O'Brien, whose Avondale home is the very essence of Irish hospitality, and for Gene Savage, who is gone but never forgotten.

Always Ireland was created with the help and inspiration of many people. The book was brought to fruition at a time when conditions on the ground were far from ideal—the very idea of masking a smile is about as alien to the Irish psyche as the notion of social distancing.

Special thanks, as always, to two imaginative project managers who somehow managed to keep me on the right track, which was never the straight and narrow, Mary Norris and Allyson Johnson. And to project editor Ashley Leath for seeing this book through. Krista Rossow is an astute photo editor whose keen eye ensured that Ireland is shown in its truest light on every page. Designers Sanaa Akkach and Lisa Monias also helped to make *Always Ireland* a beautiful book, and Jerome Cookson made sure the maps were both accurate and helpful. Mary Stephanos and Michael O'Connor shepherded my most errant words and meandering Irish thoughts into literate-looking sentences. At National Geographic, my thanks especially go to Karen Martinez, who smooths the path of my travels with much moral and digital support, and to Lisa Thomas, who every couple of years sends me careering around Ireland and further afield in search of adventure and a good story.

My thanks to two authors whose works helped direct many routes taken in this book: to Christopher Somerville, author of National Geographic Traveler Ireland guidebooks, and Jane Powers, author of that beautiful bible of Irish horticulture, *The Irish Garden*.

In Ireland, my eternal gratitude is owed to Helen and David O'Brien for their endless hospitality at Avondale, and for Helen's help with the culinary tips in this book. For sharing his endless curiosity of the great outdoors, and his wisdom on many matters while indoors, Alf O'Brien also deserves a big thank-you.

As always, my *anam cara* (soul friend) Sean Hogan and his wife, Katie Condon, extended a warm Munster welcome to me in Healy's Bridge, County Cork, and in Valentia Island, County Kerry, where the next generation of Hogans, Dan and Nancy, acted as intrepid guides to everything from dinosaur footprints to wild Atlantic swimming. Keith Brittle and Kati Schultz were great companions on the Beara Peninsula and helped with their expert knowledge of restaurants and hostelries.

Another old and dear friend who made the writing of this book a real pleasure was Tim McNulty, who always knew exactly when I was most in need of a tea break from the desk or a quick spin along the east coast. Many thanks to Tim for sharing his insightful knowledge of many aspects of modern Ireland, for pointing me in several good directions, and for his ever gregarious and often hilarious company throughout a socially distanced and difficult year. Thanks also to the gallant Galwegian Rory O'Shaughnessy for sharing his boundless knowledge of the west of Ireland on a (mostly) memorable night out in Westport. Up in Ulster, my thanks is due to Dr. Declan Bonar and his friends Pat and Jo Dunleavy for their northern hospitality and for sharing great stories and local knowledge of Donegal. To the Dunleavys and anyone who invited me in for a cuppa, thank you for making Ireland the warm and welcoming place it is.

A special word of thanks to one woman whom I *couldn't* visit on my most recent travels. But Ena Hogan well knows the gratitude I'll always have in my heart for her and her late husband, John, for the door they kept ever open to me and for the timely encouragement they gave me to persevere through hard times in Ireland, *fadó, fadó*.

And finally, to Maggie, *mo grá*, for her constant support and love throughout the writing of this book. ∎

ABOUT THE AUTHOR

Fadó, fadó (long, long ago), Justin "Jack" Kavanagh grew up in County Wicklow, the Garden of Ireland. He studied English literature and philosophy at University College Dublin before leaving his homeland to work in London, Tokyo, Philadelphia, New York, and Washington, D.C.

Kavanagh began his career in journalism at the *Irish Press* in Dublin and has gone on to write widely on travel, culture, current affairs, and sport for *National Geographic Traveler* (Washington, D.C.), *The Globalist* online magazine (Washington, D.C.), *The Independent* (London), *90:00* (San Diego), *The Title* (Dublin), and *In Dublin* magazine, among others.

He has worked as an editor for National Geographic International Editions, which publishes books, magazines, and other media in more than 35 languages; he was also a senior editor for National Geographic Books, where he wrote and edited guidebooks on Ireland, Cuba, New York City, Japan, and other destinations. Kavanagh is also author of *National Geographic Complete National Parks of Europe.* He is currently working on a book about UNESCO World Heritage sites to be published by National Geographic Books.

Kavanagh works for National Geographic Expeditions, where he leads the "Ireland: Tales and Traditions of the Emerald Isle" tour. He splits his time between Philadelphia and the west of Ireland.

Each summer, Jack takes to the highways and byways (although mainly the byways) of Ireland to meet old friends and acquaintances and to make new ones. "There is no better season," according to Kavanagh, "in which to indulge in Ireland's two unofficial national pastimes: chatting and daydreaming." You can follow his adventures and conversations with all who'll give him the time of day, around Ireland and elsewhere, on Instagram: @jkglobaltext. ∎

Justin "Jack" Kavanagh in the place that is closest to his heart, Glendalough in his native County Wicklow

ALWAYS IRELAND

Since 1888, the National Geographic Society has funded more than 14,000 research, conservation, education, and storytelling projects around the world. National Geographic Partners distributes a portion of the funds it receives from your purchase to National Geographic Society to support programs including the conservation of animals and their habitats.

Get closer to National Geographic Explorers and photographers, and connect with our global community. Join us today at nationalgeographic.org/joinus

For rights or permissions inquiries, please contact National Geographic Books Subsidiary Rights: bookrights@natgeo.com

Excerpts from "Gone Fishing" used with kind permission from Mercier Press.

Excerpt from "Stardust" by Michael D. Higgins used with kind permission from the author and Liberties Press.

Library of Congress Cataloging-in-Publication Data
Names: Kavanagh, Justin (Journalist), author.
Title: Always Ireland / Jack Kavanagh.
Description: Washington, D.C. : National Geographic, [2023] | Includes index. | Summary: "This one-of-a-kind guide will allow you to experience Ireland as the locals do"-- Provided by publisher.
Identifiers: LCCN 2022021528 | ISBN 9781426222160 (hardcover)
Subjects: LCSH: Ireland--Guidebooks. | Ireland--History, Local.
Classification: LCC DA980 .K38 2023 | DDC 914.1704--dc23/eng/20220513
LC record available at https://lccn.loc.gov/2022021528

ISBN: 978-1-4262-2216-0

Printed in South Korea

22/SPSK/1